Lecture Notes in Computer Science   14699

The series Lecture Notes in Computer Science (LNCS), including its subseries Lecture Notes in Artificial Intelligence (LNAI) and Lecture Notes in Bioinformatics (LNBI), has established itself as a medium for the publication of new developments in computer science and information technology research, teaching, and education.

LNCS enjoys close cooperation with the computer science R & D community, the series counts many renowned academics among its volume editors and paper authors, and collaborates with prestigious societies. Its mission is to serve this international community by providing an invaluable service, mainly focused on the publication of conference and workshop proceedings and postproceedings. LNCS commenced publication in 1973.

Pei-Luen Patrick Rau
Editor

Cross-Cultural Design

16th International Conference, CCD 2024
Held as Part of the 26th HCI International Conference, HCII 2024
Washington, DC, USA, June 29 – July 4, 2024
Proceedings, Part I

 Springer

Editor
Pei-Luen Patrick Rau
Tsinghua University
Beijing, China

ISSN 0302-9743   ISSN 1611-3349 (electronic)
Lecture Notes in Computer Science
ISBN 978-3-031-60897-1   ISBN 978-3-031-60898-8 (eBook)
https://doi.org/10.1007/978-3-031-60898-8

This Springer imprint is published by the registered company Springer Nature Switzerland AG
The registered company address is: Gewerbestrasse 11, 6330 Cham, Switzerland

If disposing of this product, please recycle the paper.

Foreword

This year we celebrate 40 years since the establishment of the HCI International (HCII) Conference, which has been a hub for presenting groundbreaking research and novel ideas and collaboration for people from all over the world.

The HCII conference was founded in 1984 by Prof. Gavriel Salvendy (Purdue University, USA, Tsinghua University, P.R. China, and University of Central Florida, USA) and the first event of the series, "1st USA-Japan Conference on Human-Computer Interaction", was held in Honolulu, Hawaii, USA, 18–20 August. Since then, HCI International is held jointly with several Thematic Areas and Affiliated Conferences, with each one under the auspices of a distinguished international Program Board and under one management and one registration. Twenty-six HCI International Conferences have been organized so far (every two years until 2013, and annually thereafter).

Over the years, this conference has served as a platform for scholars, researchers, industry experts and students to exchange ideas, connect, and address challenges in the ever-evolving HCI field. Throughout these 40 years, the conference has evolved itself, adapting to new technologies and emerging trends, while staying committed to its core mission of advancing knowledge and driving change.

As we celebrate this milestone anniversary, we reflect on the contributions of its founding members and appreciate the commitment of its current and past Affiliated Conference Program Board Chairs and members. We are also thankful to all past conference attendees who have shaped this community into what it is today.

The 26th International Conference on Human-Computer Interaction, HCI International 2024 (HCII 2024), was held as a 'hybrid' event at the Washington Hilton Hotel, Washington, DC, USA, during 29 June – 4 July 2024. It incorporated the 21 thematic areas and affiliated conferences listed below.

A total of 5108 individuals from academia, research institutes, industry, and government agencies from 85 countries submitted contributions, and 1271 papers and 309 posters were included in the volumes of the proceedings that were published just before the start of the conference, these are listed below. The contributions thoroughly cover the entire field of human-computer interaction, addressing major advances in knowledge and effective use of computers in a variety of application areas. These papers provide academics, researchers, engineers, scientists, practitioners and students with state-of-the-art information on the most recent advances in HCI.

The HCI International (HCII) conference also offers the option of presenting 'Late Breaking Work', and this applies both for papers and posters, with corresponding volumes of proceedings that will be published after the conference. Full papers will be included in the 'HCII 2024 - Late Breaking Papers' volumes of the proceedings to be published in the Springer LNCS series, while 'Poster Extended Abstracts' will be included as short research papers in the 'HCII 2024 - Late Breaking Posters' volumes to be published in the Springer CCIS series.

I would like to thank the Program Board Chairs and the members of the Program Boards of all thematic areas and affiliated conferences for their contribution towards the high scientific quality and overall success of the HCI International 2024 conference. Their manifold support in terms of paper reviewing (single-blind review process, with a minimum of two reviews per submission), session organization and their willingness to act as goodwill ambassadors for the conference is most highly appreciated.

This conference would not have been possible without the continuous and unwavering support and advice of Gavriel Salvendy, founder, General Chair Emeritus, and Scientific Advisor. For his outstanding efforts, I would like to express my sincere appreciation to Abbas Moallem, Communications Chair and Editor of HCI International News.

July 2024   Constantine Stephanidis

HCI International 2024 Thematic Areas
and Affiliated Conferences

- HCI: Human-Computer Interaction Thematic Area
- HIMI: Human Interface and the Management of Information Thematic Area
- EPCE: 21st International Conference on Engineering Psychology and Cognitive Ergonomics
- AC: 18th International Conference on Augmented Cognition
- UAHCI: 18th International Conference on Universal Access in Human-Computer Interaction
- CCD: 16th International Conference on Cross-Cultural Design
- SCSM: 16th International Conference on Social Computing and Social Media
- VAMR: 16th International Conference on Virtual, Augmented and Mixed Reality
- DHM: 15th International Conference on Digital Human Modeling & Applications in Health, Safety, Ergonomics & Risk Management
- DUXU: 13th International Conference on Design, User Experience and Usability
- C&C: 12th International Conference on Culture and Computing
- DAPI: 12th International Conference on Distributed, Ambient and Pervasive Interactions
- HCIBGO: 11th International Conference on HCI in Business, Government and Organizations
- LCT: 11th International Conference on Learning and Collaboration Technologies
- ITAP: 10th International Conference on Human Aspects of IT for the Aged Population
- AIS: 6th International Conference on Adaptive Instructional Systems
- HCI-CPT: 6th International Conference on HCI for Cybersecurity, Privacy and Trust
- HCI-Games: 6th International Conference on HCI in Games
- MobiTAS: 6th International Conference on HCI in Mobility, Transport and Automotive Systems
- AI-HCI: 5th International Conference on Artificial Intelligence in HCI
- MOBILE: 5th International Conference on Human-Centered Design, Operation and Evaluation of Mobile Communications

List of Conference Proceedings Volumes Appearing Before the Conference

1. LNCS 14684, Human-Computer Interaction: Part I, edited by Masaaki Kurosu and Ayako Hashizume
2. LNCS 14685, Human-Computer Interaction: Part II, edited by Masaaki Kurosu and Ayako Hashizume
3. LNCS 14686, Human-Computer Interaction: Part III, edited by Masaaki Kurosu and Ayako Hashizume
4. LNCS 14687, Human-Computer Interaction: Part IV, edited by Masaaki Kurosu and Ayako Hashizume
5. LNCS 14688, Human-Computer Interaction: Part V, edited by Masaaki Kurosu and Ayako Hashizume
6. LNCS 14689, Human Interface and the Management of Information: Part I, edited by Hirohiko Mori and Yumi Asahi
7. LNCS 14690, Human Interface and the Management of Information: Part II, edited by Hirohiko Mori and Yumi Asahi
8. LNCS 14691, Human Interface and the Management of Information: Part III, edited by Hirohiko Mori and Yumi Asahi
9. LNAI 14692, Engineering Psychology and Cognitive Ergonomics: Part I, edited by Don Harris and Wen-Chin Li
10. LNAI 14693, Engineering Psychology and Cognitive Ergonomics: Part II, edited by Don Harris and Wen-Chin Li
11. LNAI 14694, Augmented Cognition, Part I, edited by Dylan D. Schmorrow and Cali M. Fidopiastis
12. LNAI 14695, Augmented Cognition, Part II, edited by Dylan D. Schmorrow and Cali M. Fidopiastis
13. LNCS 14696, Universal Access in Human-Computer Interaction: Part I, edited by Margherita Antona and Constantine Stephanidis
14. LNCS 14697, Universal Access in Human-Computer Interaction: Part II, edited by Margherita Antona and Constantine Stephanidis
15. LNCS 14698, Universal Access in Human-Computer Interaction: Part III, edited by Margherita Antona and Constantine Stephanidis
16. LNCS 14699, Cross-Cultural Design: Part I, edited by Pei-Luen Patrick Rau
17. LNCS 14700, Cross-Cultural Design: Part II, edited by Pei-Luen Patrick Rau
18. LNCS 14701, Cross-Cultural Design: Part III, edited by Pei-Luen Patrick Rau
19. LNCS 14702, Cross-Cultural Design: Part IV, edited by Pei-Luen Patrick Rau
20. LNCS 14703, Social Computing and Social Media: Part I, edited by Adela Coman and Simona Vasilache
21. LNCS 14704, Social Computing and Social Media: Part II, edited by Adela Coman and Simona Vasilache
22. LNCS 14705, Social Computing and Social Media: Part III, edited by Adela Coman and Simona Vasilache

47. LNCS 14730, HCI in Games: Part I, edited by Xiaowen Fang
48. LNCS 14731, HCI in Games: Part II, edited by Xiaowen Fang
49. LNCS 14732, HCI in Mobility, Transport and Automotive Systems: Part I, edited by Heidi Krömker
50. LNCS 14733, HCI in Mobility, Transport and Automotive Systems: Part II, edited by Heidi Krömker
51. LNAI 14734, Artificial Intelligence in HCI: Part I, edited by Helmut Degen and Stavroula Ntoa
52. LNAI 14735, Artificial Intelligence in HCI: Part II, edited by Helmut Degen and Stavroula Ntoa
53. LNAI 14736, Artificial Intelligence in HCI: Part III, edited by Helmut Degen and Stavroula Ntoa
54. LNCS 14737, Design, Operation and Evaluation of Mobile Communications: Part I, edited by June Wei and George Margetis
55. LNCS 14738, Design, Operation and Evaluation of Mobile Communications: Part II, edited by June Wei and George Margetis
56. CCIS 2114, HCI International 2024 Posters - Part I, edited by Constantine Stephanidis, Margherita Antona, Stavroula Ntoa and Gavriel Salvendy
57. CCIS 2115, HCI International 2024 Posters - Part II, edited by Constantine Stephanidis, Margherita Antona, Stavroula Ntoa and Gavriel Salvendy
58. CCIS 2116, HCI International 2024 Posters - Part III, edited by Constantine Stephanidis, Margherita Antona, Stavroula Ntoa and Gavriel Salvendy
59. CCIS 2117, HCI International 2024 Posters - Part IV, edited by Constantine Stephanidis, Margherita Antona, Stavroula Ntoa and Gavriel Salvendy
60. CCIS 2118, HCI International 2024 Posters - Part V, edited by Constantine Stephanidis, Margherita Antona, Stavroula Ntoa and Gavriel Salvendy
61. CCIS 2119, HCI International 2024 Posters - Part VI, edited by Constantine Stephanidis, Margherita Antona, Stavroula Ntoa and Gavriel Salvendy
62. CCIS 2120, HCI International 2024 Posters - Part VII, edited by Constantine Stephanidis, Margherita Antona, Stavroula Ntoa and Gavriel Salvendy

https://2024.hci.international/proceedings

Preface

The increasing internationalization and globalization of communication, business and industry is leading to a wide cultural diversification of individuals and groups of users who access information, services and products. If interactive systems are to be usable, useful and appealing to such a wide range of users, culture becomes an important HCI issue. Therefore, HCI practitioners and designers face the challenges of designing across different cultures, and need to elaborate and adopt design approaches which take into account cultural models, factors, expectations and preferences, and allow development of cross-cultural user experiences that accommodate global users.

The 16th Cross-Cultural Design (CCD) Conference, an affiliated conference of the HCI International Conference, encouraged the submission of papers from academics, researchers, industry and professionals, on a broad range of theoretical and applied issues related to Cross-Cultural Design and its applications.

A considerable number of papers were accepted to this year's CCD conference addressing diverse topics, which spanned a wide variety of domains. A notable theme addressed by several contributions was that of user experience and product design from a cross-cultural point of view, offering insights into design, user interaction, and evaluation across different domains and how cultural contexts shape user preferences, expectations, and behaviors. Furthermore, a considerable number of papers explore how individuals perceive, attend to, and process information within cultural contexts. Furthermore, the impact of culture across different application domains is addressed, examining technologies for communication, cultural heritage, and digital transformation and bringing together cutting-edge research, innovative practices, and insightful studies. Finally, the influence of culture on emerging technologies is a prominent theme, with contributions discussing extended reality, aviation and transportation, as well as artificial intelligence, addressing a multitude of aspects such as narrative design, interaction design, evaluation of user experience and performance, artificial empathy, and ethical aspects.

Four volumes of the HCII 2024 proceedings are dedicated to this year's edition of the CCD conference:

- Part I addresses topics related to Cross-Cultural Design and User Experience, and Cross-Cultural Product Design;
- Part II addresses topics related to Cross-Cultural Communication and Interaction, and Cultural Perception, Attention and Information Processing;
- Part III addresses topics related to Cross-Cultural Tangible and Intangible Heritage and Cross-Cultural Digital Transformation;
- Part IV addresses topics related to Cross-Cultural Extended Reality, Cross-Cultural Design in Aviation and Transportation, and Artificial Intelligence from a Cross-Cultural Perspective.

The papers in these volumes were accepted for publication after a minimum of two single-blind reviews from the members of the CCD Program Board or, in some cases, from members of the Program Boards of other affiliated conferences. I would like to thank all of them for their invaluable contribution, support and efforts.

July 2024   Pei-Luen Patrick Rau

16th International Conference on Cross-Cultural Design (CCD2024)

Program Board Chair: **Pei-Luen Patrick Rau**, *Tsinghua University, China*

- Na Chen, *Beijing University of Chemical Technology, P.R. China*
- Zhe Chen, *Beihang University, P.R. China*
- Kuohsiang Chen, *National Cheng Kung University, Taiwan*
- Wen-Ko Chiou, *Chang Gung University, Taiwan*
- Zhiyong Fu, *Tsinghua University, P.R. China*
- Hanjing Huang, *Fuzhou University, P.R. China*
- Toshikazu Kato, *Chuo University, Japan*
- Xin Lei, *Zhejiang University of Technology, P.R. China*
- Sheau-Farn Max Liang, *National Taipei University of Technology, Taiwan*
- Dyi-Yih Michael Lin, *I-Shou University, Taiwan*
- Wei Lin, *Feng Chia University, Taiwan*
- Rungtai Lin, *National Taiwan University of Arts, Taiwan*
- Na Liu, *Beijing University of Posts and Telecommunications, P.R. China*
- Cheng-Hung Lo, *Xi'an Jiaotong-Liverpool University, P.R. China*
- Yongqi Lou, *Tongji University, P.R. China*
- Ta-Ping Lu, *Sichuan University, P.R. China*
- Liang Ma, *Tsinghua University, P.R. China*
- Huatong Sun, *University of Washington Tacoma, USA*
- Hao Tan, *Hunan University, P.R. China*
- Pei-Lee Teh, *Monash University Malaysia, Malaysia*
- Lin Wang, *Incheon National University, Korea*
- Hsiu-Ping Yueh, *National Taiwan University, Taiwan*
- Andong Zhang, *Shanghai Jiao Tong University, P.R. China*
- Runting Zhong, *Jiangnan University, P.R. China*
- Xingchen Zhou, *Beijing Normal University, P.R. China*

The full list with the Program Board Chairs and the members of the Program Boards of all thematic areas and affiliated conferences of HCII 2024 is available online at:

http://www.hci.international/board-members-2024.php

HCI International 2025 Conference

The 27th International Conference on Human-Computer Interaction, HCI International 2025, will be held jointly with the affiliated conferences at the Swedish Exhibition & Congress Centre and Gothia Towers Hotel, Gothenburg, Sweden, June 22–27, 2025. It will cover a broad spectrum of themes related to Human-Computer Interaction, including theoretical issues, methods, tools, processes, and case studies in HCI design, as well as novel interaction techniques, interfaces, and applications. The proceedings will be published by Springer. More information will become available on the conference website: https://2025.hci.international/.

General Chair
Prof. Constantine Stephanidis
University of Crete and ICS-FORTH
Heraklion, Crete, Greece
Email: general_chair@2025.hci.international

https://2025.hci.international/

Contents – Part I

Cross-Cultural Product Design

Cross-Cultural Design and User Experience

Persuasive Determinants of Physical Activity in Adults: Cultural Differences and the Moderating Effect of Gender and Age

Najla Almutari, Alaa Alslaity[✉], and Rita Orji

Dalhousie University, Halifax, CA, Canada
{najla.almutari,Alaa.alslaity,Rita.orji}@dal.ca

Abstract. Evidence shows that physical inactivity is one of the leading causes of mortality worldwide. A growing variety of behavioural change interventions have been developed to promote physical activity behaviour, and have shown success. However, most of these apps apply a one-size-fits-all approach focusing on individualistic cultures and neglecting collectivist cultures. We investigate the possible cultural differences between individualism and collectivism on how the behavioral determinants influence people's physical activity behaviour. We conducted a large-scale study of 430 participants from collectivist and individualist cultures using the extended Health Belief Model (HBM). We also assess the moderating effect of age and gender. We map these determinants to their corresponding persuasive strategies that can be used in operationalizing them in behaviour change applications for promoting physical activity. Our findings show that Social influence and Cue to action are the strongest determinants of physical activity for collectivists. Whereas in individualists, Cue to action, and Self-efficacy are the strongest determinants of physical activity. Finally, we discuss the implications of our findings and offer design guidelines for persuasive interventions that both appeal to a broad audience and are tailored to a particular group depending on their gender and age group.

Keywords: Physical Activity · Persuasive Technology · Health Belief Model (HBM) · Culture · Persuasive determinants · Behaviour change

1 Introduction

Physical inactivity is a significant risk factor for many non-communicable diseases, such as heart disease and diabetes. Evidence shows that physical inactivity is one of the highest risk factors for death globally [33]. Research shows that 25% of adults (18 years or older) are physically inactive [33]. This high number of inactive adults continues to rise, as it is driven by economic development and urbanization. Therefore, physical activity promotion remains an important task. However, it is not an easy task due to the interactions and interdependencies between physical activity and various factors, including demographic, psychological, social, biological, and behavioural factors. Research has shown that physical activity motivation interventions are one of the most effective ways to motivate people to be physically active [61].

P.-L. P. Rau (Ed.): HCII 2024, LNCS 14699, pp. 3–27, 2024.
https://doi.org/10.1007/978-3-031-60898-8_1

Persuasive Technology (PT) refers to apps that are intentionally designed to change behaviours and attitudes by persuasion without coercion or deception [26]. These apps have shown effective results at changing behaviours in many health domains [2, 17, 47]. Behaviour change theories are the basic building block for many persuasive and behaviour change systems [1, 69]. Over the years, various health behaviour theories have been developed that could be used to inform persuasive intervention designs [56], such as Social Cognitive Theory [12], Transtheoretical Model [64], Theory of Planned Behaviour [4], and the Health Belief Model [68]. However, the Health Belief Model (HBM) is one of the most widely applied health behaviour theories [55–57, 59, 68].

The Health Belief Model (HBM) was developed to explain why some people take actions aimed at preventing diseases or activities that can lead to health issues while others care less. The HBM proposes that the likelihood of performing a health-related behaviour is influenced by individual's perception of six determinants:

- Perceived susceptibility: "perceived risk for contracting the health condition of concern".
- Perceived severity: "perception of the consequence of contracting the health condition of concern".
- Perceived benefit: "perception of the good things that could happen from undertaking specific behaviours";
- Perceived barrier "perception of the difficulties and cost of performing behaviours";
- Cue to action "exposure to factors that prompt action";
- Self-efficacy "confidence in one's ability to perform the new health behaviour" [62]

Several persuasive applications (or apps) have been developed for promoting physical activity [11, 24, 52]; however, these apps mostly used the one-size-fits-all approaches neglecting tailoring behaviour theories and associated persuasive strategies to user groups [41, 55].

More importantly, most PT studies are based on developed countries such as American, European, and Canadian cultures, which are categorized as individualistic [47, 55], although physical inactivity remains a global challenge that affects individualist and collectivist cultures. Consequently, existing PT for promoting physical activity may not meet the needs of users from collectivist cultures, which emphasizes the need to investigate how to tailor persuasive interventions for physical activity to people from collectivist cultures. Culture has been shown to influence many aspects of our lives, including our beliefs, motivations, and even how we interact with interactive systems [46, 48, 66]. Cultural and contextual factors should be taken into consideration in designing interventions aimed at motivating healthy behaviour change to ensure the success of these interventions.

Despite the overwhelming evidence on the need to consider people's culture in designs, the effect of different cultural groups (as identified by Hofstede [76]) on the design of physical activity interventions and associated determinants has been largely ignored. Whether or not people from collectivist and individualist cultures are influenced by different physical activity determinants is an open research question which we intend to answer in the current research. Specifically, our research will investigate *if* and *how* behaviour determinants can be tailored in PT interventions targeting various cultures to promote physical activity among the target audience effectively.

In this paper, we present culturally appropriate design guidelines for tailoring persuasive physical activity interventions to collectivist and individualist cultures. Our design guidelines are based on a large-scale comparative study (N = 430) of the physical activity behaviour and associated determinants of people from collectivist and individualists cultures. Specifically, 217 participants were collectivist and 213 from individualist cultures. We used structural equation modelling (SEM) to develop models and conducted a comparative analysis of the relation between the different determinants of physical activity behaviour for people from collectivist and individualist cultures. Furthermore, we investigate possible moderating effects of age and gender both within and between the cultural groups. Finally, we offer design guidelines for both a one-size-fits-all and a personalized approach to PT intervention design.

Our study is based on the HBM determinants. We also extended the HBM and included the Social Influence because it is an important determinant of health behaviour [8].

Our findings show significant differences between the participants from collectivistic cultures and those from individualistic cultures. The *social influence, cue to action* and *perceived severity* emerged as the strongest determinants of physical activity in participants from collectivistic cultures. Whereas in the individualist culture, *cue to action, self-efficacy,* and *social influence* are the strongest determinants of physical activity. The results also demonstrated a moderating effect of gender and age. With respect to the within-group gender differences, the results show that collectivist males and females differ in social influence, severity, and susceptibility, while individualist males and females differ significantly in perceived benefit and severity. Likewise, various age groups within each culture show differences. For instance, collectivist younger and older adults perceived self-efficacy, severity, susceptibility, and social influence differently, while individualist younger and older adults perceived susceptibility, severity, social influence, self-efficacy, and benefit differently.

These differences emphasize the need to tailor PT interventions based on cultural groups (collectivism and individualism). Therefore, tailored guidelines for promoting physical activity based on the health beliefs of different cultures are necessary for an effective and successful health behaviour change.

Our work offers five main contributions. First, it extends the health belief model to include the social influence as an important determinant of health behaviour from the literature. Second, it applies the extended HBM to conduct a comparative investigation of the determinant of physical activity among collectivist and individualist cultures, creating ten unique models for different populations of users. Third, it investigates the moderating effect of age and gender on the extended HBM determinants on physical activity behaviour. Fourth, we map the determinants to their corresponding design strategies for operationalizing them in behaviour change intervention design. Finally, we offer design guidelines for persuasive interventions that appeal to both a broad audience and tailored to a particular group depending on their culture, gender, and age group.

2 Background and Related Work

This section presents background concepts and explores the related work. Specifically, we discuss culture and human behaviour in Sect. 2.1, culturally-relevent persuasive techniques in Sect. 2.2, and the HBM in Sect. 2.3

2.1 Culture and Human Behaviour

Culture can be defined as "the collective programming of the mind which distinguishes the members of one group or category of people from another" [76]. It is acquired and transmitted from one generation to another and shared by a group of people. Culture plays an important role in forming people's behaviours and attitudes. It influences almost all areas of our lives, including the way people communicate and interact with technology [59]. Social scientists have examined the differences between cultures based on the values distributed by various groups. As a result, they identified five critical cultural dimensions [76]: Collectivism versus Individualism, Femininity versus Masculinity, Long-term versus Short-term orientation, Power-distance, and Uncertainty avoidance. This paper focuses on the first dimension (i.e., Collectivism versus Individualism) as many studies have shown that these two dimensions account for most of the variation in global differences [36, 76]. Particularly, this study examines possible cultural differences in the determinants of physical activity using the extended HBM.

Studies have found several differences between individualist and collectivist cultures. In an individualist culture, there are loose ties between individuals, and individuals are expected to take care of themselves and their immediate family members [76]. People in individualist cultures tend to be more independent in making decisions, more competitive, less cooperative, and less concerned within-group goals [46, 72]. On the other hand, people in collectivist cultures get united into solid and cohesive groups from birth. The collectivist expects other in-group members to take care of them and to protect them in return for unquestioning loyalty [36, 46, 72]. In addition, group interest outweighs the individual interest in a collectivist society, and individuals behave to maintain good and tight relationships within the group to avoid loss of face [46, 76]. In terms of attitude-behaviour patterns, Collectivists are less consistent, and they work for group benefit [46, 76].

It is worth mentioning that the five cultural dimensions (known as Hofsteade's cultural model) have some limitations, such as the broad binary classification [37]. However, we decided to adopt it for several reasons; 1) it has been successfully adopted by several HCI research [13, 28, 46, 51]. 2) Recent research has confirmed the validity of the individualism/Collectivism dimension [71]. 3) research has found that the Collectivist/Individualist dimension successfully predicts individuals' behaviours, such as healthy eating [23], food overconsumption [3, 63], and smoking cessation [46].

To distinguish individualist and collectivist cultures, researchers rely on the individualist index, a 16-item scale designed to measure four dimensions of collectivism and individualism [75]. The scores of this index are presented as a spectrum from 0 to 100. The higher the score obtained, the more individualists and the lower scores are collectivists. Researchers generally categorize North America, Western Europe, and Australia as individualist nations, whereas Africa, Asia, and South America are characterized as collectivist societies [76]. Therefore, this research follows a similar classification to allocate participants into cultural groups. Canada scores 80 on the individualist index and, therefore, can be characterized as an individualist culture, whereas Saudi Arabia scores 25 and is thus considered a collectivistic culture [21, 22, 55]. The contrast between the two nations makes them of interest for this study.

2.2 Culturally Relevant Persuasive Technology

Recent research has shown that computer applications in general, and persuasive technology in particular, need to be made culturally relevant [46, 48, 68]. Persuasive Technology (PT) can be defined as technology that aims to form, alter, or reinforce attitudes and/or behaviours without using deception, coercion, or inducements [26]. PT should be designed to unobtrusively integrate into the user's daily life [19]. As mentioned above, culture plays a crucial role in shaping individuals' attitudes and behaviours. Thus, total integration of PT into human life cannot be achieved without taking into consideration various cultural aspects.

According to Grimes and Grinter [31], cultural relevance can be achieved if the intervention understands the beliefs, norms, needs, and behaviours of the target population. Accordingly, persuasive technologies (which are often informed by human behaviour theories and their associated determinants) can be made culturally relevant by adapting the fundamental theories, determinants, and strategies to the cultural beliefs, norms, and needs of the target audience. It is worth noting, however, that adapting to the cultural dimensions does not necessarily mean that the PT interventions will be successful. Rather, PT interventions that adapt to the cultural dimensions will increase the likelihood of being culturally meaningful to the target audience [31], which, in turn, will increase its effectiveness.

The research in the area of designing culturally-relevant PT is still limited, and only a few research have been done in this area. Khaled et al. [46] investigated the impact of cultural differences on the effectiveness of various persuasive strategies. They concluded that the persuasive strategies commonly used are suitable for individualists rather than for collectivists. Accordingly, the authors proposed five collectivist-focused persuasive strategies – group opinion, group surveillance, deviation monitoring, disapproval conditioning, and group customization. These strategies, however, are not theory-based and not based on a large-scale study.

In the domain of smoking cessation, a persuasive game called "Smoke?" is proposed by Khaled et al. [45]. The game targeted both collectivist and individualist cultures, and its design was informed by a set of collectivist-focused strategies – harmony, group opinion, monitoring, disestablishing, and team performance. The evaluation results of "Smoke?" demonstrated that the culturally-matched strategies yield greater persuasion.

Culturally relevant designs have also been used in other health domains. For instance, Orji and Mandryk [56] investigated culturally relevant aspects in the healthy eating domain. They proposed culturally-relevant design approaches for tailoring persuasive technology interventions to collectivists and individualistic cultures. The results of a large-scale study revealed some differences between various cultural groups and subgroups. Based on that, the authors proposed two approaches for designing culturally-relevant persuasive applications.

Despite the existence of prior work on culturally-relevant persuasive strategies, it is not a straightforward process to adopt strategies from one domain to another; Strategies that worked in one domain (e.g., smoking cessation) might not be directly transferable to another domain (e.g., physical activity intervention design) [55]. This is because each domain has special characteristics that make it different. For instance, eating is a daily behaviour that is necessary for everybody. On the other hand, physical activity, although it is as important as healthy eating, it is not necessarily a daily activity. Also, being physically active may require special types of equipment, time, and effort. This makes it more challenging to design persuasive interventions for promoting physical activity. Therefore, there is a need for more work to investigate various persuasive determinants in the physical activity domain with the aim of developing culturally-relevant PT interventions.

2.3   HBM and Theory-Driven Behaviour Change Systems

This section introduces the HBM and its determinants. Then it shows a number of empirical studies that applied the HBM in the design of the health interventions, and it discusses the effectiveness of the interventions at achieving the intended behaviour change objectives.

The Health Belief Model (HBM) was developed to explain why some people take actions aimed at preventing diseases or activities that can lead to health issues while others care less. It suggests that there are six determinants that influence people's health behaviours: *Perceived susceptibility*, *Perceived severity*, *Perceived Benefit*, *Perceived Barrier*, *Cue to Action*, and *Self-efficacy*. These determinants provide a framework for designing behaviour change interventions. The HBM is most suitable for addressing problem behaviours that have health consequences such as physical inactivity because it concentrates on health motivators [59].

Based on a literature review, we extended the HBM determinants by including the social influence as a seventh determinant because the literature recognized it as an important factor affecting physical activity behaviour [18, 52, 73, 74]. Social influence indicates the effect that other people have on us, and it occurs when an individual's behaviour or attitude is affected by others. Most of our behaviours can be shaped by the power of social influence" [58]. We included social influence for several reasons; first, while several studies have shown the major role that others play in motivating physical activity behaviour, the effects of HBM determinants and social influence together and their cultural-related impact are still unclear. Second, research has shown that the HBM can be extended and adapted to increase its predictive power and suit various health behavioural contexts (e.g., see Orji et al., [59]). Finally, social influence is found as an essential determinant of physical activity behaviour [58].

The HBM has been successfully applied in the design of many persuasive interventions for physical activity [32, 38, 49]. Some researchers focus on designing interventions for the physical activity of a particular group of people. For instance, Hoseini et al. [35] investigated the effect of an intervention based on the Health Belief Model on the physical activity of females at risk for hypertension. The intervention plan was comprised of three education sessions that were conducted in four weeks. To evaluate the effectiveness of the interventions, the authors evaluated the physical activity level of the participants before and two months after the intervention. The results showed that physical activity levels increased significantly after deploying the intervention. A more recent study [8] focused on HBM and physical activity in a collectivist culture. Saudi Arabia was considered as a use case sample. The study also investigated the moderating effect of age and gender. The results demonstrated that Social influence, Cue to action and Perceived severity are the strongest determinants of physical activity in Saudi adults.

In addition to the theoretical work on HBM and physical activity, research has led to designing mobile applications that are based on the HBM determinants to promote physical activity behaviour. For instance, *Fish'n'Steps* is a persuasive game designed to promote physical activity by mapping the growth of a fish with the user step count [52]. It employed some HBM determinants in its design. Particularly, the game adopted the Perceived Benefit determinant as follows: if the total number of steps exceeded a predefined target, the fish's appearance improved to the next growth level. The user's success in achieving the daily step goal also affected the facial expression of the fish, happy when the goal is reached, angry when the goal is partially reached, and sad if the goal is not reached. These different facial expressions can be associated with perceived susceptibility. Besides, the second version of the game adopted the Perceived Severity as follows: a team of players can play the game such that each user has one fish in a shared fish tank containing four fishes. The growth of each fish impacts the whole fish tank. If any of the team members did not achieve the step goal, the tank's coloration was gradually removed, and the water got darker. The consequences of not achieving the step goal of each member can be associated with perceived severity [52].

Time for Break [54] is another example of HBM-based apps. This app implements Cue to Action through periodic notifications adjustable via personalized settings to allow people to set up their preferred work and break duration. These notifications encourage moving and standing.

Despite the existence of prior studies in the use of HBM determinants for physical activity, the work in this domain is still limited in the sense that they do not investigate the cultural differences; Most existing research focuses on the Western audience, who are mostly individualist culture. Up to our knowledge, the literature lacks a study that evaluates the cultural impact (individualist vs. collectivist) on the effectiveness of persuasive interventions for physical activity based on the HBM determinants. Having said that, this study investigates the possible cultural differences between individualism and collectivism on how the determinants influence people's physical activity behaviour. This will inform the design of culturally-tailored persuasive interventions and increase their suitability for the target group as well as their effectiveness at motivating physical activity. Specifically, this study investigates *if* and *how* behaviour determinants can be tailored in PT interventions targeting various cultures to effectively promote physical activity among the target audience. We consider two different cultures, Individualist (presented by a Canadian sample) and collectivist (presented by Saudi sample).

3   Method

In our study, we aimed to address the HBM determinants that can guide in designing culturally relevant persuasive interventions for promoting physical activity. To uncover the HBM determinants of physical activity among Saudi adults and Canadians and the moderating effect of age and gender, we adopted a quantitative research approach. We designed an HBM based survey in which we considered the six determinants: *Perceived susceptibility, Perceived severity, Perceived benefit, Perceived barrier* and *Self-efficacy,* in addition to the *Social influence* factor. In this section, we briefly discussed the instruments used to measure the HBM determinants, the data collection and the demographics of our participants.

3.1 Measurement Instrument

Before conducting the study, we reviewed the HBM determinants, and their application for promoting physical activity. Also, the study was approved by the University Research Ethics Board. The survey involves questions about the seven determinants (six determinants of HBM and Social Influence), in addition to participants' demographics and intention to be physically active. All the survey questions were measured using a 7-point Likert scale ranging from 1 (Strongly disagree) to 7 (Strongly agree). The selected question were adapted and validated by previous research [10, 32, 43, 49, 55, 59].

Before deploying the main study, we pilot-tested the survey on 15 participants for refinement. To enable us to accommodate the Saudi audience, the survey was translated from English to Arabic by a native speaker who is fluent in both languages, and the translation was validated by two other native speakers who are fluent in both languages. Therefore, the Arabic version of the survey was distributed to the Saudi audience (collectivist audience), and the English version was shared with the Canadian audience (individualist audience). Participants in this survey are 18 or over.

3.2 Participants Recruitment

The target population for the study is Canadian and Saudi adults. Our participants were recruited via social media and through University email lists. In order to recruit public participants, we posted announcements on social media groups (e.g., Twitter and Facebook). Participation was voluntary, and no compensation was offered. Data were collected (between December 2018 and February 2019). A total of 217 Canadian responses were received, of which four were removed as they were incomplete. The total of Saudi responses received was 225, of which eight were removed as they were incomplete. Table 1 presents the participants' demographic information.

Table 1. Summary of Participants' Demography in the HBM Survey

Variables		Canada (N = 213)	Saudi (N = 217)	Total (N = 430)
Gender	Male	109	55	164
	Female	102	162	264
	Non-Binary	2	0	2
Age Group	Younger Adults (18–35)	118	144	262
	Older Adults (over 35)	95	73	168

4 Data Analysis

The main objective of our study is to conduct a systematic comparison of Saudi and Canadian audiences with respect to their determinant of physical activity. Specifically, we examine the similarities and the differences between collectivists and individualist audiences with respect to the determinants of physical activity and whether gender and age moderate the influence of these determinants on their physical activity behaviour.

After applying the reliability and validity tests, the verified data from the extended HBM survey is analyzed in two steps: First, we conducted a Confirmatory Factor Analysis (CFA) to test whether the survey data fit our hypothesized model (i.e., if the data replicate the seven determinants in physical activity behaviour [20]. SmartPLS3[1] was used to perform a component-based confirmatory factor analysis CFA for each data group. Second, we established the relationship between the extended HBM determinants and the physical activity behaviour using Partial Least Squares (PLS) Structural Equation Modeling (SEM) [44]. To do that, we developed two models of physical activity determinants: one for each culture (Saudi, and Canadian audiences). In addition, we developed eight models to investigate the impact of gender and age within and between the cultural groups (4 for the Saudi and 4 for the Canadians). PLS-SEM is powerful and it is recommended to analyze behavioural data, especially if the data includes many variables to be observed [67]. Figure 1 shows the structural model.

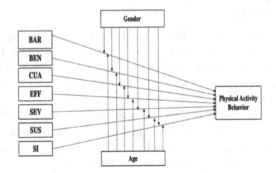

Fig. 1. PLS-SEM model structure

To explore the differences and similarities between individualists and collectivists in their physical activity determinants, we developed ten different models and conducted a multi-group comparison using the in-build SmartPLS feature for conducting multi-group comparisons. Specifically, to test if differences exist between collectivists and individualists, we separated data into two groups and built a model for each group. Then, we examined the influences of the seven determinants on physical activity behaviour in the two models.

Again, before comparing the collectivist and individualist models, we established measurement invariance between Saudi and Canadian samples. The psychometric properties from our two groups show that they have the same structure; therefore, our data

---

[1] https://www.smartpls.com/

is suitable to conduct a multi-group comparison. Measurement invariance was assessed using component-based CFA via SmartPLS 3 [34, 65].

Examining variations both within the same culture and between cultures plays a significant role in the validity and generalizability of the findings. Failure to consider variations within the same culture could lead to overgeneralization of the findings [30]. Therefore, acknowledging within-cultural variations is fundamental in cross-cultural comparisons. In our study, we consider variations both within the same culture and between cultures by examining the moderating effects of age and gender groups on collectivists and individualists. The Saudi and Canadian samples were further separated by gender and age. Hence, we developed eight additional models of physical activity behaviour: four for the culture/age groups (individualist younger and older adults, and collectivist younger and older adults) and four for the culture/gender groups (individualist males and females, collectivist males and females). To create two distinct age groups, we categorize participants into two age groups: Younger Adults (18–35) and older adults category (> 35 years old), as depicted in Table 1.

4.1 Model Validity and Reliability

Before analyzing the data, we evaluate its suitability and reliability using several recommended measures and tools for model reliability and validity [9, 56]. We follow a well-established approach that has been used by many researchers [56] in examining the model's reliability and validity.

1. Data Suitability: we used the Kaiser-Meyer-Olkin (KMO) sampling adequacies and the Bartlett Test of Sphericity [40] to assess the suitability of the data. The results show that KMO was (0.951), which is above the recommended value (0.6). The Bartlett Test of Sphericity was statistically significant ($\chi 2(3003) = 43,427.379$, $p < 0.0001$). That demonstrates the suitability of our data for analysis [50].
2. Measurement Model: the validity, reliability, and consistency in the PLS-SEM model were measured using the following criteria. First, for indicator reliability, we examined the indicators loadings of the models, and they were all above the recommended value (0.7) [15]. Second, we assessed the internal consistency and reliability using composite reliability (CR) and Cronbach's alpha. All results were higher than their threshold value of 0.7 [15, 29]. Third, the average variance extracted (AVE) [56] was used to check data for convergent reliability, and all constructs have an AVE above the recommended threshold of 0.5 [15].
3. Finally, we evaluated discriminant validity using the Heterotrait-Monotrait (HTMT) ratio of correlations and found that HTMT was all below the recommended limit of 0.9 [15].

To summarize, the scale reliability and validity for Canadian and Saudi yielded acceptable results for all indices for PLS-SEM model validity and reliability as presented in Table 2 and Table 3.

Table 2. Canadian scale validity/reliability

Variables	AVE	Composite reliability	Cronbach's alpha
Threshold values	≥0.5	≥0.7	≥0.7
BAR	0.513	0.893	0.871
BEN	0.544	0.953	0.947
CUA	0.504	0.909	0.888
EFF	0.598	0.899	0.867
SEV	0.625	0.832	0.717
SUS	1.000	1.000	1.000
SI	0.625	0.869	0.625
BEH	0.555	0.833	0.733

BAR = perceived barrier, BEN = perceived benefit, CUA = cue to action, EFF = self-efficacy, SEV = perceived severity, SUS = perceived susceptibility, SI = social influence, BEH = physical activity behaviour.

Table 3. Saudi scale validity/reliability

Variables	AVE	Composite reliability	Cronbach's alpha
Threshold values	≥0.5	≥0.7	≥0.7
BAR	0.686	0.813	0.742
BEN	0.526	0.943	0.935
CUA	0.514	0.880	0.842
EFF	0.651	0.880	0.815
SEV	0.707	0.827	0.725
SUS	1.000	1.000	1.000
SI	0.649	0.880	0.823
BEH	0.549	0.827	0.719

BAR = perceived barrier, BEN = perceived benefit, CUA = cue to action, EFF = self-efficacy, SEV = perceived severity, SUS = perceived susceptibility, SI = social influence, BEH = physical activity behaviour

5 Result

The results from our models reveal some interesting similarities and differences between participants based on their cultures, gender, and age group with respect to the influence of the six HBM determinants and social influence (SI) on their physical activity behaviour as shown in Tables 4, 5, and 6. In this section, we summarize and compare the results for various groups as well as explain the results.

5.1 General Model – Saudi Arabians vs. Canadians

The results in Table 4 shows that social influence, cue to action, and severity emerged as significant motivators of physical activity among the Saudi audience. Perceived barrier is the only determinant that influences physical activity behaviour negatively for the Saudi audience. On the other hand, for Canadians, cue to action, self-efficacy, social influence, and perceived benefit significantly influenced physical activity behaviour, while barrier does not have a significant effect on Canadians.

By comparing the results for both groups, we notice that social influence emerged as the strongest determinant for Saudi physical activity behaviour. However, the same determinant is the third-strongest determinant for Canadians. Possible interpretations of these results can be obtained from the characteristics of collectivist and individualist culture according to Hofstede [76].

Individualist cultures promote individual identity and encourage the achievement of individual objectives, whereas in collectivist cultures such as Saudi Arabia, the focus is on group identities, and individuals are encouraged to cooperate to achieve group objectives [25]. That explains why social influence is the strongest factor for motivating the Saudi audience. Perceived benefit emerged as a significant determinant for Canadians but not for the Saudi audience. A possible explanation is that the benefit of physical activity and risk (susceptibility) of inactivity are usually operationalized in persuasive applications as benefits and risks to individuals. These may not motivate people from the collectivist culture who care more about the effect on their in-group – community, family, and significant others. Similarly, self-efficacy emerged as a significant determinant for Canadians but not for the Saudi audience.

Table 4. Standardized path coefficients and Significance of the models for individualist and collectivist cultures. The numbers represent coefficients that are significant at least at p < .05, and '–' represents non-significant coefficients

	BAR	BEN	CUA	EFF	SEV	SUS	SI
Saudi Arabia	–.26	–	.15	–	.11	–	.24
Canada	–	.12	.35	.22	.13	–	.18

BAR = perceived barrier, BEN = perceived benefit, CUA = cue to action, EFF = self-efficacy, SEV = perceived severity, SUS = perceived susceptibility, SI = social influence.

The non-significant effect of self-efficacy on physical activity behaviour also speaks to the characteristics of the collectivists. They may not be motivated to engage in physical activity if their in-group are doing otherwise, even if they believe they can do it as individuals. This is supported by the emergence of social influence as the strongest determinant of physical activity among Saudi audiences. This means Saudi's are more likely to be influenced by others to engage in physical activity. They are more likely to be physically active if their in-group are physically active [8].

5.2 Moderating Effect of Gender and Age

In this section, we present and compare the results of the moderating effect of gender and age within and between the cultural groups.

Saudi Males and Females. As shown in Table 5, Saudi males and females share some significant similarities and differences with respect to how the seven determinants influence their physical activity behaviour. Self-efficacy, cue to action, and severity (in decreasing order) are the significant motivators of physical activity for the Saudi female group. For Saudi males, cue to action, social influence and susceptibility emerged as the strongest motivators of physical activity. On the other hand, barriers and susceptibility negatively influence physical activity behaviour for Saudi females, while Saudi males are negatively associated with perceived barriers only. Benefit and social influence are not significantly related to Saudi females, whereas benefit and severity are non-significant motivators for the Saudi male. Association with perceived severity and social influence emerged as the main differentiators of Saudi males and females.

Canadian Males and Females. Canadian males and females share some significant similarities and differences in the effect of the determinants on their physical activity. The determinants cue to action and social influence significantly influence behaviour for Canadian males and females (although at different degrees). Cue to action emerged as the strongest determinant for Canadian males, while social influence is the strongest determinant for Canadian females. Barriers impact physical activity behaviour negatively for Canadian males and females, whereas self-efficacy and susceptibility are not significant for both groups. Perceived Benefit is positively associated with physical activity behaviour for Canadian males, whereas it is not significant for Canadian females. Perceived benefit and severity emerged as the main differentiator of Canadian males from females.

Table 5. Standardized path coefficients and significance of the models for males and females within the individualist and collectivist cultures. The numbers represent coefficients that are significant at least at p < .05, and '-' represents non-significant coefficient.

	SI	SUS	SEV	BAR	BEN	CUA	EFF
Saudi Females	–	−.12	.25	.32	.26	–	−.25
Saudi Males	.25	.13	–	.11	.37	–	−.23
Canadian Females	.26	–	.13	–	.10	–	−.26
Canadian Males	.15	–	–	–	.21	.15	−.33

BAR = perceived barrier, BEN = perceived benefit, CUA = cue to action, EFF = self-efficacy, SEV = perceived severity, SUS = perceived susceptibility, SI = social influence.

Saudi Younger and Older Adults. As shown in Table 6, the results for younger and older Saudi adults show some interesting similarities and differences. Social influence and cue to action positively influence both younger and older Saudis' physical activity while the perceived benefit is not significant in both age groups. However, perceived barrier is perceived negatively in both younger and older Saudi adults. Younger and older Saudi adults differ in their perception of self-efficacy, severity, and susceptibility. Older Saudi adults perceive susceptibility as positive, while the same determinant is not significant for younger Saudis. Self-efficacy is not significant for younger Saudi adults, whereas it negatively affects behaviour for older Saudi adults. Finally, severity is positively associated with younger Saudi adults, whereas it is not significant for older Saudi adults.

Table 6. Standardized path coefficients and significance of the models for younger and older adults within the individualist and collectivist cultures. The numbers represent coefficients that are significant at least at p < .05, and '–' represents non-significant

	BAR	BEN	CUA	EFF	SEV	SUS	SI
Saudi Younger Adults	−.33	–	.15	–	.19	–	.16
Saudi Older Adults	−.40	–	.12	−.16	–	.13	.50
Canadian Younger Adults	−.32	.26	.28	–	–	–	–
Canadian Older Adults	−.12	–	.41	.23	.32	−.13	.17

BAR = perceived barrier, BEN = perceived benefit, CUA = cue to action, EFF = self-efficacy, SEV = perceived severity, SUS = perceived susceptibility, SI = social influence.

Canadian Younger and Older Adults. Similar to the Saudi model, the results for younger and older Canadian adults show some interesting similarities and differences as well. Both younger and older Canadian adults perceive cue to action as the strongest determinant of physical activity, whereas barrier discourages both groups from being physically active. On the other hand, younger and older Canadian adults differ in their perception of benefit, social influence, susceptibility, severity, and self-efficacy. Older Canadian adults perceive social influence, severity, and self-efficacy as positive, while these determinants are not significantly associated with physical activity behaviour for younger Canadian adults. In contrast, older Canadian adults perceive susceptibility as negative, while susceptibility is not significant in motivating physical activity behaviour for younger Canadian adults. Finally, benefit positively motivates younger Canadian adults and is not significant for Canadian older adults.

6 Discussion

This section discusses the results presented in the previous section and provides interpretations of the findings, in addition to design recommendations.

- Perceived Susceptibility: Considering the result of perceived susceptibility presented in Table 4, both Saudi and Canadian participants do not care about the risk of being physically inactive as the models show that the relationship between perceived susceptibility and the likelihood of physical activity is not significant. This is probably because, in the collectivist culture, family and other in-group members are expected to bear the possible negative consequences of risky behaviours [16]. For instance, if the person gets a physical inactivity-related disease, relatives easily take care of their sick ones. Therefore, collectivists act as a cushion against potential losses at an individual level. Thus, perceived susceptibility does not significantly impact the behaviour of people from collectivist cultures (e.g., Saudi Arabia) since it is often operationalized as a risk to an individual (rather than to a group) in intervention designs. Consequently, persuasive interventions that portray potential risks of not performing physical activity in terms of risk to oneself are not likely to motivate physical activity among Saudi adults (specifically the female and younger adult groups).

Saudi females perceive susceptibility negatively, which implies that employing susceptibility may demotivate them to perform physical activity. This is probably because, in Saudi, females are expected to live their lives with others who take care of them, such as their parents and spouses. Hence, they may have a wrong evaluation of the possible risk of physical inactivity to themselves and may view it as unrealistic. Our results also suggest that younger adults are careless about the risk associated with physical inactivity. This observation is in line with previous research, which found that young adults are more likely to care more about superficial benefits such as improvement in physical appearance rather than the possible associated risk of unhealthy behaviour (e.g., diseases) [35, 36].

Moreover, research has shown that cultural backgrounds can affect the person's perceptions about a disease, including its causes, symptoms, and treatment, and health, which reflects on the person's health beliefs [53, 56, 62]. These cultural differences can explain the variance in our results between Canadian and Saudi groups with respect to how the perceived susceptibility affects their physical activity behaviour.

Based on the results, we suggest that for people from the collectivist culture, persuasive strategies such as self-monitoring, loss-framed appeal, and simulation could be employed and operationalized in a way to show the risk associated with physical inactivity to an individual's family and other in-group members [8].

- Perceived Severity is known as "the seriousness of the consequences of developing a health condition"[56]. The results of perceived severity vary among the different groups. It is positively associated with Canadians and Saudis in general, including both Canadian and Saudi females, Saudi younger adults, and Canadian older adults. This implies that these groups may be motivated to be physically active by interventions that allow them to visualize the seriousness of the consequences of being physically inactive [42]. On the other hand, perceived severity is not significant for Saudi older adults, Canadian younger adults, and both Canadian and Saudi males. This implies that not only cultural backgrounds can affect the person's perceptions about diseases and the causes and cures, but also age and gender. This implies that individuals who associate the causes and cures for disease to external factors (such as religious beliefs or genetic makeup) will have adverse beliefs of the relationship between diseases and physical inactivity. Our results show that Saudi older adults, Canadian younger adults, and both Canadian and Saudi males belong to such a group. Therefore, they underrate the consequences of physical inactivity-related diseases such as losing work and money due to sickness-related issues [55]. Based on these results, we suggest tailoring persuasive applications that apply severity to motivate physical activity based on a person's perception of threat. For people from the collectivist culture, specifically older adults and males, the severity could be operationalized to show the seriousness of the consequences of physical inactivity with respect to the effect on an individual's family and other in-group members. For example, showing the seriousness of how getting a disease as a result of physical inactivity would affect the entire family's happiness, peace, and usual daily programs is more likely to motivate them to be physically active. Accordingly, persuasive strategies, such as *simulation,* can be employed to show the cause-and-effect linkage of physical inactivity to getting certain diseases and how that affects the group's happiness and peace.

- Perceived Barrier is significantly negatively associated with most groups, including the Saudi general model, both Canadian and Saudi females and males, and both Canadian and Saudi younger and older adults. For behaviour change to occur, perceived benefits must outweigh the perceived barriers [39]. This can explain why the perceived barrier is non-significant in the general Canadian audience, while they are significantly motivated by perceived benefits. Also, individualists (Canadians) consider self-benefit and personal achievement more than difficulties and the cost associated with performing the behaviours (barriers) compared to the collectivists (Saudis) [55]. For Saudis, our results show that among the HBM determinants, the perceived barrier is the strongest determinant that is negatively associated with physical activity in the general model. Perceived barrier show stronger relation with Saudi females than males. These results are in line with previous research [6, 8, 27]. The higher relationship with perceived barriers in Saudi females could be linked mainly to social and cultural factors, as Saudi females usually have limited opportunities compared to Saudi males to engage in outdoor activities. For instance, females are required adherence to appropriate forms of dressing and conduct code and may not be allowed to go to certain places or do certain things. They are more restricted than males [7, 70]. For example, Saudi females are not expected to engage in certain activities such as swimming in public pools. Besides, there are fewer and more expensive available female gyms compared to those for Saudi males [5]. Therefore, persuasive application designers aiming to motivate physical activity in Saudis should be aware of the inhibiting influence of perceived barrier in their design. Persuasive apps can focus on suggesting strategies and skills to overcome the barriers, such as recommending indoor activities that do not require going to the gym, recommending nearby gender-appropriate gyms, and recommending culturally and religiously acceptable exercise routines to avoid being stereotyped.

- Perceived Benefit significantly motivates Canadians in general, Canadian males, and Canadian younger adults, whereas it is not significant for Canadian older adults and all of the Saudi groups. This implies that individualists (Canadians) are more motivated to perform physical activities because of the benefit associated with physical activity [55]. Hence, an application that helps Canadians to see the benefit associated with physical activity is more likely to motivate them. Canadians are more likely to perform the behaviour if the benefits outweigh the barriers. A possible explanation for Saudi results is that Saudis view the benefits associated with performing physical activity as a shared benefit. That is, the benefit of physical activity should be reflected in terms of how it affects their community or the group they are associated with rather than personal benefit. Unfortunately, most of the benefits as operationalized in HBM are focused on personal benefits (benefits to self), not group or community-related benefits of performing physical activity. This is in line with previous research, which concluded that most existing theories and models are designed to be more appropriate for people from Western cultures [8, 55, 57]. Thus, physical activity intervention designers may employ strategies that emphasize the group/community-related benefits of physical activity for Saudi groups. By surveying the literature, we found that Rewards and Gain-framed appeal strategies are among the most common implementations of perceived benefits. Thus, PT could employ the *reward* and *gain-framed appeal* persuasive strategies to show the benefit of physical activity not only to an individual's health but reflect the happiness, peace, and stability that good health could bring to the entire family or community.

- Cue to Action "can be thought of as any event or stimuli that trigger the performance of a target behaviour" [55]. Cue to action emerged to be the only factor that is significant among all Canadian and Saudi groups. This highlights the importance of implementing various cue to action-orientated strategies such as reminders, prompts, and alerts in physical activity promotion interventions targeting the Canadian or Saudi population to promote desired behaviours. People may know the benefit of the behaviour but may still need some nudge to take action towards performing the desired behaviours. Thus, based on the literature, *persuasive strategies* such as *reminders* and *suggestion* would work well in this context [8].

- Self-efficacy can be described as "confidence in one's ability to perform the new health behaviour" [60]. Self-efficacy is positively associated with the Canadian general group, Canadian older adults, and Saudi females and males. The significant association with self-efficacy implies that these groups are more likely to perform the physical activity if the intervention is implemented to boost their self-efficacy with respect to promoting their ability to be physically active. Therefore, persuasive designers should employ strategies such as *incremental goal setting, feedback, praise* and *recognition to build self-efficacy* [8, 55]. On the other hand, self-efficacy is negatively associated with Saudi older adults. This negative association can be due to the negative believes of this group in their ability, which, in turn, is due to the lack of experience of exercising in the past that has created self-doubt.

- Social Influence refers to the influence that other people have on us and our behaviours. The results show that social influence is significant for most of the groups. It's significantly positively associated with Saudi and Canadian general audience, Saudi males, Saudi younger and older adults, Canadian males and females, and Canadian older adults. Although these groups are positively associated with social influence, they vary in the magnitude of the social influence impact. Most Saudi groups are more strongly associated with social influence than the Canadian audience. An interpretation can be derived from the characteristics of collectivists. For instance, most collectivists' behaviours are regulated by group norms and community expectations. Therefore, they are more affected by social influence. Surprisingly, the results indicate that social influence is not significant for Saudi female and Canadian younger adult groups. This contrasts with the results of a previous study that found that females are more motivated by social influence than males [14]. A possible explanation for Saudi females is that many of them believe that physical activity is not for them [5]. Persuasive intervention designers should apply strategies that promote social influence such as *cooperation, social comparison, social facilitation, and social learning* to promote physical activity in all the considered groups except for Saudi females and Canadian younger adults. To design for Saudi females, persuasive intervention designers should focus on strategies that build their confidence in their ability since self-efficacy is the strongest determinant for them. Thus, strategies such as *incremental goal setting, feedback, praise* and *recognition* could be employed to build self-efficacy.

6.1 Using Our Results to One-Size-Fits-All and Personalized Physical Activity App Design

This section presents our recommendations for designers of persuasive technologies for promoting physical activities. Based on our findings, we suggest design tips for both one-size-fits-all and personalized approaches.

- One-Size-Fits-All Approach: Many PT designers adopt a one-size-fits-all approach. Recent research found that theory-driven design has a better chance to succeed. Therefore, even a one-size-fits-all approach should be based on theory and experimental results. This section provides general recommendations for PT designers who follow a one-size-fits-all approach.

As shown in Table 7, the Perceived barrier is the only determinant that is not perceived as positive by any group; in fact, it significantly influences physical activity negatively for all the groups except the Canadian general group. Therefore, PT designers should *avoid strategies that* emphasize *barriers*; instead, they should focus on using various strategies, such as suggestions and reminders to overcome the various barriers associated with physical activity when designing for Saudi and Canadian audiences, irrespective of their age or gender.

On the other hand, Cue to action is perceived as positive by all participants, irrespective of their group. Therefore, persuasive interventions targeted at Saudis and Canadians should employ strategies that emphasize cue to action, such as *reminders and suggestions* irrespective of the group. In addition, social influence is positively associated with the majority of the considered groups, and it is not negatively associated with any group. Thus, we recommend designers employ the Social influence strategies such as *cooperation, social comparison, social facilitation, and social learning* to promote physical activities in the collectivist and individualist' groups.

- **Personalization Approach:** Although one-size-fits-all approaches show success, to some extent, researchers have found that personalizing persuasive interventions enhances their effectiveness. Therefore, this section provides recommendations for tailoring PT interventions to a particular subgroup (e.g., collectivist females and collectivist young people). Table 7 summarizes our results. It shows the association between each group and the seven determinants. Based on our results, we present the following design recommendations for tailoring persuasive interventions for promoting physical activity.

As Table 7 shows, the Perceived benefit is positively associated with the general Canadian group. So, we recommend using persuasive strategies such as Rewards and Gain-framed appeal to motivate Canadian users in general. These strategies, however, are more effective with Canadian males and younger adults. So, if the designer to provide more fine-grained design, we recommend emphasizing benefits to motivate Canadian males and younger adults. On the other hand, our results did not show any association between benefits and Saudi groups. So, we do not recommend using it for any Saudi group.

Our results also show a positive association between Self-efficacy and the general Canadian group, but it has no significant association with particular Canadian groups (Male/Female, younger/older adults). On the other hand, Self-efficacy is positively associated with both Saudi males and females groups and negatively with Saudi older adults. It is not significantly associated with the general Saudi group, however. Accordingly, persuasive technologies that are designed for the general individualist culture, regardless of the gender and age strategies, as well as males and female groups of collectivist cultures, should boost the person's ability to perform physical activity. Particularly, persuasive strategies, such as Incremental Goal Setting, Feedback, and Recognition, are good choices to motivate the aforementioned groups to engage in physical activity.

Table 7. Summary of appropriate determinants for motivating physical activity among various cultural groups. '√' represent strategies that can be used for each group, 'X' represent strategies that should be avoided, CA: Canada, SA: Saudi

Cultural Groups	BAR	BEN	CUA	EFF	SEV	SUS	SI
SA General	X		√		√		√
CA General		√	√	√	√		√
SA Females	X		√	√	√	X	
SA Males	X		√	√		√	√
CA Females	X		√		√		√
CA Males	X	√	√				√
SA Young Adults	X		√		√		√
SA Older Adults	X		√	X		√	√
CA Young Adults	X	√	√				
CA Older Adults	X		√		√	X	√

Among all the determinants, severity has the second strongest positive appeal to Canadian older adults; however, it's not significant for Canadian younger adults. Similarly, severity strongly appeals to Saudi females but not Saudi males. Therefore, PTs targeted at individualist older adults, Collectivist younger adults, or females (collectivist or individualist) should emphasize the consequences of being physically inactive. According to the literature, *Punishment*, *Negative Reinforcement*, and *Simulation* are examples of persuasive strategies that help emphasize the seriousness of the consequences of physical inactivity.

Perceived susceptibility emerged as the second least significant determinant. It is positively associated with two groups only, Saudi males and older adults. So, we suggest employing it, along with other determinants (e.g., Cue to action and Social Influence), to improve the effectiveness of the intervention. Based on that, persuasive interventions targeted individualists males, and older adults should emphasize the risks associated with being physically inactive. To do so, designers can use strategies, such as Self-monitoring, loss-farmed appeal, and Simulation.

6.2 Mapping the Determinants to Persuasive Strategies

In this section, we map the extended HBM determinants of physical activity for Saudi and Canadian adults to the appropriate persuasive strategies. In order to make our findings and recommendations actionable for persuasive interventions, we mapped every determinant to a set of persuasive strategies. The mapping was done based on an extensive literature review, opinions of seven experts in the area of HCI, Persuasive Computing, and health, while taking into consideration the main characteristic of collectivist and individualist cultures into account [55]. Specifically, we reviewed the literature and identified various approaches to implement each determinant. Then, and to ensure accuracy, we had two focus group sessions with seven researchers and experts in in the domains of HCI, persuasive computing, and health. The experts discussed and agreed on the final mapping. For example, Social influence (SI) is mapped to the cooperation, social facilitation, social learning, and comparison strategies. Table 8 shows the inferred mapping.

Table 8. Summary of the sample mapping of determinants to persuasive strategies

Perceived barrier	Perceived benefit	Cue to Action	Self-efficacy	Perceived severity	Perceived susceptibility	Social influence
Suggestion	Reward, and Gain-framed appeal	Reminder, And Suggestion	Incremental goal setting, Feedback, Praise, and Recognition	Punishment, negative reinforcement, Vicarious reinforcement, and Simulation	Self-mentoring, Loss-farmed appeal, and Simulation	Cooperation, Social facilitation, Social learning, and Comparison

We mapped cue to action (CUA) to the reminder and suggestion strategies, as suggested by previous research [59]. Perceived severity (SEV) determinant is mapped to punishment, negative reinforcement, vicarious reinforcement, and simulation strategy. These four strategies show the seriousness of the consequences of inactivity [56, 77]. We mapped Perceived barrier (BAR) to suggestion strategy because suggestion helps overcome the barriers by recommending feasible solutions, such as recommending indoor activities that may appeal to one and nearby gender-appropriate gyms. Perceived benefit (BEN) is mapped to reward and gain-framed appeal persuasive strategies with an emphasis on the group/community-related benefits of physical activity. Perceived susceptibility (SUS) is mapped to self-mentoring, loss-framed appeal and simulation that could be operationalized in a way to show the risk associated with physical inactivity to an individual's family and other in-group members. Lastly, self-efficacy (EFF) is mapped to feedback, incremental goal setting, recognition, and praise.

6.3 Limitations and Future Work

The Health Belief Model employed in this work has been widely employed in many health behaviours areas. Our results could be applied in other health domains. However, they should be applied with caution as they may not generalize. We also acknowledge the gender imbalance in our Saudi participant sample, which may limit the generalizability of our findings. As part of our future work, we will apply the guidelines we describe above to design and evaluate a persuasive intervention tailored to motivate physical activity among people from collectivist cultures. We will also investigate the generalizability of our model across other domains.

7 Conclusion

Over the past decades, many PT applications have been developed to promote physical activity behaviour by manipulating various health determinants and PT strategies. However, these applications are usually developed and evaluated in individualistic countries. As a result, there is a lack of evidence on how to make PT appropriate for collectivists. In this paper, we presented an extended HBM model to investigate and compare the determinants of physical activity among Saudi and Canadian adults as a case study and representative of collectivist and individualist cultures, respectively. Our models revealed some differences between various cultural groups and sub-groups, and we discussed these differences from the perspective of physical activity promotion and PT intervention design. We also measured the moderating effect of age and gender on Saudi and Canadian audiences and discussed their implications for designing the persuasive intervention. Then we presented design opportunities for both a one-size-fits- all and a personalized approach to PT intervention design. Finally, we map the determinants of physical activity to their corresponding persuasive strategies that can be used in operationalizing them in persuasive applications for promoting physical activity.

References

1. Abroms, L.C., Padmanabhan, N., Thaweethai, L., Phillips, T.: IPhone apps for smoking cessation: a content analysis. Am. J. Prevent. Med. **40**, 279–285 (2011). https://doi.org/10.1016/j.amepre.2010.10.032
2. Ahtinen, A., Ramiah, S., Blom, J., Isomursu, M.: Design of mobile wellness applications: identifying cross-cultural factors. In: Proceedings of the 20th Australasian Conference on Computer-Human Interaction: Designing for Habitus and Habitat, OZCHI 2008 (2008)
3. Airhihenbuwa, C.O.: Culture matters in global health. Eur. Health Psychol. **12**(4), 52–55 (2010)
4. Ajzen, I. 1991. The theory of planned behaviour. Organ. Behav. Human Decis. Processes (1991). DOI:https://doi.org/10.1016/0749-5978(91)90020-T
5. Al-Eisa, E.S., Al-Sobayel, H.I.: Physical activity and health beliefs among Saudi women. J. Nutr. Metabol. (2012). https://doi.org/10.1155/2012/642187
6. Al-Hazzaa, H.M.: School backpack: how much load do saudi schools boys carry on their shoulders? Saudi Med. J. **27**, 1567–1571 (2006)

7. Al-Nakeeb, Y., et al.: Obesity, physical activity and sedentary behaviour amongst British and Saudi youth: a cross-cultural study. Int. J. Environ. Res. Public Health **9**, 1490–1506 (2012). https://doi.org/10.3390/ijerph9041490

8. Almutari, N., Orji, R.: Culture and health belief model: exploring the determinants of physical activity among Saudi adults and the moderating effects of age and gender. In: UMAP 2021 - Proceedings of the 29th ACM Conference on User Modeling, Adaptation and Personalization (2021)

9. Alqahtani, F., Meier, S., Orji, R.: Personality-based approach for tailoring persuasive mental health applications. User Model. User-Adapt. Interact. **32**, 353–295 (2021). https://doi.org/10.1007/s11257-021-09289-5

10. Anderson, E.S., Wojcik, J.R., Winett, R.A., Williams, D.M.: Social-cognitive determinants of physical activity: the influence of social support, self-efficacy, outcome expectations, and self-regulation among participants in a church-based health promotion study. Health Psychol. **25**, 510 (2006). https://doi.org/10.1037/0278-6133.25.4.510

11. Ayubi, S.U., Parmanto, B.: PersonA: persuasive social network for physical Activity. In: Proceedings of the Annual International Conference of the IEEE Engineering in Medicine and Biology Society, EMBS (2012)

12. Bandura, A.: Social Foundations of Thought and Action: A Social Cognitive Theory/Albert Bandura. Prentice-Hall, Upper Saddle River (1986)

13. Breiner, K., Görlich, D., Maschino, O., Meixner, G., Zühlke, D.: Human-computer interaction. In: Interacting in Various Application Domains2009

14. Carli, L.L.: Gender and social influence. J. Social Issues **57**, 725–741 (2001). https://doi.org/10.1111/0022-4537.00238

15. Chin, W.W. 1998. The partial least squares approach for structural equation modeling. Modern methods for business research

16. Cho, H., Lee, J.S.: The influence of self-efficacy, subjective norms, and risk perception on behavioural intentions related to the H1N1 flu pandemic: a comparison between Korea and the US. Asian J. Social Psychol. **18**, 311–324 (2015). https://doi.org/10.1111/ajsp.12104

17. Choi, B., Lee, I., Kim, J., Jeon, Y.: A qualitative cross-national study of cultural influences on mobile data service design. In: CHI 2005: Technology, Safety, Community: Conference Proceedings - Conference on Human Factors in Computing Systems (2005)

18. Ciman, M., Donini, M., Gaggi, O., Aiolli, F.: Stairstep recognition and counting in a serious Game for increasing users' physical activity. Pers. Ubiq. Comput. **20**(6), 1015–1033 (2016). https://doi.org/10.1007/s00779-016-0968-y

19. Consolvo, S., McDonald, D.W., Landay, J.A.: Theory-driven design strategies for technologies that support behaviour change in everyday life. In: Conference on Human Factors in Computing Systems - Proceedings (2009)

20. Costello, A.B., Osborne, J.W.: Best practices in exploratory factor analysis: four recommendations for getting the most from your analysis. In: Practical Assessment, Research and Evaluation (2005)

21. Country Comparison - Hofstede Insights. https://www.hofstede-insights.com/country-comparison/saudi-arabia/. Accessed 10 Mar 2020

22. Country Comparison - Hofstede Insights: https://www.hofstede-insights.com/country-comparison/canada/. Accessed 10 Mar 2020

23. Davis, S.: The influence of collectivistic and individualistic value orientations on the acceptance of individually-tailored internet communications. J. Educ. Commun. Values **8**, 17–32 (2009)

24. Edney, S., et al.: "Active Team" a social and gamified app-based physical activity intervention: randomised controlled trial study protocol. BMC Public Health **17**(1), 1–11 (2017). https://doi.org/10.1186/s12889-017-4882-7

25. Fijneman, Y.A., et al.: Individualism-collectivism: an empirical study of a conceptual issue. J. Cross-Cult. Psychol. **27**, 381–402 (1996)
26. Fogg, B.J.: Persuasive Technology: Using Computers to Change What We Think and Do (2003)
27. Forrest, K.Y.Z., Bunker, C.H., Kriska, A.M., Ukoli, F.A.M., Huston, S.L., Markovic, N.: Physical activity and cardiovascular risk factors in a developing population. Med. Sci. Sports Exerc. **33**, 1598–1604 (2001). https://doi.org/10.1097/00005768-200109000-00025
28. Furner, C.P., George, J.F.: Cultural determinants of media choice for deception. Comput. Human Behav. **28**, 1427–1439 (2012). https://doi.org/10.1016/j.chb.2012.03.005
29. Gefen, D., Straub, D., Boudreau, M.-C.: Structural equation modeling and regression: guidelines for research practice. Commun. Assoc. Inf. Syst. **4**, 7 (2000). https://doi.org/10.17705/1cais.00407
30. Green, E.G.T., Deschamps, J.C., Páez, D.: Variation of individualism and collectivism within and between 20 countries: a typological analysis. J. Cross-Cult. Psychol. **36**, 321–339 (2005). https://doi.org/10.1177/0022022104273654
31. Grimes, A., Grinter, R.E.: Designing persuasion: health technology for low-income African American communities. In: de Kort, Y., IJsselsteijn, W., Midden, C., Eggen, B., Fogg, B.J. (eds.) PERSUASIVE 2007. LNCS, vol. 4744, pp. 24–35. Springer, Heidelberg (2007). https://doi.org/10.1007/978-3-540-77006-0_4
32. Gristwood, J.: Applying the health belief model to physical activity engagement among older adults. Illuminare Stud. J. Recreation Parks ad Leisure Stud. (2011)
33. Guthold, R., Stevens, G.A., Riley, L.M., Bull, F.C.: Worldwide trends in insufficient physical activity from 2001 to 2016: a pooled analysis of 358 population-based surveys with 1·9 million participants. Lancet Global Health **6**, 1077–1086 (2018). https://doi.org/10.1016/S2214-109X(18)30357-7
34. Henseler, J., Ringle, C.M., Sarstedt, M.: Testing measurement invariance of composites using partial least squares. Int. Mark. Rev. **33**, 405–431 (2016). https://doi.org/10.1108/IMR-09-2014-0304
35. Hoseini, H., Maleki, F., Moeini, M., Sharifirad, G.R.: Investigating the effect of an education plan based on the health belief model on the physical activity of women who are at risk for hypertension. Iranian J. Nurs. Midwifery Res. **19**, 647–652 (2014)
36. Hui, C.H., Triandis, H.C.: Individualism-collectivism. J. Cross Cult. Psychol. (1986). https://doi.org/10.1177/0022002186017002006
37. Irani, L., Vertesi, J., Dourish, P., Philip, K., Grinter, R.E.: Postcolonial computing: a lens on design and development. In: Conference on Human Factors in Computing Systems - Proceedings (2010)
38. Jalilian, F., et al.: Predicting factors related to regular physical activity among Iranian medical college student: an application of health Belief Model. Social Sci. (Pakistan) (2016). https://doi.org/10.3923/sscience.2016.3688.3691
39. Janz, N.K., Becker, M.H.: The health belief model: a decade later. Health Educ. Behav. (1984). https://doi.org/10.1177/109019818401100101
40. Kaiser, H.F.: A second generation little jiffy. Psychometrika (1970). https://doi.org/10.1007/BF02291817
41. Kaptein, M., Lacroix, J., Saini, P.: Individual differences in persuadability in the health promotion domain. In: Ploug, T., Hasle, P., Oinas-Kukkonen, H. (eds.) PERSUASIVE 2010. LNCS, vol. 6137, pp. 94–105. Springer, Heidelberg (2010). https://doi.org/10.1007/978-3-642-13226-1_11
42. Kasmaei, P., et al.: Brushing behaviour among young adolescents: does perceived severity matter. BMC Public Health (2014). https://doi.org/10.1186/1471-2458-14-8
43. Kasser, S.L., Kosma, M.: Health beliefs and physical activity behaviour in adults with multiple sclerosis. Disabil. Health J. (2012). https://doi.org/10.1016/j.dhjo.2012.07.001

44. Ketchen, D.J.: A primer on partial least squares structural equation modeling. Long Range Plan. (2013).https://doi.org/10.1016/j.lrp.2013.01.002
45. Khaled, R., Barr, P., Biddle, R., Fischer, R., Noble, J.: Game design strategies for collectivist persuasion (2009)
46. Khaled, R., Barr, P., Fischer, R., Noble, J., Biddle, R.: Factoring culture into the design of a persuasive game. In: ACM International Conference Proceeding Series (2006)
47. Khaled, R., Biddle, R., Noble, J., Barr, P., Fischer, R.: Persuasive interaction for collectivist cultures. In: Conferences in Research and Practice in Information Technology Series (2006)
48. Kimura, H., Nakajima, T.: Designing persuasive applications to motivate sustainable behaviour in collectivist cultures. PsychNology J. **9** (2011)
49. King, K.A., Vidourek, R.A., English, L., Merianos, A.L.: Vigorous physical activity among college students: using the health belief model to assess involvement and social support. Arch. Exerc. Health Dis. **4**(2), 267–279 (2014). https://doi.org/10.5628/aehd.v4i2.153
50. Kupek, E.: Beyond logistic regression: structural equations modelling for binary variables and its application to investigating unobserved confounders. BMC Med. Res. Methodol. **6**, 1–10 (2006). https://doi.org/10.1186/1471-2288-6-13
51. Li, W.-C., Harris, D., Li, L.-W., Wang, T.: The differences of aviation human factors between individualism and collectivism culture. In: Jacko, J.A. (ed.) HCI 2009. LNCS, vol. 5613, pp. 723–730. Springer, Heidelberg (2009). https://doi.org/10.1007/978-3-642-02583-9_78
52. Lin, J.J., Mamykina, L., Lindtner, S., Delajoux, G., Strub, H.B.: Fish'n' steps: encouraging physical activity with an interactive computer game. In: Dourish, P., Friday, A. (eds.) UbiComp 2006. LNCS, vol. 4206, pp. 261–278. Springer, Heidelberg (2006). https://doi.org/10.1007/11853565_16
53. Vaughn, L.M., Jacquez, F., Bakar, R.C.: Cultural health attributions, beliefs, and practices: effects on healthcare and medical education. Open Med. Educ. J. **2**(1) (2009)
54. Luo, Y., Lee, B., Yvettewohn, D., Rebar, A.L., Conroy, D.E., Choe, E.K.: Time for break: understanding information workers' sedentary behaviour through a break prompting system. In: Conference on Human Factors in Computing Systems - Proceedings (2018)
55. Orji, R., Mandryk, R.L.: Developing culturally relevant design guidelines for encouraging healthy eating behaviour. Int. J. Hum. Comput. Stud. **72**(2), 207–223 (2014). https://doi.org/10.1016/j.ijhcs.2013.08.012
56. Orji, R., Mandryk, R.L., Vassileva, J., Gerling, K.M. 2013. Tailoring persuasive health games to gamer type. In: Proceedings of the SIGCHI Conference on Human Factors in Computing Systems - CHI 2013, vol. 2467 (2013). https://doi.org/10.1145/2470654.2481341
57. Orji, R., Orji, F., Oyibo, K., Ajah, I.A.: Personalizing health theories in persuasive game interventions to gamer types: an African perspective. In: ACM International Conference Proceeding Series (2018)
58. Orji, R., Oyibo, K., Lomotey, R.K., Orji, F.A.: Socially-driven persuasive health intervention design: competition, social comparison, and cooperation. Health Inf. J. **25**(4), 1451–1484 (2019). https://doi.org/10.1177/1460458218766570
59. Orji, R., Vassileva, J., Mandryk, R.: Towards an effective health interventions design: an extension of the health belief model. Online J. Public Health Inf, **4**(3) (2012). https://doi.org/10.5210/ojphi.v4i3.4321
60. Orji, R.O.: Design for Behaviour Change: A Model-driven Approach for Tailoring Persuasive Technologies. University of Saskatchewan, Canada (2014). http://hdl.handle.net/10388/ETD-2014-06-1555
61. Oyibo, K., Adaji, I., Olagunju, A.H., Deters, R., Olabenjo, B., Vassileva, J.: Ben'fit: Design, implementation and evaluation of a culture-tailored fitness app. In: ACM UMAP 2019 Adjunct - Adjunct Publication of the 27th Conference on User Modeling, Adaptation and Personalization (2019)

62. Oyibo, K., Orji, R., Vassileva, J.: The influence of culture in the effect of age and gender on social influence in persuasive technology. In: Adjunct Publication of the 25th Conference on User Modeling, Adaptation and Personalization - UMAP 2017, pp. 47–52 (2017). DOI:https://doi.org/10.1145/3099023.3099071

63. Pooye, S.: Cultural Factors leading to overweight and obesity: a cross-cultural analysis of Japan and the United State of America (2010)

64. Prochaska, J.O., DiClemente, C.C., Norcross, J.C.: In search of how people change: applications to addictive behaviours. Am. Psychol. (1992). https://doi.org/10.1037//0003-066x.47.9.1102

65. Product I SmartPLS: https://www.smartpls.com/. Accessed 19 Mar 2020

66. Reinecke, K.: Culturally Adaptive User Interfaces. * Thesis (2010)

67. Ringle, C.M., Silva, D., Bido, D.S.: Structural equation modeling with the smartpls. REMark - Revista Brasileira de Marketing (2014). DOI:https://doi.org/10.5585/remark.v13i2.2717

68. Rosenstock, I.M.: Why people use health services. The milbank Memorial Fund Quarterly (1966). https://doi.org/10.2307/3348967

69. Rosser, B.A., Eccleston, C.: Smartphone applications for pain management. J. Telemed. Telecare **17**, 308–312 (2011)

70. Samara, A., Nistrup, A., Al-Rammah, T.Y., Aro, A.R.: Lack of facilities rather than socio-cultural factors as the primary barrier to physical activity among female Saudi university students. Int. J. Women's Health (2015). https://doi.org/10.2147/IJWH.S80680

71. Schimmack, U., Oishi, S., Diener, E.: individualism: a valid and important dimension of cultural differences between nations. Pers. Social Psychol. Rev. (2005). https://doi.org/10.1207/s15327957pspr0901_2

72. Sun, T., Horn, M., Merritt, D.: Values and lifestyles of individualists and collectivists: a study on Chinese, Japanese, British and US consumers. J. Consum. Mark. **21**(5), 318–331 (2004). https://doi.org/10.1108/07363760410549140

73. Takahashi, M., Kawasaki, H., Maeda, A., Nakamura, M.: Mobile walking game and group-walking program to enhance going out for older adults, pp. 1372–1380 (2016). https://doi.org/10.1145/2968219.2968415

74. Toscos, T., Faber, A., An, S., Gandhi, M.P.: Chick clique: persuasive technology to motivate teenage girls to exercise. In: BT - In CHI 2006 Extended Abstracts on, Human Factors in Computing Systems (CHI EA 2006) (2006)

75. Triandis, H.C., Gelfand, M.J.: Converging measurement of horizontal and vertical individualism and collectivism. J. Pers. Social Psychol. **74**, 118 (1998). https://doi.org/10.1037/0022-3514.74.1.118

76. Triandis, H.C., Hofstede, G.: Cultures and organizations: software of the mind. Adm. Sci. Q. (1993). https://doi.org/10.2307/2393257

77. Wang, Y., Fadhil, A., Lange, J.P., Reiterer, H.: Integrating taxonomies into theory-based digital health interventions for behaviour change: a holistic framework. J. Med. Internet Res. (2019)

Design Innovation Based on the Material Experience and Tactile Prompting

I-Ying Chiang[1]([✉]) [ID], Po-Hsien Lin[2] [ID], and Rungtai Lin[2] [ID]

[1] Department of Arts and Design, College of Arts, National Tsing Hua University,
Hsinchu 300044, Taiwan
iychiang@mx.nthu.edu.tw

[2] Graduate School of Creative Industry Design, College of Design, National Taiwan University
of Arts, New Taipei 220307, Taiwan
{t0131,rtlin}@mail.ntua.edu.tw

Abstract. The sense of touch has been regarded as the most initial feeling among human's five senses. Mainly relying on corporeal contact, it could process the touch data, transport the sensation information, and create haptic affection. Meanwhile, materials studies have become one of the most critical issues in craft and product design. The material is the soul of craft, and each material brings its unique character. Nevertheless, the material employment of craft objects also reflects its context and extensions of regional culture. Residents from regions with varied cultural contexts might use divergent adjective terms to describe their awareness and sense of touching material. This study aims to analyze the emotional feeling and semantics expression from the material experience and assist educators and designers reasonably in realizing and extracting these haptic elements during the product design process. This case study consults with 6 experts and recruits 10 designers to participate in this practical project. The result shows that people with various backgrounds reveal their diverse preferences and pleasures in the material experience and expression. Specifically, the authors address that employing the haptic semantic could connect and enrich the material experience, cultural elements, and design presentation. This study proposes a new prospection for product design by enhancing the connection between material experience and haptic semantics. The authors suggest that subsequent research may focus on exploiting the haptic semantics with the cultural context and relevant application of AI-co-creation for design innovation.

Keywords: Material Experience (MX) · Tactile Prompting · Haptic Driven Design (HDD) · AI-co-Creation · Process Innovation · Product Innovation

1 Introduction

At the onset of the 21st century, the narrative of an emerging global aesthetic economy signaled a pivot towards a renewed emphasis on haptic engagement. Product designers were thus prompted to focus on the role of tactile sensation and its influence on user experience [1–3]. Since 2019, however, the emergence of pandemic-induced social restrictions has necessitated a shift towards increased reliance on digital interfaces, resulting in a concomitant reduction in the diversity of physical material interactions [2, 3]. This transition has not only altered sensory engagement but also raised questions about the future of corporeal sensation and tactile consciousness, igniting the researchers' interest in exploring uncharted territories of haptic cognition in this altered landscape.

Sensory-derived aesthetic experiences act as a vital channel connecting somatic sensations and self-perception to cognitive recognition [2]. The medium of tangible materials plays a crucial role, engaging individuals through direct tactile interaction, potentially culminating in a profound sense of qualia [2]. Beyond their physical properties, materials possess a more profound, almost spiritual resonance and can evoke extensive semantic networks through the interplay of physical sensations and perceptual awareness [2, 4]. Designers, therefore, must possess a profound comprehension of material experience nuances and haptic cognitive processes to enhance the intricate interrelation between materials and the human sensorium.

This study aims to analyze the emotional feeling and semantics expression from the material experience and assist educators and designers reasonably in realizing and extracting these haptic elements during the product design process. Moreover, the authors further try to implement the constructs of material experience (MX) and haptic semantics (HS) integrated into a haptic-driven design (HDD) framework, identifying the essential components for design innovation.

2 Literature Review

2.1 Material Experience

Over the years, the discussion around the "Material Experience" framework has been a focal point for scholars and designers, leading to the evolution of numerous strategies aimed at augmenting the design process with innovative material considerations [5–7]. Despite the product industry's primary focus on functionality for market success, a cohort of researchers advocates for a broader evaluation of materials, suggesting that they should also be appraised for their capacity to engender profound user experiences [6, 8, 9]. Within this spectrum of investigation, material-driven design (MDD) has emerged as a critical methodology, distinguished by its cohesive framework. In 2015, building upon this research, Karana and colleagues put forth the MDD approach as a means to foster the creation of innovative design processes and the conception of novel product materials that offer viable alternatives to conventional choices, such as sustainable materials, bio-based innovations, and intelligent materials [10]. The goal was to harness the potential of the MDD approach to empower designers to deeply engage with and reflect on their design practices, thereby cultivating a quest for meaningful material experiences. Karana et al. proposed four steps of the MDD method: (1) Understanding the material and extracting the technical experiential characterization, (2) Creating the vision of material experience, (3) Manifesting materials experience and matching patterns, (4) Designing product concept from material experience [10].

In the elaboration of material experience, Karana and colleagues delineated its composition through four distinct yet interconnected dimensions: the sensorial, which encompasses the aesthetic facet of experience; the interpretative, referring to the imbuing of materials with symbolic meanings; the affective, which involves the emotional resonances elicited by material interaction; and the performative, highlighting the active engagement and utility of materials in human experiences [8, 10, 11]. Specifically, at the sensorial level, individuals discern materials through tactile qualities such as hardness, texture, and temperature. Materials embody attributes like wit, allure, or generosity at the interpretative dimension, thus ascribing personality to the inanimate. Emotionally, the affective dimension acknowledges that materials can provoke a spectrum of responses, from joy to anger to surprise. Lastly, the performative aspect underscores the necessity of recognizing materials' functional roles in fostering a holistic grasp of their utilization and significance in haptic cognition [1]. This study, therefore, integrates these four dimensions as fundamental to advancing our understanding of haptic cognition through the lens of material experience.

2.2 Haptic Cognition Model

Individuals experience sensations in response to external stimuli, a phenomenon extensively examined in studies focusing on human sensory perception and its underlying mechanisms [12]. This exploration not only elucidates the framework of the sensory system but also delves into how such stimuli trigger profound perceptions and cognitive processes [12]. Scholarly discourse since the 1980s has underscored the simultaneous occurrence of user engagement and experiential sensations during direct interactions with objects [13–16]. Based on the previous studies [1, 8, 10, 11, 17–22], this study explores the Haptic Cognition Model (HCM) [1], as shown in Fig. 1, within the realm of design theory and practice. Central to our investigation is the dynamic interaction between designers' conceptualizations and users' cognitive processes, mediated by haptic experiences. The HCM model elucidates two interrelated models guiding this communication process, facilitating the transition from material experience (MX) to product design through haptic semantics (HS). Material experience encompasses sensorial, interpretative, affective, and performative dimensions, while haptic semantics serves as the intermediary language for translating these experiences into tangible design elements. Through a qualitative methodology incorporating theoretical insights and empirical observations, our study unveils the nuances of the encoding and decoding processes within the HCM framework. Designers traverse three hierarchical levels—visceral (technical stratum), behavioral (semantic stratum), and reflective (effective stratum)—during encoding. In contrast, users engage in a decoding process, interpreting haptic stimuli across material sensation (aesthetic experience), semantic cognition (meaningful experience), and predicted effect (emotional, active experience). Integrating haptic semantics augments users' cognitive engagement, fostering deeper interactions with designed products. This research underscores the transformative potential of haptic interactions in enriching design practices and enhancing user experiences, paving the way for future investigations into embodied cognition's cultural and contextual dimensions in design.

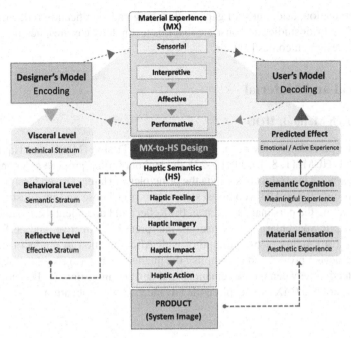

Fig. 1. Haptic Cognition Model (HCM) [1].

2.3 Tactile Prompting and AI-co-Creation

Individuals apprehend the external environment through their bodily senses and articulate their emotions or ideas through verbal language or lexical constructs. Language serves as a potent tool enabling humans to imbue significance into their experiences [1]. Contextual descriptions not only reflect our comprehension of the world around us but also represent a mechanism for cultural evolution. As highlighted by Lakoff & Wehling, the meanings embedded within words and sentences transcend mere visual perception [23]. Moreover, this study champions the utilization of haptic semantics as a catalyst for enhancing designers' comprehension and reinterpretation of materials by tactile prompting generated from the material experience.

Artificial Intelligence Generated Content (AIGC) currently finds widespread applications spanning various sectors, including media, education, entertainment, marketing, and scientific research [24]. This underscores the technology's capacity to offer users efficient, streamlined, and tailored content services [25]. AI functions as a collaborative ally, fostering a symbiotic partnership with designers and methodically guiding their innovative ideation [26–28]. A prime example is the case of Midjourney, where this tool has achieved significant advancements in the fundamental components of AI co-design and has seamlessly integrated into the design innovation process [24]. Nonetheless, AI-co-creation fosters interdisciplinary collaboration and communication, compensating for deficiencies in sketching abilities while concurrently reducing design time [24]. Research demonstrates that this technology enhances the precision and diversity of design solutions. Nevertheless, AI-co-creation fosters interdisciplinary collaboration and communication, bridging skill gaps in sketching and significantly reducing design timelines [24]. Prior studies demonstrate that this technology elevates the precision and diversity of design outcomes [29].

3   Method and Material

3.1   Research Method: HDD

Based on the preceding study of the Material Driven Design (MDD) and Haptic Cognition Model (HCM) [1, 8, 10, 11, 17–22], the authors further propose and conduct the process innovation in product design via the principles of Haptic Driven Design (HDD), as shown in Fig. 2. The HDD comprises six steps: (a) Choose and manifest the target material to create the personal experience. (b) Reflect and document the material experience via haptic vocabulary with sensorial, interpretative, affective, and performative expressions. (c) Employ tactile prompting with AI-co-creation in product design. (d) Conduct the design project and accomplish the qualia product. (e) Evaluate the correlation and affection between haptic semantics and design innovation. (f) Develop further Material Experience (MX) and explore the advanced HDD application.

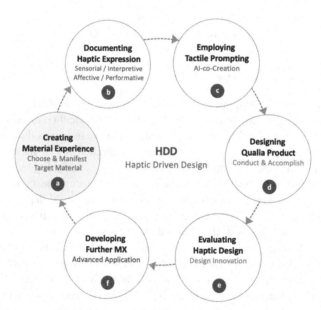

Fig. 2. Six steps of Haptic Driven Design (HDD).

3.2 Stimuli and Empirical Design Project

Based on the Haptic Driven Design (HDD) framework, this study schemes the design project, which explores and applies haptic semantics (feeling, imagery, impact, action) derived from material experience (sensorial, interpretive, affective, performative). Six kinds of materials (wood, cement, wool, RP resin, glass, and ceramic) were chosen as the stimuli by 10 designers. Then, this empirical design project developed 10 series of haptic topics and related objects, which were brought out based on designers' material experiences. The project organizer directs these young designers to develop their haptic products, focusing on the haptic discussion according to the hand's touch. Furthermore, these 10 extending objects are the advanced stimuli for experts' evaluations.

3.3 Participants and Procedures

This research invites 6 experts to execute the Focus Group Discussion (FGD) and to be the consultors who are the senior experts in craft creation, product design, and art education, advise this experimental project previously, and evaluate the design outcomes later. Besides, this case study recruits 10 designers to participate in this practical project. The young designers are students from the Department of Arts and Design in the University with mature craft creation and product design experiences who design diverse products by applying the haptic cognition approach with abundant material experiences. The project director is a skilled crafter and design educator who organizes and promotes HDD applications in this case study. The HDD project comprises three stages: reflection, execution, and evaluation, as shown in Fig. 3.

- Reflection Stage: A public exhibition was conducted to share the design outcomes of the MX-to-HS design project with the broader audience. This event also facilitated a collaborative dialogue among participants and designers on their 'material experience' and the extended expressions of 'haptic semantics.' This process guides designers in reflecting on their operational journey within the HDD framework, discussing the challenges encountered and potential solutions. Additionally, it involves suitable adjustments in further projects.
- Execution Stage: Guide participants in extending and developing suitable haptic topics based on their prior experience in the MX-to-HS design project. It encourages the ten participating designers to continue utilizing materials from the initial phase (wood, cement, wool, RP resin, glass, ceramics) as stimuli samples for advanced material experiences. Furthermore, they are to iteratively refer to and fill out the application checklist, reviewing and revising the selected haptic vocabularies and control variables for tactile sensation. This process aims to complete the design and creation of ten sets of haptic products (PP01–PP10), which will serve as the stimuli for further evaluation.
- Evaluation Stage: Six experts (EE01–EE06, comprising three with expertise in craftsmanship, two in product design, and one in art education) were invited to conduct empirical evaluations on the design outcomes of the HDD Project (consisting of ten haptic works). These evaluations were facilitated using the outcome assessment form,

employing two assessment modes: V (visual evaluation) and S (synesthetic evaluation of sight and touch). Subsequently, an analysis and discussion of the expert evaluation data results were carried out.

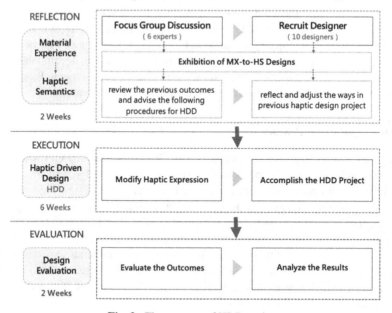

Fig. 3. Three stages of HDD project.

3.4 Research Instrument

This study proposed the "HDD Application Form" as the research instrument that guides the haptic-driven design procedures, as shown in Table 1. The designer records four parts of haptic semantics via sensorial, interpretive, affective, and performative keywords that connect to the description of material experiences in outer perception, extensional meaning, inner emotion, and associated scenarios. Besides, the experts evaluated the correlation between tactile prompting and results via the "HDD Assessment Form," as shown in Table 2.

Table 1. HDD Application Form (take D10 as an example).

Designer	D10	Provocative Material	Ceramic
Haptic Expression Based on the Material Experience			
Sensorial External Perception	1. The surface of the ceramic feels smooth, gentle, and moist to the touch, retaining a fine sandblasted texture. 2. It flows naturally along the curve with minimal bumps and undulations, ensuring smooth lines.		
Interpretive Meaning Cognition	1. It evokes an association with an elegant and graceful personality. 2. It suggests a humble and sincere character trait.		
Affective Internal Emotion	1. Aims to provide a sense of healing and peace, stabilizing the mood. 2. Hopes to represent and convey the user's elegant demeanor and humble attitude through this product.		
Performative Associate Scenario	1. Hopes to create a work that can be held and rubbed in the palm. 2. Aims to allow the toucher to caress the surface of the work back and forth smoothly.		
Tactile Prompting	*Gentle / Modest / Healingly / Caressing*		
Design Element	Undulation & Particle	**Technique/Craft**	Hand Kneading
Haptic Control (1–5: weak/low – intense/high)			
Control Factor	I (weak)	II (medium)	III (intense)
Surface undulations			
Glaze particle sizes			
AI-co-Creation			
Finalized Design (Ikebana Ware)			

(*continued*)

Table 1. (*continued*)

Production Process (180*160*230 mm)		

Reflection (Designer / Creator)

a. There should be further accumulation of knowledge and skills regarding mixing glaze particles to more precisely control the variations in the surface texture's intensity.

b. The curvature undulations of the vase's body should be adjusted to be smoother, making the hand movements more fluid during back-and-forth touches.

c. There should be more advancement in learning the display effects of floral art styles to enhance the work's sensory style and brand image.

4　Results and Discussions

4.1　The Creation of HDD Project

This study, during the "Phase II: HDD Project" (spanning 10 weeks), recruited the same 10 designers who had previously participated in "Phase I: MX-to-HS Experiment" (spanning 12 weeks). Through the exhibition of initial outcomes, a discussion and observational learning of each other's preliminary application results were facilitated among all participants, also extending their foundational experience with the application of material experience established in the earlier experiment. This allowed for a nuanced retrospection of existing material experience and enabled the extension of haptic semantics, further expanding the development of qualia products. Consequently, the participating designers in this phase II (HDD Project) will be well equipped with essential knowledge and skills in the Haptic Driven Design (HDD) method. Based on their previous design experiences with the haptic object of cup sleeve, the designers refined the ten haptic topics developed during Phase I to "angular, gravelly, coarse, fluffy, puffy, bumpy, smooth, brittle, sandy, and gentle," along with corresponding keywords as tactile prompting in four parts (sensorial, interpretive, affective, and performative semantics). Observations from the interaction between the project advisors and the designers revealed that repeated selection or careful adjustment of tactile prompting facilitated the designers' ability to employ the HDD methods. This assistance was instrumental in manifesting subsequent haptic imageries, aligning more closely with the desired quality of material experience and design development vision, culminating in the completion of ten distinctive products (including pen, candle holder, planting pot, pillow, clutch, brush bottle, lampshade, jewelry box, fragrance cup, and ikebana ware), as shown in Fig. 4.

Table 2. HDD Assessment Form (take PP06-EE02 as an example).

Product	PP06	Expert	EE02
Material	RP Resin	Technique	3D Printing
Brush Bottle (70*70*110 mm)			
Haptic Target	**Tactile Prompting** Correlation Evaluation: 1–5 (weak/low – intense/high)		
Assessment Mode	**V** (Visual)	**S** (Synesthetic of sight and touch)	
Sensorial External Perception	*Bumpy*		
	5	4	
Interpretive Meaning Cognition	*Naughty*		
	2	4	
Affective Internal Emotion	*Amusingly*		
	3	5	
Performative Associate Scenario	*Fingering*		
	4	5	
General Evaluation			
Preference	4	5	
Ranking (Top 3)	NA	Top 1	
Suggestion	When actually touching, the sense of weight and touch generated by the physical interaction dramatically enhances the degree of preference. Replacing the resin used for 3D prototyping might bring a higher evaluation. Further, the designer can try to convert it to other materials.		

Fig. 4. Overview of the HDD project outcomes.

4.2 Varying Capabilities of HDD Application

Contrasting the data from the "Evaluation results of the HDD project," as shown in Table 3, indicates that designers exhibit diverse approaches and capabilities in translating and implementing the HDD method across different tactile knowledge dimensions. Overall, the ten designers performed better in the "Performative/ Associate Scenario " level (mean: 4.10); conversely, they need to improve more in the transformation of the "Affective/Internal Emotion" level (mean: 3.63).

Table 3. Evaluation results of the HDD project (PP01 ~ PP10 by EE01 ~ EE06).

Mean	Assessment Mode	Sensorial	Interpretive	Affective	Performative	Overall	Preference	Ranking (Top 3)
PP01 **Wood** (Pen)	V	3.83	3.33	3.33	4.50	3.75	3.50	1.67
	S	4.17	3.50	3.50	5.00*	4.04	4.33*	1.83
PP02 **Cement** (Candle Holder)	V	4.33*	3.17	3.33	2.83	3.42	3.83	1.67
	S	4.50*	4.00	4.00	2.83	3.83	3.50	1.00
PP03 **Cement** (Planting Pot)	V	2.83	3.33	2.00	3.17	2.83	2.50	1.33
	S	3.00	3.83	2.67	3.50	3.25	3.33	1.50

(*continued*)

Table 3. (*continued*)

Mean	Assessment Mode	Sensorial	Interpretive	Affective	Performative	Overall	Preference	Ranking (Top 3)
PP04 **Wool** (Pillow)	V	3.33	3.33	4.67*	4.67	4.00	3.00	1.00
	S	4.17	3.83	5.00*	4.50	4.38*	4.00	2.17
PP05 **Wool** (Clutch)	V	3.50	4.33*	3.33	4.17	3.83	3.67	2.00
	S	4.00	4.50	3.83	4.00	4.08	3.83	2.00
PP06 **RP Resin** (Brush Bottle)	V	3.67	3.83	3.50	4.50	3.88	4.00	2.67
	S	3.50	3.83	4.00	4.50	3.96	4.00	2.33
PP07 **RP Resin** (Lampshade)	V	3.67	4.17	4.00	4.33	4.04*	4.17*	3.00*
	S	3.67	4.33	3.50	4.50	4.00	3.67	1.33
PP08 **RP Resin** (Jewelry Box)	V	4.33*	3.67	3.83	3.83	3.92	3.83	2.50
	S	4.50*	3.50	4.00	4.50	4.08	4.17	2.17
PP09 **Glass** (Fragrance Cup)	V	3.67	3.50	3.17	3.67	3.50	2.83	1.00
	S	4.50*	3.83	3.00	3.67	3.75	3.17	1.50
PP10 **Ceramic** (Ikebana Ware)	V	3.33	4.00	3.83	4.83*	4.00	3.83	2.17
	S	3.33	4.83*	4.17	4.50	4.21	4.17	3.17*
Overall Mean	**V**	3.65	3.67	3.50	4.05*	3.72	3.52	1.90
	S	3.93	4.00	3.77	4.15*	3.96	3.82	1.90
	V + S	**3.79**	**3.83**	**3.63**	**4.10***	**3.84**	**3.67**	**1.90**

* The start marks the best-recognized result matching each criterion's tactile prompting.
The underline marks the worst-recognized result of expert assessments in each criterion.

Taking visual assessment (associated tactile perception) as an example, when PP07 (RP resin lampshade) received a higher evaluation (4.04), it also achieved the highest preference mean (4.17), along with the best ranking for the average change in order among the top three (3.00). On the other hand, when PP03 (concrete planting pot) received a lower recognition (2.83), it led to the lowest preference score (2.50).

Furthermore, excluding PP07 (RP resin lampshade), the data reveals a consistent trend across nine out of ten works that followed the same pattern: the means from " Synesthetic assessment of sight and touch," which included physical touch, were consistently higher than those means from "Visual assessment," which only provided visual images. However, examining the overall means for tactile quality assessment across all ten products, there is an observable general improvement: the overall means across the four tactile dimensions increased from 3.72 (V) to 3.96 (S); also, the overall means of preference score rose from 3.52 (V) to 3.82 (S).

4.3   The Innovation via Tactile Prompting with AI-co-Creation

While initiating the HDD project, the director convened an FGD (Focus Group Discussion) to re-examine and modify research instruments accordingly. Consequently, an "AI-co-Creation" column was added to the "HDD Application Form" (Table 1). In the further stages of design development practice, designers participating in advanced phases were guided to establish their core haptic topics and plan the tactile knowledge dimensions during the sketching stage of design ideation. Subsequently, they integrated relevant haptic keywords with artificial intelligence image generation software (Midjourney) using Tactile Prompting, achieving innovative outcomes. Through the interactive sharing between project advisors and participating designers, the integration of "AI-Assisted Design" into the development process of qualia design was found to facilitate the external manifestation of internal tactile imageries within Haptic Driven Design (HDD). This process not only enriches the references available during design ideation but also accelerates the evolution of the design development process.

5   Conclusions

Based on the previous studies [1, 8, 10, 11, 17–22], the authors explore a design innovation connected with the material experience (haptic expression) and AI-co-creation (tactile prompting). Furthermore, the results of the Haptic Driven Design (HDD) project confirm the proposed methods and procedures. The research findings and conclusions are as follows: (a) Designers who have undergone the initial training of the 'MX-to-HS Design Project' will revise the haptic descriptors during the 'HDD Project,' making them more aptly reflect the desirable qualities and developmental vision of material experiences. (b) The precise selection or careful adjustment of haptic descriptors by designers aids in the subsequent manifestation of haptic imagery. This allows for the judgment or application of relevant reference materials or the flexible incorporation of other design methods. For instance, utilizing AI-co-creation enables more evident selection and mastery of necessary design information to optimize the quantity and quality of design sketch ideation, improving the efficiency from design development to completed work. (c) Individual designers possess distinct strengths in capturing different haptic quality aspects of design performance, which affects the preference level, acceptance, and ranking when evaluating haptic quality products. (d) In evaluating haptic quality products, the assessment that includes physical touch assistance (sympathetic haptics) yields higher ratings than evaluations based solely on visual observation (associative haptics). In other words, incorporating real material experiences in visual-haptic evaluation enhances experts' appraisal of haptic products. Finally, the authors address that employing the haptic semantic could connect and enrich the material experience, cultural elements, and design presentation. This study proposes a new prospection for product design by enhancing the connection between material experience and haptic semantics. The authors suggest that subsequent research may focus on exploiting the haptic semantics with the cultural context and relevant application of AI-co-creation for design innovation.

Acknowledgments. This research was supported by the National Science and Technology Council, Taiwan [Grant ID: NSTC 112-2221-E-007-084]. The authors would like to thank all the designers who participated and contributed their creations. In addition, the authors also appreciate the valuable suggestions of Prof. Han-Yu Lin from the Department of Industry Design at the National Kaohsiung Normal University.

Disclosure of Interests. The authors have no competing interests to declare that are relevant to the content of this article.

References

1. Chiang, IY., Lin, PH., Lin, R.: Haptic cognition model with material experience: case study of the design innovation. In: Rau, P.L.P. (ed.) Cross-Cultural Design. HCII 2023. Lecture Notes in Computer Science, vol. 14023, pp. 180–193. Springer, Cham (2023). https://doi.org/10. 1007/978-3-031-35939-2_14
2. Chiang, I.-Y., Sun, Y., Lin, P.-H., Lin, R., Lin, H.-Y.: Haptic semantics in qualia product. In: Rau, P.L.P. (ed.) Cross-Cultural Design. Interaction Design Across Cultures. HCII 2022. Lecture Notes in Computer Science, vol. 13311, pp. 21–35. Springer, Cham (2022). https:// doi.org/10.1007/978-3-031-06038-0_2
3. Masayuki, K., translated by Wang, X.: Design Focus Product Masayuki Kurokawa. Beijing: China Youth Press (2002). (Chinese version)
4. Chen, Y.-T.: A Study on Tactile Image and Style (Doctoral dissertation). National Chiao Tung University, Institute of Applied Arts, Hsinchu (2016). (in Chinese)
5. Manzini, E.: The Material of Invention. MIT Press, Cambridge (1989)
6. Ashby, M., Johnson, K.: Materials and design. In: The Art and Science of Material Selection in Product Design, 2nd edn. Butterworth-Heinemann Elsevier, Oxford (2009)
7. Yao, R.-K.: An introduction to the material experience design method and its promotion report in Taiwan crafts. J. Craftol. Taiwan **1**, 69–86 (2022). (in Chinese)
8. Karana, E., Hekkert, P., Kandachar, P.: Materials experience: descriptive categories in material appraisals. In: Proceedings of the Conference on Tools and Methods in Competitive Engineering, pp. 399–412. Delft University of Technology, Delft (2008)
9. Karana, E., Pedgley, O., Rognoli, V.: On materials experience. Des. Issues **31**(3), 16–27 (2015)
10. Karana, E., Barati, B., Rognoli, V., Zeeuw van der Laan, A.: Material driven design (MDD): A method to design for material experiences. Int. J. Des. **9**(2), 35–54 (2015)
11. Giaccardi, E., Karana, E.: Foundations of materials experience: an approach for HCI. In: Proceedings of the 33rd SIGCHI Conference on Human Factors in Computing Systems, pp. 2447–2456. ACM, New York (2015)
12. Sternberg, R.J.: Cognitive Psychology, 5th edn. Wadsworth, Belmont (2009)
13. Hutchins, E.L., Hollan, J.D., Norman, D.A.: Direct manipulation interface. Hum.-Comput. Interact. **1**, 311–338 (1985)
14. Norman, D.A., Draper, S. (eds.): User Centered System Design: New Perspectives on Human-Computer Interaction. Erlbaum, London (1986)
15. Norman, D.A. Cognitive artifact. In: Carroll, J.M. (ed.) Designing Interaction. Cambridge University Press, Cambridge (1991)

16. Chiang, I.-Y., Lin, P.-H., Kreifeldt, J.G., Lin, R.: From theory to practice: an adaptive development of design education. Educ. Sci. **11**(11), 673 (2021). https://doi.org/10.3390/educsci11110673

17. Norman, D.A.: Emotional Design: Why We Love (or hate) Everyday Things. Basic Books, New York (2004)

18. Norman, D.A.: The Design of Everyday Things: Review and Expanded Edition. Basic Books, New York (2013)

19. Lin, C.L., Chen, C.L., Chen, S.J., Lin, R.: The cognition of turning poetry into painting. J. US-China Educ. Rev. B **5**(8), 471–487 (2015)

20. Chiang, I.-Y.; Lin, R.; Lin, P.-H.: Placemaking with creation: a case study in cultural product design. In: Rau, P. (ed.) Cross-Cultural Design. Experience and Product Design Across Cultures. HCII 2021. Lecture Notes in Computer Science, vol. 12771. Springer: Cham (2021). https://doi.org/10.1007/978-3-030-77074-7_20

21. Lyu, Y., Wang, X., Lin, R., Wu, J.: Communication in human–AI co-creation: perceptual analysis of paintings generated by text-to-image system. Appl. Sci. **12**, 11312 (2022). https://doi.org/10.3390/app122211312

22. Chiang, I.Y.: From Quality to Qualia: Hi-Touch in Product Design (dissertation). National Taiwan University of Arts. Graduate School of Creative Industry Design (2023). (in Chinese)

23. Lakoff, G., Wehling, E.: The Little Blue Book: The Essential Guide to Thinking and Talking Democratic. FREE, New York (2012)

24. Yin, H., Zhang, Z., Liu, Y.: The exploration of integrating the midjourney artificial intelligence generated content tool into design systems to direct designers towards future-oriented innovation. Systems **11**, 566 (2023). https://doi.org/10.3390/systems11120566

25. Cao, Y., et al.: A comprehensive survey of ai-generated content (aigc): A history of generative AI from gan to chatgpt. arXiv (2023). arXiv:2303.04226

26. Tomasello, M.: A Natural History of Human Thinking. Harvard University Press, Cambridge (2014)

27. INCOSE Systems Engineering Handbook Working Group. Systems Engineering Handbook, 4th edn. INCOSE: San Diego, CA, USA (2015)

28. Jarrahi, M.H., Askay, D., Eshraghi, A., Smith, P.: Artificial intelligence and knowledge management: a partnership between human and AI. Bus. Horiz. **66**, 87–99 (2023)

29. Kelly, K.: What AI-Generated Art Really Means for Human Creativity (2022). https://www.wired.com/story/picture-limitless-creativity-ai-image-generators/. Accessed 11 Nov 2024

Behavioral Lock Screen Application Practice Based on Gamification Design Method

Feng Gao[1]([⊠]), Chaoyang Yu[2], Huihong Zhou[2], and Lanxi Xie[2]

[1] ZTE Corporation, Shenzhen, China
18204012@qq.com
[2] ZTE Corporation, Shanghai, China

Abstract. Gamification design is an important and engaging design method in experience design, currently widely explored and discussed in various fields. This paper adopts gamification design as a method, focusing on the "task, measurement, metric" cycle, to redesign and iteratively design the basic mobile application "Behavioral Lock Screen Application." The study validates the positive impact of gamification design on user retention and usage rates in fundamental applications.

Keywords: Gamification design · Task-measurement-metric cycle · Flow · Fogg Behavior Model · Behavioral Lock Screen Application

1 Introduction

Gamification design involves incorporating elements and designs from games into non-gaming contexts, aiming to enhance the enjoyment of experiences, attract users, and stimulate their interest and motivation to increase user engagement, ultimately assisting users in achieving their goals more effectively. Initially prevalent in the education sector, gamification strategies gained popularity in various internet products after 2010, aiming to enhance user engagement and improve overall user experiences. The design of basic applications on mobile devices has become increasingly internet-oriented in recent years, with a growing reliance on user data and a faster pace of iterative design. Exploring the application of gamification design in suitable basic mobile applications is a key consideration for terminal designers. This paper will elaborate on the implementation of gamification design, focusing on the basic application "lock screen," for further discussion and exploration.

2 Gamification Theories and Methods

The concept of 'gamification' was initially introduced by Richard Bartle, a professor at the University of Essex and a pioneer in multiplayer online games, in his work 《The Game of Work》 in 1980 [1]. The original intention was to "turn non-gaming things or work into a game" by leveraging the positive effects and motivating factors of gamification. In 2002, Nick Pelling-Smith first used the term "gamification" on his website to describe a design

P.-L. P. Rau (Ed.): HCII 2024, LNCS 14699, pp. 43–57, 2024.
https://doi.org/10.1007/978-3-031-60898-8_3

method that applies gamified user interfaces to business electronic devices. This approach aimed to make electronic transactions more enjoyable and efficient. The popularity of gamification surged after 2010, leading to the emergence of various gamification design methods and theories. It began to be applied in diverse fields such as education and the internet.

PBL System. The elements of Points, Badges, and Leaderboards (PBL) are considered the three major features of gamification. These elements were frequently employed in early gamification studies and designs. Points, Badges, and Leaderboards are regarded as the presentation elements of gamification. However, as later gamification theories and practices have demonstrated, PBL represents only a small fraction of the elements commonly used in gamification [2, 3].

DMC Theory. The DMC theory of gamification design was introduced by American gamification experts Kevin Werbach and Dan Hunter in their 2012 book "For the Win: How Game Thinking Can Revolutionize Your Business." The DMC theory is a method that applies game design principles to non-game contexts, encompassing three levels of game elements: Dynamics, Mechanics, and Components.

Dynamics, the most abstract level, refers to the psychological factors that drive user behavior, such as goals, progress, and feedback. Mechanics, the intermediate level, pertains to the rules and methods used to implement dynamics, including challenges, competition, cooperation, and more. Components, the most concrete level, represent the gamified elements that users can see and interact with, such as points, badges, leaderboards, and other tangible rewards.

The authors argue that gamification design is inherently user-centric, aiming to stimulate users' intrinsic motivation and enhance engagement and loyalty by leveraging the three levels of game elements: Dynamics, Mechanics, and Components. This user-focused approach utilizes game elements to tap into users' internal motivations, ultimately fostering a more engaging and loyal user experience [4] (Fig. 1).

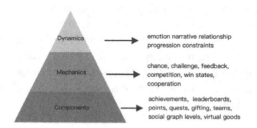

Fig. 1. DMC theory

Software Gamification Analysis Method. In 2017, Wang Yaqian et al., in their paper "A Goal-Oriented Software Gamification Analysis Method," built upon previous theories and proposed a more practical analysis method for software gamification. Drawing inspiration from the core elements of challenge tasks, measurement, and evaluation within a cyclic system, they aimed to provide a systematic and actionable approach.

The authors transformed challenge tasks into a goal model, defining gamified activities. To facilitate the completion of challenge tasks, they suggested measuring user activities in gamification through quantifiable indicators (resembling the Mechanics layer in DMC theory) [5] (Fig. 2).

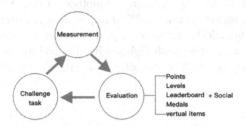

Fig. 2. Task, Measurement, Evaluation Circle

The aforementioned theories and methods dissect the gamification process, particularly the DMC model and the software gamification approach, providing insights into constructing gamified products. Another category of theories delves into exploring the underlying reasons behind why "gamification" can captivate users, encouraging them to continuously engage.

The Flow Model. The Flow Model is one of the most widely recognized and accepted theories in the industry. It emphasizes aligning task difficulty with user abilities, providing clear goals, guiding attention appropriately, and offering immediate feedback. This is done to lead users into a state where they engage in an activity for an extended period with high levels of concentration. As illustrated in the diagram below, it is evident that task difficulty should be set at an appropriate level. For individual users, the ideal scenario is a gradually increasing level of difficulty, forming a spiral that effectively captures user attention and engagement [6] (Fig. 3).

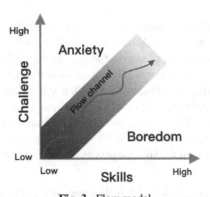

Fig. 3. Flow model

BJ Foog's Behaviour Model. The model comprises three fundamental elements: Motivation, Ability, and Prompts. For any behavior to occur, these three factors must be simultaneously satisfied—people need motivation for the behavior, the ability to execute it, and a suitable trigger or prompt. The model assumes that a behavior is most likely to occur only when an individual has sufficient motivation, the ability to perform the action, and there is a trigger to remind them. All three conditions are essential [7, 8].

A classic example is Ant Forest, where the motivation is tree planting, the ability involves activities like walking or using public transportation, and the trigger is the Alipay app reminding users to collect energy. The trigger condition is easily accessible within the daily software usage routine, with high reachability and low ability requirements. Consequently, the design of Ant Forest is effective in attracting users to engage with the application (Fig. 4).

Fig. 4. BJ Foog's Behaviour Model

In summary, the current state of gamification theories and methods is characterized by ongoing discussions with different emphases and analytical perspectives. For the practical design of specific products in the industry, it is essential to integrate gamification concepts and theories into a workflow and methodology with strong practical applicability.

Combining the widely used design process double diamond theory, we have integrated gamification design. In a typical design flow of Discover −> Define −> Develop −> Deliver, gamification design primarily focuses on the Define and Develop stages. During these stages, gamified elements and motivational mechanisms are integrated and refined. The process evolves from Discovery −> Define Problems −> Determine Gamification Theme Story −> Design Game Model (challenge goals, measure user gaming behavior, evaluate behavior loop) −> Deliver Implementation. This integration aims to provide a robust and practical framework for incorporating gamification into product design, aligning it with established design processes for effective implementation.

3 Introduction of Behavioral Lock Screen Application

Lock screen applications are the first local applications that users encounter when using their phones, and they are also the most frequently used applications. With the development of smartphones, these devices have become an indispensable part of users' lives as crucial components of their mobile terminals. According to a report from the 360 Mobile User Research Center in 2016, the average smartphone user unlocks their phone screen 122 times per day, with some "enthusiastic users" unlocking it up to 850 times. A more recent study by Accesspath indicates that users check their phones an average of 58 times per day. Picking up the phone may become a habitual behavior, as data shows that half of the phone usage occurs within 3 min of the previous usage, with an average duration of approximately 1 min and 15 s each time.Different research institutions have reported varying frequencies of daily phone checks and unlocks for different sample groups, both in China and globally. However, they all reach a consistent conclusion: users frequently unlock their phones to perform various operations. As the first interface users see when interacting with their phones, the lock screen is of paramount importance. Recognizing this, mobile phone manufacturers began redesigning lock screen applications around 2015, providing not only the time and new information but also visually appealing wallpapers and relevant content recommendations to enhance the user experience.

Behavioral Lock Screen Application was conceived to enhance the user experience of unlocking screens by delivering a product that goes beyond the conventional. By presenting users with exquisite photographic images on the lock screen, users not only check the time and notifications but also enjoy various photography wallpapers, such as scenic views, food, still life, pets, and lifestyle. The lock screen also provides functions like liking and bookmarking, allowing users to express preferences. Through user likes, the system tailors wallpaper recommendations based on user interests.However, over time, the usage rate of the original Behavioral Lock Screen application decreased, along with a decline in user engagement metrics such as likes and shares for the images. In order to enhance the user experience of the ZTE lock screen product, we have decided to undergo a redesign using gamification design principles in the process.

4 Practical Implementation Process

4.1 Discovery

Through user interviews, competitive analysis, and data analysis, we identified the following reasons for the decline in the original lock screen usage:

- **Product Homogenization:** The market is saturated with similar products, offering users various types of aesthetically pleasing images, leading to a lack of product differentiation.
- **Limited and Monotonous Content Resources:** The available content is limited, and there is a lack of variety. Users easily encounter repetitive images as they scroll through, diminishing the overall appeal.
- **Passive Interaction Format:** The interaction format is passive, as users merely need to swipe left or right to view images. This lack of active participation results in a diminished sense of engagement, leading to a rapid decline in novelty and reduced product stickiness.

4.2 Problem Definition

Given the identified reasons, it is evident that the original Behavioral Lock Screen application, unchanged for several years, lacks significant appeal to users. The existing product primarily involves passive receipt of aesthetically pleasing images. Initially, users may be interested in swiping and viewing due to the novelty of the content. They might even engage with features like liking and sharing. However, over time, as there is no meaningful connection established between the content and users' personal lives or habits, the initial novelty diminishes, leading to a natural decline in usage.

To sustain user interest, Behavioral Lock Screen application needs to establish a meaningful connection with users' lives. This could involve fulfilling desires that are challenging to achieve in their daily lives or assisting in achieving personal goals. By creating a connection between the product and users' aspirations or objectives, the lock screen can foster a sense of novelty and engagement, thus preventing a decline in usage over time.

4.3   Determine Gamification Theme

During the product redesign, we found ourselves amidst the COVID-19 pandemic, a period marked by relatively enclosed lifestyles. Recognizing the challenges and seeking to provide users with new experiences and a positive mindset during this time, we aimed to build on the existing Behavioral Lock Screen application.

In our brainstorming sessions, considering the prevailing circumstances, we envisioned promoting a healthy lifestyle from a humanistic perspective. We wanted "Behavioral Lock Screen Application" to offer users a sense of "Life is not just the temporary hardships we face but also the unrestrained spirit and the beauty of distant landscapes." Subsequently, we formulated three gamification themes:

- **Health and Fitness:** Using the "Cloud Mountaineering" theme, we showcase mountainous landscapes on the lock screen to motivate users to engage in regular physical activity.
- **Travel:** Employing the "Cloud Tourism" theme, we present scenic views from various parts of the country, allowing users to virtually travel and fulfill their desires during the pandemic.
- **Intangible Cultural Heritage:** Leveraging the "Cloud Tour of Intangible Cultural Heritage" theme, we offer virtual tours of China's intangible cultural heritage, showcasing images that provide insights into the diverse cultural heritage of the country.Due to practical considerations in product design and implementation, we initially focused on refining the gamification design for the "Cloud Mountaineering" theme. We defined this theme as the "Climber."

4.4   Develop

Designing User Gamified Challenge Goals, Measuring User Behavior, and Evaluating Behavior Loop.

- **Gamified Challenge Goals:** The "Climber," as the name suggests, aims to ascend to great heights, with the ultimate goal being the summit of Mount Everest. Throughout this journey, users need to climb various mountains of different heights as sub-goals, completing each sub-goal before reaching the summit of Mount Everest.

- **Measuring User Behavior:** Measure the number of steps taken by users daily and track the number of days, converting their steps into climbing heights.
- **Evaluating User Behavior:** Establish an evaluation system to assess user behavior, i.e., climbing heights, and create incentives.
- **Mountain Views:** Display different picturesque mountain images based on the ascent of various mountains, providing users with visual enjoyment while inheriting the core content of the ZTE lock screen.
- **Medals:** Award different medals based on the climbed height and time taken.
- **Ranking:** Daily/monthly/total climbing heights ranked among numerous users.
- **Achievements:** Number of peaks corresponding to daily/monthly/total climbing heights.
- **Sharing:** Users can share the scenic images of the climbed mountains and the achieved climbing heights with friends (Fig. 5).

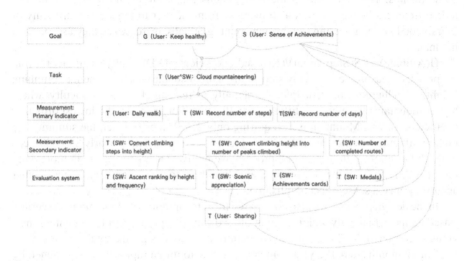

Fig. 5. Task, Measurement, Evaluation Relationship Diagram

The gamified design for the "Climber" involves the task T (User: Cloud Mountaineering, ultimately reaching the summit of Mount Everest), representing the gamified goal. In this gamification process, the ZTE Lock Screen App converts the user's step count into climbing height and translates the accumulated steps into the number of ascents of different mountain peaks. Throughout this process, the app provides information on climbing height, ascent frequency, displays scenic images of different mountains, and awards achievement cards and medals based on climbing height and frequency.

Additionally, the app shows the user's ranking among numerous users, encourages sharing of this information with friends, and aims to increase user engagement by making them aware of their walking step count. By comparing their steps with previous records and others' step counts, the app seeks to motivate users to continuously challenge themselves, fostering a sense of achievement during the climbing process.

In establishing the loop of challenge tasks, measurement, and evaluation, especially establishing a strong relationship between measurement and evaluation is crucial. According to the Flow Model, the game difficulty should not be too high, meaning high evaluations should not be overly challenging. If the difficulty is too great, it may lead users to give up, but it also shouldn't be too boring or easy. The difficulty should spiral up gradually, turning the ultimate challenge task into a series of sub-challenges. Users progress through these sub-challenges by continuously "clearing" them, ultimately completing the entire challenge task.Sub-challenges are typically arranged from easy to difficult. Through timely evaluation feedback, users gain a sense of achievement, enticing them to engage in the next sub-goal challenge, immersing themselves in the game. This sequential, gradually increasing difficulty keeps users motivated and immersed in the gaming experience, aligning with the principles of the Flow Model.

Based on the specific analysis of the gamified design above, combined with information on major mountains in China, we have compiled climbing routes for the top 20 mountains. The elevations of these mountains vary from low to high, and the altitude differences between peaks also increase from smaller to larger. The difficulty of users' cloud mountaineering (target step count) gradually increases as they ascend each mountain.

H(Altitude) $= S$(Step count)$/(K$(Fixed coefficient)$*D$(Difficulty coefficient).From the primary measurement of daily step count to the secondary measurement of climbing height, we adhere to the principle of gradually increasing challenge difficulty, where higher mountains have higher difficulty coefficients. For example, the lowest difficulty coefficient for She Mountain is 1, requiring only 2,800 steps to reach the summit. The highest difficulty coefficient for Mount Everest is 3.4, necessitating nearly 850,000 steps to reach the summit. In the gaming process, we motivate users to engage in more daily physical activity (walking or running), enabling them to ascend one peak after another and experience a sense of accomplishment.

In the design process, we also considered the total duration of cloud mountaineering. Based on the actual daily walking situation of different types of people (sedentary individuals, average individuals, and fitness enthusiasts), we designed a total duration ranging from 2 months to half a year, which, according to initial rapid surveys, is generally acceptable to most users as a suitable gaming length.

During communication with the implementation team for the climber's gamified design, due to practical constraints such as implementation time, server limitations, and user data privacy concerns, we decided to exclude ranking from the evaluation and incentive components.

4.5 Delivery and Implementation

Based on the gamified design process outlined above, we proceed with a detailed interface design for the measurement and evaluation system.

Measurement Design. Real-time display of climbing height and the conquered peaks, providing users with information reminders and indicating the effort required to achieve their goals.

We have meticulously crafted a climber-exclusive display for both the lock screen and the screen-off state, taking into account the characteristics of lock and screen-off functionalities (Fig. 6).

Fig. 6. Measurement interface

Evaluation System Design. Different evaluation incentives are provided during and after the climbing process, encompassing four distinct types:

- **Scenic Appreciation:** Upon reaching the altitude of a corresponding peak during each climb, Behavioral Lock screen will showcase the beauty of the mountain along with corresponding poetic phrases.
- **Achievements:** Users are rewarded with achievement cards based on their daily, monthly, yearly, and cumulative step counts.
- **Medals:** Corresponding medals are awarded upon completing a climb.
- Social Interaction:All scenic images, achievements, and medals can be shared, fostering social discussions and a sense of accomplishment among users (Fig. 7).

4.6 Data Feedback

With the release and market availability of the mobile Z40s Pro, we captured the climber usage data from April to December, as shown in the following chart (Table 1).

From the chart, it can be observed that the usage rate peaked after four months, aligning with our initial estimation of the average time for climbers to complete one route. Subsequently, the usage rate experienced a slight decline but stabilized at over 50%. The increase from the previous average usage rate of 32% to a stable rate of over 50% indicates the success of this iterative update. Gamified design, providing users with clear gaming objectives and evaluative incentives at each stage, contributes to increased user engagement. Additionally, the slight decrease in usage after four months can be

Fig. 7. Evaluation system interface

Table 1. Climber usage

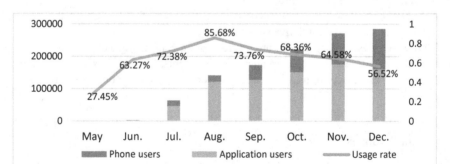

attributed to users completing a route climb without new goals. After experiencing all the incentives in the evaluation system, users no longer have new motivations, and they naturally exit the climber's journey.

4.7 Iterative Design Based on Data Feedback

To retain existing users and attract new ones, we iteratively optimized the gamified model in terms of goals, metrics, and evaluations.

- **Establish New Routes:** Introducing new routes and challenges provides a sense of novelty, enticing users to engage in the game.
- **Introduce New Metrics:** Bringing in additional metrics enriches users' gaming behaviors, providing a more comprehensive measurement of their activities.
- **Optimize and Enrich the Evaluation System:** Enhancing the evaluation system offers more appealing incentives, encouraging users to immerse themselves in the game for a longer duration.

Following the climber's ascent routes, we designed new routes like the Cool Runners, the Qinghai Lake Circuit, the Forbidden City and Bird's Nest Scenic Route, the West Lake Rose Route, the Huangpu River Riverside Route, and more, providing users with a diverse selection of routes (Fig. 8).

Fig. 8. New routes

To broaden the target audience, in addition to the existing metric of step counting, we introduced a step count for running. This allows users who engage in running and fitness activities to play the game while tracking their running statistics. According to the Fogg Behavior Model, the trigger cost for this user segment is relatively low. Users who already have a habit of running can easily enter the game by choosing the "Cool Runners" feature. Furthermore, we added a running button on the lock screen slide interface, making it more convenient and faster to open compared to third-party running apps that require navigating into a separate module. This design places "Cool Runners" in the Fogg Behavior Model with low ability requirements and a large effective trigger zone, enabling users to engage in the game for an extended period (Fig. 9).

Fig. 9. Lock screen of Cool Runner

For the design of the evaluation system, we have the following goals:

1. Provide recognition for users' repeated actions to accumulate acknowledgment, thus increasing participation time.
2. Demonstrate that users have enough qualifications or authority to express affirmation for their sustained participation.
3. Encourage users to explore as much content within the application as possible.

To address these goals, we have formulated three optimization directions:

1. Expanded the original climber's performance record interface to separately display the achievements obtained from running and walking.
2. Introduced variations in achievement records and sharing cards based on different performance accomplishments.
3. Added a historical record query feature for users to easily review their past achievements.

In response to this, we have made the following iterative improvements to achievement cards, medals, and achievement sharing.

- **Achievement Cards:**

On the main interface data cards, in comparison to the climber, we added the display of running data. To accommodate this change, achievement cards are divided into two types: data when using routes and data when initiating running. There may be data overlap between the two, for example, initiating a cool run while using a route. To encourage users to continue using the app, we compared running data with half marathon and full marathon achievements. By comparing the data with marathons, a well-known high-difficulty running activity, users can be motivated to continue participating and have the desire to share, especially considering that only a small percentage of people in life can complete a marathon (Fig. 10).

Fig. 10. Achievement cards

- **Medals:**

We have enriched the types of medals, introducing six different medals based on time and speed. In comparison to the previous climber, we made differentiated improvements. Depending on the performance achieved, medals now have distinct colors and display elements, motivating users to undertake multiple challenges to achieve better results (Fig. 11).

- **Achievement Sharing:**

Achievement sharing has been enriched compared to the climber, divided into route history and cool running history. It records the time and athletic achievements of each completion, making it convenient for users to share afterward and enhancing stickiness (Fig. 12).

"Cool runner" is currently in internal testing. After the official launch, we will continue to improve the "Goal, Metric, Evaluation" cycle based on user feedback and data feedback, ensuring that users maintain continuous interest and engagement in the gamified Behavioral Lock Screen application.

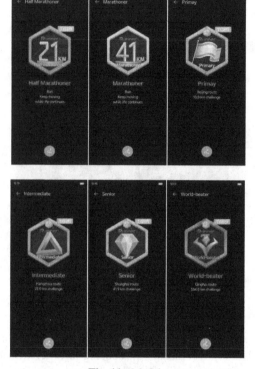

Fig. 11. Medals

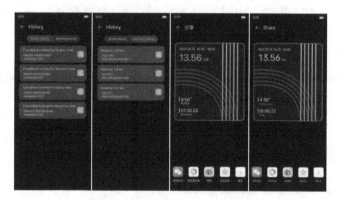

Fig. 12. Achievement records and sharing

5 Conclusion

This paper introduces the theories and methods of gamification design, summarizing a practical workflow and methodology for product design. Using the example of the Behavioral Lock Screen application, it illustrates how gamification design and iterative design can be applied to terminal product systems. Data feedback indicates that gamification design has a positive impact on product stickiness and user engagement. However, to maintain user engagement over a longer period, iterative design is crucial in the "Goal, Metric, Evaluation" cycle of gamification, keeping users in a state of flow.

For the Behavioral Lock Screen application, we will continue to iterate and develop using gamification design, advancing the concept of "healthy living." We plan to further productize "cloud tourism showcasing the beauty of various regions in the country" and "cloud participation in national intangible cultural heritage activities." This will present the scenic beauty and outstanding intangible cultural heritage from different parts of the country to ZTE smartphone users, contributing to the dissemination of traditional culture and the inheritance of traditional skills.

References

1. Coonradt, C.A., Nelson, L.: The Game of Work. Gibbs Smith (2017)
2. Jurado, J.L., Fernandez, A., Collazos, C.A.: Applying gamification in the context of knowledge management, In: 15th International Conference on Knowledge Technologies and Data-driven Business on Proceedings, pp 1–4 (2015)
3. Chou, Y.K.: Actionable Gamification. Huazhong University of Science and Technology Press, Wuhan (2017)
4. Werbach, K., Hunter, D.: For the win: How Game Thinking Can Revolutionize Your Business. Zhejiang People's Publishing House, Zhejiang (2014)
5. Wang, Y., Liu, C., Yu, Y., Jin, Z.: A goal-oriented software gamification analysis method. J. Chin. Mini-Micro Comput. Syst. **38**(4), 683–689 (2017)
6. Csikszentmihalyi, M., Abuhamdeh, S., Nakamura, J.: Flow: In Flow and the Foundations of Positive Psychology. Springer, Heidelberg (2014)
7. Fogg, B.J.: Tiny Habits: The Small Changes That Change Everything. Houghton Mifflin Harcourt, Boston (2020)
8. https://behaviormodel.org/

Shaping a Longevity Service Through Visual, Tangible, Cultural, and Social Artifacts

Sheng-Hung Lee[✉]

Massachusetts Institute of Technology, Cambridge, MA, USA
shdesign@mit.edu

Abstract. In the era of longevity economics, people not only live longer, but also desire a better quality of life. People are living longer, but our social infrastructure—including healthcare, education, and finance—is not equipped to deal with the socio-technological challenges that come with aging, like health and money problems. According to research conducted by the World Health Organization (WHO) in 2022, most countries are grappling with the need to transform their health and social systems to address the rapidly expanding aging population. The research discussed in this paper aims to develop an effective longevity service by employing visual and tangible artifacts through four co-creation workshops and 12 semi-structured interviews. The 20 Cambridge- or Boston-based participants engaged with a prototype longevity coaching service, in an attempt to identify and reflect on their needs for a longer life and to project their future selves through the lens of a longevity service. This study addressed four questions: 1. How can people's ideas and visual concepts be effectively translated into tangible prototypes in a co-creation workshop? 2. What are the advantages of incorporating visuals and tangible artifacts in a longevity coaching service to reframe and address longevity-related challenges? 3. How can subtle needs and insights be discerned through the cultural and social perspectives integrated into a longevity coaching service? 4. In what ways can tangible artifacts, complemented by visuals and text, be used to raise awareness about the longevity coaching service and culture, thereby enhancing people's understanding of their holistic well-being in the future? The study explored and discussed the concept of Design for Longevity (D4L) enriched by the integration of visual, tangible, cultural, and social dimensions, which serves as a framework for building and refining a more meaningful, respectful, and inclusive longevity coaching service.

Keywords: service design · longevity planning · tangible artifact · design for longevity

1 Introduction

1.1 Longevity Economics and Experience-Driven Service Industries

In the era of longevity economics [1], experience-driven service industries [2, 3] are emerging to meet the desire of sophisticated users to satisfy their vision of quality of life [4]. People are seeking not only ownership of tailor-made products, but also the

P.-L. P. Rau (Ed.): HCII 2024, LNCS 14699, pp. 58–71, 2024.
https://doi.org/10.1007/978-3-031-60898-8_4

experience of memorable, respectful, and unique services [5, 6]. People live longer [7] and want to live better with meaning and dignity [8].

The scholar Golden (2022) mentioned that the traditional three stages of life—birth, study/work, and retirement—need to change to embrace multiple life stages, complexity, and ambiguity, especially in the context of transformational organizational cultures, multi-generational environments, a diverse workforce, inclusive policies, and longevity economics [9].

For example, instead of saying people are retiring, let's say people are "rewiring" to move towards different life stages and to continue learning, creating, and experimenting with new challenges. Meanwhile, society is shifting individuals' perception of what planning for the future looks like at all ages—from the traditional financial planning approach for design for retirement to a holistic longevity coaching service: Design for Longevity (D4L). This transformational shift has shaped the fundamental mindset and systems that individuals must re-consider when designing and using financial planning strategies and services.

The idea of D4L originally emerged from the world of product design (i.e. the fashion industry, product lifecycle, and manufacturing process). The intent is to design resilient, sustainable, repairable, and modular systems of products, services, and experiences to form circular economics to reduce environmental impact, promote responsible culture, and generate long-lasting value.

Regarding the economic and financial side, the concept of D4L has expanded the definition and scope of financial planning and become more critical than ever to connect with people's different stages of life in preparation for the socio-technological challenges in a super-aging society: mobility, education, home, family, community, investment, risk, and future [10].

1.2 Research Hypothesis and Questions

This is a descriptive qualitative research study that explores, observes, documents, and analyzes the data from four co-creation workshops [8, 9] and 12 pilot tests conducted with Longevity Planning Blocks (LPBs) to build a longevity coaching service with visual, tangible, and cultural perspectives. Broadly speaking, a longevity coaching service is an extension of typical financial planning services that empower and educate individuals to adapt and learn the concept of longevity planning and longevity literacy.

A good longevity coaching service might consider learnability, efficiency, safety, trustworthiness, confidence, and perceived service quality. Our hypothesis is that creating visual and tangible artifacts in a co-creation workshop can make participants more engaged with the longevity coaching service process by 1. Understanding and embracing the new concept of longevity planning; 2. Reflecting and identifying their longevity desires based on demographics, including culture, age, gender, expertise, and education; and 3. Projecting their future selves through the lens of longevity planning.

Thus, this study explored four research questions: 1. How do participants translate their ideas and visuals into tangible prototypes through a co-creation workshop? 2. How do participants consider the advantages and disadvantages of applying visuals and tangible artifacts to reframe and solve longevity-relevant challenges during the longevity coaching service process? 3. What subtle human needs can be observed through cultural and social lenses in the process of creating a longevity coaching service? 4. How do people use tangible artifacts with provocative questions, representative icons, and visuals to raise awareness of the longevity coaching service and emphasize its importance in enhancing the understanding of people's future holistic well-being?

2 Literature Review

This section covers three areas—creative artifacts, experience prototypes, and a think-aloud approach—to contextualize the connections between a longevity coaching service and visual, tactical, cultural, and social artifacts.

2.1 Longevity Planning Blocks (LPBs) and Tangible Artifacts

There are many ways to define artifacts. Think about why people keep ordinary things, such as a vase, a table, or a clock. Sometimes it is because they care about status-signaling and find that to be much more important than high use-value [12–15]. This is often common with objects that are memorable, unique, personal, and irreplaceable, whether three-dimensional objects or two-dimensional photos or graphics.

In this study, we are curious to explore not only the functional side of objects, but also the cultural parts of artifacts to discover political meanings and systems implications in a broader social context for longevity.

The scholar Turkle coined the term "evocative objects" to connect two less familiar or relevant concepts or ideas to spark new meanings, feelings, and perceptions that impact our relationships with things [16]. Evocative artifacts can reveal the value of status-signaling that makes us think about the root cause of the object we are passionate about. One example is the design and development of the 12 Longevity Planning Blocks (LPBs) by Lee and Coughlin from the MIT AgeLab in 2022 shown in Table 1 and Fig. 1 [11].

Table 1. The design of 12 Longevity Planning Blocks (LPBs) including four stages of retirement, provocative questions, and representative icons. (LPBs was co-created by Sheng-Hung Lee and Joseph F. Coughlin)

Managing complexity	Making big decisions	Managing complexity	Living solo
• How will you manage your health? • Where will you live?	• What will you do on Tuesday morning? • Who will you have lunch with?	• How will I get an ice cream cone? • How will you provide care?	• Who will change your light bulbs? • Who will care for you?

The LPBs consisted of 12 tangible artifacts with 8 provocative questions (e.g., these life-relevant questions enable individuals to reconsider elements of their environment, families, and communities), representative icons, and textures to help financial service providers and recipients envision a possible future longevity coaching service. This study used the early stage of the LPB design and development process to explore the broader perspective from visual and tangible to cultural and social.

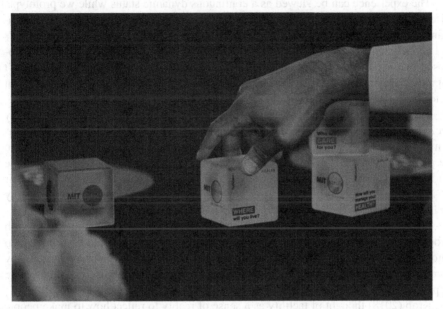

Fig. 1. The design and development of 12 Longevity Planning Blocks (LPBs) co-created with the MIT AgeLab (Credit: Amanda Macchia)

2.2 Cultural and Social Artifacts

Payne, a design educator and a design leader of a nonprofit, public-interest organization, explained that not many disciplines can create cultural artifacts, processes, services, and events [17]. Further, we can think of cultural and social artifacts that are rooted in the complex ecology-driven systems that might impact longevity coaching service design.

The idea of cultural or social artifacts can be traced back to the understanding of design as a diverse discipline. The design domain cannot be fully speculated, created, and implemented by itself without collaboration and extension with other disciplines. Therefore, design can be considered not only a catalyst, but also a product of cultural inventions. It can bridge times from the past to the future and be associated with deeper and broader environmental, cultural, economic, and social contexts.

2.3 Experience Prototype

Instead of discussing the traditional approach of experience prototypes in a design process [18], such as Human-Centered Design [19] or Design Thinking, from IDEO, a leading global design and innovation company transforming businesses, society, and technologies [20], this study explores how people interact with experiences empowered by visual or tangible artifacts to learn new longevity-related knowledge.

The experience can be viewed as a continuous dynamic status while we prototype, discuss, and analyze echoing Erwin's (2018) perspectives that it's not about visualization, it is about visualizing; it's not about user research, it is about the researching; it's not about the prototype, it is about the prototyping [17]. In addition, Larsen (2018) proposed that experience always has a social body based on the assumption that it isn't human consciousness that determines people's existence, but their social existence that determines their consciousness [21].

The first interaction with artifacts is through touch. But what do people actually feel when they touch things? Larsen (2018) indicated that we can consider tactility as a mix of a physical sensation and a mental experience. The concept of tactility is to be perceptible on the skin's surface while keeping the remaining part as an intangible underneath. People thought what they could see is the part of objects they touch, but their obsessions and personal preferences of how to use specific objects might also directly or indirectly change their behavior or perceptions "interacting" with the objects [21].

For example, individuals might integrate their habits because of their interaction with products. Since the popularity of using smartphones has increased and been integrated into our lives seamlessly, for most young generations, smartphones have replaced many electrical devices (e.g., cameras and tablets) and services. People also use smartphone apps for calling food delivery services or car transportation services.

Krop (2018) thought of tactility as a sense of reality to reflect how to make people feel: smooth, rough, soft, etc. [21]. Sonneveld (2018) considered touch as a full-body experience that can give people a sense of being in control, discovery, and navigating the world around them. People's touch experience can also make them vulnerable and sentimental. For instance, when we're touched, we might feel harmed or irritated [21].

In summary, this study experimentally prototyped and tested a longevity coaching service. The primary goal was to capture, synthesize, and analyze participants' reactions, emotions, and decision-making processes concerning visual and tangible artifacts associated with provocative scenarios within cultures and social contexts.

2.4 Think-Aloud Approach

Think-aloud is one of the qualitative research approaches to study any words in participants' minds that are expressed through verbal, visual, and behavioral formats while performing a designated task [21–23]. Previously, Ericsson & Simon (1980) treated participants as quasi-researchers, since to some degree, the experiment's results were co-created with researchers [24].

Olson et al. (1984) considered the think-aloud approach an effective research tool to access people's working memory from a higher-level thinking process [25]. It could also be a helpful way to observe and study individual differences while performing the same task.

To successfully apply this method, researchers should consider their own specific roles, relatable triangulation sources, and methods for data interpretation [22]. The think-aloud technique originated from the field of cognitive and psycholinguistic theory. At the time, scholars from cognitive psychology wanted to understand the connections between human working memory, thoughts, and words. For example, the idea of "inner speech" and working memory was used in Vygotsky's (1962) *Thought and Language* to study people's thought processes, cognitive workload, and expression [26].

However, one critical concern is when participants' expressions are not displayed verbally– such as showing physical actions, visual interpretations, or emotions while finishing tasks. The study result might then be distorted in the midst of verbal translation to satisfy the requirements of the think-aloud approach. Eccles and Arsal (2017) also mentioned three common pitfalls of using the think-aloud approach [27]. Participants don't need to explain their thoughts verbally or through other means; instead, they only need to think aloud retrospectively or concurrently.

A researcher also needs to guide participants before they start to think aloud, such as using warm-up exercises to instruct participants about the method. Lastly, the time of a think-aloud approach is important, due to the limitation of participants' attention and the quality of the research result.

In this study, a think-aloud approach was applied to four co-creation workshops and 12 semi-structured user interviews [28, 29]. The experiments were designed to ensure that 20 participants were less influenced by the research team. To gain a more accurate analysis, the discussion between a participant and facilitator during the longevity coaching experiment and then post-experiment interviews were all recorded through Zoom cloud. Researchers also reviewed discussions and interviews through the video transcriptions.

3   Research Methods, Process, and Results

Figure 2 demonstrates the research flow of study 1 and study 2. The study was a qualitative research project hosting four co-creation workshops [11, 12] and conducting 12 semi-structured interviews to gather data. A think-aloud method, prototyping result, and design process were applied to analyze information to address the four initial research questions and three hypotheses.

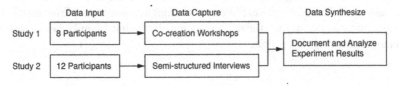

Fig. 2. Research flow overview of Study 1 and Study 2 from data input, capture, to synthesize

Two results were presented: 1. Participants' visuals and tangible design prototypes; 2. Keywords, quotes, and stories from semi-structured interviews. These learnings enabled us to better translate information into insight and helped us propose the D4L service considerations diagram (Fig. 4) to address the four research questions.

3.1 Recruitment

The author used his connections to invite 20 volunteer participants based in either Cambridge or Boston. Most had backgrounds in design (i.e. industrial, graphic, interaction, advertisement, business, and architecture design). Additionally, some had engineering, education, finance, and communications backgrounds. Regarding the demographics, 25% were males and 75% were females, with an average age of 35 years old. Significantly, 90% of participants had little or limited financial planning experience. Among the 20 participants, we conducted two studies.

In Study 1 (Fig. 2), eight female participants, each with expertise in diverse design disciplines, were divided into four workshop groups (two participants per group), creating a more intimate 1:1 co-creation setting to delve into the sensitive and challenging longevity planning and design topic.

Within each co-creation workshop, participants were equipped with accessible prototyping materials (e.g., form core board, thick paper, LEGO, glue gun, Post-its, Sharpies) and allocated approximately one hour to collaboratively create and engage in team discussions and sharing. In Study 2, the author conducted the semi-structured interviews with 12 participants.

3.2 Visual and Tangible Prototypes of Longevity Services

Selected prototypes and ideas came from four co-creation workshops designed by eight designers from various backgrounds (Fig. 3). The intention was to envision future longevity coaching services through visual and tangible artifacts in response to the first research question: How do people translate their ideas and visuals into tangible prototypes through a co-creation workshop?

Since each co-creation workshop was conducted for approximately 45–60 min, the use of a think-aloud approach and role-playing had an effective influence to help participants better express and think in the shoes of both a service provider and recipient, and facilitate more constructive conversations. In a 10–20-min post-workshop session, a quick interview and reflection were shared by participants to help us understand their sketches, drawings, and tangible prototypes with stories.

In summary, the deliverables are inspired by a great interest in how to make longevity coaching services more engaging and gamified (and not gimmicky) and an experience that builds trust and creates a safe exploratory environment where people are encouraged to consider many angles beyond finance: education, community, family, home, mobility, risk, relationship, trust, future, etc.

Fig. 3. Idea sketches, storytelling, visual expressions of longevity planning strategies, and low-resolution tangible prototypes (Credit: Sheng-Hung Lee)

3.3 Semi-structured Interview

In pilot tests of Study 2 (Fig. 2), the 12 participants were provided with the high-fidelity tangible artifacts—LPBs—to experience a longevity coaching experience for approximately 35–45 min followed by a 10–15-min semi-structured interview. The research result was documented and organized from 12 post-experiment interviews.

During the 12 experiments, the verbal and behavioral data were captured, such as participants' quotes, stories, the number of Post-it notes they used, the number of times they touched the LPBs, and also their gestures: leaning against the edge of the table or occupying the whole table and thinking it to be a learning zone.

However, due to the focus of this study and scope of the paper, we emphasized verbal discussion of interviews to present the advantages and disadvantages of using visual and tangible artifacts for future longevity coaching services (Table 2).

The intention was to gather participants' feedback in response to the first research question: What do people consider the advantages and disadvantages of applying evocative visuals (e.g., the image of a lonely cat that enables participants to express their thoughts about the stage of living alone), representative icons (e.g., the icons that encapsulate the concrete life examples from four retirement stages), and tangible artifacts (e.g., LPBs) to reframe and solve longevity-relevant challenges during the design process? Table 2 provides useful evidence and references to re-design the visual and tangible artifacts.

Table 2. Participants' direct quotes on using visual and tangible artifacts (LPBs) in a future longevity coaching service.

Advantages	Disadvantages
• "When I flip each LPB, I can naturally have more thoughts." • "The icons on LPBs can give me a direct idea." • "I enjoy the translucent texture of matte surface. It makes me want to see through the opposite side of a cube. I just want to keep touching them (LPBs)." • "The dimension of one LPB is a decent design that I cannot hold it with my full hand, but I can move it around, especially the rounded radius makes it smooth and pleasant to touch." • "The weight of each LPB is satisfying. It makes me feel the design is premium and important."	• "The realistic photos on LPBs are a bit hard to read on a translucent face and some photos might be too complicated to understand." • "LPBs should leave some white space, so I won't feel confused." • "I need more LPBs that can reflect my longevity coaching needs. Maybe we can DIY to make our own LPBs." • "Instead of adding questions, visuals, icons, and logos, I think it would be interesting to create a LEGO-style of structure to trigger more possibilities of playing and various configurations."

3.4   D4L Service Considerations Through Various Lenses

The first two sessions of the experiment were to address the first two research questions. The above preliminary results better enabled us to synthesize and discuss the last two research questions about identifying subtle needs and observations from cultural and social perspectives and raising awareness of the longevity coaching service to enhance people's understanding of their future holistic well-being by using tangible artifacts with visuals and messages in the context of a longevity service.

Therefore, in the study, the conceptual D4L service considerations (Fig. 4) were proposed to explore this complex, sensitive, and integral topic. By using visual and tangible artifacts (LPBs) as assisting tools or creative props, the insights and learnings were translated from participants' verbal and behavioral data into many provocative prototypes, compelling stories, intimate feelings, short-term plans, long-term goals, and even strategic longevity planning actions.

Cultural and social contexts might directly or indirectly shape the content of longevity coaching services and experiences. Participants' nationality, language, ritual, behavior, gender, age, value of money, and life expectations belong to the realm of culture and society that could all contribute to and change the visions, approaches, designs, systems, and impact of future longevity coaching services.

Additionally, observations, role-playing performances, interviews, and these multi-faceted qualitative research approaches could help us identify more evidence that participants' domain knowledge, levels of financial literacy, diverse nationalities, and living and working experiences can affect their ability to understand and articulate this new concept of a longevity service. The human side was complex and affected the design attributes of D4L services.

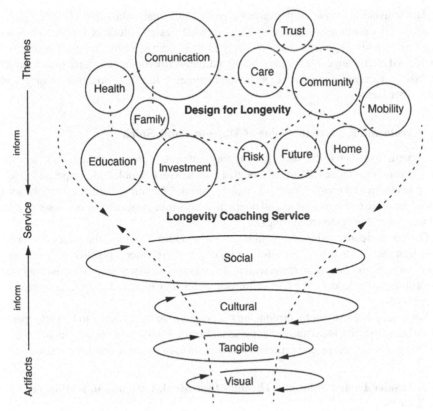

Fig. 4. Proposed D4L service considerations presenting complex, diverse, and systemic contexts and challenges in relation to applying visual, tangible, cultural, and social artifacts. The size of the circles doesn't represent the hierarchy or importance.

4 Discussion and Next Steps

Three discussions were highlighted to reflect this sensitive, personal topic: how to project your future self and shape longevity services. The discussion not only addressed four research questions but also included 1. How participants translated their ideas between three different formats (verbal, visual, and tangible); 2. What the value of make-to-think is; and 3. How we reconsider design solutions through the lens of individuals, community, and society.

4.1 Translated Three Different Formats: Verbal, Visual, and Tangible

Based on in-person observation and four workshop video recordings, most participants spent the first half of their time sparking ideas for brainstorming and ideations in co-creation workshops. However, the accessible prototyping materials encouraged participants to draw and visualize their ideas from their verbal discussion to more visual and tangible on paper. The "prototyping-friendly" environment also enabled them to turn their two-dimensional ideas into three-dimensional objects.

The translations between participants' verbal to visual to tangible ideas were also meaningful to observe and discuss. The extended design solutions for the future of longevity coaching services could not only exist in verbal, visual, tangible, and more flexible and interchangeable formats, but also strategically encompass participants' backgrounds, genders, ages, expertise, interests, incomes, education, financial literacy, and many other factors.

4.2   Create and Explore the Value of Make-to-Think Spirit

When participants have accessible prototyping materials in front of them (five letter-size white paper, Post-it notes, Sharpies, hot glue gun, scissors, double-sided tape, and glue), it inspires them and enables them to "make to think." Creating tactility can make idea generation more fluent, concrete, and interactive, according to the fieldwork observations and four workshop video recordings.

Once participants had made tangible objects and idea drawings, they started to build upon each other's ideas with more focused goals. It also created a positive and engaging momentum to circulate these ideas with more constructive discussion. We observed that this prototyping-friendly vibe had an impact on all four groups during the co-creation experiments.

Further study can explore introducing the prototyping stage earlier to let participants achieve more creative ideas and richer personal stories. Future studies can also investigate which types of prototyping significantly impact the quality and quantity of ideas.

4.3   Consider Design Solutions Through Individual, Communal, and Social Lenses

The concept of a longevity coaching service is innovative, complex, and full of business potential in both expanding financial planning services and creating a whole new service. In Study 1, four design solutions from co-creation workshops revealed the complexity of building an effective, trusted, and delightful longevity coaching service.

The complexity of longevity planning services and systems arises not only from the diverse array of key stakeholders involved but also due to the intricate interplay of an individual's educational background, aspirations, financial circumstances, family status, cultural influences, and various other demographic factors.

In both Study 1 and 2, participants underscored the intricate challenges related to longevity planning and design during discussions with a facilitator and researcher. For instance, they highlighted factors such as individuals' educational backgrounds, mobility levels, and financial conditions, which significantly influence their ability to formulate effective future aging-in-place plans.

Most participants' initial ideas came from their life and work experiences. For example, participants were asked to act as a longevity coach (a service provider) or a user (a service recipient) in a role-playing exercise, which enabled them to consider more comprehensive aspects (e.g., social, political, and cultural perspectives) of the possible scenario. If played as a longevity coach, a participant needs to think of their user's demographics, financial and family conditions, investable liquid income, monthly savings, yearly income, and other personal information.

In contrast, acting as a service recipient, a participant needed to think about the needs, constraints, and areas of interest beyond financial planning. A few participants proposed platform-level design solutions (e.g., how we establish a robust financial planning system), but most considerations only stayed at the individual level.

For further study, the structure of a co-creation workshop can be designed to put more emphasis on how we can shift the participants' conversation from the desires of individuals to the culture-shaping and system-building of communities. For instance, how do we address the low financial and longevity literacy rate through transforming our current education system, taking into account all that comes with that: students, faculty, curriculum design, environment, longevity learning toolkit design for both educators and students, and other learning resources.

Essentially, the generative design solutions—from personal needs to collective social values—should be emphasized more. Ultimately, the aim is not only to improve people's quality of life, but also to promote a society with higher longevity literacy, longevity strategies, and longevity planning.

5 Conclusion

In the 21st century, humans are witnessing a transformative revolution in technology, science, and society. Advances in computational science, artificial intelligence (AI), digital transformations, experience-led products, and longevity economics are reshaping how we live and what we value, especially as we face challenges like the energy crisis, climate change, and demographic shifts resulting in a longer healthspan and lifespan along with a low birth rate. The concept of Design for Longevity (D4L) could serve as a useful approach to empower researchers, designers, and scientists to review our existing systems sustainably and comprehensively. What's more, it has greatly impacted the researchers of this study in terms of focus, shifting from object-level problem-solving to system-level cultural integrations [17].

Based on the four co-creation workshops and 12 semi-structured user interviews, the preliminary result of this study demonstrated the opportunities of using visual and tangible artifacts to assist in the creation of a holistic longevity coaching service integrating cultural and social aspects of proposed D4L service considerations. In this study, we used a traditional financial planning service and industry as a referencing experience to shape a longevity coaching service, leveraging the value of visual and tangible artifacts to discuss the importance of 1. Translation of ideas and visual concepts into tangible prototypes through a participatory approach; 2. Demonstrating perceived advantages of employing visuals and tangible artifacts to reframe and address challenges related to longevity; 3. Identifying subtle needs and interpreting them through the cultural and social perspectives of people; and 4. Utilizing tangible artifacts e.g., Longevity Planning Blocks (LPBs) coupled with provocative questions, representative icons, and visuals, to raise awareness of the longevity coaching service that enhances people's literacy of holistic well-being.

Acknowledgments. This study is a component of the author's doctoral research specifically focused on Design for Longevity (D4L) service systems through the lens of visual, tactical, cultural, and social artifacts. This research is generously sponsored by MIT AgeLab and MIT Ideation Lab and is guided by the author's Ph.D. committee affiliated with the Massachusetts Institute of Technology (MIT): Professor Maria C. Yang, Dr. Joseph F. Coughlin, Professor Olivier de Weck, Professor Eric Klopfer, and Professor John Ochsendorf. The author extends heartfelt gratitude to Dr. Lisa D'Ambrosio, Research Scientist at MIT AgeLab, and Professor Sofie Hodara, Northeastern University College of Arts, Media, and Design, for their constructive comments on an earlier version of the manuscript. Additionally, the author sincerely appreciated the great contribution, invaluable feedback, and stories provided by 20 volunteer participants.

Disclosure of Interests. The author has no competing interests to declare that are relevant to the content of this article.

References

1. Coughlin, J.F.: The Longevity Economy: Unlocking the World's Fastest-Growing. PublicAffairs, New York, NY, Most Misunderstood Market (2017)
2. Pine, B.J., Gilmore, J.H.: The Experience Economy, With a New Preface by the Authors: Competing for Customer Time, Attention, and Money. Harvard Business Review Press, Boston, Massachusetts (2020)
3. Lai, M., Huang, J.: X Thinking: Building Better Brands in the Age of Experience, X Thinking Institute. Shanghai (2022)
4. Coughlin, J.F.: Disruptive demography: the new business of old age. In: Irving, P.H., Beamish, R. (eds.) The Upside of Aging, pp. 51–62. Wiley, Hoboken (2014)
5. Lee, S.-H., Yang, M.C., De Weck, O.L., Lee, C., Coughlin, J.F., Klopfer, E.: Macro-trend study under service system: preliminary research in service innovation and emerging technology. In: Hamid, U.Z.A., Suoheimo, M. (eds.) Service Design for Emerging Technologies Product Development, pp. 45–72. Springer, Cham (2023). https://doi.org/10.1007/978-3-031-29306-1_4
6. Lee, S.-H., De Weck, O.L., Yang, M.C., Coughlin, J.F.: The transformation of design platform under system thinking. Int. J. Perfor. Arts Digital Media **19**(3), 1–29 (2023). https://www.tandfonline.com/doi/full/10.1080/14794713.2023.2271820
7. WHO. Ageing and Health (2022). https://www.who.int/news-room/fact-sheets/detail/ageing-and-health
8. Irving, P.H., ed.: The Upside of Aging: How Long Life Is Changing the World of Health, Work, Innovation, Policy and Purpose. Wiley, Hoboken (2014)
9. Golden, S. Stage (Not Age).: How to Understand and Serve People over 60-the Fastest Growing, Most Dynamic Market in the World, Harvard Business Review Press, Boston (2022)
10. Lee, S.-H., et al.: Designing healthcare services for longevity. In: Narratives of Love: Towards Healing, Transformation, and Transcendence (2023)
11. Lee, S.-H., et al.: Co-create financial planning services for an aging population: designers' perspectives. Proc. Des. Soc. **3**, 947–956 (2023)
12. Lee, S.-H., et al.: Service design in action: transformation, consideration, and system thinking. Proc. Des. Soc. **3**, 3145–3154 (2023)
13. Atenao, E. M.: Famous Ordinary Things. Dabook, Lausanne (2017)
14. Fukasawa, N., Morrison, J.: Super Normal: Sensations of the Ordinary. Lars Müller, Baden (2007)

15. Yanagi, M., Brase, M.: The Beauty of Everyday Things. Penguin Books, London (2018)
16. Turkle, S. (ed.): Evocative Objects: Things We Think With. MIT press, Cambridge, Mass (2007)
17. Fuller, J. (ed.): Where Must Design Go Next? Oro Editions (2023)
18. Buchenau, M., Suri, J.F.: Experience prototyping. In: Proceedings of the 3rd Conference on Designing Interactive Systems: Processes, Practices, Methods, and Techniques, pp. 424–433. ACM, New York (2000)
19. IDEO, ed., Human Centered Design Toolkit, IDEO, San Francisco, Calif. (2011)
20. Brown, T., Katz, B.: Change by Design: How Design Thinking Transforms Organizations and Inspires Innovation. Harper Business, New York (2009)
21. Can You Feel It? Effectuating Tactility and Print in the Contemporary, Onomatopee, Eindhoven (2018)
22. Charters, E.: The use of think-aloud methods in qualitative research an introduction to think-aloud methods. Brock Educ. J. 12(2) (2003)
23. van Someren, M.W., Barnard, Y.F., Sandberg, J.A.: The Think Aloud Method: A Practical Guide to Modelling Cognitive Processes. Academic Press, London (1994)
24. Ericsson, K.A., Simon, H.A.: Verbal reports as data. Psychol. Rev. 87(3), 215–251 (1980)
25. Olson, G.M., Duffy, S.A., Mack, R.L.: Thinking-out-loud as a method for studying real-time comprehension processes. In: Kieras, D.E., Just, M.A. (eds.) New Methods in Reading Comprehension Research, pp. 253–286. Routledge, Abingdon (2018)
26. Vygotskij, L.S., Vygotskij, L.S.: Thought and Language. MIT Press, Cambridge, Mass (1985)
27. Eccles, D.W., Arsal, G.: The think aloud method: what is it and how do i use it? Qual. Res. Sport Exerc. Health 9(4), 514 (2017)
28. Lee, S.-H., Coughlin, J.F., Yang, M.C., Balmuth, A., de Weck, O., Ochsendorf, J.: Design Artifacts and Gaming Transform Financial Planning Services. Industrial Designers Society of America, New York, NY, The Watering Hole (2023)
29. Lee, S.-H., Yang, M.C., Coughlin, J.F., Lee, C., Klopfer, E.: From Brainstorming to Bodystorming: Co-Creation Workshop Analysis Using Applied Video Ethnography. Industrial Designers Society of America, New York, NY, The Watering Hole (2023)

Room Acoustic Design for Open Plan Interior in Dwelling House

Wei Lin[1(✉)], Chun-Pin Huang[2], Fei-Ran Lu[1], and Qing-Feng Lin[1]

[1] School of Architecture, Feng Chia University, Taichung, Taiwan, R.O.C.
wlin@fcu.edu.tw
[2] Yangger Interior Design Co., Ltd., Taipei, Taiwan, R.O.C.
tc@yangger.com

Abstract. Taiwanese dwelling house designs prioritize open space flexibility while also addressing the high-quality sound field requirements, which can be objectively simulated and verified post-construction. The living room, serving as the primary area for leisure activities, is often adjacent to the dining area or others. Ensuring optimal sound quality, necessitating control over sound reflection volumes in both the living room and adjoining areas. Firstly it is achieved by mitigating outdoor noise intrusion and minimizing indoor noise sources through strategic room acoustic design approaches that integrate broadband absorptive materials capable of effectively absorbing sound across various frequencies. Utilizing computer predictions alongside corresponding material performance allows for the reinforcement of sound magnitude while enhancing speech intelligibility and hearing intimacy during the early stages of design. Overall, This study aims not only to explore these issues but also to establish a sound environment conducive to achieving a basic quality listening field.

Keywords: Open plan interior house · room acoustics · computer simulation · sound field verification

1 Introductions

1.1 Research Background

Noise has been the world health organization is defined as one of the biggest environment problem in [1], it can lead to cardiovascular disease, children's cognitive dysfunction, sleep disorders and annoyance. Noise causes sleep disturbances that lead to subsequent cascading health problems such as obesity [2], diabetes, and cardiovascular disease [3]. Especially if the housing unit is located near the transportation network [4], such as close to the vehicle road, rail system and airport area, it will be the main source of sound pollution. In the city, there are other noise sources, including construction noise and neighborhood living noise, especially during the COVID-19 lockdown in 2020, noise complaints showed a 48% increase in the number of noise complaints compared to the same period in London in spring 2019, more due to working from home, noise sources shifting to construction work noise (36%), and a significant increase in complaints about neighborhood living noise (50%) [5]. Thanks to the COVID-19 pandemic, lockdown and restrictions in many countries have reduced noise pollution levels. For example, after two weeks of lockdown in Barcelona, Spain, noise pollution levels dropped by 11 dB (A)(Lday) [6], the average reduction was 5.4 decibels (lAeq) in London [7]. Despite the decrease, London experienced a 47.5% increase in noise complaints during lockdown, due to people working from home and staying longer, combined with a combination of work accumulation and emotional frustration, making them more sensitive to nearby outdoor noise [5]. As a source of outdoor noise penetrate into building envelope, windows (such as openings) are one of the weakest elements, and only windows are the most cost-effective solution to control the outdoor noise penetration. After the epidemic, people prefer to do work and leisure at home because of the heightened awareness of public health and the risk of upper respiratory tract infection that may be increased by engaging in outdoor leisure activities. For the home space, the composite space combined with the living room, dining room and kitchen space, combined with audio-visual perception, has become a trend. Modern home space tends to be small space, generally less than $100 \, \text{m}^2$, for the family to attach importance to the interaction with the family, making the open space favored by more and more people, in the design of ingenious combination with other spaces, not only has a visual extension effect, but also makes the space transparent and bright. Based on the above description, Fig. 1 demonstrated a typical house prefers to adopt an open design in the planning of entry way, dining, kitchen, living and study room, so that the sense of lighting and space is more extended, and the middle island is installed in the middle of the kitchen and dining room to increase its permeability and openness with remote living and study space elastically.

Entry way

Dining

Kitchen

Living

Study

Fig. 1. Typical open plan with a $100 \, \text{m}^2$ dwelling house, the functional space was separately brought into the room through the color notation, including the representative five locations of the entry, dining, kitchen, living and study room, respectively.

Some researches discuss the configuration pattern of home kitchen space and adjacent public areas (Dining room and living room), summarizes the corresponding relationship between modern kitchen and interior space through spatial mapping of various cases, provides interior designers with reference indicators for interior space design when planning kitchen and adjacent space, and completes the combination of customized dining room, kitchen and living room [8]. Opposite the configuration of the space set; the living room still plays a master role in con-ducting family members to do leisure activities with adjacent dining space. Considering the sound quality and speech intelligibility, the volume of sound reflection will not only be restrained in the living room, but the other volumes with dining and kitchen parts may continue to connect with coupled effects. Engaging in cognitive use from the perspective of different family members, ironically, the main benefits of a shared work environment and ease of interaction actually become the source of the problem. This study will not first explore this issue, but to provide a sound environment to achieve basic quality listening field. Audiovisual equipment currently combines 5.1 channels or 7.2 channels with home theater speaker hearing equipment. To be able to hear the high-quality sound, outdoor noise must be shielded and indoor noise sources must be eliminated, and then room acoustic design strategies were proposed which included indoor absorptive material with broadband. When sound waves strike an object's surface at an angle, they are reflected at the same angle. This reflection effect is similar to seeing a mirror image, and it results in specular reflections occurring [9]. A textured and decorated surface that reflects acoustic energy causes the sound to scatter in different directions, reducing its intensity. This is known as diffuse reflection [10, 11]. The natural sound field is subject to various physical limitations, such as the size of the space and the distance from the sound source. In large hall spaces, it can be challenging to achieve optimal sound quality without the use of amplification. To address this, sound amplification technology is utilized to enhance the sound quality, ensuring that the audience can hear every note and nuance of the performance. The use of loudspeaker equipment is critical during performances, allowing for the adjustment of sound characteristics, the balance of parts, and sufficient volume. These adjustments help to create a more immersive and enjoyable experience for the audience while ensuring that every part of the performance is heard clearly. Furthermore, this technology allows for recordings to be reproduced with high fidelity in other spaces. The sound amplification and loudspeaker equipment can be adjusted to suit the characteristics of the recording space, ensuring that the listener hears the performance as intended. Overall, sound amplification technology and loudspeaker equipment play a vital role in enhancing the quality of live performances and reproducing them with high fidelity in other spaces. The interior space radiation affects the way sound travels by causing a series of reflections. When sound travels, it is mainly distributed through direct sound and reflected sound. The volume of sound will not decrease significantly except for when there is a distance between the source of the sound and the listener. The way sound is distributed is also related to the size of the space. To fully comprehend the complex interplay between the initial reflections and the direct sound, it is essential to delve deeper into the intricate details. The late energy response, which captures the arrival time and acoustic energy of the direct sound, along with the subsequent reflections, plays a crucial role in shaping the overall sonic character of any given space. Therefore, it is imperative to gain a comprehensive understanding of this relationship to accurately analyze and manipulate sound in any acoustic environment [12]. The ideal amount of reverberation time (RT) for a room is determined by its volume. It is recommended that the RT be planned accordingly to ensure optimal sound quality. In order to regulate the acoustical parameters of a room, such as RT30, C80, D50, Ts, and EDT, it is important to measure them as physical quantities. These parameters are regulated based on the impulse response of an international standard ISO 3382, as specified by Bradley in 2004. The impulse response is a measurement of how a room responds to a sound wave, and it is used to determine the acoustical properties of the room. By measuring the impulse response of a room and comparing it to the international standard, one can ensure that the room is acoustically optimized for its intended purpose [13]. Additionally, many dwelling houses have a middle island that is installed in the kitchen and dining areas for increased permeability and flexibility in the living and study areas. The living room is the main area for leisure activities and is typically adjacent to the dining area. To ensure good sound quality and speech intelligibility, it is important to control the volume of sound reflection in the living room and other adjoining areas. This is achieved by blocking outdoor noise and minimizing indoor noise sources, room acoustic design strategies are used to ensure high-quality sound in the space. By using these materials, sound reflections can be reinforced, and speech intelligibility can be improved.

1.2 Research Purposes

Dwelling houses in Taiwan typically have a design that prioritizes open spaces for the entryway, dining, kitchen, living room, and study areas. This design allows for an extended sense of lighting and space throughout the home. Additionally, many dwelling houses have a middle island that is installed in the kitchen and dining areas for increased permeability and flexibility in the living and study areas. The living room is the main area for leisure activities and is typically adjacent to the dining area. To ensure good sound quality and speech intelligibility, it is important to control the volume of sound reflection in the living room and other adjoining areas. This is achieved by blocking outdoor noise and minimizing indoor noise sources, room acoustic design strategies are used to ensure high-quality sound in the space. For instance, indoor absorptive materials with broadband are often used to absorb sound waves of different frequencies. By using these materials, sound reflections can be reinforced, and speech intelligibility can be improved. Overall, the design of houses in Taiwan prioritizes open space and flexibility while also considering the quality of the sound field. The four objectives of this research are as follows: 1. Taiwanese dwelling houses are designed with a strong emphasis on open space and flexibility. 2. Achieve unparalleled sound quality with advanced technology that proofs outdoor noise and facilitate indoor sound absorption, resulting in a truly immersive listening experience. 3. The living room is the primary space for leisure activities, and its acoustics are optimized for using with reinforcement sound system. 4. Dwelling houses in Taiwan are designed to meet acoustical standards of comfort and quality, with careful attention paid to noise control and acoustical design.

2 Project Practices

2.1 The Design Implement

This study aims to improve the quality of sound in residential spaces, with a specific focus on noise control and background noise. The goal is to create a pleasant and comfortable sound field indoors. The study looks at how interior design projects can help achieve this goal through collaboration with homeowners. The impact of noise disturbances on our lives cannot be underestimated, as studies have consistently shown that they have a range of negative effects. These include a reduction in the quality of our sleep, a decrease in our ability to be productive at work, and a decline in our overall mental well-being. Such findings have been repeatedly documented in research literature, highlighting the need for effective measures to mitigate the adverse effects of noise pollution. The ultimate aim of undertaking noise control and interior decoration turnkey projects is to deliver a tranquil and luxurious living experience that exceeds all expectations. By eliminating disruptive noises and incorporating aesthetically design elements, the resulting living space will provide a serene atmosphere that promotes a ideal and peaceful lifestyle. This approach is focused on delivering a dwelling house environment that is not only visually appealing but also creates a sensation of relaxation while satisfying the highest standards of quality of living. The study thoroughly analyzes multiple acoustical issues and budget constraints, and provides a clear and definitive directional reference for subsequent design decisions. The numerical calculation and computer simulation evaluations are meticulously scrutinized to ensure precise and accurate results. Furthermore, the study offers practical and feasible solutions for optimizing the acoustic plant in the living space, ensuring a high-quality sound experience for all.

2.2 Indoor Sound Environment

The study object is indisputably located on the 7th floor of a residential building in the Nei-Hu District of Taipei. The surrounding area is significantly impacted by noise pollution, emanating primarily from the following three noise sources: (1). Traffic noise refers to the sound produced by vehicles moving on a road. (2). It's important to note that this project is situated right next to Songshan Domestic Airport, which means that it is highly to be affected by noise from aircraft during takeoff and landing. (3). Sounds from nearby construction activity or other building facilities. The ongoing study project is dedicated to creating a design that emphasizes open space and flexibility. The entryways are designed to provide a grand welcome, with ample space for guests to move freely. The dining area is spacious enough to accommodate a large family. The kitchen is designed to be open and airy, with plenty of counter space and storage for all needs. The living room is a generously sized area that creates a cozy and comfortable space for family time. The plane configuration design is shown in Fig. 2.

Typically have a design that prioritizes open spaces for the entryway, dining, kitchen, living room, and adjacent toilet areas. The research exclusively focused on the open plan area highlighted with red color blocks. The primary objective was to optimize sound quality by facilitating absorption. The sound field area spans 150 m^2, and its volume is 350 m^3, which effectively contributes to achieving the appropriate reverberation time for

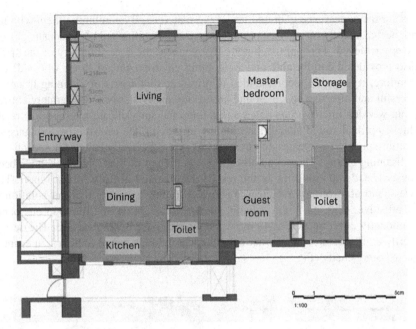

Fig. 2. Figure is the interior design diagram of the plan configuration. The sound field evaluation of the open plan includes the living room, dining room, kitchen and adjacent toilet and guest space. The indoor sound field evaluation is the area marked with red color blocks.

the living area. Determining the appropriate reverberation time for a room is crucial for achieving the desired sound quality. This time is determined by the room's volume and finishes, but what really matters is the intended use of the room. While lively and active areas may prefer a longer reverberation time, other spaces that require clear speech and comfortable sound demand shorter reverberation times. Follow the guidelines below to determine the optimal reverberation time for your room and use proper acoustical design to achieve it with confidence. The criteria of reverberation time is set as 0.45 s at middle frequency. The reverberation time criteria, which is the time required for sound to decay in a room, has been specifically set to 0.45 s for the middle frequency. This means that any sound produced in the room will take 0.45 s to decay to 60 dB at the middle frequency.

2.3 Sound Absorption Usage

In order to ensure optimal sound quality, the open plan has been designed with utmost care and attention. To avoid acoustic obstacles in a sound field, such as echoes and total harmonic standing wave effects, it is imperative to arrange the layout of the room's furniture and materials to guarantee an even distribution of sound absorption effects when installing acoustic panels on the ceiling and walls. The living, dining, and listening areas are equipped with sound-absorbing materials that have been carefully selected for their superior sound-absorbing properties installation locations have been strategically chosen to maximize the effectiveness of the sound-absorbing materials. It's essential to consider the appearance of sound-absorbing materials. By combining them with the interior design shape, you can ensure that long-term durability and high acoustic performance are achieved. This approach not only enhances the overall quality of the space but also provides a comfortable and welcoming environment for those who will use it. Therefore, it is highly recommended to prioritize this aspect of planning to create a successful and effective space. Sound absorption materials were deliberately chosen a 15 mm wooden microporous panel and a 9mm calcium silicate microporous panel to achieve optimal sound absorption, thereby improving the acoustic performance of the interior space. This creates an environment that is perfectly suited for speech and music listening clarity. The sound absorption coefficient of these materials have been rigorously tested and conforms to the results documented in ISO354 test report. The average sound absorption coefficient is above 0.76, thus ensuring that our solution is highly effective. With its 9 mm calcium silicate construction, the microporous panel can confidently cover an area of 49 m^2 while modeling the ceiling surface. The design is expertly crafted to meet the owner's preferences, and the sound field design ensures complete homogeneity (Fig. 3).

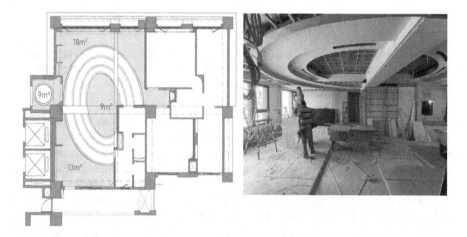

Fig. 3. The ceiling is designed with a curved surface and the 9mm calcium silicate microporous panel covers a total area of 49 m2. This design is visually and acoustically pleasing. Ceiling construction on the right side of the picture.

3   Objective Evaluation

3.1   Computer Simulation

Indoor sound field performance planning requires a thorough understanding of sound energy and its distribution. By confirming the independence and correlation of acoustic parameters, we can determine the objective of this planning with greater certainty. Therefore, it is crucial to consider sound energy when adjusting indoor spaces. Computer simulations offer an array of evaluation techniques, specifically designed to analyze the effectiveness of indoor sound insulation in various locations. These techniques have been developed to provide the most accurate results, ensuring that be able to make informed decisions about the soundproofing needs. After the verification measurement is completed, the physical properties in real time are collected through objective testing, and the corresponding relationship between objective physical measurements is explored. At this stage, computer simulation is used to predict and evaluate the indoor sound field model and sound insulation performance. With the continuous advancement of software and hardware technology, the computer simulation software for hall sound quality has matured and is now widely used in research on sound quality design and evaluation of sound field characteristics in halls. According to the principle of geometric acoustics, the indoor sound field is simulated by computer, and the actual room is built to simulate the propagation law of sound wave in the room. In order to reduce the time required for computer simulation to generate sound energy distribution, a measurement based rendering software was developed. ODEON software is used to analyze the actual measurement and draw the distribution map of sound energy. It has a trend prediction function in research projects, especially when the sound source is stable, such as a fixed sound source (P1) like a home theater speaker position, and measurement of multiple points (1, 2, and 3) (Fig. 4).

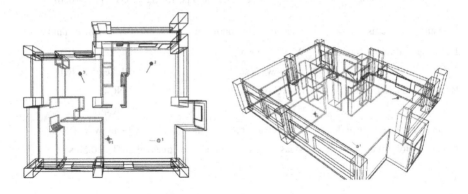

Fig. 4. Odeon computer simulation software sets the sound source (P1 is the location of the speaker for home theater set) and the sound field of three measurement points (1, 2 and 3).

3.2 Field Verification

The filed verification are performed after the completion of indoor acoustics, the main evaluation items include indoor environment sound, background with HVAC system, sound insulation performance of entrance, and reverberation time. For room acoustical verification of measurement, several important considerations are necessary: indoor environment sound analyze the distribution of sound pressure levels across different locations within the room to identify variations and optimize acoustics, background noise levels to assess their impact on the overall acoustical environment and identify potential sources of interference, sound proof, Assess the ability of building materials and structures to block the transmission of sound across various frequencies, measured in Dntw ratings, reverberation time in a room to determine its acoustic properties and suitability for various applications. The indoor environment is based on measurement results with the equivalent average volume $LAeq$ (dB) as the evaluation index and the A-weighted noise intermittently exposed in a certain period of time in the selected position in the sound field are averaged by the energy. The parameter index formula is shown in Eq. 1. The acceptance work has been completed and carried out, the project and performance standards, the range of measurement, as shown in Table 1.

$$LAeq = 10log\frac{1}{T}\int_{t}^{t+T} (\frac{Pt}{P0})^2 dt \tag{1}$$

$LAeq$: A-weighted average energy level dB (A) in period time;
T: measurement time in seconds;
Pt: measure sound pressure in Pa;
P0: reference sound pressure, based on 20 μPa.

Table 1. Conditions of acoustic measurement and performance criteria standard.

Measurement items	Measurement conditions	Performance standards
Indoor environment sound	Window open	$\leq$LAeq 55 (dB)
	Window close	$\leq$LAeq 50 (dB)
Background noise level	HAVC on	$\leq$NC45
	HVAC off	$\leq$NC40
Sound proof of entrance door	1.5 m away from entrance door	$\geq$Dnt, w = 35 (dB)
Reverberation time	Measurements at open plan areas	$\leq$RT = 0.55 s

3.3 Sound Proof Exterior

The building structure reduces the noise interference between conjunction indoor rooms through the performance of sound insulation. There are many reasons for the treatment of the indoor acoustic environment, including adjacent space and outdoor air noise and noise vibration generated by the equipment. Noise is introduced which is penetrated into the room through building doors, windows, walls, and floors, and the vibration of building internal equipment and indoor activities of residents constitute the increase of environmental noise, which has become one of the reasons for disturbing life and affecting environmental quality. The existing standards and specifications for sound insulation aim to strengthen the whole system of sound insulation, not to regulate individual components or materials, reduce the disturbance and influence of residents' living sound independently, and improve the quality of the quiet environment of the residential area.

Air insulation design and floor impact insulation design, according to the code has its scope of application. 150 mm thick reinforced concrete walls were used for the interior space in Taiwan; Surface cement mortar paint, the field sound insulation grade can reach more than 42 dB, has good sound insulation performance, the glass sound insulation performance specification standard is also more than 36 dB, can provide professional manufacturers in the development of materials in the process of benchmark reference. As long as the mass per unit area (m) and the Modulus of Elasticity (E) of the panel are known, the sound transmission through a single-layer plate can be approximated to a good accuracy. At low and mid frequency bands, the Acoustic transmission loss (TL) is calculated according to the mass law [11, 12]. The prediction formula is shown in Eq. 2 and Eq. 3, Eq. 4 *is addressed for building element* (Door) insulation performance, *DnTw*.

The prediction formula is shown in *Eq. 2*.

$$TL = 20 \log (mf) - 48 \text{ dB} \tag{2}$$

At high frequencies, the coincidence effect weakens the acoustic transmission, and the transmission loss is given by *Eq. 3*

$$TL = 20 \log (mf) + 10 \log (f/fc) - 44 \text{ dB} \tag{3}$$

The field measurement of sound insulation performance is based on the background noise correction of the receiving room, and the sound field transmission loss of the sound insulation performance of building components is based on the specification formula of CNS8465-1 as explained in Eq. (4).

$$DnT, w = D + 10 \log (T/T0) \text{ dB} \tag{4}$$

4 Results

4.1 Computer Simulation

This study attempts the dwelling house under the guidance of objective measurements which include simulation in design phase and field verification, interior designers can understand the nature of interior sound field and effectively engage to support the design plan systematically. Differ from the indoor sound field discussion, the paper proposes a kind of solution to issues, which will bring out a jade effect for interior designers engaged in the field of specialized indoor sound study. Odeon simulation was development by DTU and main algorithms were constructed based on ray tracing and image source modelling. In 1984, ray-tracking algorithms were discussed, An improved hybrid model combining ray tracing and image source methods was proposed in 1990, followed two years later by a secondary source method. Later, in 1995, a more efficient ray-tracing method based on vector scattering was implemented. A special application of ray tracing is a particle tracking, which means that the radiation is considered to be sound energy carrier of the plaques, along the ray to sound velocity spread around the room, after each reflection, based on the absorption characteristics of the surface energy decreases.

All the total energy of the particle can be displayed as a function of time, this is the global attenuation function of the room can calculate the quite accurate reverberation time estimates. This approach takes into account the location of the source, the location of the absorbing material in the room, and the degree of scattering, that is, the lack of diffusion in the room. However, there is no receiver; Calculate the volume of energy attenuation. This method was introduced in ODEON in 1995 along with vector-based scattering. In an empirical case, a fixed sound source (S1), such as a home theater speaker position, and a receiving point for a multi-point (R1, R2, R3) sound field measurement are set up, especially when the location of the sound source is known and the directivity is confirmed, total energy of the particle can be displayed as a function of time was performed in Fig. 5.

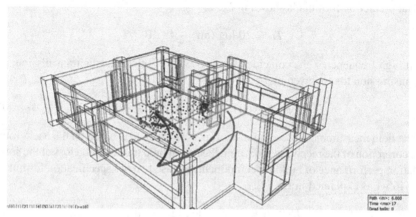

Fig. 5. All the total energy of the particle can be displayed as a function of time, this is the global attenuation function of the room calculation.

For predicting the reverberation time (RT) using computer simulations, accurate predictions of reverberation time can be obtained, aiding in the design and optimization of acoustically sound environments. Accurate room dimensions and geometry into the simulation software to reflect the actual physical space being analyzed. Incorporate data on the surface materials present with design in the room, along with their corresponding absorption coefficients, to accurately model sound absorption and reflection properties. Specify the locations of sound sources and receivers within the room to simulate sound propagation paths and calculate reverberation time at various points. Consider the frequency-dependent absorption properties of materials in the room to account for variations in reverberation time across different frequency bands. However, this time may not account for the presence of furniture, occupants, and other objects in the room that may affect sound absorption and reflection properties. Table 2 and Fig. 6 addressed simulation result of reverberation time which show that the average value of the middle frequency band (500 Hz, 1000 Hz) is 0.44 s and 0.43s , separately.

Table 2. Simulation results of RT(s) at middle frequency (500 Hz and 1000 Hz)

RT (s)Measurement points / middle at frequency	500Hz	1000Hz	Distribution of sound source and measurement points
R1	0.41s	0.40s	
R2	0.42s	0.46s	
R3	0.48s	0.47s	
Average	0.44s	0.43s	

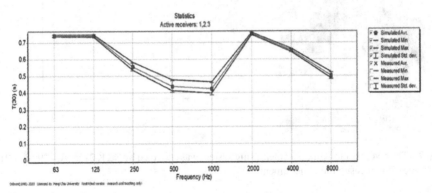

Fig. 6. Statistic results of Odeon calculation results at 1/1 octave (63-8 KHz) broad band

4.2 Field Verification

Ensure that room acoustics comply with relevant standards, applicable to the specific use of the space, such as ISO standards or CNS. Assess the reverberation time to understand the sound decay characteristics within the room, ensuring it aligns with the intended purpose of the space. Evaluate the distribution of sound reflections and absorption within the room to optimize acoustics and minimize room echoes and reverberations. Background noise levels with HVAC to ensure they are within acceptable limits and do not interfere with intended activities or occupant comfort. Bedside the above the measurements parameters, effectiveness of sound isolation measures to prevent sound transmission between adjacent spaces and minimize noise leakage. Reverberation time (s) measurements are used as an evaluation correction of the equivalent acoustic absorption area of the receiving chamber and are calculated as twice the elapsed time after attenuation regression from the first 5 to 35 dB of the attenuation curve. Refer to ISO 3382 (Measure of the reverberation time of rooms with reference to other acoustical parameters), through the pulse signal generation, the sound energy will be sent out the test signal, 1/2 "measurement microphone, the received signal back to the workstation for calculation. The measuring equipment and process shall comply with ISO3382 measurement specification, including a sound source generator or other measuring device that can measure T30 from 100 Hz to 3150 Hz frequency band, the measurement system adopts equipment systems such as B&K 2755-A, 4292-L-001 and Type-4966 for collection, as shown in Fig. 7. The signal to noise ratio of the above INR values must be greater than 35 dB or 45 dB to confirm the accuracy of determining the reverberation time (T30) and the correct interpretation of the measuring system and impulse response. On-site measurement of reverberation time T30 which show that the average value of the middle frequency band (500 Hz, 1000 Hz) is 0.42 s and 0.47 s, separately.

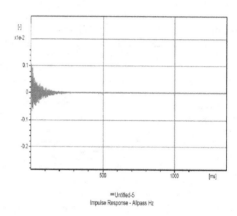

Fig. 7. The reverberation time T30 measuring system was collected by B&K 2755-A, 4292-L-001 and Type-4966 measurement instrument

It has a trend prediction function indoor, especially when the sound source is from outside of dwelling house, such as noise source alone street and (fixed and moveable sound, such as vehicle and mechanical sound). Measurement results with the equivalent average volume $LAeq$ (dB) as the evaluation index and the A-weighted noise intermittently exposed in a certain period of time in the selected position in the sound field, are averaged by the energy. In the indoor environment, the $LAeq$ (dB) value of sound energy is measured after the window is opened and the adjacent window faces the outdoors. B&K 2250 real-time analyzer was used for the measurement and 49.4 dB(A), measurement result is shown as a Fig. 8.

By adhering to these important considerations during on-site NC measurement of HVAC systems, considering factors such as proximity to HVAC equipment, occupant areas, and potential sources of noise interference. Measure noise levels under various operating conditions and modes of the HVAC system, including startup, normal operation, and shutdown, to capture the full range of noise emissions. The results of on-site

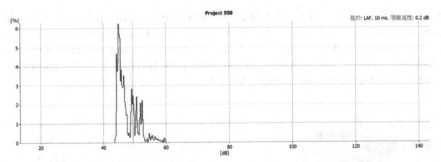

Fig. 8. B&K 2250 real-time analyzer was used for measurement and average of sound level is 49.4 dB(A).

noise criteria (NC) measurement of HVAC systems normally operated was performed as 55.5 dB which is approximately equivalent to NC48, sound magnitude of each board band was shown in Fig. 9.

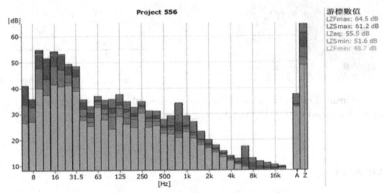

Fig. 9. B&K 2250 real-time analyzer was used for measurement and average of sound level 55.5 dB.

The entrance door with entry hall is considered for air sound insulation, and the measured content conforms to the sound insulation performance specification ISO140-4_6.2~6.3, and the declared value of ISO 717-1. The overall sound insulation performance (DnT,w) of the entrance door may exceed 35 dB, the distribution of measuring equipment and measuring points is described as follows; The sound insulation performance of the building construction door was measured by B&K 2250 real-time analyzer (noise meter) (sound pressure meter in accordance with IEC6167–2 type1 class), and the test sound source was pink noise. According to the sound insulation performance specification 140-4_part 4, it meets the requirements of the sound source point and the receiving point. Constructed in the adjacent chamber volume space, with a large volume space as the sound source room, the frequency spectrum of the sound source room (100 Hz–3150 Hz) in the adjacent third octave band between the step difference shall not be greater than 6 dB. Configure an active speaker equipment system as a single sound source. The receiving point is a mobile microphone, the measuring point is 1.2 m high, the measurement time of each point is 30 s, and the sound pressure level of 1/3 of the 30-s integral of each point is 100–3150 kHz. Figure 10 addressed sound proof of door verification which show that the average parameter value (DnT,w) $\geqq$ 35 dB between the sound source side and the sound receiving side.

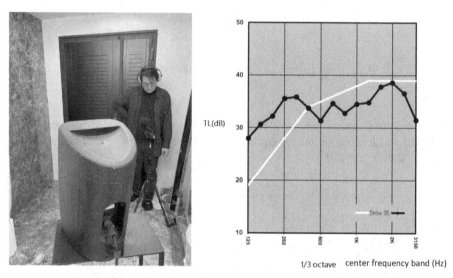

Fig. 10. Sound insulation performance of the door sound insulation parameter value (DnT,w) $\geqq$ 35 dB between the sound source side and the sound receiving side.

5   Discussion

The design of dwelling houses in Taiwan typically emphasizes open spaces to create a sense of extended lighting and spaciousness throughout the home. Moreover, many dwellings feature a middle island installed in the kitchen and dining areas to enhance permeability and flexibility in the living and study spaces. The living room serves as the primary area for leisure activities and is usually adjacent to the dining area. To ensure optimal sound quality and speech intelligibility, it is crucial to control sound reflection volumes in both the living room and adjoining areas. Primary task may be achieved by mitigating outdoor noise intrusion and minimizing indoor noise sources through strategic room acoustic design approaches that incorporate broadband absorptive materials capable of effectively absorbing sound with various frequencies. By utilizing the computer prediction with corresponding materials performance, sound magnitude can be reinforced while improving speech intelligibility and hearing intimacy at earlier stage. Overall, house designs in Taiwan prioritize open space and flexibility while also considering high-quality sound field requirements may approve through the objective simulation and verification after construction. This study will not first explore this issue, but to provide a sound environment to achieve basic quality listening field.

Acknowledgements. This study was subsidized and supervised by Research Project of Feng Chia University, and design director of Yangger Interior Design Co. Ltd. Mr.Huang Chun-Pin who are kindly share the verification of design dwelling housing venue for achieving the results. At the same time, the author hereby extends sincere gratitude to the reviewers who gave many valuable suggestions for revision of this paper.

References

1. World Health Organization. Environmental noise guidelines for theEuropean region, ed., World Health Organization. Regional Office for Europe (2018)
2. Oftedal, B., et al.: Road traffic noise and markers of obesity – a population-based study. Environ. Res. **138**, 144–153 (2015)
3. Sørensen, M., et al.: Long-term exposure to road traffic noise and incident diabetes: a cohort study. Environ. Health Perspect. **121**(2), 217–222 (2013)
4. Buratti, C.: Indoor Noise Reduction Index with an open window (Part II). Appl. Acoust. **67**(5), 383–401 (2006)
5. Tong, H., Aletta, F., Mitchell, A., Oberman, T., Kang, J.: Increases in noise complaints during the COVID-19 lockdown in Spring 2020: a case study in greater London, UK. Sci. Total Environ. **785**, 147213 (2021)
6. Ajuntament de Barcelona. Informe COVID-19 d'alteració dels nivells sonors. Medi Ambient i Serveis Urbans – Ecologia Urbana (2020)
7. Aletta, F., Oberman, T., Mitchell, A., Tong, H., Kang, J.: Assessing the changing, urban sound environment during the COVID-19 lockdown period using shortterm, acoustic measurements. Noise Mapp. **7**(1), 123–134 (2020)
8. Chen, P.L.: The influence of interior design floor plans on family relationships take the kitchen as an example. In: Proceeding of Interior Design Education Forum 2022, pp. d30–08 (2022)
9. Barron, M.: Auditorium Acoustics and Architectural Design. E & FN Spon, London (1993)
10. Beranek, L.L.: Concert Halls and Opera Houses: How They Sound. Springer, New York (1996)
11. Beranek, L.L.: Concert Halls and Opera Houses: Music, Acoustics, and Architecture, 2nd edn. Springer, New York (2004)
12. Long, M.: Archtectural Acoustics. Elservier Academic Press, London (2006)
13. Bradley, J.S.: Using ISO3382 measures to evaluate acoustical conditions in concert halls (2004)

Designing Virtual Spaces for Cross-Cultural Engagement: A Focus on Young Adults and Regional Cultural Elements

Jie Ling[1] , Danqi Xie[1] , Li Ouyang[2]([✉]) , Qiyang Lei[1] , Zihuan Xu[1] , and Zihong Wu[1]

[1] Zhongkai University of Agriculture and Engineering, Guangzhou 510220, Guangdong, China
[2] The Guangzhou Academy of Fine Arts, Guangzhou 510261, Guangdong, China
oylee@163.com

Abstract. This study is dedicated to creating a cross-cultural interactive virtual space aimed at individuals aged 18 to 25, with the goal of fostering deeper cultural understanding and interaction through unique regional cultural elements and virtual simulation technology. As globalization accelerates, virtual spaces have become a crucial platform for cross-cultural communication, yet they also present challenges such as cultural misunderstandings and superficial interactions. Through literature review, survey research, and initial user testing, this study explores how to enhance user interactivity and immersion using Virtual Reality (VR) and Augmented Reality (AR) technologies, and assesses the cultural acceptance and interactive behaviors of young people from various cultural backgrounds. Findings indicate that young individuals show significant interest in cultural exchange and social functionalities within virtual spaces, particularly within gaming and modern-style environments. However, there are discrepancies in the understanding of cultural symbols, highlighting the need for greater emphasis on cultural education and user experience in the design of cross-cultural virtual spaces. Additionally, participants prefer using lightweight and accessible devices, such as smartphones and computers, over VR headsets. The study suggests that the design of cross-cultural virtual spaces should delve into young people's cultural preferences and technology acceptance, offering diverse communication methods and rich cultural educational content. Furthermore, technology development should focus on enhancing user experience to make cross-cultural virtual spaces more inclusive and appealing to young users. The limitations of this study include its sample range and data collection methods, indicating the need for future research to encompass a broader sample and diverse data collection techniques. The findings provide new insights for virtual space design, aiming to facilitate cultural understanding and communication among young adults globally through technological innovation.

Keywords: Cross-cultural communication · Virtual space · Young adults · Cultural symbols · Virtual Reality

P.-L. P. Rau (Ed.): HCII 2024, LNCS 14699, pp. 88–103, 2024.
https://doi.org/10.1007/978-3-031-60898-8_6

1 Introduction

1.1 Background

As globalization accelerates, communication between different cultures becomes particularly important. The rapid development of internet technology and virtual reality plays a crucial role in eliminating geographical boundaries and promoting instant interaction and sharing. However, this progress also introduces new challenges, including cultural misunderstandings and impacts on deep cultural exchanges. While social media platforms like Weibo, Instagram, and TikTok play significant roles in global information dissemination, the phenomenon of "cultural fast food" and superficial communication methods on these platforms raise concerns about the depth of cultural understanding and authentic communication. Moreover, although virtual reality technology offers the potential for immersive cultural experiences, its popularity among young people is limited by costs and device comfort. This study aims to explore how to overcome these challenges by designing a future-themed cross-cultural interactive virtual space, integrating unique regional cultural elements, and promoting communication and interaction among young adults through virtual simulation devices. Through literature review and preliminary surveys, this study has collected and analyzed iconic cultural elements from East Asian regions, assessed the appeal of different visual elements to a diverse group of young people, aiming to enhance the efficiency and depth of cross-cultural communication by designing architectural spaces with communication functions. Preliminary research results show that participants displayed significant interest in such futuristic virtual environments, despite biases in interpreting cultural symbols, which did not hinder the smoothness of communication and overall satisfaction. These findings highlight the importance of correctly expressing and understanding multicultural elements in virtual spaces, providing new directions for future research.

1.2 Research Objectives and Significance

Research Objectives. The aim of this study is to design and implement a cross-cultural interactive virtual space targeted at young adults aged 18 to 25, with a particular emphasis on integrating regional cultural elements to foster deeper cultural understanding and communication. By incorporating the latest virtual simulation technologies, this study not only explores innovative methods of communication but also aims to assess the impact of these methods on cross-cultural understanding and interaction. The core objectives of the research include:

Analyzing the challenges and opportunities of current cross-cultural communication: Through literature review and empirical research, evaluate the challenges faced and opportunities provided by internet technology and virtual reality technology in facilitating communication between different cultures.

Designing a future-themed cross-cultural interactive virtual space: Utilizing selected regional cultural elements to create a virtual environment that not only attracts young people's participation but also promotes deep cultural exchanges.

Assessing the role of virtual spaces in promoting cross-cultural understanding: Collecting preliminary feedback from participants on their experiences in the virtual space through surveys, with a special focus on their understanding of cultural elements, the smoothness of interaction, and overall satisfaction.

Proposing new models and strategies for cross-cultural communication: Based on the findings, discussing how technological innovations can enhance the effectiveness and inclusiveness of cross-cultural communication.

Significance. The significance of this research lies in providing a new perspective for understanding and improving how people from different cultural backgrounds communicate and interact in virtual spaces. As globalization progresses, cross-cultural communication becomes increasingly important yet more complex. By constructing a cross-cultural virtual communication space specifically designed for young adults, this study not only helps to promote understanding and respect between different cultures but also provides new solutions for modern challenges such as the cultural fast-food phenomenon and cultural misinterpretation.

Furthermore, the outcomes of this research hold significant implications for both academic and practical fields. For academia, it enriches the theoretical foundations of cross-cultural communication and the use of virtual reality technology, offering new data from empirical research. For the practical field, especially in education, cultural exchange, and technology development, the design principles and strategies proposed by this study can guide the development of more effective tools and platforms for cross-cultural communication.

2 Literature Review and Related Work

2.1 Exploration and Challenges in the Design of Cross-Cultural Virtual Spaces

In a globalized society, virtual spaces have become an important platform for cross-cultural communication. Designers apply cross-cultural theories, such as Hofstede's cultural dimensions theory, Hall's high-context and low-context cultural theory [1], the SMCR communication model [2], embodied cognition's "4E" approach [3], and Lefebvre's spatial theory [4], to explore ways of integrating diverse cultural elements such as painting [5], ceramics [6], and Peking opera masks [7] into virtual design. Simultaneously, with the development of augmented reality (AR) and virtual reality (VR) technologies, researchers are investigating how these technologies can enhance user interactivity and immersive experiences. Currently, designers frequently use 3Dmax [8] for model construction, and implement interaction design with devices like Arduino, Track IR [9], HTC VIVE, Leap Motion, combined with the Unity3D engine [10]. Virtual space design also incorporates multi-dimensional analysis centered on user experience, emphasizing the importance of sensory, emotional, and interaction experiences [11, 12]. However, further research is needed to deepen the understanding of the needs of users from different cultural backgrounds and to enhance their sense of immersion. Designers are exploring the application of different space designs from a cross-cultural perspective, such as exhibition design [13], dining space design [14], concept bookstore design [15], campus space design [16], and luxury brand stores [17]. The challenge lies in how to effectively integrate cross-cultural theories with technological innovations to create more inclusive and interactive virtual spaces. The Importance of Spatial Cognition in Environmental Design.

2.2 The Application of Virtual Reality in Cross-Cultural Communication and Education

Virtual reality technology has demonstrated its new potential in the fields of social interaction and education during the pandemic. For example, the Virtual Burning Man Festival [18] held online in 2021 provided a low-risk social platform for users. Originally an offline event held in the desert, where participants would create large public art installations and conclude with a burning ceremony, the pandemic made such gatherings impossible. Consequently, the organizers of Burning Man turned to virtual design, creating a large virtual space for people to experience. Studies have shown that VR technology can effectively serve as a tool for remote communication and large-scale project management. For instance, research by Ali Abbas et al. [19] indicates that with precise spatial quantification through BIM software, VR technology can act as a supplementary means of communication, assisting in the better management of large-scale global projects and facilitating real-time connections between participants from afar. In the realm of cross-cultural education, VR technology has been proven to help promote the development of cross-cultural knowledge, attitudes, and beliefs. Research by Berti et al. [20] revealed that language learners' perceptions of foreign cultures and their attitudes towards the use of virtual reality can change through VR experiences. An experiment involving undergraduate students enrolled in a basic Italian language course allowed them to explore typical Italian settings using smartphones, earphones, and Google Cardboard, enabling learners to uncover new cultural layers missing from traditional teaching materials, thereby enhancing their understanding and cognition of foreign cultures (Fig. 1).

Fig. 1. Virtual Burning Man Festival. Source: https://virtualburn.burningman.org/booth/

2.3 Cultural Acceptance and Interactive Behavior of Young Adults

Researchers have shown great interest in the effectiveness and acceptance of virtual simulation technology across different domains. The Technology Acceptance Model (TAM) has been widely used to evaluate the effectiveness and user-friendliness of virtual simulation technologies. Specifically, researchers have investigated the application of virtual simulation technology in fields such as tourism planning [21], sporting events [22], and luxury retail [23]. Xuili Zhu [24] believes that enhancing the cultural acceptance among young people requires widespread promotion and dissemination from within and beyond, which could be achieved through combining exhibitions with events, enhancing the training of technical talents, expanding the mass base of intangible cultural heritage, and promoting it internationally, and relying on ancient buildings to create intangible cultural heritage tourism routes and characteristic towns for heritage conservation. Moreover, Jung Hyo Lee [25] has expanded the original TAM by emphasizing the importance of perceived enjoyment, social interaction, and the intensity of social connections for young users' acceptance of virtual simulation technologies. This indicates that virtual simulation technology is not only a tool but also an effective platform for enhancing user experience and promoting social interaction. However, critical commentary points out that although technologies such as 360-degree real-scene virtual simulation can improve learners' sense of presence and immersive experience, as demonstrated by Shadiev et al. [26], the effectiveness of this technology may vary across different cultural backgrounds. Young people lacking in cultural background knowledge may have misunderstandings about other cultures, and reliance solely on technology cannot fully resolve these cultural misunderstandings. Therefore, virtual simulation technology still needs to be combined with in-depth cultural education and interaction to increase young people's awareness and interest in different cultures. Ghanbarzadeh et al. [27] have tested Second Life among higher education users, pointing out that the design of virtual learning environments needs to be user-friendly and appealing, as well as realistic to increase student engagement and learning outcomes. This highlights the aesthetic and practical factors that need to be considered in the design and development of virtual simulation environments.

In the application of virtual simulation technology, the cultural acceptance and interactive behavior of young adults are complex and multidimensional. While existing research has demonstrated the potential of virtual simulation technology in enhancing user experience and promoting social interaction, it also reveals limitations and challenges in cultural education and communication. Therefore, future development and application of virtual simulation technology need to focus more on the deep integration of cultural content and personalized experiences, as well as providing more diverse and interactive learning environments. In this way, the cultural acceptance of young adults can be effectively enhanced, promoting understanding and communication between different cultural backgrounds.

2.4 Cultural Symbols and High-Low Context Virtual Spaces

In the context of globalization, the application of cultural symbols and high-low context in virtual space design is crucial for facilitating effective cross-cultural communication. Although advancements in technologies such as Virtual Reality (VR) and Augmented

Reality (AR) enhance the immersion and interactivity of virtual spaces, technological progress alone does not guarantee the accurate transmission and reception of cultural information. Therefore, designers must deeply understand and apply cultural symbols, optimizing user experience according to the needs of different contextual cultures (Fig. 2).

Fig. 2. Qin Dynasty Terracotta Warriors and Horses in VR Art Museum. Screenshot by Greener

Firstly, the accurate selection and presentation of cultural symbols are key to achieving cultural authenticity and resonance with users. For instance, The VR Museum of Fine Art on the STEAM platform recreates classic works such as the Mona Lisa's smile, the statue of David, and Buddha figures, accompanied by their history and explanation. Integrating Peking opera masks into virtual spaces interactively, allowing users to understand their history and cultural significance by clicking on different masks, not only adds educational value but also prevents cultural misunderstandings. Additionally, demonstrating how to balance user needs and expression methods in different cultural contexts will help strengthen the cultural inclusivity and diversity of virtual spaces.

Secondly, applying the high-low context cultural theory to virtual space design requires a deep understanding of different users' communication styles and preferences. High-context culture users may prefer communication through environmental context and non-verbal cues, whereas low-context culture users may favor direct verbal information. Hence, virtual spaces should offer adjustable communication settings to meet the needs of different users, for example, providing rich background information and symbolic images for high-context culture users and clear, explicit text explanations for low-context culture users.

Critically speaking, although the Technology Acceptance Model (TAM) and other theories provide a framework for evaluating the acceptance of technology in cross-cultural applications, existing research often overlooks the complexity of cultural dynamics and the actual needs of users. Therefore, future research should focus more on integrating cultural symbols and contextual differences, as well as users' cultural experiences and interactive behaviors, rather than solely concentrating on technological implementation.

In summary, the design of virtual spaces needs to go beyond technology itself, to deeply explore and integrate cultural symbols and the theory of high-low contexts, designing environments that not only reflect multiculturalism but also promote effective communication between users from different cultural backgrounds. At the same time, the role of user research and cultural education in the design process should be emphasized, ensuring that virtual spaces are not only technologically advanced but also culturally inclusive, meeting the cross-cultural communication needs of young adults in a globalized era.

3 Methodology

3.1 Data Collection

Survey: A survey was designed to gather extensive quantitative data, incorporating both closed-ended questions and Likert scale items, to evaluate young adults' preferences towards cross-cultural virtual spaces and their ability to understand culture in high-context scenarios. The survey was distributed online using the Questionnaire Star platform, targeting individuals aged 18 to 25 from various regions across the nation. The survey sources were divided into two parts: one portion of the sample was collected using a WeChat snowball distribution method, and the other was gathered using the sample service provided by Questionnaire Star.

3.2 Quantitative Data Analysis

The survey results were analyzed using the statistical software Excel, which included calculations of frequencies, means, and standard deviations to identify relationships and trends among different variables. This involved compiling the collected data into Excel spreadsheets, using formulae to compute the necessary statistical measures, and interpreting these results to understand the patterns and insights within the young adult responses regarding cross-cultural virtual spaces.

3.3 Ethical Considerations

Before conducting the study, all participants were informed about the research's purpose, process, and their rights through the questionnaire sent via Questionnaire Star, including the freedom to withdraw from the study at any time. All collected data were treated with confidentiality and used solely for academic research purposes.

Table 1. Virtual space and different design styles

	Ethnic style	Modern style	Fantasy style
Res-tau-rants			
Tea rooms			
Stages			
Class-rooms			
Inns			

Note: Design by Danqi Xie

3.4 Virtual Space Design Samples

The questionnaire included sections on virtual spaces involving everyday social scenarios, categorized by function, including restaurants, tea houses, stages, classrooms, and hostels. The styles of these spaces ranged from ethnic and modern to fantasy themes, encompassing the various aspects of daily social interaction within a virtual context (Table 1).

4 Data Collection and Analysis

4.1 Data Preparation and Preprocessing

Before the analysis, 137 surveys were collected, out of which five were discarded due to age incompatibility. The remaining responses were from users aged 18 to 25. Surveys were distributed via WeChat and the Questionnaire Star platform, ensuring complete responses. To ensure the quality of the analysis, 32 surveys with response times under 120 s were eliminated, leaving 100 valid questionnaires. All participants were fully informed about the purpose and process of the research and their rights, including the freedom to withdraw at any time. All data were anonymously collected and used solely for academic purposes.

4.2 Descriptive Statistical Analysis

Descriptive statistics were performed on basic user data, including gender distribution and ethnic composition. The sample included both male and female users from 16 provinces and cities in China, involving Han, Miao, and Buyi ethnic groups (Table 2).

Table 2. Number and percentage of user basic information

Category	Content	Quantity	Percent (%)
Sex	Male	49	49
	Female	51	51
Nationality	Han	97	97
	Miao	2	2
	Buyi	1	1
Province	Guangdong	29	28.71
	Henan	6	5.94
	Sichuan	6	5.94
	Chongqing	5	4.95
	Hunan	5	4.95
	Jiangsu	5	4.95
	Shanxi	4	3.96

(*continued*)

Table 2. (*continued*)

Category	Content	Quantity	Percent (%)
	Shaanxi	4	3.96
	Fujian	4	3.96
	Hebei	4	3.96
	Guangxi	3	2.97
	Anhui	3	2.97
	Yunnan	3	2.97
	Zhejiang	3	2.97
	Beijing	2	1.98
	Guizhou	2	1.98
	Jiangxi	2	1.98
	Liaoning	1	0.99
	Jilin	1	0.99
	Shanghai	1	0.99
	Heilongjiang	1	0.99
	Xinjiang	1	0.99

Frequency analysis was conducted on four basic questions designed to gather user preferences for virtual socialization and tool usage. For example, 65% preferred interacting with others in virtual spaces, while 35% preferred solitary experiences. Over half of the respondents were "very interested" in virtual space social features, while 41% showed moderate interest. For preferred activities, 90% favored competitive gaming, indicating a significant preference for social interaction through gaming. In terms of preferred devices, 47% opted for VR headsets, while 29% preferred smartphones, showing a tendency towards more accessible and lightweight devices (Table 3).

Table 3. User preferences for using social functions in virtual spaces.

Category	Content	Frequency	Percent (%)
1. In a virtual space, do you prefer to communicate with other users or enjoy the experience alone?	Communicate with other users	65	65
	Enjoy the experience alone	35	35
2. Are you interested in social functions in virtual space?	Very interested	55	55
	Generally interested	41	41

(*continued*)

Table 3. (*continued*)

Category	Content	Frequency	Percent (%)
	Not interested	4	4
3. What type of activities do you prefer to participate in virtual space?	Party/Social Event	65	65
	Game competition	90	90
	Learning/Educational Activities	52	52
	Creative/Artistic Activities	60	60
	Others	2	2
4. Which device do you prefer to use to experience in virtual space?	Computer	23	23
	Cell phone	29	29
	VR head display	47	47
	Others	1	1

4.3   Inferential Statistical Analysis

The distribution among the three virtual space styles showed the least number of users interested in ethnic styles and the most in fantasy styles, potentially reflecting the majority Han ethnicity's lack of novelty in ethnic styles. However, the preference among different virtual spaces like restaurants and tea rooms showed no significant variation among the three styles. Notably, fantasy style stages had a clear advantage, possibly due to their attractive lighting and themes. Modern style was preferred for classrooms, likely aligning with a quiet study atmosphere, while for lodging spaces, young users favored modern and fantasy styles, indicating a preference for modern interpretations of traditional elements.

Regarding space style preferences, users showed varied preferences correlating with the function of the space, especially noticeable in entertainment-oriented stages and study-focused classrooms. For leisure spaces like restaurants, tea rooms, and lodges, preferences were more evenly distributed, indicating diverse tastes among the users (Table 4).

Table 4. User preferences for virtual space style types.

Space type	Ethnic style (Number of Selections)	Modern style (Number of Selections)	Fantasy style (Number of Selections)
Restaurants	31	33	36
Tea rooms	29	31	40
Stages	27	19	54
Classrooms	31	44	25
Inns	23	36	41
Total Selections	141	163	196

The analysis of cultural understanding based on space preference revealed that average scores for cultural comprehension did not exceed four points. Modern style spaces received the highest average understanding score, suggesting a correlation between user identity and cognition. High scores in cultural understanding for fantasy-style stages and modern-style classrooms suggest confidence in these choices, indicating interest and comprehension among users (Table 5).

Table 5. Users' cultural understanding of virtual space style.

Space type	Ethnic style (The average score)	Modern style (The average score)	Fantasy style (The average score)
Restaurants	3.76	4.03	3.64
Tea rooms	3.67	3.95	3.87
Stages	3.69	3.57	3.82
Classrooms	3.7	4.00	3.63
Inns	3.79	3.86	3.76
overall average score	3.722	3.882	3.744

In the final overall evaluation, the scores for all three styles were higher than the total average scores for cultural understanding, suggesting that despite not having a high level of cultural understanding, users showed significant interest and satisfaction with the virtual spaces (Table 6).

Table 6. Overall user satisfaction with virtual space style.

Space type	Ethnic style (The average score)	Modern style (The average score)	Fantasy style (The average score)
overall satisfaction	3.88	4.08	4

4.4 Discussion and Limitations

This study employed quantitative methods to explore young adults' preferences and cultural understanding within cross-cultural virtual spaces. Results indicate significant interest in social functions and cultural elements within virtual spaces, particularly in gaming competitions and modern-styled environments. However, the level of understanding of cultural elements varied among users, suggesting the need to consider the demands and cognitive differences of users from diverse cultural backgrounds when designing virtual spaces.

This research has limitations; for instance, the sample was confined to young people in China, which may not fully represent the preferences and behaviors of young adults globally. Additionally, while we attempted to collect data through survey methods, self-reported data might be influenced by social desirability bias and not accurately reflect individuals' experiences and preferences. Future studies should consider a broader sample and employ a variety of data collection methods to enhance the depth and breadth of research.

Despite these limitations, this study provides valuable insights into young adults' cross-cultural communication in virtual environments and offers empirical evidence for designing more inclusive and interactive cross-cultural virtual spaces. Future research should further investigate the effective application of cultural elements in virtual space design to promote deeper cultural understanding and communication.

5   Conclusion

This study aimed to explore and evaluate the effectiveness of cross-cultural interactive virtual spaces in promoting cultural understanding and communication among young adults. Utilizing Hall's high-context and low-context cultural frameworks, this research conducted surveys to gather preferences and understandings of individuals aged 18 to 25 regarding various cultural symbols and virtual communication spaces.

5.1   Key Findings

Preferences and Needs for Cultural Communication: Young adults show significant interest in utilizing virtual spaces for cultural communication, especially within gaming competitions and modern-styled environments. They expressed a high interest in the social functions of virtual spaces, yet there were differences in their levels of cultural understanding.

Understanding and Application of Cultural Symbols: While participants were interested in the cultural symbols presented within virtual spaces, their levels of understanding these symbols varied. This indicates the need for more cultural education and explanations in the design of cross-cultural virtual spaces.

Technology Acceptance and User Experience: Participants were open to using virtual reality technology for cultural communication but preferred more accessible and lightweight devices like smartphones and computers over VR headsets.

5.2   Conclusions and Recommendations

This research underscores the importance of deeply understanding the cultural preferences and communication needs of young adults when designing cross-cultural virtual spaces. Designers should accommodate the needs of users from various cultural backgrounds by providing diverse communication methods and rich cultural educational content to facilitate more effective cross-cultural understanding and interaction. Additionally, technological development should focus on user experience, adopting devices and platforms that are more widely accepted to attract a broader range of young users.

5.3 Limitations and Future Directions

The study's limitations primarily lie in its sample range and data collection methods. Future research should extend the sample size to include young people from a broader range of cultural backgrounds and employ diversified data collection methods, such as in-depth interviews and observational studies, for a more comprehensive understanding. Furthermore, future studies should explore how to effectively integrate different cultural elements to design virtual spaces that both reflect multiculturalism and promote effective communication.

In summary, this research offers valuable insights and recommendations for the design of cross-cultural interactive virtual spaces, aiming to enhance cultural understanding and communication among young adults, thereby contributing to building a more inclusive and connected global society.

Acknowledgments. This study was funded by several esteemed institutions and projects: the Guangzhou Academy of Fine Arts for the 2020 first-class course "Design Basics" (6040320127), the 2021 Ideological and Political Demonstration Course "Design Basics (Three-Dimensional Space)" (6040321061), Zhongkai University of Agriculture and Engineering for the top virtual simulation course "Design Composition", the Guangdong Provincial First-Class Offline Course "Design Composition", and The 2023 school-level new agricultural science teaching research and reform practice project is an in-depth practice of information technology and "Design Composition" education and teaching under the concept of "Tolerating Mistakes and Seeking Beauty, Integrating Skills to Have Beauty, and Honoring Schools to Promote Beauty". Their generous support greatly facilitated the research.

Disclosure of Interests. The authors have no competing interests to declare that are relevant to the content of this article.

References

1. Lu, Z.: Research on the Application of Catering Space Design Based on the High-context Cultural Perspective (2022). https://kns.cnki.net/kcms2/article/abstract?v=Y2wviAwYlnLk conlxvBinq0s56UcSFi9k04BoAf5l2yp0mVQPDqES8mADELBlRXSoBo-BTRShF6VN-oXGYE1ECjr3zWyxoPw9RUtiWxEZD0M7w9pDMIFvQ==&uniplatform=NZKPT&language=gb
2. Kang, X.: Research on Virtual Community Promotion of Yao Zhou Kiln Ceramic Mobile Terminal under SMCR Theory (2023). https://kns.cnki.net/kcms2/article/abstract?v=Y2wviAwYlnKzzlrqD64UdmssHNf7iFcSpKatQFNXK80nGAfwWr13in6uc7Zw5Wk90b bvP2ahze-8thgFrtgZHbaWNlT0FQ0ffE67QvDNyz0Agb2s-QV4Kw==&uniplatform=NZKPT&language=gb
3. Yang, J.: Interaction of the Virtual and the Real: The Construction of New Space Based on Embodied Cognition. New Architecture. 87–91 (2022)
4. Yang, C., Ren, W.: When lefebvre meets VR painting: the production of space and the problem of the body in virtual worlds. J. Hubei Univ. Educ. **40**, 88–97 (2023)
5. Wang, X.: Spatial Narration and Digital Representation of the Picture of Xiyuan Gathering in Song Dynasty——A Case Study of Li Gonglin's the Picture of Xiyuan Gathering (2022). https://kns.cnki.net/kcms2/article/abstract?v=Y2wviAwYlnIuWDs1La6s3GZx8Qi IPIvFmreOepXPexIsI1GDrh5kMFbvFuJfEgrRXPRW6cJ0RqS4nqr28s6ylTgq68kSDCWc oiSxXD_8JSqLvHrzjqdoCw==&uniplatform=NZKPT&language=gb

6. Zhu, B.: The Design of Dai Ceramics Art Digital Display Based on VR Technology (2019). https://kns.cnki.net/kcms2/article/abstract?v=Y2wviAwYlnJQ-SMz_PCQJhkcYxK24p8i 2yW99M5aiy7jtXXTMYU2yxV5oDmWwoTLlL86l2h-W2MK86CoausXW-6QiGbia0j QTgW41gHVS0sO7jQjo_hZkQ==&uniplatform=NZKPT&language=gb

7. Li, X.: Research on the application of virtual reality in the inheritance of painted peking opera masks (2022). https://kns.cnki.net/kcms2/article/abstract?v=Y2wviAwYlnLdgJK1iJO6rJJh QoOO0UjEd2kMwBbr_aGf402VbT_SFhXImuFhneY4PFsh6ahskjxGmvm01dlqKsLSGn eFSj7hikkXXHWzdjyQRT0DJW96gw==&uniplatform=NZKPT&language=gb

8. Shi, S.: Research and practice on virtual simulation experimental teaching of exhibition space design. Packa. Eng. **41**, 147–150 (2020). https://doi.org/10.19554/j.cnki.1001-3563. 2020.S1.037

9. Wang, H.: Yueyang Tower Virtual Space Design Based on Arduino and Experience Research (2015). https://kns.cnki.net/kcms2/article/abstract?v=Y2wviAwYlnKg_r7dQXJn7haTfXDF HAEopABstUBlrc3e_VZOsHWSEyN4lrmzkCugzfI4wwjgL3cU48-eRPsDCIXxPtMIJD hWqkntbNl_K1ECcVE0Ibp88Q==&uniplatform=NZKPT&language=gb

10. Tang, S.: Research on Virtual Interactive Experience Design of Ancient Looms for Future Museum (2023). https://kns.cnki.net/kcms2/article/abstract?v=Y2wviAwYlnKmjaS_Cim 8wL0T4KAGaMKPpBcTL--ADYXoNbw-24a_3mRlhUTLGWTjknJ5fQb82rY2XmCqG0 0I4LAUqyI8OXayRVFDciOmlM63Jv3gVuffIA==&uniplatform=NZKPT&language=gb

11. Shao, Y.: Research on Virtual Home Furnishing Exhibition Design Based on User Experience (2015). https://kns.cnki.net/kcms2/article/abstract?v=Y2wviAwYlnL0tVjvUlObsM8Csmd HZ4ebsBt0wLdR8_klyxXYT9yIkJ7oxKDkznNg12D0MGynLkzzd_IuTCTm0RZdgn8yh JvHznSWrVUx873_JO59DvuvbQ==&uniplatform=NZKPT&language=gb

12. Du, Y.: On Experience Design: A Case Study of the Exhibition Design of Chinese Minority Literature Museum (2010). https://kns.cnki.net/kcms2/article/abstract?v=Y2wviAwYlnIl uITgqS3QIdWojCOEdktZabaFRgZvbJw-Gn4i-BtZ2TaPAtCxxxf4qjTFsePYK0ebfpBjK8 heiACfY8ElGCOQtNTA64yPONMhWKQpqSqmMA==&uniplatform=NZKPT&langua ge=gb

13. Pang, Y., Cao, Y.: The spreading of the traditional chinese culture under the intercultural background——the analysis on the designing plan of the "Tang: Art from the Silk Road Capital" exhibition. In: Wenbo, pp. 90–96 (2017)

14. Xu, Y.: Contemporary Chinese space consumption in a cross-cultural context (2013). https:// kns.cnki.net/kcms2/article/abstract?v=Y2wviAwYlnKrOBvuzeC6m0cQdoI1qAUMw8Bl WwKMX6VNfJL4N7sf7P-4qXx5XzvjnZ8O_QXvpISJvFOvpjt-oT5h4Eqyhb5Ej30jKc V2PxKSOspxSsfm-A==&uniplatform=NZKPT&language=gb

15. Tian, Y.: The innovative design hyperspace based on high emotion in new concept bookstore. Design **33**, 153–155 (2020)

16. He, X.: The Effect of Cross-cultural Differences on the Thermal Comfort of University Campus Open Spaces (2022). https://kns.cnki.net/kcms2/article/abstract?v=Y2wviAwYl nIaQSrJcPs3cBTyl32UC-X9ubvp0hn2yRmOflRuHCyEzhQ3vq8_hGTGpqPbFhBO4iQRqi msK_KTy0kxvKptf_geINLaJG0rAadiyIKq-tRLrg==&uniplatform=NZKPT&language=gb

17. Xin, Z.: Research on the Application of Typical Chinese Elements in Luxury Brand Exclusive Shops (2023). https://kns.cnki.net/kcms2/article/abstract?v=Y2wviAwYlnL6E-0gXRnQXI1 hiPi4PU6Xbwr1q1rwZWMILkmfnyI22MYmNJJ4g_QM_Ob_ZAcY1lG1EN_nba4gho4Ra IUzCJd49i32ia3aaEoRHjKGIkLnBQ==&uniplatform=NZKPT&language=gb

18. Virtual Burn | Burning Man. https://virtualburn.burningman.org/booth/. Accessed 20 Feb 2024

19. Abbas, A., Choi, M., Seo, J., Cha, S.H., Li, H.: Effectiveness of immersive virtual reality-based communication for construction projects. KSCE J. Civ. Eng. **23**, 4972–4983 (2019). https://doi.org/10.1007/s12205-019-0898-0

20. Berti, M., Maranzana, S., Monzingo, J.: Fostering cultural understanding with virtual reality: a look at students' stereotypes and beliefs. Int. J. Comput.-Assist. Lang. Learn. Teach. **10**, 47–59 (2020). https://doi.org/10.4018/IJCALLT.2020010104
21. Disztinger, P., Schlögl, S., Groth, A.: Technology acceptance of virtual reality for travel planning. In: Schegg, R., Stangl, B. (eds.) Information and Communication Technologies in Tourism 2017, pp. 255–268. Springer, Cham (2017). https://doi.org/10.1007/978-3-319-51168-9_19
22. Capasa, L., Zulauf, K., Wagner, R.: Virtual reality experience of mega sports events: a technology acceptance study. JTAER **17**, 686–703 (2022). https://doi.org/10.3390/jtaer1702 0036
23. Altarteer, S., Charissis, V.: Technology acceptance model for 3D virtual reality system in luxury brands online stores. IEEE Access. **7**, 64053–64062 (2019). https://doi.org/10.1109/ACCESS.2019.2916353
24. Zhu, X.: Research on the protection strategy of Ningbo Zhujin lacquer wood carving intangible heritage. In: Ningbo Economy (Sanjiang Forum), pp. 36–38 (2019)
25. Lee, J., Kim, J., Choi, J.Y.: The adoption of virtual reality devices: the technology acceptance model integrating enjoyment, social interaction, and strength of the social ties. Telematics Inf. **39**, 37–48 (2019). https://doi.org/10.1016/j.tele.2018.12.006
26. Shadiev, R., Wang, X., Huang, Y.-M.: Cross-cultural learning in virtual reality environment: facilitating cross-cultural understanding, trait emotional intelligence, and sense of presence. Educ. Tech. Res. Dev. **69**, 2917–2936 (2021). https://doi.org/10.1007/s11423-021-10044-1
27. Ghanbarzadeh, R., Ghapanchi, A.H.: Antecedents and consequences of user acceptance of three-dimensional virtual worlds in higher education. JITE Res. **19**, 855–889 (2020). https://doi.org/10.28945/4660
28. Steam: The VR Museum of Fine Art. https://store.steampowered.com/app/515020/The_VR_Museum_of_Fine_Art/. Accessed 22 Feb 2024

Interactive Experience Design of Indoor Lamps Based on the Concept of Emotionalization

XinRen Miao, Feng He[✉], and XiaoFang Lin

Guangxi Normal University, Guilin 541006, China
2952540006@qq.com

Abstract. To combine the emotional concept with Maslow's hierarchy of needs theory to design an interactive experience design for indoor lighting with the meaning of self-actualization and value creation. Methods: Taking indoor lighting as an example, using the theory of three levels of emotion, combining people's needs for emotional interaction and creative experience design for the pleasure of using indoor lighting, and remote control of APP interaction, we design a design of indoor lighting that can be learned while using. Conclusion: The final design of the interior lamps is a good experience with a beautiful shape and rich functions. Through the design of the warm Sinusoidal sensation product, it can relieve people's fatigue and anxiety, and at the same time, it can also help people to improve themselves and realize their self-worth.

Keywords: Interior Lighting · Emotional Concept · Experience Design · Interaction Design

1 Introduction

Any upgrading or change in technology will lead to a series of disruptions in the way of life of the society. More importantly, it will redefine the way of communication and connection between human beings and the world. Human-computer interaction will become more convenient and faster. According to the research of the three-level concept of emotionalization, people's emotional needs and the concept of self-improvement have risen to the highest demand point, and people want to enjoy the functions of the products while bringing new learning and cognitive concepts to themselves. Emotional needs are an important branch of people's spiritual needs. People are no longer satisfied with just facing the cold functional parts of the machine, letting the machine as a carrier to convey people's thoughts. People are more willing to let the machine become emotional interaction, value creation can better support people's emotions, bring the use of pleasure at the same time, but also lead us to new progress, breakthroughs in their own, to achieve self-worth. The design and development of indoor lighting programs in the current market has brought people a more pleasurable experience. Officials can be placed in the bedroom, hall, restaurant decoration, used to adjust the light and illumination, can make the surrounding atmosphere to become more in line with the mood of the environment. But indoor lighting can create more value than that.

P.-L. P. Rau (Ed.): HCII 2024, LNCS 14699, pp. 104–115, 2024.
https://doi.org/10.1007/978-3-031-60898-8_7

2 Indoor Lamps and Lanterns Development Status and Inter-issues (Problems)

2.1 Analysis of Market Conditions

With the continuous development and breakthrough of LED lighting technology, the lighting efficiency of indoor lamps and lanterns has been significantly higher, and the development of indoor lamps and lanterns has shown the trend of diversification, intelligence, environmental protection, customization and so on [1].At the same time, intelligent lighting system has gradually become the development trend of indoor lighting, through the cell phone APP remote control of lights, according to the environment, the lighting system can be customized. The automatic adjustment of the brightness of the environment and other functions are gradually popularized. In addition to the basic lighting function of indoor lamps and lanterns, there are also many other functions. The LED light bulbs have many additional functions, such as saving atmosphere, energy saving and environmental protection. For example, LED bulbs with adjustable brightness and color temperature. Intelligent ceiling lamps can automatically adjust the brightness according to the environment. Indoor lighting can also be connected to the smart home system to realize the linkage control with other devices. For example, voice control, timer switch and other intelligent functions. With people's health concerns continue to improve, indoor lighting is also to the direction of healthier development. For example, lamps with eye protection, lamps and lanterns that can regulate the body's biological clock. Indoor lighting is divided into five types of lighting: overall lighting, local lighting, accent lighting, background lighting, decorative lighting. These include table lamps, floor lamps, spotlights, chandeliers, down lights, and ceiling lamps [2].

Desk Lamps. Children's function classification, desk lamps can be divided into reading desk lamps, decorative desk lamps, work desk lamps and other types. Reading lamps are mainly used for reading and writing, the light is softer, not blinding, package temperature is moderate, can reduce visual fatigue. Decorative table lamps focus on the appearance of design and style, according to different decorative styles and personal preferences to choose. Desk lamps emphasize the lighting function, the light is bright enough, irradiation area is large enough.

Floor Lamps. Floor lamps are usually divided into two types of up lighting and direct illumination, up lighting floor lamps are usually illuminated figural panels, the use of diffuse reflection principle to illuminate the entire room, so that the light is more soft and comfortable; direct illumination floor lamps are directly irradiated where the need for illumination, the light is more centralized, suitable for the need to focus on the lighting of the place.

Spotlights. Spotlight is a typical non-main light, no rules and regulations of the modern genre of lighting, can create an atmosphere of indoor lighting. Through the free change of the angle of the small spotlight, the combination of a variety of lighting effects.

Wall Lamps. Are installed on the interior walls of the auxiliary lighting decorative lamps and lanterns, light and elegant, can be embellished with elegant, rich and beautiful, especially the newlywed room is particularly suitable. Wall lamps of more types and styles, general common ceiling lamps, color-changing wall lamps, bedside wall lamps, wall lamps in front of the mirror and so on.

Chandeliers. Is a high-level decorative lighting hanging on the indoor ceiling? nowadays, the pendant lamp has been equipped with spring or height adjuster, which can be suitable for different heights of the floor and needs.

Down Light. Is a kind of recessed lighting fixture embedded in the ceiling, usually installed in the group room, living room, bathroom on the perimeter of the ceiling? This embedded in the ceiling inside the hidden lamps and lanterns, all the light is projected downward, the exhibition of direct light distribution, the lamps and lanterns of the metal body as well as the plastic lamp body has a good performance of flame retardant?

Ceiling Lamps. Are installed in the interior of the room, the appearance of the lamps and lanterns are close to the ceiling, the light is emitted from the interior, for the interior of the dike for lighting. Ceiling lamps can be divided into incandescent ceiling lamps, fluorescent ceiling lamps, tungsten halogen ceiling lamps, LED ceiling lamps, etc. according to the light source.

2.2 Problems with Indoor Lighting

Light is too bright or too dark: some indoor lamps really light too harsh, or too dim, does not meet the needs of human clothing on the comfort of light, prolonged use will cause eye fatigue and discomfort. The light should be adjustable in terms of warmth, coldness and strength. [3].

Color: some indoor lamps and lanterns of light color deviation is serious, so that the entire choking environment of the package tone is not coordinated, affecting the living and working environment.

Higher energy consumption: the energy consumption of the existing room lamps and lanterns is usually higher, long-term use will consume a lot of electricity, not conducive to energy saving and emission reduction. Should be combined with green design concepts and environmental awareness.

2.3 Trends in Interior Lighting Design Under Emotional Demands

With the advent of smart home, there is a growing demand for intelligent control of indoor lights. For example, through the cell phone APP or voice tapping system, to achieve a variety of colors, brightness and mode of adjustment, as well as with the music, the environment of the linkage, to enhance the user and the indoor environment of the interaction and experience. The design of indoor lighting also requires customization. Consumers can choose the style, color and brightness of the lighting to suit their preferences and needs, creating a unique indoor atmosphere [4]. This enhances the user's sense of participation and creativity, and allows for a deeper emotional interaction between people and products.

Indoor lighting design really need to pay attention to the emotional needs of people, through the light and dark, color and brightness of the predicate, to create a comfortable, romantic, warm and other different atmospheres and environments, to meet the different emotional needs of people. Also need to consider the physiological and psychological needs of people, in different environments, dais for different comfortable light, to avoid problems such as packet difference and glare, to improve the use of experience and relief [5]. These are the functional requirements for the protection of eyesight at the reflective level.

In the context of increasing environmental awareness, the design of indoor lighting also need to consider the green bad security factors [6]. The use of low-energy LED light source, renewable materials made of lamps and other real materials, reduce energy consumption, reduce the impact on the environment and the abuse of energy. Focusing on the concept of green design enhances people's reflection and choice in value creation. According to the existing problems and design trends in the design of indoor lighting, summarizes the design of indoor lighting products. The steps involved in the actual study (see Fig. 1).

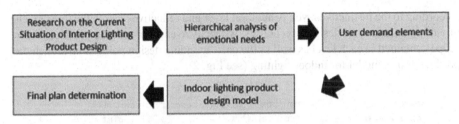

Fig. 1. The actual study of interior lighting design and related steps

3   Related Theories

3.1   Emotional Design Concepts

Emotional design is a design concept that focuses on users' inner emotion, so that users can enjoy the social value of the products from the physiological, psychological and spiritual levels, guiding them to the pursuit of happiness, and improving the quality of people's life through design. Emotional design creatively integrates the interaction mode, form, color, structure, decoration, material, function, and the elaboration of facts and other elements of the product, integrates the expected emotional feeling into the constituent elements of the product, highlights the product's aesthetic characteristics and interactive session, and starts from "useful" to "good to use" [7]. The aesthetic characteristics and interactivity of the product are emphasized, and the user satisfaction is enhanced from three levels of "useful", "good" and "want to use", so that the user can have an emotional experience in the process of using the technical functions of the product. Donald Norman, a psychologist in China, divided the human emotional system into three levels, the instinctive level, the behavioral level, and the reflective level in his "Emotional Design".

Instinctive layer design focuses on the physical attributes of the product, such as shape, material, structure, color, etc., on the five senses of vision, hearing, smell, taste, and erosion to bring the sense of the Palace; behavioral layer design focuses on the product's interactive mode of operation and use of the product's functions, and how to make the user in the process of interacting with the product to generate positive, positive emotions, to obtain the sense of convenience and pleasure: Reflective layer design focuses on the deeper meaning and value of the product, and will continue to cause the user to reflect on the product to generate emotional resonance and a sense of belonging, but also to stimulate the creativity and experience of the user. Reflective layer design focuses on the deeper meaning and value of the product, which will continuously lead to the reflection of the user, the emotional resonance and sense of belonging of the user to the product, and at the same time stimulate the user's creativity and sense of experience.

4   Emotional Expression of Interior Lighting Design

According to the instinctive layer, behavioral layer and reflective layer in the three levels of emotional theory of design psychology, we analyze and pray for the product design scope contained in each level as well as the corresponding design points, and launch the product design model for indoor lighting (see Fig. 2).

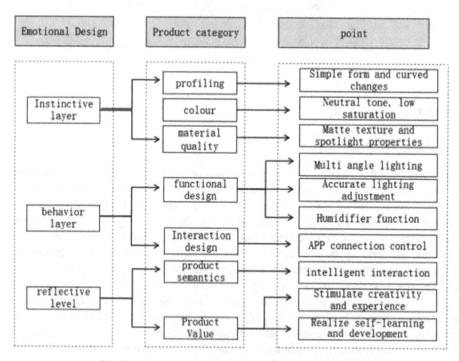

Fig. 2. Indoor lamps and lanterns product design model

4.1   Emotional Design at the Instinctive Level

Modeling. Indoor lamps and lanterns of different forms, diverse shapes, mainly in the form of the following lighting presentation: table lamps, Chandeliers, simple lamps, wall lamps, floor lamps, spotlights, ceiling lamps. Among them, wall lamps can be installed in the indoor Jing wall on the auxiliary lighting decorative lamps, its light elegant and harmonious, the environment can be decorated with elegant, rich, calm, 5/13 to the basic modeling of the interior lamps and lanterns are basically divided into two kinds of abstract and figurative. Figurative interior lamps usually have _ bright form and image, their design inspiration usually comes from real life in the concrete Hugh things, such as animals, Plants, characters and so on. This design style is enough to make people feel friendly and familiar, giving people a warm, comfortable feeling. And it is more suitable for children's furniture and women's groups. Abstract indoor lighting real appearance is inclined to minimalist Fengge and Levitical style, emphasizing simplicity, functionality and elegance, the design of indoor lighting can be a simple lines or shapes, without excessive decorations and details. The color can be white, black or grey, giving people a sense of purity and elegance. At the same time, it emphasizes innovation, technology and futuristic sense, and can adopt the appearance of streamlined, geometric shapes or irregular shapes to give people a sense of coming and avant-garde.

The combination of figurative and abstract modeling is more innovative, layered, emotional and flexible. Innovative: This kind of design breaks the traditional design thinking and creates a unique and novel shape, which can attract people's eyes and add the highlight of the interior.

Layers. The design is rich in layers. Figurative elements provide the foundation and landscape for the design, while abstract elements add dynamism and vitality to the design.

Emotional Expression. Figurative elements can trigger people's emotional resonance, while abstract elements can stimulate people's imagination and creativity. These elements can convey a specific sense of meaning and mood.

Flexibility. Makes the design more flexible and versatile. Creates a variety of interior lighting shapes. For example, the 0SGONA indoor bedside wall lamp uses a combination of abstract and figurative design, so that the illumination is full of dynamism and vitality, and the light and shadow shapes are vivid and rich in layers.

Color. From the point of view of the instinctive level, neutral color will bring people a sense of calm, comfort and relaxation, and it will not stimulate people's vision or psychology too much. For example, in interior design, neutral color walls and furniture products will bring people a warm and comfortable feeling. Modern interior design focuses more and more on individuality and innovation, so the color package of lighting is also more diverse. In addition to the traditional white and gold, neutral colors such as grey, black, etc. are becoming popular. At the same time, in the minimalist look and feel of the design, choking the interior lighting color selection of black, gray and other neutrals, can create a simple and elegant atmosphere. Because Therefore, in designing the color application of the indoor lighting, black color design was chosen as the main color to enhance the product's appearance. It emphasizes the quality, elegance and low profile of the lamps, while attracting the value of the lamps and the sense of the clinch.

The Material. Of the visual party performance is also an important factor to consider the impact of emotion. After researching and analyzing, the most Metal is the material used for indoor lighting. There are two types of metal: smooth and frosted. Smooth metal surfaces reflect light and give people a sense of sophistication and elegance, while frosted metal surfaces are more understated and subdued. Secondly, the durability of the material will also give people an emotional response. A strong and durable metal will give people a sense of reliability and longevity. In the process of product consideration and design, we need to choose the appropriate material according to the product positioning and user groups, in order to enhance the attractiveness and emotional value of the product. Indoor wall lamps also have a functional role. Compared with other materials such as wood and textile, the use of frosted metal surface not only enhances the texture and feel of the lamp, but also has a certain degree of corrosion and abrasion resistance. In addition, frosted metal can also provide a soft lighting effect, making discreet indoor lighting more cozy and comfortable. Therefore, frosted metal as the contact surface of the product is more suitable for indoor lighting, which can add a sense of sophistication and futuristic feeling to the indoor space.

4.2 Emotional Design at the Behavioral Level

Indoor ambient lighting at the behavioral level of the functional aspects of the main considerations are based on different the festival lights are used to adjust the color, brightness and luminous part of the festival lights to create the atmosphere, regulate the mood and enhance the life experience of the scene and demand.

For example, intelligent control, you can use the smart phone APP remote control lights, convenient to use the user at anytime and anywhere I control the lights, to achieve self-tuning section lights, intelligent sensing and other functions. Such as solaraxy intelligent ambient light, Bluetooth networking, APP control of light brightness and color temperature, not only the sound function, there are colorful mode and timer function. Second is the timer function, you can set a timer to turn on and off the light, to help users develop good habits, such as automatically turn on the light in the morning to help users wake up, and automatically turn off the light in the evening to help users fall asleep. In terms of voice control, you can control the light by voice, for example, "Xiao Ai Classmate, turn on the reading light" or "Xiao du Xiao du, lower the brightness of the light in the cellar room", which provides users with a more convenient operation experience. There is also an automatic sensor system for lamps and lanterns, which can be set up to automatically turn on and off the lamps or adjust the brightness of the lamps and lanterns according to the user's activities, such as automatically turning off the lamps and lanterns when people leave the room and automatically turning on the lamps and lanterns when people enter the room. The most important thing is energy saving and environmental protection, the use of low energy consumption LED lamp beads, can save energy, reduce environmental pollution.

In summary, the functional design of interior ambient lighting at the behavioral level needs to take into account factors such as intelligent tapping, timer function, voice control, automatic sensing, and energy-saving protection, in order to communicate with the needs of the users in different scenarios, and to provide a more convenient, comfortable, and energy-saving living experience.

The Interaction Design. Of indoor lighting at the behavioral level mainly refers to the interaction and communication between the user and the ambient light. The aim is to enhance the user's experience and feelings through the performance of the light, as well as to provide a more intelligent I, comfortable and personalized eye service. Because interaction is a two-way street, indoor lighting can increase the interaction and exploration between people and products while providing a sense of experience, and achieve emotional communication between people and Light in the actual.

In the process of interaction design, various operation functions and modes are designed for indoor luminaires, so that people can learn and use them through exploration, learning through interaction, and interacting through learning.

4.3 Emotional Design at the Reflective Level

Product semantics: The semantics of indication is utilized in the interaction of intelligent Lee, so that the design of the lamps and lanterns can convey the indication information clearly, so that the users can operate and use the lamps and lanterns correctly. For example, the smart switch series can express its switching status through the appearance design, such as through the change of the LED indicator light or the change of the packet.

Product value: The value of the product itself is not only the appearance, convenient function and emotional interaction, but also the value creation is an important demand point for a product to be able to establish a lasting connection with the users. Self-actualization is the highest level of human needs, which refers to the individual's pursuit of the full play of their potential, the urge to realize and enhance their self-worth, and in the process experience inner satisfaction and a sense of well-being. Self-actualization is the pursuit of higher spiritual needs on the basis of satisfying physiological needs, safety needs, social needs and respect needs, including. It includes the exploration of reason, the pursuit of envy, and the perfection of morality. Similarly, self-actualization is also a process of continuous pursuit of progress and improvement. People will discover their own defects in the process of continuous learning and growth, and will improve themselves through learning and upgrading. In the Reflective Dimensions indoor lighting project, the shape of the moon is projected into the room using virtual reality, and when users control the project through an app, information about the moon's crust and meteorological changes pops up, so that people can click on it when they want to learn, which promotes learning and enhances the value of the product itself.

5   Indignant Interior Luminaire Design Practices

5.1 Design Orientation

According to the user scenarios and demand points, the design of indoor lamps and lanterns is positioned for the youth group and working people, the basic function of the product is lighting, in addition to lighting additional functions are: warm and cold light switching mode, through gestures and touch mode control of brightness, package temperature adjustment, timing and automation functions, humidifier mode, as well as through the APP connection operation of the science and technology mode. Increase the adhesion between the user and the product.

5.2 Product Design Innovation Points

The product design of indoor interactive lamps and lanterns under the concept of emotionality is carried out from the theory of three levels of emotion, namely, the appearance design at the instinctive level, the interaction and functional design at the behavioral level, and the semantic connotation of the product and the design to satisfy people's self-actualization at the level of friendship, which can help people to explore the connotation and role of the product from different levels, and let people realize their self-worth in the process of adopting and reflecting on the use of the product.

Mainly manifested in the appearance of indoor lighting products modeling, color and material selection of three aspects. In the appearance modeling design, we take the simple abstract art form as the design element, and the abstract graphic contour adopts the soft curve and round form, which makes people feel soft and comfortable, adds the dynamics to the overall shape, and makes people feel friendly, comfortable and warm. In the color design, part of the hot gold as the background color, so that the scenery under the curtain has a warm atmosphere, and silver as a cold color decorative moonlight scenery appears more vivid, outlining a gentle sunset scene, so that the interior of a unique style. The material selection is made of frosted metal, and the frosted surface makes the product appear more low-key and calm. Secondly, the durability of gold will also bring people a reliable and long-lasting feeling. As an indoor product lighting, it should also have a low-key, calm mood and infectious force to bring pleasure and relaxation to the users. Indoor lighting design (see Fig. 3).

Is mainly reflected in the functional diversity design and emotional interaction design of lamps and lanterns. In the functional design, users can connect the APP to adjust the color temperature, brightness and light position by themselves through gestures and touch control functions, and can pre-set the working mode of the lamp through timing and automation modes. The design page of the APP is divided into two alternating modes, day and night. When you are not at home, you can enter commands through the APP connection to operate the timing and automation modes in advance. At night, gestures and touch control, lighting timing, and moon projection can be carried out through the mobile phone connection. The mobile phone will carry out science popularization according to the shape changes of the moon on the day. After the connection, it can automatically synchronize the shadow and breath form of the moon, and adjust the color temperature and brightness of the light according to needs when reading in the bedroom at night, giving the user the greatest humanized and comfortable experience. The interface design of indoor lighting APP (Hello, small view) (see Fig. 4).

When the weather is dry, you can enable the humidifier mode, which is like a mountain stream cloud and mist when it is opened, showing the beauty of nature, as if it brought nature to the room, borrowing the scenery to generate emotion, which is the emotional interaction between people and indoor lamps. As an additional function of

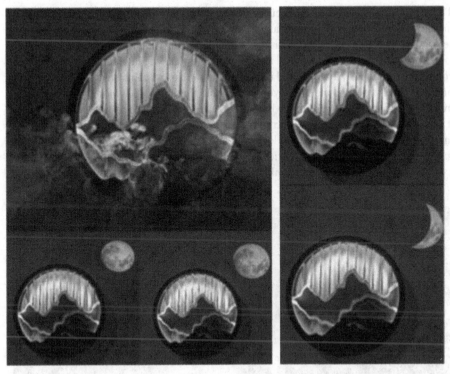

Fig. 3. Interior Lighting Design under the Concept of Emotionalization

Fig. 4. Interior Lighting APP interface design (Hello,Xiao Jing)

the product, it adds a variety of sensory experience for the user and enriches the level of product experience.

The Emotional Design of Reflection Level. Is mainly manifested in the process of interaction between people and lamps, and also the improvement and realization of self-value. Through the popularization of the change of the moon projection of indoor lamps and the precise touch control and adjustment mode, the interaction process is more conducive to people's learning and improvement, and users can also learn in the process of use. When the weather is dry, you can enable the humidifier mode, which is like a mountain stream cloud and mist when it is opened, showing the beauty of nature, as if it brought nature to the room, borrowing scenery and feeling, which is the emotional interaction between people and indoor lamps. As an additional function of the product, it adds a variety of sensory experience for the user and enriches the level of product experience. Among them, the thinking generated by the interaction between the user

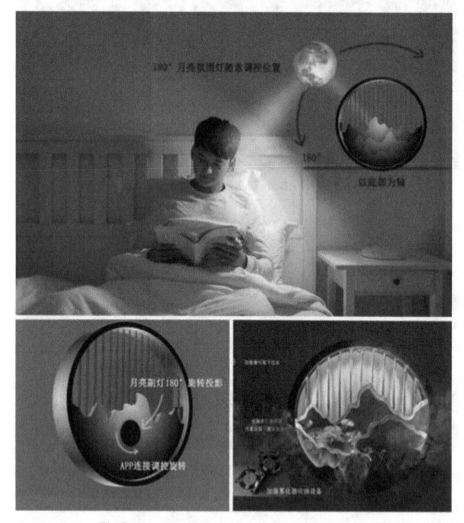

Fig. 5. Simulation and operation mode of indoor lighting

and the product, as well as the beautiful emotional experience brought to the user in the process of using the product, is also the original intention of using the emotional design concept. The simulation and operation mode of indoor lamps and lanterns (see Fig. 5.).

6 Conclusion

Through the interaction and research of indoor lamps and lanterns, combined with the concept of emotional design, the design reflection and research are carried out on the user's aesthetic, use, demand point and emotional experience from the instinct level, behavior level and reflection level, and the design method of indoor lamps and lanterns to meet the highest level of human needs is summarized. On the basis of the basic lighting function of indoor atmosphere lamps, the emotional experience and interaction between people and lamps are increased.

Comprehensive design is carried out from the appearance, the cold and warm color temperature oflights, the touch adjustment mobility of light position, the function of humidifier, APP connection control and science popularization, and finally the indoor lamps are designed with beautiful appearance, rich functions and good experience value. This lamp can relieve people's fatigue and anxiety at the same time, but also help users to self-improvement and growth, improve the quality of life of users. The research combines the concept of emotional design and emotional interaction design to explore and study the design of indoor lighting products, in order to provide research reference for the design of relevant indoor lighting products that can be adapted.

References

1. Zhang, Y.L., Zhang, H.W.: Research on emotional design of intangible cultural heritage apps at the reflective level: a case study of Nantong Tie-dye. West. Leather (03), 81–83 (2024). https://doi.org/10.20143/j.1671-1602.2024.03.081
2. Zhou, W.X.: Research on human-machine emotional experience design based on action intention understanding. Design (02), 124–127 (2024). https://doi.org/10.20055/j.cnki.1003-0069.001477
3. Gong, Q.M.: Research on the design of intelligent indoor lighting based on user demand -- taking "bright light" lighting design as an example. Hunan Packing (01), 154–156 (2021). https://doi.org/10.19686/j.carolcarrollnkiissn1671-4997.2021.01.046. (2021)
4. Gao, L.Y., Zhang, Z.W.: The App interface to guide the emotional concept. Art Appreciat. (05), 92–93 (2021)
5. Zhang, Z.W.: Master's Thesis on Artistic Expression and Application of Emotionalized (2020). https://doi.org/10.27357/d.cnki.gtgyu.2020.000837
6. Zhang, S.J.: Master's thesis on Home Lighting Design Research based on Emotion (2020). https://doi.org/10.26932/d.cnki.gbjfc.2020.000305

Developing a Co-eating Agent for Food Education

Jui-Ying Wang[1] and Tomoo Inoue[2]([✉]) [iD]

[1] Graduate School of Comprehensive Human Sciences, University of Tsukuba, Tsukuba, Japan
[2] Institute of Library, Information and Media Science, University of Tsukuba, Tsukuba, Japan
inoue@slis.tsukuba.ac.jp

Abstract. Food education, called Shokuiku in Japanese that teaches about the agricultural environment, food cherishing, nutrition, and healthy eating through lectures and practice, is getting attention. Based on the demand for diversified food education for different age groups, digital food education has been promoted. Besides, lack of encouragement to eat healthily poses risks of unhealthy eating. Some agents developed for caring needs that monitor the users' diet but could not eat together and did not provide structured food education content. Inspired by these problems, we intended to achieve effective food education by developing a virtual co-eating agent with the capability of eating virtual food and teaching structured food education. We developed a co-eating agent for food education and conducted user studies with 6 Japanese students and 6 international students. Participants attended a one-on-one lab-based food education workshop with an agent, including a 5-min co-eating and a 15-min food education lecture. The results showed that the participants felt the sense of eating together with the agent, had a positive impression of the agent, had positive learning satisfaction and their sugar literacy scores were improved. Based on the results, the effectiveness of the co-eating agent for food education and the relationship between the impression and learning outcome were discussed. It is suggested to provide co-eating activities with structured educational content and explore how to maintain the perceived meal similarity of co-eating agents for food education.

Keywords: co-eating agent · food education · dietary similarity

1 Introduction

Improving the understanding of food and nutrition knowledge can help people make positive and informed food choices. Food education takes place in school, family, and community, which teaches about the agricultural environment, food cherishing, nutrition, and healthy eating through lecture and practice. In Japanese Shokuiku (food education) 4th Promotion Basic Policies, the goals were set as increasing awareness of the food environment, maintaining a balanced diet, eating three meals a day, and increasing the number of co-eating for building a more energetic life [1]. Moreover, based on the demand for diversified food education for people of different ages, digital food education has got attention and implemented in multiple countries [2–4]. How to connect virtual learning content with real-life experience has become an issue.

P.-L. P. Rau (Ed.): HCII 2024, LNCS 14699, pp. 116–128, 2024.
https://doi.org/10.1007/978-3-031-60898-8_8

Besides, co-eating is an important social activity that connects people. People chat, share information, enrich their eating experience, and encourage healthy eating while eating together [5, 6]. It has been found that adolescents having more meals with their family were more likely to have parents' encouragement on healthy eating [6]. However, some people are separated from their eating partners because of distance or irregular eating time. Lack of encouragement to eat healthfully poses risks of unhealthy eating. Previous research has shown that people working irregularly time could not eat with their family members but with co-workers, and it was hard to get encouragement for a healthy diet from them [7].

On the other hand, some co-eating agents have been used around the dining table for caring needs that monitor the users' diet and encourage a healthy diet [8, 9]. However, these agents did not eat and did not provide structured food education content. Though it has been found that showing agents' eating actions influenced the enjoyment and the eating amount [10], whether it could connect the learner, agent, and food in the food education context needs to be explored. Although the supervisory function of co-eating agents was discussed, their effectiveness on food literacy remained unknow. Inspired by these problems, we intended to achieve effective food education by developing a virtual co-eating agent with the capability of eating virtual food and teaching structured food education. The research questions RQ1 and RQ2 are as follows:

RQ1. Does the food education provided by the co-eating agent improve participant's food literacy?
RQ2. Is the impression of the co-eating experience and co-eating agent related to participants' learning in food education?

To answer these questions, we conducted user studies with 12 students to explore the effectiveness of co-eating agent for food education. They attended a one-on-one lab-based food education workshop with an agent, which included a 5-min co-eating and a 15-min food education lecture. Based on the user studies, we investigated their co-eating experience in the workshop, the impression of the co-eating agent for food education, and the learning outcome. We discussed how the impression of the virtual food and co-eating agent influences their learning.

2 Method

2.1 Participants

To explore the effectiveness of co-eating agent for food education, we conducted an experiment with a co-eating agent for food education. Before conducting the experiment, we obtained ethical approval from the Research Ethics Review Committee of the Department of Library, Information, and Media Studies of the University of Tsukuba (No. 22–134).

The participants were recruited through social networking services and a local recruitment website. A total of 12 students (6 male, 6 female) joined voluntarily, 6 of them were Japanese students and the other 6 of them were international students. 3 of them were from China, 2 of them were from Taiwan and 1 was from Indonesia. The average age was 23.6 ($SD = 3.80$), ranging from 20 to 32. Every participant received a 960-yen Amazon gift card for participation in the one-hour experiment.

2.2 Co-eating Agent

The co-eating agent was developed and improved based on the agent from previous research focused on eating [11]. The character model was cartoon style and from © Unity Technologies Japan/UCL. In this study, the agent ate with participants and gave the lecture about food with the slides (see Fig. 1). The eating actions were set as a conditional repeating sequence of the "Home position", "Preparation", "Hold", "Stroke", and "Recovery". The virtual food was presented in a plate on the table. It showed the eating process and eating trimming clearly. The dialogues were pre-scripted with some multiple-dimensional branching in CSV file, and the sound was created through Google Text-to-Speech speech synthesis. The participants interacted with the agent mainly by clicking the sliders and buttons.

To better connect the user and the food, it is suggested to make user felt the food and told it to the agent [12]. The agents asked some question about food in the aspect of smells, interest, taste, sugar content and likable. After participant answered it, the agent gave feedback based on the answer and also shared it's feeling. For example, the agent asked "How does the chocolate smell? Do you feel any flavor when you chew it?" If the answer was positive, agent said "It is fun to experience smells. Isn't it?", if not, the agent said "It is sometimes hard to tell the smells. Isn't it?" Then, the agent shared its feelings by saying "I slightly feel some flavors like flower." (see Fig. 2).

For that self-disclosure of the agent was effective in encouraging healthy behaviors [13], the agent talked about some healthy tips it took in the daily life conversation, such as "I am trying to go to sleep early and get up early recently. Then, I can make breakfast myself." The healthy tips were not directly related to the food educational contents but revealed the role of the agent.

Fig. 1. The agent ate with participant (left) and gave food education lecture (right).

2.3 Food Education Workshop

The topic of food education workshop was set as "free sugars intake". Some people eating alone were faced with the risk of unhealth diet included sweet snacks and sweet beverage [7, 14]. According to WHO's guidance, free sugars is monosaccharides and disaccharides added to foods and drinks, and sugars in honey and fruit juice. For both children and adults, it is strongly recommends reducing the intake of free sugars to less than 10% of total energy intake to avoid the risk of chronic disease [15]. On the other

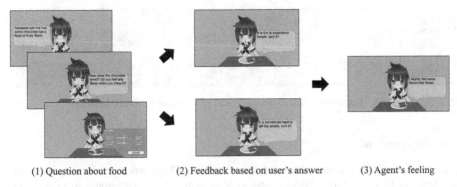

| (1) Question about food | (2) Feedback based on user's answer | (3) Agent's feeling |

Fig. 2. An example of the flows of dialogue about food between participant and the agent.

hand, sugar (monosaccharides and disaccharides) is not specifically listed in Japanese Nutrition Facts Label. People need to extrapolate the sugar content from amount of carbohydrates, and it may cause some difficulties to grasp and control the sugar intake.

In the food education workshop, there was an online pre-test, a co-eating session, a food education session, and a post-test. There were three goals of the workshop in knowledge, skills, and attitudes respectively, which were (1) understanding methods and resources to promote sugar control, (2) being able to use effective information to develop sugar control strategies, and (3) respecting norms, attitudes, and values about sugar control.

Co-eating Session. In the co-eating session, both the agent and the participant ate dark chocolate. Compared to other sweet snacks, dark chocolate was relatively low in sugar, low in glycemic index, and contained cocoa daphne and minerals. There were 4 pieces of dark chocolate for the agent and the participant. The agent ate half the chocolate at a time and the cycle of eating was about 45 to 50 s. For participants, the eating amount and eating timing were decided by themselves. During co-eating, the agent and participants had conversations about daily life and food. The co-eating was at least 5 min and if the conversation was not completed within 5 min, the co-eating continued.

Food Education Session. The lecture on food education given by the agent was made by the experimenter based on a supplementary teaching material called "Healthy eating out skills for school children" published at Taiwan Health Promoting School [16] and adjusted to match the situation in Japan. It contained three parts and one in-class question at the end of each part (see Fig. 3). The first part was "Definition and guidance of free sugar", which was about knowledge of WHO's guidance and skill of calculating daily sugar intake limit [15]. The second part was "Nutrition facts label and Standard Tables of Food Composition in Japan", which was about the skill of accessing nutrition information and calculating sugar content from labels on food products or standard tables made by MEXT [17]. The third part was the "Traffic light diets system", which was about the skill of long-term sugar control. The lecture was about 15 min, and it varied depending on the speed of answering the questions.

Fig. 3. The in-class questions at the end of each part of food education.

2.4 Environment

The experiment was conducted in a lab at a university. There was a seat for the co-eating session and food education session and another seat for the participant to take a rest between sessions. In both sessions, the participant sit in front of a table with a large screen (32 inches), a keyboard, and a mouse for interacting with the agents. A cup of water, disinfectant alcohol, and Kleenex were also placed on the table, which participants could use as they liked. In addition, there was a plate with four pieces of chocolate in the co-eating session (see Fig. 4). Two cameras recorded the experiment.

Fig. 4. The environment in the co-eating session (left) and the food education session (right).

2.5 Data Collection and Analysis

The data of the co-eating experience in the workshop, the impression of the co-eating agent for food education, and the learning outcome were collected. The question used for co-eating experience and impression of the co-eating was adapted from previous co-eating agent research [11].

Co-eating Experience. Eating amount and the subjective feeling of co-eating were investigated. The eating amount was counted by the experimenter after the experiment and the smallest unit was 0.5 pieces. A 7-point Likert scale questionnaire (1: strongly disagree, 7: strongly agree) was used to investigate the subjective feelings, including "perceived meal similarity" (CE1-CE3), "tastiness" (CE4-CE6) and "feeling of having meal together" (CE7-CE9).

Impression of the Co-eating Agent for Food Education. A 7-point Likert scale questionnaire (1: strongly disagree, 7: strongly agree) was used for investigating impression of the co-eating agent, including "closeness" (Cl1-Cl4), "trust" (Tr1-Tr5), "social presence in the aspect of reality" (SP1-SP5), and "social presence in the aspect of companionship" (SP6-SP12). In "social presence in the aspect of reality", items were about whether participants felt the agent as real beings [18]. In "social presence in the aspect of companion", items were about whether participants and agents maintain attention to each other [19].

Learning Satisfaction. Learning satisfaction was investigated in the aspects of knowledge, skill, attitude, and confidence via a 7-point Likert scale questionnaire (1: strongly disagree, 7: strongly agree) was used for investigating the learning satisfaction, including "knowledge" (LS1), "skill" (LS2), "attitude" (LS3), "confidence" (LS4) and the satisfaction in the workshop (LS5-LS7). LS5-LS7 were adapted from the questionnaire in online course research that asking the satisfaction on the instructor and course [20], and other 4 item were self-made.

Learning Outcome. The learning outcome was investigated in the aspects of knowledge (0–9 points), skill (0–9 points), and attitude (1–7 points). The questions were check box questions, fill-in questions, short answer questions, and 7-point Likert scale questions. There were 9 items for knowledge, which measured the understanding of which food contains free sugar, and the daily sugar daily sugar intake limit according to WHO guidance were measured. There were 9 times for skill, which measured the ability to use the energy intake table, nutrition label, available carbohydrates table, and traffic light diet system to develop sugar control strategies. There were 10 items of 7-point Likert scale questions for attitude, which measured the attitude toward sugar control and paying attention to sugar content. The score of attitudes was the average level of the 10 items. Because the scores in the pre-test and post-test were paired and normally distributed, a paired samples t-test was conducted to explore the learning outcome.

Free Description Question and Interview. There was a free description question in the questionnaire and an interview participant to describe the felt and thought in the experiment. The interview was semi-structured with some behavior events questions, asking the general feeling and when the participant felt eat together, closeness, trust and the social presence. Their thoughts on sugar and nutrition labelling were also asked.

2.6 Experimental Procedures

The experiment consisted of the co-eating session and the food education session. It lasted about 60 min in total. The following procedure was followed:

1. Explain the experiment to the participant in writing, then obtain the signatures on a consent form through email.
2. Let participant fills in the online pre-test.
3. Invite participant to the lab and conduct digital food education workshop.
   a. Let participant and an agent greet each other, and then eat with the agent for about 5 min.
   b. Let participant take a rest and set the table.
   c. Let participant take an interactive lecture from the agent for about 15 min.
4. Let participant fill in the post-test, questionnaire and conduct the interview.

3 Results

3.1 Co-eating Experience

On average, the co-eating agent ate 3.5 ($SD = 0.26$) pieces of chocolate, and the participant ate 2.8 ($SD = 1.06$) pieces of chocolate. According to the 7-point Likert scale questionnaire, the participants had a positive attitude toward the "perceived meal similarity" ($M = 6.3$, $SD = 0.79$), "tastiness" ($M = 5.6$, $SD = 0.96$) and "feeling of having meal together" ($M = 5.9$, $SD = 0.99$). Participants agreed that they felt the agent's virtual dark chocolate similar to their dark chocolate, felt the dark chocolate was tasty and felt eating together with the agent (Fig. 5).

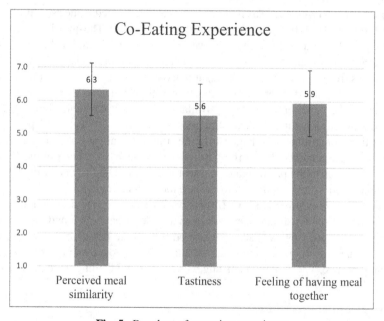

Fig. 5. Bar chart of co-eating experience

3.2 Impression of the Co-Eating Agent

According to the 7-point Likert scale questionnaire, the participants had a positive attitude toward "closeness" ($M = 5.2$, $SD = 1.01$), "trust" ($M = 5.9$, $SD = 0.57$), "social presence in the aspect of reality" ($M = 4.6$, $SD = 1.14$) and "social presence in the aspect of companion" ($M = 4.6$, $SD = 1.05$) (see Fig. 6). Participants agreed that they trust the agent and slightly agreed that they felt close, reality and companion to the agent.

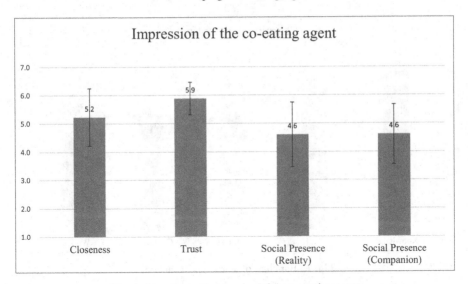

Fig. 6. Bar chart of impression of the co-eating agent

3.3 Learning Satisfaction and Learning Outcome

According to the 7-point Likert scale questionnaire, the participants had a positive attitude toward learning satisfaction in "knowledge" ($M = 6.7$, $SD = 0.49$), "skill" ($M = 6.1$, $SD = 0.90$), "attitude" ($M = 6.3$, $SD = 0.78$) and "confidence" ($M = 5.5$, $SD = 1.00$) and also had a positive attitude toward the satisfaction of the food education workshop ($M = 5.6$, $SD = 1.16$) (see Fig. 7). They strongly agreed that "the workshop helps them understand the knowledge of sugar intake", agreed that "the workshop is helpful for their future regulation of sugar intake", "makes them pay attention to sugar intake", "increases their confidence in the regulation of sugar intake" and thought the workshop and the agent were worth recommending.

In the pre-test, participants' average scores were 5.0 ($SD = 2.66$), 2.6 ($SD = 1.49$) and 4.7 ($SD = 0.79$) in knowledge, skill and attitude respectively. In the post-test, participants' average scores were 7.6 ($SD = 0.90$), 5.8 ($SD = 2.46$) and 5.6 ($SD = 0.58$) in knowledge, skill and attitude respectively. To compare the scores in the pre-test and post-test, a paired samples t-test was conducted. It was significantly different in knowledge ($t(11) = 3.15$, $p < 0.01$), skill ($t(11) = 4.46$, $p < 0.01$), and attitude ($t(11) = 3.95$, $p < 0.01$) (see Fig. 8). It suggested that their scores were significantly improved.

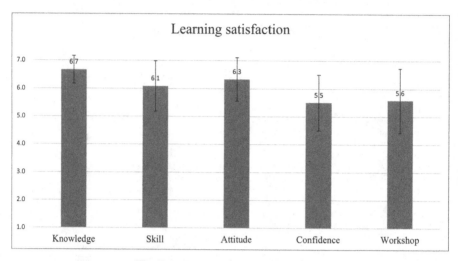

Fig. 7. Bar chart of learning satisfaction

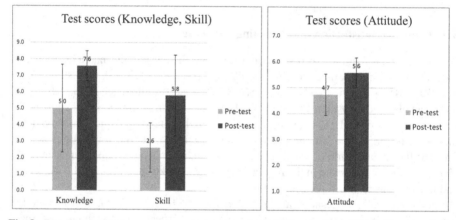

Fig. 8. Bar charts of test scores in pre-test and post-test in knowledge, skills (left) and attitude (right).

3.4 Relationship Between the Impression and Learning Outcome.

In order to explore whether the impression of the virtual food and co-eating agent related to their learning in food education, we calculated the learning outcome as the total score of the post-test minus the total score of the pre-test and conducted Pearson correlation coefficient tests. Pearson correlation coefficient showed that perceived meal similarity significantly highly correlated with the learning outcome (correlation coefficient = 0.84, $p < 0.01$). Though the social presence in the aspect of companion moderately correlated with the learning outcome, it was not significant (correlation coefficient = 0.42, $p = 0.18$). No other significant relationships were found between the impression and learning outcome (Figs. 9 and 10).

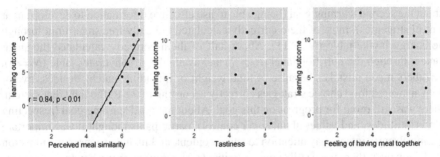

Fig. 9. Scatter plots of co-eating experience and learning outcome.

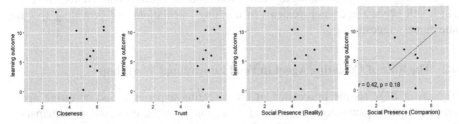

Fig. 10. Scatter plots of impression of the co-eating agent and learning outcome.

4 Discussion

To achieve effective co-eating agent for food education, this study aimed to explore how learners thought about food educational co-eating agent and whether their food literacy have been improved. In addition, intended to explore the role of co-eating agent with virtual food in food education, we have investigated the relationship between the participants' impression of food educational co-eating agent with virtual food and learning outcome.

4.1 Learning Satisfaction and Learning Outcome in Food Education Provide by Co-eating Agent

To answer RQ1 (Does the food education provided by the co-eating agent improve participant's food literacy?), we have developed a food education workshop given by the co-eating agent and evaluated participants' learning satisfaction and learning outcome. The questionnaire showed that participants were satisfied with learning and felt the agent as an instructor and the workshop to be recommended. The pre-test and post-test showed that participants' food literacy about sugar was significantly improved in knowledge, skill, and attitude.

In the post-test, we have estimated the degree of achievement of each learning goal. About the first learning goal (understanding methods and resources to promote sugar control), most of the participants ($N = 11$) answered the daily free sugar intake limit in the WHO guidance correctly. They got a general understanding of the definition of free sugar and the accuracy of identifying food with free sugar was 6.6 out of 8 on average.

About the second learning goal (being able to use effective information to develop sugar control strategies), most of them correctly calculated the daily free sugar limit through the energy intake table ($N = 11$). About half of them correctly calculated the sugar content through the nutrition label ($N = 7$) and available carbohydrates table ($N = 5$), the others made mistakes because of total weight or including starch. Besides, five of them answered food choice strategies correctly according to the traffic light diet system. There was still room for progress on this goal. About the third learning goal (respecting norms, attitudes, and values about sugar control), participants thought it was important to control sugar intake, pay attention to sugar content, and include sugar in the nutrition label. However, there were still some participants who thought that when he/she is busy, he/she tends to get energy from food with a lot of sugar ($N = 7$).

It is suggested that co-eating agents for food education could improve food literacy, but it still needs some improvements in teaching calculations and providing specific situational suggestions.

4.2 The Role of Co-eating Agent in Food Educational Workshop

To answer RQ2 (Is the impression of the co-eating experience and co-eating agent related to participants' learning in food education?), we have evaluated participants' impression of the co-eating experience, the impression of the co-eating agent, and the learning outcome. The questionnaire showed that participants had a good time co-eating and had a positive impression of the co-eating agent in general. The co-eating agent could act as a close and trustworthy food educational instructor by having co-eating activities and giving food education with well-structured and reliable sources.

The Pearson correlation coefficient showed that perceived meal similarity significantly highly correlated with the learning outcome. The more participants thought the agent's food was similar to their own, the better the learning outcome. It has shown a potential of providing similar food to support food education, which needs further study with comparison. In addition, it is needed to explore how to maintain or improve the perceived meal similarity, such as customize the eating time or impression of the food of the co-eating agent.

5 Conclusion

In this study, we intended to achieve effective food education by developing a virtual co-eating agent with the capability of eating virtual food and teaching structured food education. We explored the subjective feelings and learning outcomes in food education provided by a co-eating agent. The results showed that the participants felt the sense of eating together with the agent, had a positive impression of the agent, had positive learning satisfaction and their scores were improved. In addition, a relationship was found between perceived meal similarity and learning outcomes. Based on the result of the user study, the effectiveness and role of the co-eating agent for food education were discussed. It is suggested to provide co-eating activities with structured educational content and explore how to maintain the perceived meal similarity of co-eating agent for food education.

References

1. Ministry of Health, Labor and Welfare: Shokuiku 4th Promotion Basic Policies (in Japanese). https://www.mhlw.go.jp/content/000770380.pdf. Accessed 2 Feb 2024
2. Ministry of Agriculture, Forestry and Fisheries: Digital food education guidebook (in Japanese). https://www.maff.go.jp/j/syokuiku/network/movie/index.html. Accessed 2 Feb 2024
3. Diamantis, D.V., et al.: Improving children's lifestyle and quality of life through synchronous online education: the nutritional adventures school-based program. Nutrients **15**(24), 5124 (2023)
4. Murimi, M.W., Nguyen, B., Moyeda-Carabaza, A.F., Lee, H.J., Park, O.H.: Factors that contribute to effective online nutrition education interventions: a systematic review. Nutr. Rev. **77**(10), 663–690 (2019)
5. Pedersen, S., Grønhøj, A., Thøgersen, J.: Following family or friends: social norms in adolescent healthy eating. Appetite **86**, 54–60 (2015)
6. Poulos, N.S., Pasch, K.E., Springer, A.E., Hoelscher, D.M., Kelder, S.H.: Is frequency of family meals associated with parental encouragement of healthy eating among ethnically diverse eighth graders? Public Health Nutr. **17**(5), 998–1003 (2014)
7. Gupta, C.C., Coates, A.M., Dorrian, J., Banks, S.: The factors influencing the eating behaviour of shiftworkers: What, when, where and why. Ind. Health **57**(4), 419–453 (2019)
8. McColl, D., Nejat, G.: A socially assistive robot that can monitor affect of the elderly during mealtime assistance. J. Med. Devices **8**(3), 030941 (2014)
9. Randall, N., Joshi, S., Liu, X.: Health-e-eater: dinnertime companion robot and magic plate for improving eating habits in children from low–income families. In: Companion of the 2018 ACM/IEEE International Conference on Human–Robot Interaction, pp. 361–362. ACM (2018)
10. Fujii, A., Kochigami, K., Kitagawa, S., Okada, K., Inaba, M.: Development and evaluation of mixed reality co-eating system: Sharing the behavior of eating food with a robot could improve our dining experience. In: 2020 29th IEEE International Conference on Robot and Human Interactive Communication (RO-MAN), pp. 357–362. IEEE (2020)
11. Wang, J.-Y., Inoue, T.: The similarity of virtual meal of a co-eating agent affects human participant. In: International Conference on Collaboration Technologies, pp. 115–132. Springer, Cham (2023). https://doi.org/10.1007/978-3-031-42141-9_8
12. Esau, M., Lawo, D., Neifer, T., Stevens, G., Boden, A.: Trust your guts: fostering embodied knowledge and sustainable practices through voice interaction. Pers. Ubiquit. Comput. **27**(2), 415–434 (2023)
13. Jeong, S., Aymerich-Franch, L., Alghowinem, S., Picard, R.W., Breazeal, C.L., Park, H.W.: A robotic companion for psychological well-being: a long-term investigation of companionship and therapeutic alliance. In: Proceedings of the 2023 ACM/IEEE International Conference on Human-Robot Interaction (HRI 2023), pp. 485–494. ACM (2023)
14. Reicks, M., et al.: Frequency of eating alone is associated with adolescent dietary intake, perceived food-related parenting practices and weight status: cross-sectional family life, activity, sun, health, and Eating (FLASHE) Study results. Public Health Nutr. **22**(9), 1555–1566 (2019)
15. World Health Organization: Guideline: sugars intake for adults and children. World Health Organization, Geneva, Switzerland (2015)
16. Liu, Y.: Healthy eating out skills for school children (in Chinese), Taiwan Health Promoting School. https://hps.hphe.ntnu.edu.tw/files/201904/topic_promote-file/a651c087f7f85683e8d757d13e53d4ef.pdf. Accessed 2 Feb 2024
17. Ministry of Education, Culture, Sports, Science and Technology: Standard Tables of Food Composition in Japan. https://www.mext.go.jp/en/policy/science_technology/policy/title01/detail01/1374030.htm. Accessed 2 Feb 2024

18. Heerink, M., et al.: A field study with primary school children on perception of social presence and interactive behavior with a pet robot. In: 2012 IEEE RO-MAN: The 21st IEEE International Symposium on Robot and Human Interactive Communication, pp. 1045–1050. IEEE (2012)
19. Lubold, N., Walker, E., Pon-Barry, H.: Effects of adapting to user pitch on rapport perception, behavior, and state with a social robotic learning companion. User Model. User-Adap. Inter. **31**(1), 35–73 (2021)
20. Eom, S.B., Ashill, N.: The determinants of students' perceived learning outcomes and satisfaction in university online education: an update. Decis. Sci. J. Innov. Educ. **14**(2), 185–215 (2016)

The Impact of Short-Video Application Affordances on Cross-Cultural User Engagement Behavior Intention: Based on SOR Model

Wu Wei[1], Na Li[1], and Yunjie Chen[2(✉)]

[1] School of Film Television and Communication, Xiamen University of Technology, Xiamen, Fujian, China
[2] School of Management, Ming Chuan University, Taipei, Taiwan
417167945@qq.com

Abstract. Nowadays, short-videos have become one of the most popular applications worldwide. Statistics indicate that short-video applications have more than 1 billion users around the world, which means that the contents in different platforms come from different countries and regions, and also represent various societies and cultures. In other words, short-videos have become an important medium for cross-cultural communication today. For users, if they cannot use short-video applications, they will lose the channel for cross-cultural content production, communication and reception. Therefore, the issues related to the media technology of short-video applications have become the objects that must be considered in the field of human-computer interaction research. This study believed that in the current age, on the one hand, research on technology affordance needs to be conducted continuously; on the other hand, how the impact of technology on user behavior would change is also a question to be concerned about. Consequently, based on the theoretical framework of the stimulus-organism-response (SOR) model, this study explores the impact of different affordances on the internal state of the organism and the correlation with cross-cultural usage responses.

According to the SOR model, this study adopted the four dimensions of technological affordance - association, visibility, persistence, and editability - as the source of stimuli for cross-cultural users of short-video applications; perceived self-efficacy as an organism's internal state; and response was investigated by measuring users' behavioral engagement intentions. Under the quantitative approach, this study found through data analysis that technology affordance as a stimulus can influence an individual's internal state and thus the response, generating a behavioral intention to continuously participate. Finally, with the findings, this study made some suggestions for short-video applications on subsequent cross-cultural practices.

Keywords: Technology Affordance · Cross-Cultural Communication · SOR Model · Self-Efficacy · Short-Video Application

P.-L. P. Rau (Ed.): HCII 2024, LNCS 14699, pp. 129–146, 2024.
https://doi.org/10.1007/978-3-031-60898-8_9

1 Introduction

Nowadays, short-video has become one of the most popular modes of communication in the world, and short-video platforms have also become indispensable application programs in media devices for users. According to publicly available data released by FastData in July 2023, TikTok - the world's most downloaded mobile short-video application in 2022 - has more than 1.6 billion users worldwide [1]. Based on the statistics of statista.com in October 2023, the countries with the largest number of TikTok users are the United States (143.4 million), Indonesia (106.52 million), Brazil (68.89 million), Mexico (62.61 million) and Vietnam (59.12 million). Although statistically speaking a large number of TikTok users are located in Asia and America, in fact, there are a considerable number of users in Europe (such as Turkey with 35.74 million users), Africa (such as 34.85 million in Arab countries) and Oceania (such as 8.5 million in Australia) [2]. This means that the short-video content in the TikTok application is being generated by users in different countries throughout the world, and that the content being generated by these users originates from the different societies and diverse cultures all over the planet. Therefore, some studies [3–5] have provided support for the argument that short-videos, represented by TikTok, are an important means of cross-cultural communication in today's era.

In the past, cross-cultural studies related to short-video mostly focused on communication strategies [6], symbolic narration [7], usage behavior [8] and media literacy [9]. Among these studies, the Chinese academia has focused in particular on studying the construction of the national image through short-videos. For example, Li et al. believed that it is necessary to actively explore "Chinese Story" in the dimension of daily life based on the concept of the human community with a shared fate and the concept of facing the common feelings and values of human beings [5]; Xiao and Zhang have advanced the argument that that creators should pay special attention to the narrative function of non-verbal symbols in Chinese short-videos [10]; Wang and Sun believed that in the process of cross-cultural communication attention should be accordance to the identification and maintenance of short-video in its emotional aspects, which result in empathic communication [11]. In point of fact, the perspectives offered by Chinese research on short-video have not departed from the range of existing studies. At the same time, the importance of technology is broached to a greater or lesser degree in these studies. However, there have been relatively few studies about short-video media technology in cross-cultural contexts. The importance of technology in the future, especially in the development of human-computer interaction, is unquestionable [12].

When short-video bears the function of cross-cultural communication, the issues related to its application technology become objects requiring consideration. Although this study did not adopt the position of technological determinism, it is equally undeniable that the development of communication technology and changes in media forms are key components of social evolution [13]. Given such a background, on the one hand, research on media technology needs to be carried out on an ongoing basis. For users, the lack of technology to support the use of short video applications prevents the communication of their cross-cultural content. On the other hand, based on the users' use of technology to their perception of technology (including the content presented through technology) as well as their feedback, we can discuss the influence of technology on user behavior.

Therefore, based on the theoretical model of stimulus-organism-response (SOR), this study took the technology affordances of short-video applications as the external stimulus, and explored the influence of different affordances on the internal state of users (organisms) and the relationship with the cross-cultural content use responses.

2 Theoretical Background and Hypothesis Building

2.1 SOR Model

In 1974, the SOR model was proposed to describe how the environment affects human behavior, thereby exploring the role of various stimuli on an individual's cognitive or psychological responses and the subsequent generation of behavioral responses. According to Mehrabian and Russell, the model has three key elements, namely, environmental stimuli (S), internal states of users (O) and responses (R) [14]. Environmental stimuli refer to the people's external stimuli such as the store atmosphere and the website's quality [15]. User internal states refer to the users' internal state, including their emotional state and cognitive state [16]. Responses refer to the reactions of their perceptions, including the approach response and the avoidance response [14]. After years of development, the SOR model has been widely used in studies related to user behavior, providing an important theoretical basis for studying the formation path and influencing factors of user behavior [17].

In prior studies, the SOR model has been used frequently to investigate issues related to new media and new technologies. For example, Sohaib et al. applied the SOR model to the study of perceived website characteristics on consumers' responses [18]. Tian and Lee studied the relationship among social media interactivity, perceived value, an immersive experience, and continued purchase intentions [19]. Hu et al. suggested that with the superiority of the online environment, cues and signals from online store elements become stimuli in the virtual space of human-computer interaction, as studied through the SOR model [20]. In addition, Lv et al. adopted the SOR model to study short videos, and noted that the generation of the information-sharing willingness of short video marketing users is a typical dynamic process of external information stimulation causing changes in the organism and generating information-sharing willingness [21].

Thus, this study used the SOR model to explore the relationship between media technology and users' perception and behavioral intention. The three components of the SOR model are described in the following sections.

2.2 Technology Affordance as Stimulus

In 1979, Gibson proposed the concept of affordance in ecological psychology. According to him, there is objective information in the environment, and it marks the possibility of interaction between the animal body and the environment, so the "pick up" of the objective information should become the main contents of psychological research or sensory research [22]. Accordingly, he argued that the concept of affordance should be used to describe what a specific environment provides for animals, that is, what the environment provides or furnishes - whether it is good or bad - there is complementarity between animals and the environment [22]. Today, this concept of affordance has gradually become clearer, and it now emphasizes the relationship between the actor and his environment, the characteristics that the environment possesses to meet the needs of users [21], and the behavior offered to actors as possibilities [22]. In 1988, Norman adopted a functional definition of affordance and introduced affordance into the field of industrial design and created "design psychology", thereby marking the first time that the concept of affordance appeared in inter-disciplinary research. Although some researchers have counterargued that affordance is a fictional chimera [23], the concept of affordance has nonetheless been deployed by an increasing number of scholars in a wide array of fields, including information, communication, technology and cultural research.

Along with the ongoing deepening of the concept of affordance, the theoretical focus of scholars has gradually shifted from attaching importance to environmental changes to discussing the relationship between users and technology. For example, Markus et al. [24] advanced the concept of affordance related to information technology, which is called "functional affordance", which denotes the goal action-oriented possibilities provided by technology to specific user groups. This conceptualization of technological affordances has emphasized human agency [25], and a potential for action [26]. Chang argued that digital technology has special effects that affect people's cognition, attitudes, emotions and even behavior due to some of its natural characteristics [27]. There are also scholarly perspectives that covered both users and technology. For example, Erofeeva believed that the technology affordance is neither part of the natural or artificial environment, nor of the perceiving subject, but is a product of their interaction [28]. In sum, the prior literature has identified several affordances, including reviewability, recombinability, and experimentation [29]; persistence, visibility, association, and editability [30]; and network-informed associating, metavoicing, generative role-taking, and triggered attending [26], and it has been demonstrated that these have differing effects on such things as organizational knowledge collaboration, socialization, flow of knowledge, power relations, and knowledge sharing [31].

In this study, association, visibility, persistence and editability were adopted from Treem and Leonardi's study as the external manifestations of affordance of short-video applications. According to Treem and Leonardi, association denotes the established connections between individuals, between individuals and content, or between an actor and a presentation [30]. It has been found through past research that two forms of association affordance exist in social media. The first type of association, that of one individual to another, is most commonly referred to as a social tie, while the other form of association is that of an individual to a piece of information. In other words, association affordance refers to the possibility of establishing connections between individuals or between individuals and content [32]. And this is in line with the characteristics of the new medium of short-video applications - that is, interactivity. When users browse cross-cultural short-video contents on short-video platforms, they not only can view other users' comments on the short-video, but also browse other videos of the same type due to the algorithm of the platforms.

Visibility, according to Treem and Leonardi, is tied to the amount of effort people must expend to locate information [30]. Leonardi suggested that the consciousness of "who knows what" and "who knows whom" will increase through visibility, thus enabling users to identify experts in relevant fields and acquire related knowledge from other users [33]. Meanwhile, visibility affordance also makes users' behaviors and social information widely known within the organization [34]. And thus drives users to manage their self-presentation through information contribution to create a more favorable impression, which is helpful to gain access to key resources in organizations [35]. Based on the findings of previous studies, this study assumed that that when browsing cross-cultural short-videos, a user will look for what he perceives as an expert based on from the publishers, commenters, and will express his/her own views and opinions on some specific short-videos.

Some scholars have argued that communication persists if it remains accessible in the same form as the original display after the actor has finished his or her presentation [36]. Persistence as used here refers to the notion that information remains available to users and does not expire or disappear [30]. Such an affordance has also been referred to as reviewability [37], recordability [38], or permanence [39]. As Erickson and Kellogg have noted, this concept of persistence entails a variety of new uses and practices: persistent conversations may be searched, browsed, replayed, annotated, visualized, restructured, and recontextualized, with what are likely to be profound effects on personal, social, and institutional practices [40]. This study concluded that persistence affordance results in the long-term existence of cross-cultural content in short-video applications, thereby allowing users to view and reuse it whenever they need it, and this is moreover helpful in improving users' perceptions and recognition of cross-cultural contents.

Editability refers to the fact that individuals can spend a good deal of time and effort crafting and recrafting a communicative act before it is viewed by others [41]. Sun et al. suggested that editability affordance allows users to codify their tacit knowledge into explicit knowledge, and in addition to modify or revise content progressively, thereby reducing the time and effort normally required to organize and compile knowledge from scratch [31]. Editability can also refer to the ability of an individual to modify or revise content that he or she has already communicated, including such straightforward acts as editing a spelling error or deleting content [42]. As such, editability is a function of two aspects of an interaction: communication formed in isolation from others, and asynchronicity [30]. In short-video applications, editability is manifested as a function whereby users modify and delete the comments published by themselves. At the same time, their published comments can be browsed by other users for a long time (unless the short-video is deleted by its publisher), so asynchronicity is also reflected.

2.3 Perceived Self-efficacy as Organism

In 1977, Bandura first conceptualized self-efficacy [43], and believed that a person's self-efficacy was based on four sources of information: past performance or mastery experiences; vicarious experiences of observing the experiences of others; verbal persuasion or social feedback and affective or physiological states [44]. According to Bandura, self-efficacy is defined as an individual's ability to deal with and cope with circumstances in the face of unpredictable and stressful situations [45]. Specifically, self-efficacy influences people's choice of activities, how much effort they will expend, and how long they will sustain effort in dealing with stressful situations [46]. Pajares asserted that self-efficacy is central to human behavior [47], because it influences people's thought patterns, emotions, and actions, which means, it can influence the totality of human behavior [48]. This is the reason why self-efficacy has generated research in several areas such as health management [49], computer use [50], psychology [51], work-related performance [52], information literacy [48], and web-based learning [53].

The influencing factors for an organism's perceived self-efficacy to be elicited vary across studies. For users of short-video social media, the influencing factors include technical pressure, environmental stimulation and emotional fluctuation [54]. The present study similarly argued that the rules of media use shaped by the technological affordance of short-video applications constitute technological pressures on users in the process of using them. Such a media environment can stimulate the perceived self-efficacy of short-video application users, and then determine their perseverance and resilience in the face of adversity, as well as the extent of that efforts that they exert in completing a task [55]. Therefore, the following hypotheses were proposed in this study:

- **H1:** Association affordance can positively influence users' perceived self-efficacy.
- **H2:** Visibility affordance can positively influence users' perceived self-efficacy.
- **H3:** Persistence affordance can positively influence users' perceived self-efficacy.
- **H4:** Editability affordance can positively influence users' perceived self-efficacy.

2.4 Behavioral Engagement Intention as Response

Engagement is the behavior of a user who interacts with the media consistently [56]. The concept of engagement has attracted considerable attention in multiple fields of research including social psychology, organizational behavior, marketing, service management, and information systems [57]. Although some studies have suggested that user engagement behavior is a behavioral indicator of user satisfaction and loyalty [58–60], the term "engagement" has generated a tremendous amount of debate and disagreement regarding its definition, dimension, and operationalization. Moreover, the interpretation of user participation remains fraught with ambiguity and controversy [58]. In spite of the wide range of conceptualizations that have been proposed for it, researchers have chiefly studied user involvement from three main perspectives [58], which are the psychological process [61], behavioral performance [62], and motivational psychological state [63]. In particular, from the psychological process perspective, researchers have considered engagement as a psychological process that leads to rewards and loyalty from customers [61]. Thus, psychological processes can be considered as a convergence perspective of the motivational psychological state and the behavioral performance.

Previous empirical studies have found that users' perceived self-efficacy affects the extent of their behavior [55]. For short-video applications, user engagement can not only improve users' perceived value, satisfaction and loyalty but also attract new users [64]. Therefore, this study focused on the individual's behavioral engagement intention, which is the user's willingness to continue to use the short video application to engage in cross-cultural interactions. Although there are conceptual differences between actual engagement behavior and behavior engagement willingness, the two are thought to be closely related [63]. This study hypothesized:

- **H5:** Users' perceived self-efficacy can positively influence their behavioral engagement intentions.

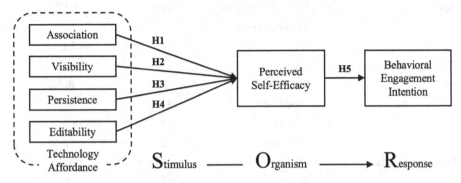

Fig. 1. Proposed theoretical framework and hypotheses

The SOR theory is used in this study to build a clear theoretical framework and to formulate hypotheses (see Fig. 1) by considering the technology affordance of short-video application as the stimulus (S), the perceived self-efficacy of short-video application users as the organism (O), and the users' behavioral engagement intention as the response (R). In doing so, it explored how the external environment stimulates the experience of users of short-video applications and further generates an intention to continuously engage.

3 Methodology

3.1 Data Collection and Analysis

This study collected data through an online questionnaire. The questionnaire included a question designed to determine whether the respondent had experience in watching cross-cultural content short-videos. A total of 400 questionnaires were distributed and 327 valid questionnaires (81.75%) were obtained. After the data collection, the respondents' demographic information was obtained through descriptive analysis. The sample comprised 168 (51.4%) men and 159 (48.6%) women (see Table 1). Exploratory factor analysis was performed to test the reliability and validity of the variables, and structural equation modeling (SEM), completed in AMOS 26.0, was used to determine the confirmatory factor analysis and model fit indices of the theoretical framework.

3.2 Measurements

The questionnaire was developed on the basis of instruments described by other studies (see Table 2). Specifically, association affordance was measured using scales adapted

Table 1. Respondent Demographics

Category		Frequency	%
Gender	Male	168	51.4
	Female	159	48.6
Age	Under 30 years old	206	63.0
	31–50 years old	101	30.9
	Over 51 years old	20	6.1
Country of Residence	Asian	133	40.7
	European	100	30.6
	American	33	10.1
	African	29	8.9
	Oceanian	32	9.8
Region of Residence	City	230	70.3
	Town	63	19.3
	Village	34	10.4
Education	Under Bachelor	44	13.5
	Bachelor	211	64.5
	Master	44	13.5
	Ph.D	28	8.6

from Pee [32]. The scale used to measure visibility affordance was from Treem and Leonardi [30]. The items for persistence and editability affordance came from Sun et al.'s and Rice et al.'s previous research [39]. User's perceived self-efficacy was measured through a scale developed by Tsai and Tsai [65]. The question items used to measure short-video applications users' behavioral engagement intentions for cross-cultural content came from the study by Fang et al. [57]. A 5-point Likert scale ranging from 1 ("strongly disagree") to 5 ("strongly agree") was used to measure the items of the constructs.

3.3 Reliability and Validity

Cronbach's alpha (CA), factor loadings (FLs), composite reliability (CR), and average variance extracted (AVE) were used to test the reliability and validity of the questionnaire (in Table 3). The CA, FL, CR, and AVE values were all within the acceptable range recommended by Hair et al. [66]. In addition, as indicated in Table 4, all square roots of the AVE (in **bold**) for the variables were greater than the intercorrelations of the variables, indicating discriminant validity. To test for common method bias, this study referred to Podsakoff et al. [67] and performed the Harman single-factor analysis [68]. The results showed the variance explained by the first factor was below the cutoff value of 50%, indicating that this study was not disturbed by common method bias.

Table 2. Measurement Scales

Construct	Items	Ref
Association (AS)	Through short-video applications, I can...	(Pee [32])
	AS1: connect with users of different cultures	
	AS2: find new cross-cultural content through what I know	
	AS3: find new users who don't recognize this content through cultures I'm familiar with	
Visibility (VI)	Short-video applications allow me to...	(Treem and Leonardi [30])
	VI1: show my cultural content to others	
	VI2: show others what I know about my culture	
	VI3: capture the attention of specific users in a cross-cultural community	
Persistence (PE)	With short-video applications, I can...	(Sun et al. [31])
	PE1: find previous information about other different cultures	
	PE2: stay in touch with others while my activities, work, or location changes	
	PE3: find content or comments after they have been posted	
Editability (ED)	Short-video applications allow me to...	(Rice et al. [42])
	ED1: create and revise content before other users see it	
	ED2: edit content in a short-video after posting	
	ED3: collaborate with others to create or edit cross-cultural contents	

(continued)

Table 2. (*continued*)

Construct	Items	Ref
Perceived Self-Efficacy (PSE)	PSE1: I think I know how to use a short-video application like 'Reels' or 'Tik Tok'	(Tsai and Tsai [65])
	PSE2: I think I know what 'short-video' is about	
	PSE3: I usually feel lost or confused when I am seeking cross-cultural content on the short-video application	
	PSE4: I am good at searching for information on the short-video applications	
	PSE5: I am confident in handling a short-video application like 'Reels' or 'Tik Tok'	
	PSE6: I think I am the kind of person who can make good use of the short-video applications	
Behavioral Engagement Intention (BEI)	I would like to...	(Fang et al. [57])
	BEI1: continue to use the short-video applications	
	BEI2: participate in events organized by the short video applications	
	BEI3: recommend the short-video applications to other users who are looking for cross-cultural content	

Confirmatory factor analysis was conducted using AMOS 26.0, and the results are within a widely accepted range ($\chi 2/df = 1.106$ RMSEA $= 0.018$, CFI $= 0.994$, NFI $= 0.941$, IFI $= 0.994$, TLI $= 0.993$, and AGFI $= 0.931$). All values indicated that model fit indices met the recommended values [69]. Therefore, the construct validity of the questionnaire was acceptable.

3.4 Structural Equation Model

To further explore the correlations between the variables, a structural equation model was developed. The results of the fit indices are presented in Table 5. The results indicated that all model fit indices meet the recommended values [69]; therefore, the structural

Table 3. Reliability and Validity

Construct		Loadings	Cronbach's alpha	AVE	CR
Association (AS)	AS1	0.706	0.770	0.531	0.771
	AS2	0.703			
	AS3	0.771			
Visibility (VI)	VI1	0.766	0.816	0.599	0.817
	VI2	0.771			
	VI3	0.783			
Persistence (PE)	PE1	0.739	0.827	0.620	0.829
	PE2	0.796			
	PE3	0.816			
Editability (ED)	ED1	0.794	0.799	0.575	0.801
	ED2	0.710			
	ED3	0.762			
Perceived Self-Efficacy (PSE)	PSE1	0.757	0.888	0.570	0.888
	PSE2	0.736			
	PSE3	0.758			
	PSE4	0.739			
	PSE5	0.763			
	PSE6	0.775			
Behavioral Engagement Intention (BEI)	BEI1	0.747	0.817	0.597	0.816
	BEI2	0.824			
	BEI3	0.749			

AVE, Average Variance Extracted; CR, Composite Reliability.

equation model of this study was determined to have good fit. The β values derived for the proposed framework are presented in Fig. 2.

The data showed that users' perceived self-efficacy was positively and significantly correlated with their behavioral engagement intentions ($\beta = 0.510$, p < 0.001). Therefore, hypothesis 5 proposed in this study is supported. Regarding technical artifacts, there was a significantly positive correlation between the association affordances of short-video applications and users' perceived self-efficacy ($\beta = 0.314$, p < 0.01). Therefore, H1 was supported. Also, visibility affordances of short-video applications can positively influence users' perceived self-efficacy ($\beta = 0.157$, p < 0.05). Hence, H2 was supported. During the process of using a short-video application, there were significantly and positively related between users' perceived self-efficacy and the persistence affordances and editability affordances of the technological device ($\beta = 0.225$, p < 0.01; $\beta = 0.216$, p < 0.01, respectively). Therefore, both H3 and H4 were supported.

Table 4. Mean, Standard Deviation, and Correlation

	M	SD	1	2	3	4	5	6
1.AS	3.417	0.883	**(0.728)**					
2.VI	3.277	0.872	0.535***	**(0.774)**				
3.PE	3.192	0.900	0.615***	0.423***	**(0.787)**			
4.ED	3.721	0.828	0.583***	0.496***	0.467***	**(0.758)**		
5.PSE	3.352	0.815	0.589***	0.479***	0.525***	0.537***	**(0.755)**	
6.BEI	3.692	0.875	0.590***	0.393***	0.474***	0.439***	0.498***	**(0.773)**

$p < 0.05$, **$p < 0.01$, ***$p < 0.001$; AS, Association; VI, Visibility; PE, Persistence; ED, Editability; PSE, Perceived self-efficacy; BEI, Behavioral Engagement intention; Bolded values indicate discriminant validity.

Table 5. Structural Equation Model

Fit Indices	Recommended Value	Value
χ^2/df	< 3.0	1.299
Root Mean Square Error of Approximation (RMSEA)	< 0.08	0.03
Comparative Fit Index (CFI)	> 0.90	0.983
Normed Fit Index (NFI)	> 0.90	0.929
Incremental Fit Index (IFI)	> 0.90	0.983
Tuckere Lewis index (TLI)	> 0.90	0.979
Adjusted Goodness of Fit Index (AGFI)	> 0.80	0.921

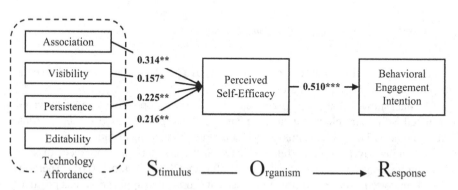

Fig. 2. Proposed framework with β values (*$p < 0.05$, **$p < 0.01$, ***$p < 0.001$.*)

4 Discussion

Based on the results of the data analysis, all of the hypotheses proposed in this study are valid. These findings suggested that users' intention to engage in usage behaviors (R) for short-video applications increases as their perceived self-efficacy (O) for technology affordance (S) increases. Consistent with the results of previous studies about SOR modeling [21, 64, 70], the results of this study indicated that the SOR model is applicable to the short-video application context.s Also, this study found that self-efficacy can affect users' behavioral engagement intention, which is also in line with previous study findings [46, 54, 71]. With respect to media technology, the affordances of association, visibility, persistence and editability all affect users' perceptions of and subsequent use behavior of media technology, and this finding substantiates the results of prior related research [72–74]. Therefore, this study concluded that users' perceived self-efficacy can be enhanced by reinforcing their perceptions of technology affordances when they use short-video applications to browse cross-cultural content, which ultimately makes it possible to boost their intention to continue engaging with the use of short-video applications.

Through the findings of this study, some practical recommendations can be proposed for the development of short-video applications and the communication of cross-cultural short-video contents. In the future, providers of short-video applications need to design simple and easy-to-operate systems to the maximum extent possible in order to enhance users' positive perception of media technology. Previous studies have found that short-video users' perceived usability and availability of media technology stimulate their intention to continue watching [75]. According to this study, users' perceived self-efficacy can also have a positive effect on their behavioral engagement intention. That is, when users find short-video applications to be good, useful, and functional, they will use them more actively, which in turn will lead to the communication of cross-cultural content in the applications. In this regard, many researchers have offered in previous studies such recommendations as incorporating a light-weight interface design [54] to make interaction easier and more flexible [64] as a way to build a unique "circle" culture [76].

Building on past recommendations and considering the findings of this study, clearer suggestions can be made from the perspective of technology affordance. First of all, designers and operators of short-video applications should pay attention to the association, persistence, and editability of short-video contents. According to this study, the association, persistence and editability affordances of short-video applications can result in users continuing to use media with confidence. Accordingly, the designers and operators of short-video applications can encourage users to actively obtain cross-cultural contents through short-videos by setting specific themes, topics and activities in order to garner more user activity. At the same time, the easy-interaction features of new media can be used to stimulate users to publish information (short-videos, comments, or forwards) in order to help promote the communication of multi-cultural contents. However, the maintainers of short-video applications must strictly supervise short-video contents, especially cultural contents from different regions, so as to prevent the negative perceptions received by cross-cultural users due to misinformation and cultural conflicts.

Furthermore, this study found that the positive correlation between visibility and users' psychological perception is relatively weak. In the future, designers and operators of short-video applications may be able to improve the system algorithm and recommendation mechanism so as to make it easier for users to obtain high-quality cross-cultural contents during use. Alternatively, the user engagement mechanism of gamification [77] can be added to encourage users to produce cultural content related to their own regions. This requires the improvement of the association and editability of short-video applications in order to take into account the creative needs of user generated content. As Norman - the first scholar to introduce the concept of affordance into the field of product design - expressly emphasized, a designer's job involves knowing the psychology of people in relation to how things work [78]. In summary, short-video applications may strive to design features that can afford or expand the association, visibility, persistence and editability affordances to increase the possibility of users utilizing short-videos for cross-cultural communication.

Finally, there are some shortcomings in this study that will require improvement and development in the future. First, based on the sampling results, the samples in this study are youths, and they may be less interested in cross-cultural contents than the general population. In addition, young people usually have a higher acceptance of media technology. Accordingly, relevant research should be carried out for older populations in the future. Second, although the samples in this study have diverse cultural backgrounds as well as social experiences with a certain degree of diversity, their understanding of the environment (including technical and humanistic) may differ. In addition, affordance itself has the characteristics of diversity [78], which will affect the universality of research findings and recommendations. Studies in the future may involve carrying out comparative research on specific regions in order that these studies can propose more effective specific recommendations. Finally, this study has adopted only association, visibility, persistence and editability as the component dimensions of technology affordance. In previous studies, scholars also extracted such other dimensions of affordance as portability, availability, locatability, multimedia [74] modality, agency, interactivity, navigability [79], etc. For the future, For the future, different dimensions of affordance can be taken to develop further research to deepen the interpretation and application of technology affordances.

Funding. This Study Was Supported by the High-Level Talent Research Project of Xiamen University of Technology (YSK22019R).

References

1. FastData: TikTok eco-development white book (FY2023 - 1st half). https://new.qq.com/rain/a/20230705A07KMN00. Accessed 31 Jan 2024. (in Chinese)
2. Statista: Countries with the largest TikTok audience as of October 2023. https://www.statista.com/statistics/1299807/number-of-monthly-unique-tiktok-users/. Accessed 31 Jan 2024
3. Yang, Y.: TikTok/Douyin use and its influencer video use: a cross-cultural comparison between Chinese and US users. Online Media Glob. Commun. **1**(2), 339–368 (2022)
4. Piao, Y.: Study on the spread of Chinese short video in South Korea against the background of cross-cultural communication. In: 2nd International Conference on Language, Communication and Culture Studies (ICLCCS 2021), pp. 325–330. Atlantis Press (2021)

5. Li, Y., Chen, X., Mao, T., Huang, G.: Analysis on the influencing factors and framework of new media's cross-cultural communication effect - taking the Li Ziqi Video on YouTube as an example. Libr. Tribunue **42**(07), 132–142 (2022). (in Chinese)
6. Wang, Y., Chen, W.: Cross-cultural communication strategies research of socializing apps during internet era. In: 2021 5th International Seminar on Education, Management and Social Sciences (ISEMSS 2021), pp. 454–460. Atlantis Press (2021)
7. Vizcaíno-Verdú, A., Abidin, C.: Cross-cultural storytelling approaches in Tiktok's music challenges. AoIR Sel. Pap. Internet Res. (2021)
8. Zhang, N., Hazarika, B., Chen, K., Shi, Y.: A cross-national study on the excessive use of short-video applications among college students. Comput. Hum. Behav. **145**, 107752 (2023)
9. Bloom, K., Johnston, K.M.: Digging into youtube videos: using media literacy and participatory culture to promote cross-cultural understanding. J. Media Literacy Educ. **2**(2), 3 (2013)
10. Xiao, J., Zhang, C.: A study of symbolic narratives in cross-cultural communication of short videos. News Writ. **3**, 24–31 (2020). (in Chinese)
11. Wang, C., Sun, Y.: The tension between technology and culture: creative short video cross-cultural empathy communication. J. Commun. **1**, 27–31 (2021). (in Chinese)
12. Riva, G. (Ed.): Ambient Intelligence: The Evolution Of Technology, Communication And Cognition Towards The Future Of Human-Computer Interaction (Vol. 6). IOS Press (2005)
13. Yu, G.: The evolution logic of future media: the iteration, reorganization and sublimation of human connection. J. Mass Commun. **10**, 54–60 (2021). (in Chinese)
14. Mehrabian, A., Russell, J.A.: An Approach to Environmental Psychology. MIT Press, Cambridge (1974)
15. Zheng, X., Men, J., Yang, F., Gong, X.: Understanding impulse buying in mobile commerce: an investigation into hedonic and utilitarian browsing. Int. J. Inf. Manage. **48**, 151–160 (2019)
16. Parboteeah, D.V., Valacich, J.S., Wells, J.D.: The influence of website characteristics on a consumer's urge to buy impulsively. Inf. Syst. Res. **20**(1), 60–78 (2009)
17. Song, Z., Liu, C., Shi, R.: How do fresh live broadcast impact consumers' purchase intention? Based SOR theory. Sustain. **14**, 14382 (2022)
18. Sohaib, O., Kang, K., Miliszewska, I.: Uncertainty avoidance and consumer cognitive innovativeness in e-commerce. J. Glob. Inf. Manag. **27**(2), 59–77 (2019)
19. Tian, H., Lee, Y.: Factors affecting continuous purchase intention of fashion products on social e-commerce: SOR model and the mediating effect. Entertain. Comput. **41**, 100474 (2022)
20. Hu, X., Huang, Q., Zhong, X., Davison, R.M., Zhao, D.: The influence of peer characteristics and technical features of a social shopping website on a consumer's purchase intention. Int. J. Inf. Manage. **36**(6), 1218–1230 (2016)
21. Lv, X., Chen, L., Liang, Y.: The influence of WeChat friends' characteristics on consumers' willingness to share in the SoLoMo model. In: Proceedings of the 2019 5th International Conference on Humanities and Social Science Research (ICHSSR 2019), pp. 627–633 (2019)
22. Gibson, J.J.: The Ecological Approach to Visual Perception. Houghton Mifflin, Boston, MA (1979)
23. Jenkins, H.: Affordances: evolution of a pivotal concept. J. Sci. Psychol. **101**(2), 34–45 (2008)
24. Markus, M.L., Silver, M.S.: A foundation for the study of IT effects: a new look at DESANCTIS and Poole's concepts of structural features and spirit. J. Assoc. Inf. Syst. **9**(10), 5 (2008)
25. Leonardi, P.M.: When flexible routines meet flexible technologies: affordance, constraint, and the imbrication of human and material agencies. MIS Q., 147–167 (2011)
26. Majchrzak, A., Faraj, S., Kane, G.C., Azad, B.: The contradictory influence of social media affordances on online communal knowledge sharing. J. Comput.-Mediat. Commun. **19**(1), 38–55 (2013)

27. Chang, J.: The Internet, technological affordance and the emotional public. Youth Journalist. **25**, 92 (2019). (in Chinese)
28. Erofeeva, M.: On multiple agencies: when do things matter? Inf. Commun. Soc. **22**(5), 590–604 (2019)
29. Faraj, S., Jarvenpaa, S.L., Majchrzak, A.: Knowledge collaboration in online communities. Organ. Sci. **22**(5), 1224–1239 (2011)
30. Treem, J.W., Leonardi, P.M.: Social media use in organizations: exploring the affordances of visibility, editability, persistence, and association. Ann. Int. Commun. Assoc. **36**(1), 143–189 (2013)
31. Sun, Y., Wang, C., Jeyaraj, A.: Enterprise social media affordances as enablers of knowledge transfer and creative performance: an empirical study. Telematics Inform. **51**, 101402 (2020)
32. Pee, L.G.: Affordances for sharing domain-specific and complex knowledge on enterprise social media. Int. J. Inf. Manage. **43**, 25–37 (2018)
33. Leonardi, P.M.: Ambient awareness and knowledge acquisition. MIS Q. **39**(4), 747–762 (2015)
34. Evans, S.K., Pearce, K.E., Vitak, J., Treem, J.W.: Explicating affordances: a conceptual framework for understanding affordances in communication research. J. Comput.-Mediat. Commun. **22**(1), 35–52 (2017)
35. Van Osch, W., Steinfield, C.W.: Strategic visibility in enterprise social media: implications for network formation and boundary spanning. J. Manag. Inf. Syst. **35**(2), 647–682 (2018)
36. Bregman, A., Haythornwaite, C.: Radicals of presentation in persistent conversation. In: Proceedings of the 34th Annual Hawaii International Conference on System Sciences, IEEE (2001)
37. Clark, H. H., Brennan, S. E.: Grounding in communication. In L. B. Resnick, J. M. Levine, S. D. Teasley (Eds.), Perspectives on Socially Shared Cognition, pp. 127–149. American Psychological Association, Washington, DC (1991)
38. Hancock, J. T., Toma, C., Ellison, N. B.: The truth about lying in online dating profiles. In: Proceedings of the SIGCHI Conference on Human Factors in Computing Systems. New York: ACM, 449–452 (2007)
39. Whittaker, S.: Theories and methods in mediated communication. In: Graesser, A.C., Gernsbacher, M.A., Goldman, S.R. (eds.) Handbook of discourse processes, pp. 243–286. Erlbaum, Mahwah, NJ (2003)
40. Erickson, T., Kellogg, W.A.: Social translucence: an approach to designing systems that support social processes. ACM Trans. Comput. Hum. Interact. (TOCHI) **7**(1), 59–83 (2000)
41. Walther, J.B.: Impression development in computer-mediated interaction. West. J. Commun. (Includes Commun. Rep.) **57**(4), 381–398 (1993)
42. Rice, R.E.: Computer-mediated communication and organizational innovation. J. Commun. **37**(4), 65–94 (1987)
43. Bandura, A.: Self-efficacy: toward a unifying theory of behavioral change. Psychol. Rev. **84**(2), 191–215 (1977)
44. Bandura, A.: Social Foundation of Thought and Action. Prentice Hall, Englewood Cliffs, NJ (1986)
45. Bandura, A., Schunk, D.H.: Cultivating competence, self-efficacy, and intrinsic interest through proximal self-motivation. J. Pers. Soc. Psychol. **41**(3), 586–598 (1981)
46. Bandura, A., Barbaranelli, C., Caprara, G.V., Pastorelli, C.: Multifaceted impact of self-efficacy beliefs on academic functioning. Child Dev. **67**(3), 1206–1222 (1996)
47. Pajares, F.: Gender and perceived self-efficacy in self-regulated learning. Theor. Pract. **41**(2), 116–125 (2002)
48. Kurbanoglu, S.S.: Self-efficacy: a concept closely linked to information literacy and lifelong learning. J. Docum. **59**(6), 635–646 (2003). https://doi.org/10.1108/00220410310506295

49. Schwarzer, R., Fuchs, R.: Self-efficacy in health behaviors. In: Conner, M., Norman, P. (eds.), Predicting Health Behaviour: Research and Practice with Social Cognition Models. Open University Press, Buckingham (1995)
50. Downey, J.P., McMurtrey, M.: Introducing task-based general computer self-efficacy: an empirical comparison of three general self-efficacy instruments. Interact. Comput. **19**(3), 382–396 (2007)
51. Kear, M.: Concept analysis of self-efficacy. Grad. Res. Nurs. **13**, 142–156 (2000)
52. Sonnentag, S., Kruel, U.: Psychological detachment from work during off-job time: the role of job stressors job involvement, and recovery-related self-efficacy. Eur. J. Work Organ. Psy. **15**, 197–217 (2006)
53. Cheng, K.H., Tsai, C.C.: An investigation of Taiwan University students' perceptions of online academic help seeking, and their web-based learning self-efficacy. Internet High. Educ. **14**(3), 150–157 (2011)
54. Chen, T., Li, X., Duan, Y.: Research on discontinuous usage intention of short video social media users based on cognitive dissonance and self-efficacy. J. Intell. **41**(10), 199–207 (2022). (in Chinese)
55. Bronstein, J.: The role of perceived self-efficacy in the information seeking behavior of library and information science students. J. Acad. Librariansh. **40**(2), 101–106 (2014)
56. Khan, M.L.: Social media engagement: what motivates user participation and consumption on YouTube? Comput. Hum. Behav. **66**, 236–247 (2017)
57. Fang, J., Zhao, Z., Wen, C., Wang, R.: Design and performance attributes driving mobile travel application engagement. Int. J. Inf. Manage. **37**(4), 269–283 (2017)
58. Cheung, C.M., Shen, X.L., Lee, Z.W., Chan, T.K.: Promoting sales of online games through customer engagement. Electron. Commer. Res. Appl. **14**(4), 241–250 (2015)
59. Kim, Y.H., Kim, D.J., Wachter, K.: A study of mobile user engagement (MoEN): engagement motivations, perceived value, satisfaction, and continued engagement intention. Decis. Support. Syst. **56**, 361–370 (2013)
60. Oh, C., Roumani, Y., Nwankpa, J.K., Hu, H.F.: Beyond likes and tweets: consumer engagement behavior and movie box office in social media. Inform. Manage. **54**(1), 25–37 (2017)
61. Bowden, J.L.H.: The process of customer engagement: a conceptual framework. J. Mark. Theor. Pract. **17**(1), 63–74 (2009)
62. Van Doorn, J., Lemon, K.N., Mittal, V., Nass, S., Pick, D., Pirner, P., et al.: Customer engagement behavior: theoretical foundations and research directions. J. Serv. Res. **13**(3), 253–266 (2010)
63. Peters, T., Işık, Ö., Tona, O., Popovič, A.: How system quality influences mobile BI use: the mediating role of engagement. Int. J. Inf. Manage. **36**(5), 773–783 (2016)
64. Gong, Y., Cao, Y., Li, J.: The impact of short-video application characteristics on user engagement behavior: the mediating role of psychological engagement. Inform. Sci. **38**(7), 77–84 (2020). (in Chinese)
65. Tsai, M.J., Tsai, C.C.: Information searching strategies in web-based science learning: the role of Internet self-efficacy. Innov. Educ. Teach. Int. **40**(1), 43–50 (2003)
66. Hair, J.F., Gabriel, M., Patel, V.: AMOS covariance-based structural equation modeling(CB-SEM): guidelines on its application as a marketing research tool. Braz. J. Mark. **13**(2), 169–183 (2014)
67. Podsakoff, P.M., MacKenzie, S.B., Lee, J.Y., Podsakoff, N.P.: Common method biases in behavioral research: a critical review of the literature and recommended remedies. J. Appl. Psychol. **88**(5), 879–903 (2003)
68. Harman, H.H.: Modern Factor Analysis. University of Chicago Press, Chicago, IL (1976)
69. Arpaci, I., Baloğlu, M.: The impact of cultural collectivism on knowledge sharing among information technology majoring undergraduates. Comput. Hum. Behav. **56**, 65–71 (2016)

70. Shi, R., Wang, M., Liu, C., Gull, N.: The Influence of short video platform characteristics on users' willingness to share marketing information: based on the SOR model. Sustain. **15**(3), 2448 (2023)

71. Lee, Y.K.: Impacts of digital technostress and digital technology self-efficacy on Fintech usage intention of Chinese Gen Z consumers. Sustain. **13**(9), 5077 (2021)

72. Tsai, J.P., Ho, C.F.: Does design matter? Affordance perspective on smartphone usage. Ind. Manag. Data Syst. **113**(9), 1248–1269 (2013)

73. Mao, C.M., Hovick, S.R.: Adding affordances and communication efficacy to the technology acceptance model to study the messaging features of online patient portals among young adults. Health Commun. **37**(3), 307–315 (2022)

74. Schrock, A.R.: Communicative affordances of mobile media: Portability, availability, locatability, and multimediality. Int. J. Commun. **18**(9), 1229–1246 (2015)

75. Wei, W., Chen, Y.: The impact of technology affordance of short videos on users' health information acceptance: a study based on Chinese short video users. In: Marcus, A., Rosenzweig, E., Soares, M.M. (eds.) Design, User Experience, and Usability: 12th International Conference, DUXU 2023, Held as Part of the 25th HCI International Conference, HCII 2023, Copenhagen, Denmark, July 23–28, 2023, Proceedings, Part V, pp. 465–479. Springer Nature Switzerland, Cham (2023). https://doi.org/10.1007/978-3-031-35705-3_34

76. Tian, K., Xuan, W., Hao, L., Wei, W., Li, D., Zhu, L.: Exploring youth consumer behavior in the context of mobile short video advertising using an extended stimulus-organization-response model. Front. Psychol. **13**, 933542 (2022)

77. Zhu, Y., Pei, L., Shang, J.: Improving video engagement by gamification: a proposed design of MOOC videos. In: Cheung, S.K.S., Kwok, L.F., Ma, W.W.K., Lee, L.K., Yang, H. (eds.) ICBL 2017. LNCS, vol. 10309, pp. 433–444. Springer, Cham (2017). https://doi.org/10.1007/978-3-319-59360-9_38

78. Norman, D.A.: The Psychology of Everyday Things. Basic Books, New York (1988)

79. Sundar, S.S.: The MAIN model: a heuristic approach to understanding technology effects on credibility. In: Metzger, M.J., Flanagin, A.J. (eds.) Digital media, youth, and credibility, pp. 73–100. The MIT Press, Cambridge, MA (2008)

A Gamified Approach on Inducing Energy Conservation Behavior

Dian Yu, Ari Yue, and Pei-Luen Patrick Rau[✉]

Department of Industrial Engineering, Tsinghua University, Beijing 100084, China
rpl@tsinghua.edu.cn

Abstract. Motivating individuals to adopt energy-saving behaviors is critical for promoting environmental sustainability and addressing environmental issues. Gamification, which involves incorporating game features into non-game environments, has emerged as a potential strategy for promoting behavior change in various domains. This study aimed to examine the relationship between gamification elements, self-determination theory (SDT)-based motivational constructs, and motivation for energy-saving behaviors. Specifically, it investigated the impact of six game elements (personal profile, non-fixed structure, feedback, challenges, competition, and social network) on individuals' motivation towards energy-saving behaviors. An experiment with a simulated game and questionnaire was conducted at Tsinghua University with 40 participants. The measurement data were analyzed using factor analysis and multiple regression analysis. Using a novel combination of simulated games and questionnaires, the study assessed the impact of different game elements on energy consumption. The study revealed a substantial reduction of 49% in overall energy usage compared to the baseline, indicating the effectiveness of gamification in promoting energy-saving behaviors. Additionally, the findings also underscored the practical application of gamification elements for energy conservation, emphasizing the importance of incorporating challenges, feedback, and social network to satisfy psychological needs and enhance motivation in designing impactful interventions.

Keywords: Gamification · Self-Determination Theory (SDT) · Energy conservation · Game elements

1 Introduction

The use of game design and game components has a long history in human-computer interaction [1, 2]. Gamification is defined as the use of game design elements in non-game contexts [3]. An aspect of gamification is the use of motivating affordances to encourage specific behaviors [4]. Positive motivation is at the heart of gamification, with an emphasis on exploiting the game's inherent features to elicit an emotional reaction from the player. The success of applying gamification strategies has paved the way for empirical research into the effect of gamification on altering users' perceptions of gamified items and potential motivational elements for behavior changes in a variety of situations involving diverse applications and designs.

© The Author(s), under exclusive license to Springer Nature Switzerland AG 2024
P.-L. P. Rau (Ed.): HCII 2024, LNCS 14699, pp. 147–160, 2024.
https://doi.org/10.1007/978-3-031-60898-8_10

Energy conservation is a major and urgent problem in today's society. In an age of unprecedented population increase and excessive consumption, the emission-intensive energy production that causes anthropogenic climate change is a serious global challenge [5]. Emerging countries' expanding energy-hungry middle classes and diminishing natural resources exacerbate the intensity of the dilemma. The increased cost of living is a direct result of scarcity and the pressing need to conserve and reduce energy use. Since 1990, both residential $CO2$ emissions and overall home energy use have been on the rise, making households a prime demographic to target [6]. Although human behavior and the factors that influence it have a significant impact on energy consumption, there has been mixed success in attempts to modify people's behaviors.

Motivating individuals to adopt energy-saving behaviors is a critical aspect of promoting sustainability and addressing environmental concerns [7]. Both intrinsic and extrinsic motivation variables might contribute to the lack of desire to participate in energy-saving actions [8]. While some individuals are intrinsically motivated by their values and beliefs, others may require external incentives, rewards, or social influences to stimulate their motivation. A combination of both intrinsic and extrinsic motivation strategies can be employed to effectively motivate individuals to adopt and sustain energy-saving behaviors.

The utilization of gamification presents a promising approach that harnesses the power of motivation and self-reflection [9]. This aligns with the principles of the Self-Determination Theory (SDT), a psychological framework that delves into human motivation and the factors that drive people to participate in specific actions. Incorporating the principles of Self-Determination Theory (SDT) in designing gamified interventions for energy conservation provides a strong rationale for enhancing motivation and promoting sustainable behavior change. This research has important theoretical implications as it provides empirical evidence for the application of Self-Determination Theory (SDT) in the domain of energy conservation behavior.

2 Literature Review

2.1 Gamification and Behavior Change

Gamification is a powerful approach that capitalizes on the principles of game design to enhance user engagement, motivation, and behavior change [3]. By incorporating game elements and mechanics into non-game contexts, it transforms mundane tasks into enjoyable experiences, driving individuals towards desired behaviors.

The appeal of gamification lies in its ability to leverage elements like challenges, rewards, competition, and storytelling, which are inherent to games and capture individuals' interest and attention. In the realm of behavior change interventions, gamification proves to be a valuable tool, utilizing game-like elements to influence and promote positive behaviors [10]. It draws upon psychological mechanisms such as positive reinforcement, goal-setting, feedback, and social influence to motivate individuals toward behavior change [11]. Through elements like points, badges, levels, leaderboards, and virtual rewards, gamification provides immediate feedback and tangible rewards, reinforcing desired behaviors and boosting individuals' motivation and engagement. The social aspect of gamification, which may involve collaborative gameplay or sharing achievements with others, taps into social influence and social norms, further amplifying the potential for behavior change [12].

2.2 Energy-Saving Behaviors and Motivation

Energy-saving behaviors refer to conscious actions taken by individuals to reduce their energy consumption and promote sustainable energy practices [13, 14]. These behaviors play a crucial role in addressing environmental challenges and achieving long-term sustainability. By conserving energy, individuals can contribute to the reduction of greenhouse gas emissions, mitigate climate change, and preserve valuable natural resources. Understanding the factors that motivate individuals to engage in energy-saving behaviors is therefore of paramount importance in promoting environmental sustainability.

Self-determination theory (SDT) is a psychological framework that emphasizes intrinsic motivation and the fulfillment of basic psychological needs as key drivers of behavior [15]. SDT posits that individuals are motivated when their three basic psychological needs are satisfied: autonomy (the desire for choice and control), competence (the need to feel capable and effective), and relatedness (the need for social connection and belongingness) [16]. In the context of energy-saving behaviors, SDT provides a valuable lens to understand the underlying motivations and psychological processes that influence individuals' engagement in sustainable energy practices. Several studies have examined the motivational aspects of energy-saving behaviors, with a particular focus on the three basic psychological needs outlined by SDT: autonomy, competence, and relatedness.

2.3 Gamification in the Domain of Energy

The conservation of energy is a critical global issue due to the continued reliance on fossil fuels and the resulting impact on climate change [17]. Households, as significant energy consumers, are a key target group for intervention [18]. While behavioral change is crucial for reducing energy usage, previous efforts have shown mixed results. Gamification has emerged as a promising tool to motivate and educate individuals about energy consumption and related concerns. Several studies have explored the application of gamification in the energy-saving domain, providing valuable insights into its effectiveness and potential. Geelen et al. [19] introduced a game-based intervention among student households, which featured direct feedback, an online platform, team rankings, and a game interface. The results showed significant enhancement in motivation to save energy, with average savings of 24%. Moreover, Orland et al. [20] conducted a study using a virtual pet game called "Energy Chickens" in a mid-size commercial office setting. The results showed a significant decrease in energy consumption, with an average reduction of 13%. Participants reported increased energy consciousness, highlighting the efficacy of gamified interventions for plug-load energy conservation in commercial offices.

Although the game-based intervention among student-households demonstrated increased awareness, positive attitudes, and motivation to save energy, it is essential to examine the long-term sustainability of behavior change and the extent to which these game behaviors translate into lasting habits. Additionally, while studies like Orland et al. [20] have shown significant reductions in energy consumption through gamified interventions, it is necessary to investigate the scalability and applicability of these findings across different settings and populations. Therefore, further research is needed to critically assess the effectiveness of specific game elements, scalability, and long-term impact of gamification in stimulating energy savings and fostering sustainable behavior change.

3 Research Framework and Hypotheses

3.1 Theoretical Framework

Aparicio et al. [21] presented a selection of game elements that match the objective and satisfy the needs of human motivation based on the SDT is an effective framework of gamification. In recent years Wee and Chong [22] adopted this framework and proposed a categorization of nine core game elements into the three categories of SDT to predict the usefulness of these elements in boosting the intrinsic motivation of users to engage in energy-saving behavior in an energy campaign. The chosen game design elements that enhance players' satisfaction with autonomy, competence, and relatedness needs were all validated by the study results. However, as of yet, this framework has not been tested for its relationship with decreasing users' energy consumption with measurements. To fill the gap, this research introduces a suitable framework that integrates established measurements and objective metrics in data collecting to increase the validity and dependability. The model for the proposed gamified energy system is depicted in Fig. 1.

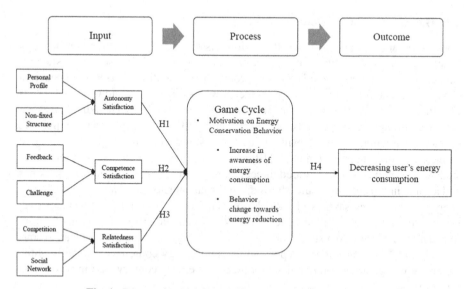

Fig. 1. Proposed model for gamified energy conserving system

The model is divided into three stages: input, process, and outcome. Personal profiles, non-fixed structures, feedback, challenges, competition, and social network, were selected to initiate a game cycle that includes judgments, knowledge of energy consumption, and actions toward energy reduction. Throughout the process, users are expected to be intrinsic and extrinsically motivated by the satisfaction of the three psychological needs, which leads them to translate motivation into energy-conserving actions. As a result, the consequence of using the system would encourage users to reduce their energy consumption.

This study's purpose is to evaluate the efficacy of gamification components in encouraging energy-saving behaviors in a simulated environment. The specific objective is to investigate the relationships between gamification elements based on self-determination theory (SDT) and users' motivation in energy-saving behaviors. The following research questions are presented to guide the study:

1. How can self-determination theory (SDT)-aligned gamification elements affect the motivation of individuals to engage in energy-saving behaviors?
2. What effect do gamification elements have on individuals' energy-saving behaviors and consumption?

3.2 Hypotheses

The following are proposed using SDT as the theoretical framework and taking into account the aforementioned literature:

- H1: Motivation for energy-saving activities is positively associated to satisfaction with autonomy needs.
- H2: Motivation for energy-saving activities is positively associated to satisfaction with competence needs.
- H3: Motivation for energy-saving activities is positively associated to satisfaction with relatedness needs.
- H4: The motivation on energy-reducing behaviors has a positive effect on decreasing energy consumption.

Motivation for energy conservation practices includes boosting energy consumption awareness and pushing behavior change toward energy reduction. Increasing environmental awareness entails several steps, including identifying specific energy-saving actions, acquiring knowledge, developing a deeper understanding of environmental and energy-related issues, learning about electrical appliances explicitly, and comprehending energy consumption patterns. Users may improve their energy awareness and knowledge by using a gamification-based energy conservation system. This may be accomplished by offering real-time insights into their energy use and allowing comparisons with typical energy demand for comparable equipment. Such interactive elements help users understand their energy consumption and promote a feeling of responsibility toward energy saving.

4 Methodology

4.1 Experiment Design

The Sims 4 was utilized as the experiment game, due to its inherent suitability for testing the desired game elements in this study. It is a well-known life simulation computer game that Maxis created and Electronic Arts distributed. Sims are virtual characters that may be created and controlled by users to be guided through many areas of their life, such as relationships, careers, and everyday activities. The Sims 4 offers a rich virtual environment that allows for the simulation of various aspects of daily life, including household management and resource consumption. By leveraging the existing features and mechanics of The Sims 4, the research objectives can still be effectively addressed. The game provides a platform that contains the six core game elements summarized in Table 1.

Table 1. Game Element details of The Sims 4

Game Element	Elaboration
Personal Profiles	Allow players to create and customize unique characters with distinct personalities, appearances, and aspirations
Non-fixed structure	Players are free to explore and shape their virtual home in the world according to their preferences
Challenge	Players have to manage their characters' needs, relationships, and aspirations etc
Feedback	Feedback mechanisms, such as meters and indicators, inform players about their characters' well-being, satisfaction, and progress
Social network	Interact and form relationships with other virtual characters in the game and engage in social interactions in a group chat for discussion with other players
Competition	Competition is introduced in the form of career progression, achieving goals, and building successful virtual lives. In addition, all participants are ranked by their energy usage for each round of the experiment for competition

The Sims 4 offers a utility bill for the controlled sim's household every game week. In The Sims 4, utility bills are simulated expenses that players' virtual households incur for the consumption of various resources, such as water, and electricity. These utility bills reflect the in-game usage of these resources by the Sims and their households.

Utility bills in The Sims 4 serve as a financial mechanism within the game, encouraging players to consider the resource consumption habits of their virtual households. This simulates the real-life costs associated with resource usage and provides a means for players to understand and manage their Sims' household expenses.

4.2 Experiment Tasks

The experiment design for this study involves two rounds of gameplay in The Sims 4, to examine the impact of energy-saving behaviors on utility bills in the game. The experiment is conducted with a group of participants who have signed a consent form and provided their personal information, including their name, and student ID.

In the first round, participants are introduced to the game and its basic controls. They are guided through the process of creating their Sims characters, with instructions to select young adults and personalize their characters based on their characteristics. Participants then enter the game and select a specific house to move in. During the first round of gameplay, participants are instructed to play for one game week, making decisions for their sims, taking care of their sims' needs, and managing their households. They are specifically asked to mirror their daily routine in real life and make every decision for their sim's actions. Participants' utility bills were recorded at the end of the first-round experiment as a baseline measurement of their energy consumption.

After the first round of the game, participants are put together into a group chat for further communication. The energy usage ranking from the first round is shared with the participants, and they are informed about the energy-saving goal for the next round of the experiment. Participants are then asked to share their thoughts on energy-saving strategies within the game in the group chat. Suggestions include turning off lights when not in use, removing non-essential appliances in build mode, or upgrading to higher-rated appliances.

For the second round of the experiment, participants resume the game from where they left off in the first round and continue playing for another game week. They are reminded of the energy-saving goal and provided instructions on how to check their energy usage throughout the week.

Before the end of the second round, the participants' utility bills were recorded once again. This enables a direct evaluation of any changes in energy usage induced during gameplay. The players are then requested to complete a post-experiment questionnaire.

4.3 Measurements

During each round of the experiment, the resulting utility bills of each player were recorded to measure the energy consumption of the simulated households. The utility bills served as an indicator of the energy usage within the game and provided valuable insights into the players' virtual energy consumption behavior. Changes in energy use were noted and the impact of energy-saving methods taken by the participants was determined by examining the utility bills throughout two rounds of the experiment. Since majority of the players were observed to perform energy-saving behavior, we denote positive changes as energy-saving. A higher value indicated greater amount of energy being conserved in the game.

The post-experiment questionnaire was divided into five sections. Section A consisted of demographic information and game experience. Section B measured satisfaction with autonomy (H1) included 3 items on personal profile and 4 items on non-fixed structure. Section C measured satisfaction with relatedness (H2) included 7 items on challenge and 3 items on feedback. Section D measured satisfaction on competence

(H3) included 5 items on competition and 3 items on social network. Section E consisted 7 items measuring motivation on energy saving behaviors. The assessment items used in this study were modified and adapted from a previous study by Wee & Choong [22].

5 Results

5.1 Participants' Profile

A total of 43 students from Tsinghua University were recruited to attend as the participants of the experiment. Recruitment was conducted through messages sent in WeChat groups consisting of Tsinghua University students. Of the 43 students recruited, 40 ultimately participated in both rounds of the experiment. The sample consisted of 22 male (55%) and 18 female (45%) participants. 52.5% were postgraduate students, while 47.5% were undergraduates. The sample was primarily composed of mostly local students (87.5%), with only 12.5% being foreign students. The mean age of the participants was 22.8 years, with a standard deviation of 3.006.

5.2 Model Evaluation

Confirmatory Factor Analysis. Since the questionnaire items were adopted from previous study, confirmatory factor analysis was performed to ensure that the items accurately reflected the measurements in this study. Based on the results, we deleted items with a factor loading of below 0.5, which included Ppro2, Ppro3, Ch2, Ch6, and Fb3. There were only three items in personal profile while two had to be deleted, we found it unfit to only use one item to measure this factor, therefore we decided to remove the entire factor, which left us with only non-fixed structure under the autonomy scale. It could be due to the irrelevance of personal profile in affecting energy conservation actions and the final utility bills.

Internal Consistency. After deleting the items, internal consistency was tested using the Cronbach's alpha coefficient. A value of above 0.7 showed good internal consistency for each factor and satisfaction scale. The reliability coefficients for all four sections of the questionnaire were found to be acceptable. Non-fixed structure ($\alpha = 0.805$), challenge ($\alpha = 0.840$), feedback ($\alpha = 0.817$), competition ($\alpha = 0.873$), and social network ($\alpha = 0.825$) were all well above 0.8. The coefficient for section B (Autonomy Satisfaction) was $\alpha = 0.805$, for section C (Competence Satisfaction) it was $\alpha = 0.845$, for section D (Relatedness Satisfaction) it was $\alpha = 0.882$, and for section E (Motivation) it was $\alpha = 0.896$.

Regression Model. The data passed the normality test ($p > 0.05$) and a multiple regression analysis was conducted on the five game elements and the motivation on energy conservation behaviors. The model is statistically significant ($F(5,34) = 7.717, p < 0.001$) with an adjusted R Square value of 0.463. Table 2 showed the detailed multiple regression analysis. Challenge ($t = 2.35, p = 0.025$), feedback ($t = 2.50, p = 0.017$), and social network ($t = 2.46, p = 0.019$) were all statistically significant, indicating a strong positive relationship between satisfaction of these three factors with motivation for energy conservation behaviors. This also indicated that competence needs have a strong positive relationship with motivation, as both challenge and feedback fall under this scale, supporting hypothesis 2. In contrast, non-fixed structure under autonomy satisfaction and competition under relatedness satisfaction, although not statistically significant, were found to be inversely related to motivation. As such, hypothesis 1 was not supported, while hypothesis 3 was partially supported

Table 2. Multiple regression analysis

Coefficients:	Beta	Std. Error	t	p
(Intercept)	0.983	0.569	1.73	0.093
Non-fixed structure	−0.205	0.140	−1.47	0.152
Challenge	0.421	0.180	2.35	**0.025***
Feedback	0.254	0.102	2.50	**0.017***
Competition	−0.162	0.127	−1.28	0.209
Social network	0.379	0.154	2.46	**0.019***

5.3 Energy-Reducing Behavioral Results

Hypothesis 4 examined the positive influence of motivation for energy-reducing behaviors on decreasing energy consumption in the game environment. Means and standard deviations of the utility bills before and after informing participants on the goal were recorded in Table 3. Utility bill before is indicative of the user's baseline energy consumption. Baseline data was found to be normal ($p > 0.05$) whereas utility bills after did not pass normality ($p < 0.05$), we assumed normality and used paired t test for comparing means between these two groups.

Table 3. Descriptive statistics of measured energy consumption

	Mean	SD
Utility bills before	148	35
Utility bills after	75	47

Based on the paired t test, the utility bills after significantly lowered ($t = 8.58$, $p < 0.001$) when participants were told to conserve energy. With the exception of three participants who had higher utility bills after, the remaining participants all demonstrated energy conservation behavior. On average, the amount saved is 73 with a standard deviation of 54. The findings revealed a significant reduction in overall energy consumption, with a 49% decrease from baseline, indicating the efficacy of the gamification intervention.

5.4 Correlation Test

Pearson's correlation test was conducted on the three psychological needs and motivation with actual behavioral changes observed in the game. From Table 4, autonomy ($t = 2.21$, $p = 0.03$, corr $= 0.34$) and competence ($t = 2.24$, $p = 0.03$, corr $= 0.34$) were shown to have a low positive correlation with the behavioral changes. As with regards to the self-reported motivation scale, competence ($t = 5.38$, $p < 0.001$, corr $= 0.65$) had a high positive correlation, while relatedness ($t = 2.37$, $p = 0.02$, corr $= 0.36$) had a low positive correlation.

Table 4. Pearson's correlation test

	t	p	Cor
Psychological needs with behavioral data			
Autonomy	2.21	**0.03***	0.34
Competence	2.24	**0.03***	0.34
Relatedness	0.52	0.60	0.08
Motivation	1.19	0.24	0.19
Psychological needs with motivation			
Autonomy	1.36	0.18	0.22
Competence	5.28	**< 0.001***	0.65
Relatedness	2.37	**0.02**	0.36

The difference in result of significant scales indicated that self-reported values may not be representative of how an individual would actually perform in real life. Non-fixed structure under autonomy gave players the freedom to navigate around in the game, which caused them to behave differently, although they may not feel that it is this flexibility that shaped their behavior. Competition and social network under relatedness were more actively experienced by the participants, which spurred their motivation to react differently in and out of the game.

6 Discussion and Conclusion

6.1 Discussion

The findings of this study are partially in line with the results of a previous study by Wee and Choong [22], which suggested that gamification is an effective way to increase university students' motivation for energy-saving behaviors. The results showed that satisfaction with competence needs had a significant positive effect on users' motivation for energy conservation behavior, which is consistent with this research. However, in contrast to previous studies, this study did not find a significant relationship between satisfaction with autonomy, and only partial relevance to relatedness needs, on users' motivation to conserve energy. While Wee and Choong [22] focused on the effect of game elements before implementing a gamified energy-saving campaign, this study contributes to the literature by incorporating a simulation game to measure the actual energy consumption of motivated users. These findings suggest that incorporating actual experiments to measure energy consumption data could result in different conclusions compared to relying solely on questionnaires.

A notable finding emerged regarding three participants who exhibited a significant decrease in utility during the second round of the experiment compared to the first round. Interestingly, these participants actively embraced energy-saving practices by opting for more energy-efficient appliances and implementing various conservation actions. Their conscientious efforts included actions such as consistently turning off lights, reducing cooking activities and minimizing computer usage. This substantial reduction in utility among these participants reflects the positive impact of their behavioral changes on energy consumption. Their proactive approach toward adopting energy-efficient appliances and engaging in energy-saving behaviors demonstrates a promising trend in achieving sustainable energy practices. Specifically, participants diligently replaced their outdated appliances with energy-efficient alternatives, contributing to a more environmentally conscious lifestyle. These findings provide valuable insights into the effectiveness of gamification strategies and the integration of Self-Determination Theory in motivating individuals to adopt energy-saving behaviors.

The theoretical implications of this research include providing empirical evidence for the application of Self-Determination Theory (SDT) in the context of energy conservation behavior. This highlights the relevance and utility of SDT in understanding the motivational factors that influence behavior in various domains. Additionally, this research presented a novel research design that combines a simulation game and questionnaire to measure the relationship between three psychological needs based on the SDT and energy conservation behavior. By incorporating actual consumption data this study avoided the desirability bias of using self-report data only.

The practical implications of this study are significant for researchers and developers in the field of energy conservation and sustainability. The findings suggest that when designing gamified energy saving systems, it is crucial to carefully consider design factors such as game elements, goals, and game mechanics to satisfy players' three basic needs based on the SDT. Implementing game design elements that promote users' sense of competence to motivate energy-saving behaviors could be effective in fostering energy conservation behavior among users. Therefore, greater emphasis of future developers should be placed on designing game elements specifically on challenge, feedback, and social network to push for greater motivation in energy conservation behaviors.

6.2 Limitations and Future Recommendations

Although the study showed promising results, there were limitations. The sample size of the experiment was small, with only 40 valid responses on the questionnaire and experimental measurements. The small sample size might have affected the experiment's statistical significance, which could explain why two of the hypotheses were not supported. In this study, only six game elements were selected based on the framework developed in Aparicio et al. [21] to meet the environment of the selected simulation game. Other game elements could potentially be a good fit for increasing the three psychological needs satisfaction. In the future, when designing an energy-conserving game system, it is recommended to explore the effect of more game elements on satisfying the three psychological needs. Another limitation was the experiment was conducted in the simulation game "The Sims 4", as a well-developed role-playing game, the game includes many other unnecessary features that could distract or affect the players. In the future, it is recommended to conduct actual measurements of users' energy consumption in real-life using a well-developed serious game and to observe the long-term effect of such a system on users' changes in lifestyle and habits.

6.3   Conclusion

Recognizing a gap in the existing research, this study adopted a unique research design that incorporated both a simulation game and a comprehensive questionnaire. By employing this innovative approach, this study examined the influence of six-game elements (personal profile, non-fixed structure, feedback, challenges, competition, and social network) in enhancing the motivation of individuals on energy-saving behaviors. Out of which, only five elements were used in the final data analysis, with challenge, feedback, and social network found to positively impact the fulfillment of the basic psychological needs specified by SDT. Additionally, the results demonstrated a substantial reduction of 49% in overall energy usage compared to the baseline, indicating the effectiveness of gamification in promoting energy-saving behaviors. This highlights the significance of addressing users' competence needs and an emphasis on social network when designing effective interventions to promote energy-saving behaviors. By understanding the effects of gamification elements on motivation, policymakers, designers, and researchers can develop effective interventions to promote sustainable energy consumption practices.

Disclosure of Interests. The authors do not have conflict of interest.

References

1. Jensen, R. H., Strengers, Y., Kjeldskov, J., Nicholls, L., Skov, M. B.: Designing the desirable smart home: a study of household experiences and energy consumption impacts (2018). Paper No. 4. https://doi.org/10.1145/3173574.3173578
2. Schaffer, O., Fang, X.: Digital game enjoyment: a literature review. In: Fang, X. (ed.) HCI in Games: First International Conference, HCI-Games 2019, Held as Part of the 21st HCI International Conference, HCII 2019, Orlando, FL, USA, July 26–31, pp. 191–214. Springer, Cham (2019). https://doi.org/10.1007/978-3-030-22602-2_16
3. Deterding, S., Dixon, D., Khaled, R., Nacke, L.: From game design elements to gamefulness: defining gamification. In: Proceedings of the 15th International Academic MindTrek Conference: Envisioning Future Media Environments, pp. 9–15. (2011). https://doi.org/10.1145/2181037.2181040
4. Hamari, J., Koivisto, J., Sarsa, H.: Does gamification work? – a literature review of empirical studies on gamification. In: 2014 47th Hawaii International Conference on System Sciences, pp. 3025–3034 (2014). https://doi.org/10.1109/HICSS.2014.377

5. Albertarelli, S., et al.: A survey on the design of gamified systems for energy and water sustainability. Games **9**(3), 38 (2018). https://doi.org/10.3390/g9030038
6. Nejat, P., Jomehzadeh, F., Taheri, M.M., Gohari, M., Abd Majid, M.Z.: A global review of energy consumption, CO2 emissions and policy in the residential sector (with an overview of the top ten CO2 emitting countries). Renew. Sustain. Energy Rev. **43**, 843–862 (2015). https://doi.org/10.1016/j.rser.2014.11.066
7. Carrus, G., et al.: Psychological predictors of energy saving behavior: a meta-analytic approach. Front. Psychol. **12**, 648221 (2021). https://doi.org/10.3389/fpsyg.2021.648221
8. Sweeney, J.C., Webb, D., Mazzarol, T., Soutar, G.N.: Self-determination theory and word of mouth about energy-saving behaviors: an online experiment. J. Psychol. Mark. **31**, 698–716 (2014). https://doi.org/10.1002/mar.20729
9. Morganti, L., Pallavicini, F., Cadel, E., Candelieri, A., Archetti, F., Mantovani, F.: Gaming for earth: serious games and gamification to engage consumers in pro-environmental behaviours for energy efficiency. Energy Res. Soc. Sci. **29**, 95–102 (2017). https://doi.org/10.1016/j.erss.2017.05.001
10. Dichev, C., Dicheva, D.: Gamifying education: what is known, what is believed and what remains uncertain: a critical review. Int. J. Educ. Technol. High. Educ. **14**(1), 9 (2017). https://doi.org/10.1186/s41239-017-0042-5
11. Krath, J., Schürmann, L., von Korflesch, H.F.O.: Revealing the theoretical basis of gamification: a systematic review and analysis of theory in research on gamification, serious games and game-based learning. Comput. Hum. Behav. **125**, 106963 (2021). https://doi.org/10.1016/j.chb.2021.106963
12. Hamari, J., Koivisto, J.: Social motivations to use gamification: an empirical study of gamifying exercise. In: ECIS 2013 Proceedings of the 21st European Conference on Information Systems (2013)
13. Zhang, C.Y., Yu, B., Wang, J.W., Wei, Y.M.: Impact factors of household energy-saving behavior: an empirical study of Shandong Province in China. J. Clean. Prod. **185**, 285–298 (2018). https://doi.org/10.1016/j.jclepro.2018.02.303
14. Hong, J., She, Y., Wang, S., Dora, M.: Impact of psychological factors on energy-saving behavior: moderating role of government subsidy policy. J. Clean. Prod. **232**, 154–162 (2019). https://doi.org/10.1016/j.jclepro.2019.05.321
15. Ryan, R.M.: The Oxford Handbook of Self-Determination Theory. Oxford University Press, Oxford (2023)
16. Ryan, R.M., Deci, E.L.: Intrinsic and extrinsic motivation from a self-determination theory perspective: definitions, theory, practices, and future directions. Contemp. Educ. Psychol. **61**, 101860 (2020). https://doi.org/10.1016/j.cedpsych.2020.101860
17. Höök, M., Tang, X.: Depletion of fossil fuels and anthropogenic climate change-a review. Energy Policy **52**, 797–809 (2013). https://doi.org/10.1016/j.enpol.2012.10.046
18. Johnson, D., Horton, E., Mulcahy, R., Foth, M.: Gamification and serious games within the domain of domestic energy consumption: a systematic review. Renew. Sustain. Energy Rev. **73**, 249–264 (2017). https://doi.org/10.1016/j.rser.2017.01.134
19. Geelen, D., Keyson, D., Boess, S., Brezet, H.: Exploring the use of a game to stimulate energy saving in households. J. Des. Res. **10**, 102–120 (2012). https://doi.org/10.1504/JDR.2012.046096
20. Orland, B., Ram, N., Lang, D., Houser, K., Kling, N., Coccia, M.: Saving energy in an office environment: a serious game intervention. Energy Build. **74**, 43–52 (2014). https://doi.org/10.1016/j.enbuild.2014.01.036

21. Aparicio, A., Francisco Luis, Gutiérrez Vela, José Luis González, Sánchez: Analysis and application of gamification. In: Proceedings of the 13th International Conference on Interacción Persona-Ordenador (2012). https://dl.acm.org/doi/abs/10.1145/2379636.237 9653

22. Wee, S.-C., Choong, W.-W.: Gamification: predicting the effectiveness of variety game design elements to intrinsically motivate users' energy conservation behaviour. J. Environ. Manage.iron. Manage. **233**, 97–106 (2019). https://doi.org/10.1016/j.jenvman.2018.11.127

The Impact of Color-Touch Cross-Modal Correspondence on the Temporal Integration of Multimodal Information

Tianyi Yuan◉ and Pei-Luen Patrick Rau(✉) ◉

Department of Industrial Engineering, Tsinghua University, Beijing 100084, China
rp1@tsinghua.edu.cn

Abstract. Based on the previous outcomes [1], the study utilized a laboratory experiment including 30 participants to explore the impact of color-touch cross-modal correspondence on the temporal integration of multimodal information. This experiment adopted an intra-group design, and all participants were required to complete a series of multimodal perception tasks and stimulation level judgment tasks in the same environment. In each trial, a vibration stimulus, and a color stimulus, each lasting 100 ms would appear. There might be a stimulus onset asynchrony (SOA) between two stimuli. After the stimuli combination, participants had to finish a temporal judgment task to determine the order in which two stimuli appeared. The independent variables of this experiment were stimuli combination type and SOA. Among them, the stimuli combination type is also tied with color chroma level (2 levels, high or low), vibration amplitude level (2 levels, high or low), and cross-modal correspondence (2 levels, high or low). There were two dependent variables in the experiment to evaluate the judgment process, namely accuracy and reaction time. As for results, firstly, cross-modal correspondence had no significant impact on temporal judgment. Besides, other independent variables (SOA, stimuli combinations, vibration amplitude levels, color chroma levels and the sequence of stimuli) had some impacts on accuracy and reaction time (RT). Although the experiment did not discover the relationship between color-touch cross-modal correspondence and temporal integration of multimodal information, further research could adjust the experimental design based on this to further explore related fields.

Keywords: Multimodal Perception · Cross-Modal Correspondence · Time Perception

1 Introduction

1.1 Significance

Multimodal information bombardment is pervasive, and the redundant and complex information may increase an individual's cognitive load. Many studies have shown consistent correspondence between stimulus features in different sensory modes. For example, people always associate louder sounds with brighter objects [2], and this mapping

P.-L. P. Rau (Ed.): HCII 2024, LNCS 14699, pp. 161–177, 2024.
https://doi.org/10.1007/978-3-031-60898-8_11

relationship is defined as cross-modal correspondence. In traditional research methods, research on multimodal perception only focuses on the role played by spatiotemporal factors. Considering that academia has generally accepted the existence of cross-modal correspondence at present, it is not comprehensive to explore the multimodal integration process from the perspective of time, space, and other environmental factors, and the correspondence relationship between each single mode may also have a significant impact on multimodal spatiotemporal integration. Therefore, we should incorporate the correspondence between cross-modal correspondence into the research process of multimodal spatiotemporal integration, and conduct research and exploration on it. By utilizing the relevant achievements of cross-modal correspondence, we can help general users reduce cognitive load, improve the efficiency of information processing, and thereby enhance individual efficiency and comfort.

The previous human-computer interaction interface mainly focused on the output of sound and vision. In future multimodal interfaces, more types of information will enhance the user experience from different perspectives. People have begun to attach importance to the multimodal user experience, by matching color and vibration in the interaction system. This study contributes to recommendations for multimodal interface design, promoting multimodal perception integration, avoiding the confusion of similar stimuli in time and space, improving the information processing efficiency of target modalities, and guiding the allocation of attentional resources.

1.2 Theoretical Background

Cross-modal Perception. Cross-modal perception refers to the perception process in which humans use two or more different sensory modalities, and there are interactive relationships between each modality [3]. So far, researchers still tend to believe that in multimodal perception, each sensory channel maintains relative independence, but at the same time, some factors influence each other. The definition of cross-modal perception is relatively broad, and in a broad sense, cross-modal perception even includes synesthesia. Multimodal information presentation can provide users with more information presentation paths during the interaction process, which helps to establish a more comprehensive information presentation system. Having more effective modal channels can enable the system to provide users with stronger accessibility. When certain modal channels cannot be perceived normally, other modal channels can serve as backup communication methods [4].

Cross-modal Correspondence. Cross-modal correspondence can generally be defined as non-random associations of cross-modal sensations [5]. Numerous studies have shown that, apart from some special cross-modal correspondence, perceptual mapping between different modalities is more common in the general population. Most cognitive neuroscience research on multisensory perception is attempting to understand cross-modal mechanisms, model them theoretically [6], and investigate the spatiotemporal factors of multisensory channel integration [7]. In a broad sense, the more different forms of stimuli can appear simultaneously, the more likely cross-modal perceptual integration is to occur [8].

Color-touch Cross-modal Correspondence. Although there have been many studies on the relationship between color vision and other sensory perceptions [9–12], only a few have explored the cross-modal correspondence between color vision and touch. In related research, tactile feedback is generally presented in the form of simulating touch or simulating vibration, making the tactile experience of the participants controllable while maintaining authenticity. Martino and Marks studied the systematic correspondence between visual brightness (black and white) and vibration frequency [13]. Ludwig and Simner also explored the non-random cross-modal correspondence relationship between color and tactile stimuli [14]. In addition, in a study by Elliot and Arts, participants were required to manually pinch open a small metal clip after seeing red, blue, or gray paper. The results showed that participants who saw red had the highest average force and speed when pinching things, indicating that red perception may be closely related to stronger force perception [15]. Another study by Kahol et al. showed that color perception through tactile feedback can assist visually impaired patients. After encoding a specific color using tactile feedback, participants were able to reproduce the approximate area and range of a specific color using only tactile feedback [16]. A study by Delazio et al. showed a significant positive correlation between color concentration (chrome) and vibration amplitude [17]. Slobodenyuk et al. investigated the cross-modal correspondence between touch and color. Participants need to use colors to describe simulated tactile stimuli of different frequencies and intensities [18]. After analyzing hue, saturation, and brightness, it was found that under the strongest tactile stimulation, the selected hue features of the participants tended to be red, purple, and blue spectra; Under the weakest tactile stimulation, the color scheme chosen by the participants tends to be yellow and green spectra [18]. Based on these studies, our previous study once again demonstrated a strong correspondence between color perception and vibration perception. At the same time, this correspondence will affect the accuracy and reaction time of single mode judgment in multimodal perception [1]. Except for it, there is limited research on the impact of color-touch cross-modal correspondence. It is expected that in this experiment, the influence of cross-modal correspondence of visual touch perception on various factors in multimodal temporal integration would be explored.

1.3 Related Temporal Concepts

This section provides a description of 3 different temporal indicators (simple reaction time, temporal order judgment, and stimulus onset asynchrony).

Simple Reaction Time (RT). Since the beginning of time dimension research in psychology, simple reaction time (RT) has always been the simplest and most popular method. In specific tasks, participants need to press the button as soon as they receive the stimulus. We refer to the time difference between the stimulus appearing and the button being pressed as simple reaction time. The simple reaction time decreases with the increase of stimulus intensity [19] and cross-modal correspondence [1].

Temporal Order Judgment (TOJ). Time perception can be evaluated through temporal order judgment (TOJ) tasks [20]. Researchers present two types of stimuli with different properties (such as vibration and color) using different stimulus intervals, and the task of participants is to indicate which stimulus appears first.

Stimulus Onset Asynchrony (SOA). Stimulus onset asynchrony (SOA) is a time measurement method used in experimental psychology, which represents the length of time between the start of one stimulus S1 and the start of another stimulus S2. The definition of stimulation is relatively broad and can include information from various modalities such as images, sounds, words, vibrations, etc. The short time interval between S1 and S2 may lead to the interaction of information processing between these two different modalities, so we need to explore the subjective time perception of the human body under different time asynchronies [21].

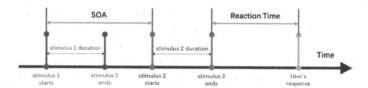

Fig. 1. Stimuli, SOA and RT

2 Research Framework

In previous studies, the existence of cross-modal correspondence in color tactile perception has been explored. Among them, the cross-modal correspondence between color chroma and vibration amplitude is the most common [1]. In the following text, "cross-modal correspondence" specifically refers to "cross-modal correspondence between color chrome and vibration amplitude.". The study aims to explore the impact of color tactile cross-modal correspondence and other factors on the accuracy of temporal judgment and RT in multimodal time integration perception. To study the issue, several hypotheses are listed as follow:

H1A. In multimodal perception of color and touch, cross-modal correspondence would have a significant negative impact on the accuracy of temporal judgment tasks. That is, color-vibration stimuli combinations with strong cross-modal correspondence can hinder participants from accurately judging the order in which stimuli appear first.

H1B. In multimodal perception of color and touch, other variables (SOA, ABS, stimuli combination type, stimuli sequence, vibration amplitude level and color chroma level) would have the impact on the accuracy of temporal judgment tasks.

H2A. In multimodal perception of color and touch, cross-modal correspondence would have a significant negative impact on the RT of temporal judgment tasks. That is, color-vibration stimuli combinations with strong cross-modal correspondence can hinder participants from rapidly judging the order in which stimuli appear first.

H2B. In multimodal perception of color and touch, other variables (SOA, ABS, stimuli combination type, stimuli sequence, vibration amplitude level and color chroma level) would have the impact on the RT of temporal judgment tasks.

The current related research is still in a blank stage, and the series of hypotheses are entirely based on deductive reasoning. We speculate that in multimodal perception, stimuli with high cross-modal correspondence are more likely to generate coupling, and multiple stimuli are more likely to generate associations in cognition, making it more difficult for participants to distinguish them.

3 Methods

3.1 Participants

G * Power was used to calculate the number of participants. Under the condition of one-way ANOVA, the effect size is taken as $f = 0.7$, and the confidence level is taken as $\alpha = 0.05$, and the statistical power is taken as $(1-\beta) = 0.8$, with a level of 4. The total sample size was 28, requiring at least 28 participants.

In the formal experiment, a total of 30 students from Tsinghua University participated in the experiment. All 30 individuals had no color perception disorders such as color blindness or color weakness, and their vision or corrected vision were normal without any tactile damage. Their naked or corrected vision was 4.8 or above. There are 14 male participants and 16 female participants in the test group, with an average age of 22.23 years. All participants had not participated in any other cross-modal correspondence experiments before the experiment and did not have any relevant knowledge background. After completing the experiment, each participant received a participant fee of 45 yuan as experimental compensation.

3.2 Apparatus and Stimuli

iPhone 11 was used as the operating device, with a system of iOS 14.0.1. A flat tabletop provided the support for the participants' arms. In addition, a series of disposable earplugs were prepared for the experiment to isolate noise. The experimental development is based on the iOS system and uses XCode 12.4 as the platform.

Based on the previous study, the 2 groups of stimuli were selected [1]. For vibration stimuli, we fixed frequency of vibration and changed the vibration perception by changing amplitude. The two vibration stimuli are as follows: (1) High-level vibration stimulation: $F = 180$, $A = 90$; (2) Low-level vibration stimulation: $F = 180$, $A = 40$.

For color stimuli, The CIELCh(uv) color model was adopted for data collection and analysis, including lightness, chroma, and hue. We fixed the lightness and hue, and achieved the correspondence by setting different chroma levels, shown in Fig. 2: (1) High-level vibration stimulation: $L = 50$, $C = 130$, $H = 12°$; (2) Low-level vibration stimulation: $L = 50$, $C = 60$, $H = 12°$;

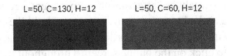

L=50, C=130, H=12   L=50, C=60, H=12

Fig. 2. Color stimuli used in the experiment

3.3 Experimental Design

This experiment adopted an intra-group design, and all participants were required to complete a series of vibration perception tasks and color selection tasks in the same environment. The pre-experiment covered various levels of SOA and different combinations of stimuli, allowing participants to become familiar with specific operating methods and perceive different time differences in advance.

This experiment included two main independent variables: stimulus modality combination and SOA. **(1) Stimulus modality combination.** The main independent variable was stimulus mode combination, which included different levels of color mode chroma and vibration mode amplitude, as shown in Table 1. In the experiment, we designed the order of appearance of stimulus mode combinations through factor design. **(2) SOA.** SOA refers to the time between the appearance of the previous stimulus and the appearance of the next stimulus. Due to the different sequence of stimuli, SOA was defined as the time between vibration and color, consisting of 16 different preset time interval levels, namely +500 ms, +300 ms, +200 ms, +150 ms, +100 ms, +50 ms, +50 ms, +25 ms, +25 ms, 0 ms (repeated once), −25 ms, −50 ms, −100 ms, −150 ms, −200 ms, −300 ms, −500 ms, −500 ms. Besides, the variable ABS was defined as the absolute value of SOA (ABS = |SOA|). For SOA, the symbol represented the order in which the stimulus appeared. "+" represents the color appearing first, and "−" represents the color appearing later. The relationship between sequence and SOA is shown in Fig. 1(a).

Table 1. Stimuli Combination Type

Stimuli Type	Amplitude Level	Chroma Level	Correspondence Level
1	High	High	High
2	High	Low	Low
3	Low	High	Low
4	Low	Low	High

3.4 Tasks and Procedures

The participants came to the laboratory and read and signed the informed consent form before the experiment began. The experimenter explained the basic process, operation methods, and precautions of the experiment to the participants, and disinfected the mobile phones. Before the experiment begins, the color weakness test was conducted to avoid color blindness and color weakness affecting the experimental results.

Each participant was asked to use a stable posture to hold the phone with one hand. They chose to hold it with either hand according to their preference, while they needed to use their other hand to click on the phone screen. Throughout the process, the relative spatial position and clicking method of their hands were required to remain stable. Participants would be informed that their accuracy and RT would not be included in the

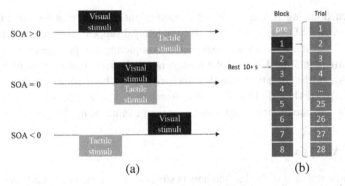

Fig. 3. Experimental design: (a) SOA settings and (b) the experiment procedure

performance evaluation, but would be used as indicators to judge whether they answer seriously, ensuring that they were focused and relaxed.

There are 9 groups in the experiment, with the first group being a pre-experiment and the following 8 groups being formal experiments, shown in Fig. 3(b). In the pre-experiment, participants could be familiar with different levels of single-mode stimulus and the formal experiment procedure. The formal experiment was arranged on factor design, with fixed intra-group order and random inter-group order. Each group had 28 sequence judgment tasks, with the first 4 being warm-up tasks to avoid the turbulence. During the process, the brightness settings remained constant. There was a total of 224 temporal judgment trials, including $4 * 8 = 32$ warm-up tasks and $16 * 4 * 3 = 192$ effective judgment tasks. In the formal experiment, there were 16 levels of SOA and 4 types of stimuli combinations, with 3 repeated measurements under each condition. After completing each group of experiments, participants needed to hold their phones steadily, rest for at least 10 s, and follow the instructions to input the parameter settings for the next group. After completing all tasks, the experimenter would conduct interviews with the participants. Each participant would receive 45 RMB as a reward.

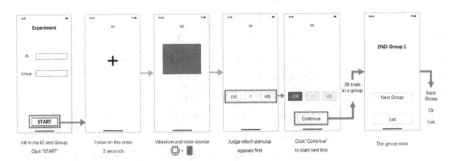

Fig. 4. Experimental design: the procedure of a certain trial

The process of a single trial was shown in Fig. 4. Before each task, a crosshair would appear in the center of screen to help the participants maintain focus. The crosshair disappeared automatically after two seconds, followed by a vibration stimulus and a color stimulus, each lasting 100 ms. The two stimuli might not appear at the same time with different levels of SOA. After the stimuli completely disappears, the participants needed to perform a sequence judgment task. After completing the perception of combined stimuli, participants needed to make a sequence judgment, that is, the color stimulus appears first, or the vibration stimulus appears first, or both appear at the same time. Then participants should click the button to make a choice. The stimuli combination could not be repeatedly perceived, and the answer cannot be modified.

3.5 Data Analysis

The experimental data of the participants is stored in real-time in the CSV document of the mobile phone, and each participant will provide 224 valid data points. After using Python for data preprocessing such as format conversion, merging, and correction, the final data form is obtained, which includes a series of variables, as shown in Table 2. After testing, the data of 30 participants showed no outliers and passed the Shapiro Wilk normality test. The experiment used Minitab 19 and Python 2.7.1 to analyze the data. In the analysis process, the significance level is taken as $\alpha = 0.05$. We conducted variance analysis on each variable combination and obtained a series of significant effect terms that affect the accuracy and RT of judgment.

Table 2. Variables and descriptions

Variables	Descriptions
soa	soa = vibration appearance time − color appearance time
abs	abs = |soa|
symbol	symbol = |soa|/soa (while soa = 0, symbol = null), represents the sequence of stimulus occurrence
correspondence (corres)	{0, 1}, 0 for high correspondence, 1 for low correspondence, named consistency in figures
type	{1, 2, 3, 4}, as Table 1
vib	{0, 1}, 0 for low-level vibration, 1 for high-level vibration
color	{0, 1}, 0 for low-level color, 1 for high-level color
key	{−1, 0, 1}, the key for the task
answer	{−1, 0, 1}, the answer for the task
result	{0, 1}, if key ≠ answer, result = 0; key = answer, result = 1
accuracy	accuracy = the mean of result
RT	unit in seconds, as shown in Fig. 1, named delta_t in figures

4 Results

4.1 Cross-Modal Correspondences

The descriptive statistics of accuracy and RT under different levels of correspondence, as Table 3. On this basis, analysis of variance was performed. Cross-modal correspondence had no significant impact on accuracy and RT. In other words. The cross-modal correspondence would not significantly impact the accuracy and RT of sequence judgment tasks under parameters selected. H1A and H2A were rejected.

Table 3. Descriptive Statistics and ANOVA for full SOA levels - correspondence

corres	result (F = 0.04, p = 0.842)		RT (F = 1.86, p = 0.173)	
	Mean	Std	Mean	Std
0	0.6879	0.4635	0.9690	0.2313
1	0.6854	0.4644	0.9896	0.6159

4.2 One-Way ANOVA to Accuracy and Reaction Time

To explore the impact of various independent variables on asynchronous stimulation, we would now explore the case where the SOA is not zero. As shown in Table 4, one-way ANOVA was conducted on the accuracy and RT using the first seven independent factors from Table 2. "*" represents $\alpha \leq 0.05$ and "−" represents $0.05 < \alpha \leq 0.1$ The results were shown in Table 4. For accuracy, type, SOA, ABS, sequence of stimulus occurrence (symbol), and vibration level (vib) had a significant impact on accuracy, while color level (col) had a slightly significant impact on accuracy. For RT, only SOA and ABS had a significant impact on RT.

Table 4. One-way ANOVA (soa $\neq$ 0)

Resource	D.F.	result			RT		
		F	p	R-sq	F	p	R-sq
corres	1	0.00	1.000	0.00%	1.59	0.207	0.03%
type	3	2.79	0.039*	0.17%	1.59	0.190	0.09%
soa	13	452.16	0.000*	53.91%	47.22	0.000*	53.91%
abs	6	970.16	0.000*	53.63%	100.37	0.000*	10.69%
symbol	1	9.14	0.003*	0.18%	0.01	0.931	0.00%
vib	1	4.55	0.033*	0.09%	3.00	0.083	0.06%
col	1	3.82	0.051-	0.08%	0.16	0.685	0.00%

4.3 SOA, ABS and Occurrence Sequence

SOA. Based on each level of SOA, accuracy and RT were briefly described in Table 5 and Fig. 5. When soa = 0, the accuracy reaches 0.9125. The simultaneous occurrence of different modal stimuli can guide participants to make relatively stable and accurate judgments. Overall, the larger the absolute value of SOA, the higher the accuracy. Intuitively, when the SOA is negative (symbol < 0), that is, when the color appears first, the average accuracy of the participants is higher.

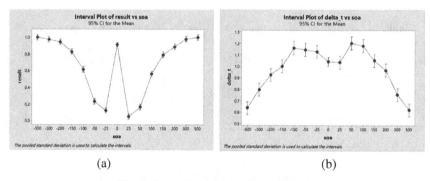

(a)   (b)

Fig. 5. Interval plot of result and RT (soa)

The RT indicator directly reflects the degree of confusion of the participants when making choices, that is, to what extent this combination of stimuli and judgment tasks will cause hesitation, thereby improving the participants' RT. Under the same conditions, there should be a trend of shortening the RT as the correctness improves. As shown in Table 5, the difference between the RT at soa = 0 ms and the average RT at soa = 25 ms in the experiment is less than 1%. The average accuracy of soap at 25 ms is only 0.05, and most participants may mistake it for simultaneous occurrence, meaning that when the vibration appears slightly earlier than the color, the participants have a very similar perception of the two. In the subsequent analysis, in addition to SOA itself, we will also perform variance analysis on the ABS factor and the sequence of stimulus occurrence (symbol).

ABS. As shown in Fig. 6(a) and Table 6, except for *soa* = 0, the larger the ABS, the better the accuracy. If accuracy were required to reach 80%, the interval between stimuli should be at least 150 ms, that is, the interval between stimuli should be 50 ms. If the accuracy was desired to reach over 90%, the interval between stimuli should be at least 200 ms, which means the interval between stimuli should be 100 ms (one stimulus duration). When *abs* < 100 ms, participants are prone to misjudging combinations with time differences as occurring simultaneously, resulting in an accuracy rate below 0.5. While *abs* = 25 ms, participants tend to believe that stimuli occur simultaneously and are prone to making incorrect choices without thinking.

As Fig. 6(b), RT reached its peak at abs = 50 ms, while abs = 100 ms was close to it. However, there was a significant difference in accuracy ($M_{result(abs=50)}$ =

Table 5. Descriptive statistics of result and RT (soa)

soa	result		RT	
	Mean	Std	Mean	Std
−500	1.000	0.000	0.6359	0.3108
−300	0.9750	0.1563	0.7969	0.3990
−200	0.9444	0.2294	0.9260	0.5686
−150	0.8278	0.3781	0.9991	0.5079
−100	0.6167	0.4869	1.1592	0.6146
−50	0.2333	0.4235	1.1449	0.5847
−25	0.1250	0.3312	1.1273	0.6348
0	0.9125	0.2828	1.0400	0.5057
25	0.0500	0.2182	1.0336	0.5712
50	0.1667	0.3732	1.2019	0.8413
100	0.5611	0.4969	1.1785	0.6361
150	0.7917	0.4067	1.0493	0.5745
200	0.8889	0.3147	0.9650	0.5222
300	0.9805	0.1383	0.7524	0.3330
500	1.000	0.000	0.6186	0.3285

0.2000, $M_{result(abs=100)} = 0.5889$). When $abs > 100$ ms, the RT of the participants gradually decreased. The greater the absolute value of asynchronous stimulus occurrence time, the shorter the RT. When $abs \leq 100$ ms, there is no trend and the RT was relatively long. It can be considered that participants will feel confused when the stimulus is not completely separated in the time dimension.

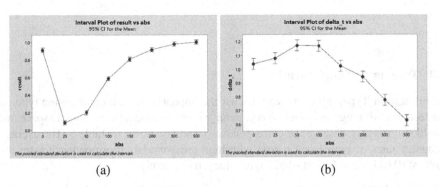

(a)   (b)

Fig. 6. Interval plot of result and RT (soa)

Table 6. Descriptive statistics of result and RT (abs)

abs	result		RT	
	Mean	Std	Mean	Std
0	0.9125	0.2828	1.04	0.5057
25	0.0875	0.2828	1.0805	0.6052
50	0.2000	0.4003	1.1734	0.7245
100	0.5889	0.4924	1.1689	0.6251
150	0.8097	0.3928	1.0242	0.5424
200	0.9167	0.2766	0.9455	0.5458
300	0.97778	0.14751	0.7747	0.3679
500	1.000	0.000	0.6272	0.3197

Occurrence Sequence. In terms of the order in which stimuli appear, it can be found that when symbol $= -1$, its average accuracy is higher. The appearance of colors first helps participants make judgments, thereby improving the accuracy of temporal judgment tasks. This result is consistent with our intuitive observation in Table 7, and the impact of the sequence of stimuli may come from the characteristics of different stimuli.

Table 7. Descriptive statistics of result and RT (sequence)

Symbol	result		RT	
	Mean	Std	Mean	Std
−1	0.6746	0.4686	0.9699	0.5594
0	0.9125	0.2828	1.04	0.5057
1	0.6341	0.4818	0.9713	0.6016

4.4 Types and Stimuli Intensity

Combination Type. Next, we will discuss the impact of stimuli combination type on correctness. Although the conclusion of *delta_t* is not significant in the sample space, we could still roughly observe the corresponding trend, as shown in Table 8. The average accuracy rates of type 1 and type 4 with high cross-modal correspondence were the highest (0.6817) and lowest (0.6270) accuracy, respectively.

Stimuli Intensity. Compared to cross-modal correspondence, the level of stimulus intensity is more likely to affect the accuracy of judgment. As shown in Table 9, the stronger the vibration amplitude level, the higher the accuracy of the participants, and the results are significant. A stronger vibration amplitude helps judge the sequence of

Table 8. Descriptive statistics of result and RT (combination type)

type	result		RT	
	Mean	Std	Mean	Std
1	0.6817	0.4660	0.9521	0.475
2	0.6556	0.4754	0.9826	0.5978
3	0.6532	0.4761	0.9965	0.6336
4	0.6270	0.4838	0.9859	0.5708

the stimulus more accurately. Similarly, higher color chroma helped participants make more accurate judgments, but it was only slightly significant, as shown in Table 4.

Table 9. Descriptive statistics of result and RT (combination type)

vib	result		RT	
	Mean	Std	Mean	Std
0	0.6401	0.4801	0.9848	0.6143
1	0.6687	0.4708	0.9564	0.5451

4.5 Other Conclusions Regarding Specific Levels of SOA

Considering that when abs = 100 ms, accuracy significantly improved, while the vibration and color just did not coincide. When $abs < 100$ ms, overlapping stimuli on the time scale can cause significant interference. In addition, when $abs = 500$ ms, no one made incorrect judgments. Therefore, considering levels that are easy to perceive, we reduced the sample space of ABS to the $abs = 100, 150, 200, 300$ ms. One-way ANOVA was conducted on accuracy and RT using 7 factors from Table 2, and results are shown in Table 10. For accuracy, all variables had the significant impact except for correspondence. For RT, combination type, SOA, ABS and vibration level had a significant impact. The correspondence still has no significant influence, while SOA and ABS can still significantly affect the judgment. The appearance of colors first can still help participants make accurate judgments, but it cannot help with RT.

Besides, the impact of combination type and vibration level on RT is significant for the first time. As shown in Fig. 7(a), type 1 with high amplitude and high chroma levels had the highest average accuracy, while the average accuracy of type 4 with low amplitude and low chroma levels is the worst. Meanwhile, as shown in Fig. 7(b), the RT of type 1 and type 2 was significantly shorter than the other 2 types.

Like previous results, the amplitude increase helps to promote the accuracy and RT of temporal judgment. The interaction plots can also illustrate this issue. As shown in Fig. 8, regardless of the level of cross-modal correspondence, stronger amplitudes

Table 10. One-way ANOVA (*soa* = 100, 150, 200, 300 ms)

Resources	D.F.	Result			RT		
		F	p	R-sq	F	p	R-sq
corres	1	0.06	0.807	0.00%	1.69	0.193	0.05%
type	3	5.59	0.001*	0.58%	2.80	0.039*	0.27%
soa	13	74.65	0.000*	15.39%	30.44	0.000*	6.89%
abs	6	170.12	0.000*	14.98%	69.63	0.000*	6.76%
symbol	1	6.22	0.013*	0.22%	0.66	0.418	0.02%
vib	1	11.4	0.001*	0.39%	6.66	0.010*	0.39%
col	1	5.28	0.022*	0.18%	0.04	0.842	0.18%

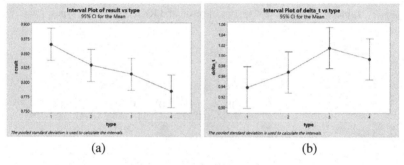

(a)   (b)

Fig. 7. Interval plots of result and RT (type, 100 < soa < 500)

correspond to higher accuracy and shorter RT. There was also a significant relationship between color chroma level and accuracy.

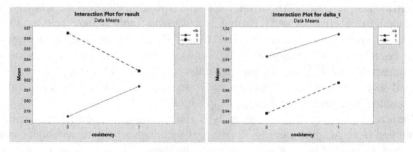

Fig. 8. Interaction plots of result and RT (vib × consistency, 100 < soa < 500)

4.6   Discussion

Cross-modal correspondence would not have a significant impact on accuracy and RT. H1A and H2A were rejected. On the contrary, time variables including SOA and ABS significantly affected accuracy and RT. The stimuli sequence (symbol), combination type, and intensity of stimuli would partially affect the judgment of sequence, which mean H1B and H2B were partially supported. Discussion would be expanded abound 3 aspects: stimuli time interval, stimuli sequence and stimuli intensity.

Firstly, the stimuli interval had impacts on temporal judgment. The group with a high time interval ($abs = 500$ ms) or a low time interval ($abs = 25$ ms, 50 ms) was less affected by stimuli levels, and the group with a time difference of 0 is not sensitive to changes in other variables. Factors irrelevant to time had the more significant effect when the SOA is moderate. When the stimulus interval is too short, participants find it difficult to make accurate judgments. When the stimulus interval is too long, the judgment task is too simple, and the role of external factors may also be greatly limited.

Secondly, the sequence of stimuli had impacts as well. When colors appear first, participants are better able to make temporal judgments. Color is a stable linear stimulus that appears and disappears instantly, while vibration is a process of appearing and disappearing. When color stimuli appear, participants perceive more immediately, while when vibrations first appear, participants cannot perceive due to the presence of tactile perception thresholds, as shown in Fig. 9. For example, when $soa = +25$ ms, the vibration objectively appears slightly earlier. However, participants might feel both of stimuli occur simultaneously. In the design of multimodal interaction, we need to consider the delay and duration of vibration, to provide users with a better user experience.

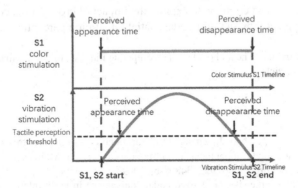

Fig. 9. Temporal characteristics of vibration and color stimuli

Finally, the level of vibration intensity has a significant impact on accuracy of temporal judgment tasks. Within a certain range, the stronger stimuli can help participants make judgments more accurately. Besides, the vibration amplitude level also directly affects the RT. However, the impact of color on RT is not significant. In practice, the impact of vibration and stimuli intensity on multi-modal temporal judgment should be emphasized to ensure the consistency between different modalities.

5 Conclusion

In conclusion, the study explored the impact of various factors (cross-modal correspondence, SOA, ABS, stimuli combination type, stimuli sequence, vibration amplitude level and color chroma level) in multimodal perception on the accuracy of temporal judgment tasks and RT in color tactile multimodal time integration perception. After analysis and discussion, we have overturned the hypothesis proposed in this chapter and obtained the following conclusions: (1) Cross-modal correspondence has no significant impact on accuracy and RT of temporal judgment task; (2) The time interval between 2 stimuli (SOA and ABS) have a significant impact on accuracy and RT, with longer time differences leading to higher accuracy. The RT first prolonged and then shortened as the time interval increased; (3) The order in which stimuli appear significantly affects the accuracy of temporal judgment tasks. When colors appear first, the accuracy is significantly improved; (4) The stimuli combination type has a significant impact on accuracy. A similar effect appeared for RT as well, only within the range of $100\,ms \leq soa \leq 300\,ms$. The combination type 1 (high amplitude & high chroma) had the highest average accuracy and the shortest RT; (5) The level of vibration amplitude significantly affects the correctness of temporal judgment tasks. Within a specific range of $100\,ms \leq soa \leq 300\,ms$, the level of color chroma can also affect accuracy, and the level of vibration amplitude can also affect RT. The stronger the level of stimulation, the higher the accuracy and the shorter the RT.

This study didn't find the relationship between color-touch cross-modal correspondence and multimodal time integration perception tasks, possibly due to the lack of a significant tendency, or limitations in the experimental design. Based on this experiment, we can continue to explore the correlation between the two in the future. In addition, subsequent research can continue to explore the impact of cross-modal correspondence of color tactile perception on multimodal spatial integration perception.

Disclosure of Interests. The authors have no competing interests to declare that are relevant to the content of this article.

References

1. Yuan, T., Rau, P.-L., Zhao, J., Zheng, J.: Color-touch cross-modal correspondence and its impact on single-modal judgement in multimodal perception. Multisensory Res. **36**, 1–25 (2023). https://doi.org/10.1163/22134808-bja10098
2. Lewkowicz, D., Turkewitz, G.: Cross-modal equivalence in early infancy: auditory-visual intensity matching. Dev. Psychol. **16**, 597–607 (1980). https://doi.org/10.1037/0012-1649.16.6.597
3. Lalanne, C., Lorenceau, J.: Crossmodal integration for perception and action. J. Physiol. Paris **98**, 265–279 (2004). https://doi.org/10.1016/j.jphysparis.2004.06.001
4. Grifoni, P.: Multimodal human computer interaction and pervasive services (2009). https://doi.org/10.4018/978-1-60566-386-9
5. Spence, C.: Crossmodal correspondences: a tutorial review. Atten. Percept. Psychophys. **73**, 971–995 (2011). https://doi.org/10.3758/s13414-010-0073-7
6. Alais, D., Burr, D.: The ventriloquist effect results from near-optimal bimodal integration. Curr. Biol. CB. **14**, 257–262 (2004). https://doi.org/10.1016/j.cub.2004.01.029

7. Driver, J., Spence, C.: Attention and the crossmodal construction of space. Trends Cogn. Sci. **2**, 254–262 (1998). https://doi.org/10.1016/S1364-6613(98)01188-7

8. Dong, C., Wang, Z., Li, R., Wang, S.: Individual variations in McGurk illusion susceptibility reflect different integration-segregation strategies of audiovisual speech perception (2023). https://doi.org/10.1101/2023.12.15.571270

9. Gilbert, A., Martin, R., Kemp, S.: Cross-modal correspondence between vision and olfaction: the color of smells. Am. J. Psychol. **109**, 335–351 (1996). https://doi.org/10.2307/1423010

10. Spence, C., Levitan, C., Shankar, M., Zampini, M.: Does food color influence taste and flavor perception in humans? Chemosens. Percept. **3**, 68–84 (2010). https://doi.org/10.1007/s12078-010-9067-z

11. Zampini, M., Sanabria, D., Phillips, N., Spence, C.: The multisensory perception of flavor: assessing the influence of color cues on flavor discrimination responses. Food Qual. Prefer. **18**, 975–984 (2007). https://doi.org/10.1016/j.foodqual.2007.04.001

12. Al-Ayash, A., Kane, R., Smith, D., Green-Armytage, P.: The influence of color on student emotion, heart rate, and performance in learning environments (2016)

13. Martino, G., Marks, L.: Cross-modal interaction between vision and touch: the role of synesthetic correspondence. Perception **29**, 745–754 (2000). https://doi.org/10.1068/p2984

14. Ludwig, V., Simner, J.: What color does that feel? Tactile-visual mapping and the development of cross-modality. Cortex J. Devoted Study Nerv. Syst. Behav. 49 (2012). https://doi.org/10.1016/j.cortex.2012.04.004

15. Elliot, A., Aarts, H.: Perception of the color red enhances the force and velocity of motor output. Emot. Wash. DC. **11**, 445–449 (2011). https://doi.org/10.1037/a0022599

16. Kahol, K., French, J., Bratton, L., Panchanathan, S.: Learning and perceiving colors haptically (2006). https://doi.org/10.1145/1168987.1169017

17. Delazio, A., Israr, A., Klatzky, R.: Cross-modal correspondence between vibrations and colors (2017). https://doi.org/10.1109/WHC.2017.7989904

18. Slobodenyuk, N., Jraissati, Y., Kanso, A., Ghanem, L., Elhajj, I.: Cross-modal associations between color and haptics. Atten. Percept. Psychophys. 68 (2015). https://doi.org/10.3758/s13414-015-0837-1

19. Jaśkowski, P.: Temporal-order judgment and reaction time for short and long stimuli. Psychol. Res. **54**, 141–145 (1992). https://doi.org/10.1007/BF00922093

20. Gibbon, J., Rutschmann, R.: Temporal order judgment and reaction time. Science **165**, 413–415 (1969). https://doi.org/10.1126/science.165.3891.413

21. Lable, I.: Conscious and unconscious processes: psychodynamic, cognitive, and neurophysiological convergences. Neuropsychoanalysis Interdiscip. J. Psychoanal. Neurosci. **2**, 99–102 (2014). https://doi.org/10.1080/15294145.2000.10773290

Exploring Cross-Disciplinary Design Dialogues: A Case-Study Workshop on Designing Medical Interfaces and the Integration of the 'Check' Methodological Canvas

Mariia Zolotova[1]([✉]) and Angelina Kablova[2]

[1] Xi'an Jiaotong-Liverpool University, Suzhou, Jiangsu, People's Republic of China
mariia.zolotova@xjtlu.edu.cn
[2] St Petersburg University, St Petersburg, Russia

Abstract. This paper addresses the topic of designing medical interfaces as a scenario which fosters cross-disciplinary design dialogues. It demonstrates this through a case-study workshop where MA students conducted user research and proposed a re-design of an inhalation anesthesia device interface. It represents a tester of a new methodological canvas "Check" tool and how it was integrated into the established methods of UX/UI design. The paper shares pedagogical reflections as well as feedback from the design team on the process of analysis and design of user interfaces and on the characteristics of collaboration between designers and medical companies. Findings suggest that designers should be trained to research the unintended use of medical devices (the UX component), including the emotional component of interaction. "Check" tool can support them in doing so through differentiating rational and emotional components of interaction and structuring them according to principles of cognitive ergonomics. The paper also emphasizes the need to conveniently and comprehensively integrate medical standards into interaction analysis, while advocating for improved communication, formalization, and potential standardization of collaborations between designers and the healthcare industry.

Keywords: Communication barriers · Cross-cultural communication · Cross-cultural product and service design · Cultural differences · Medical Interface Design

1 Introduction

In this paper, the author would like to share a case-study workshop that is a result of a collaboration between designers and a medical company producing hospital medical devices, in particular, inhalation anesthesia devices. Such devices incorporate several user interfaces, including digital interfaces. The interaction with such devices demands from its users adaptability to the constantly updating technologies and user interface design. This case-study represents a good platform to delve into the topic of a cross-disciplinary dialogue. Therefore, there are three main topics that will receive focus in this paper:

- The challenges and opportunities of a collaboration between different fields and cultures of knowledge (design and medical business), which can lead to innovation, but is characterized by barriers to mutual understanding: how to maneuver in such an interdisciplinary context? What methods and tools can help?
- The interface design culture, which includes Human-Centered Design approach and the importance of user research, the role of designers and design-specific methods;
- An integration of the above into pedagogy to form new design professionals.

1.1 Challenges and Opportunities of a Collaboration Between Designers and Medical Companies

Collaboration between designers and medical companies offers several opportunities and can address various challenges in the healthcare industry. The competition among the companies producing medical equipment is high, and each company seeks to stand out in the market with attractive yet safe designs. This is why Design Thinking is more and more involved in healthcare product development (Roberts et al., 2016) and not only engineers and medical specialists are involved in the product development but more and more often UX/UI and Industrial designers.

Designers have the skills to improve user experience of medical devices through clear visual communication and ergonomics considerations. Designers possess expertise in user-centered design, which enables them to create intuitive and user-friendly interfaces, devices, and environments that meet the needs of healthcare professionals and patients (Bardram et al., 2018). By incorporating design principles and methodologies, medical companies can enhance the usability, efficiency, and effectiveness of their products, leading to better patient outcomes and increased user satisfaction.

Another opportunity is related to the integration of Design Thinking and innovation into the development process. Designers are trained at identifying unmet needs, generating creative solutions, and prototyping ideas. Through a collaboration with medical companies, designers can contribute to the creation of innovative healthcare solutions, such as new medical devices, digital health platforms, and patient-centered services (Kimbell, 2011). This collaboration can stimulate a culture of innovation within medical companies, aiming at the advancements in healthcare design, technology and delivery.

However, there are also challenges associated with the collaboration between designers and medical companies. One challenge is the complexity and regulatory nature of the healthcare industry. Healthcare standards and regulations develop slowly in respect to the new technologies (Vincent et al., 2015). Medical products and services must comply with strict regulatory requirements, including safety, privacy, and data protection regulations (ISO 14971; GDPR). The standards vary also from country to country, which adds an additional layer to the overall complexity. Designers need to be aware of these regulations and work closely with medical companies to ensure that the designed solutions meet the necessary standards and guidelines (Borycki et al., 2010).

Another important challenge is the integration of design processes into the traditionally conservative and hierarchical structures of medical companies. Design thinking and user-centered design approaches may require a shift in the mindset and culture within these organizations. Lack of experience from both sides can create tensions that may block implementation and development of certain ideas.

In summary, the collaboration between designers and medical companies presents opportunities to improve the user experience, drive innovation, and create better health-care solutions. However, it also requires navigating the complexities of the healthcare industry and integrating design processes within established company structures. In this paper, we will have a look into the design process of a medical interface and how a methodology could support both sides of the collaboration.

1.2   The Culture of Designing Interfaces

The culture of designing interfaces encompasses the methodologies, practices, and values that guide the design process. One widely used methodology in interface design is the Human-Centered Design (HCD) approach. HCD places the user at the center of the design process, emphasizing the importance of understanding user needs, goals, and behaviors. User research plays a crucial role in interface design culture. It involves gathering insights about users through various methods such as interviews, observations, surveys, and usability tests. This knowledge enables designers to make informed design decisions that are rooted in user needs and preferences (Norman & Draper, 1986). Designers will translate user research findings into tangible design solutions, such as wireframes, prototypes, and visual designs that effectively communicate the structure, functionality, and aesthetics of the interface. Additionally, designers should collaborate with other stakeholders, such as developers and product managers, to ensure the successful implementation of the design vision, which may incorporate other factors such as business goals, technological constraints, and industry best practices. Design principles followed in the interface design include simplicity, consistency, and visual hierarchy, to create interfaces that are intuitive, aesthetically pleasing, and aligned with the brand identity of the product or company.

The culture of designing interfaces and the HCD embrace an iterative and user feedback-driven approach. Designers continuously refine and improve their designs based on user feedback, usability testing, and real-world usage data. This iterative process enables designers to address usability issues, identify opportunities for enhancement, and ensure that the interface is being improved to meet user needs.

If we observe user interface design in the medical field, we may note the following trends:

- Portability and maneuverability of medical devices (Fig. 1): This includes the dimensions and the composition of the device so that it can be displaced according to the needs. This requires interfaces to adapt to the dimensions and interaction styles of smartphones, tablets, and wearable devices.
- Intuitive visuals for a better user experience and patient-centered design (Fig. 2): As the healthcare industry generates huge amounts of data, there is an increasing need for effective data visualization and analytics in medical interfaces. The obstacle to radically innovative solutions lay in the need to strictly follow the medical standards.

In summary, the culture of designing interfaces revolves around user research and iterations to achieve interfaces that are empathetic, user-friendly, effective, and aligned with the broader goals of the company and a context in which product or service operate.

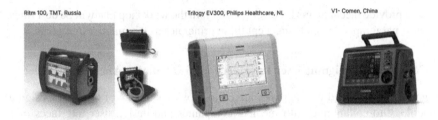

Fig. 1. Portability and maneuverability of medical devices, demonstrated via: V1-Comen, China; Trilogy EV300, Philips Healthcare, NL; Ritm 100, TMT, Russia.

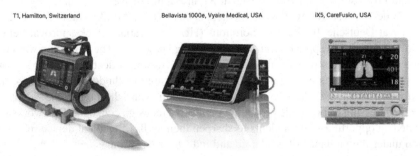

Fig. 2. Intuitive visuals for a better user experience and patient-centered design, demonstrated via: T1, Hamilton, Switaerland; Bellavista 1000e, Vyaire Medical, USA; iX5, CareFusion, USA.

2 Methods

2.1 General Principles of Designing Interfaces

In the previous paragraph, the following principles have been already mentioned: simplicity, consistency, visibility, feedback. Affordances also play a crucial role in assisting users understanding the functionality of the device (Norman, 2013; Shneiderman & Plaisant, 2004). These principles are derived from various design theories and frameworks, such as the Gestalt principles and HCD principles, and are widely recognized in the field of interface design.

When designing interfaces for medical applications, additional principles should be taken into account to ensure the safety, efficiency, and effectiveness of healthcare delivery. Such authors as Carayon et al. (2015) and Kushniruk & Patel (2004) suggest the following principles as key for designing medical interfaces. One crucial principle is the principle of clarity, which highlights the importance of presenting medical information in a clear and easily understandable manner, considering both healthcare professionals and patients. One more is the principle of hierarchy, which involves organizing information and functions in a logical and prioritized manner, allowing users to quickly access the most critical information and actions. The principle of context sensitivity in medical interfaces involves tailoring the interface to the specific task, workflows, and scenarios of healthcare professionals. Furthermore, the principle of error prevention and recovery is fundamental, as medical interfaces must incorporate features that minimize the risk of errors and provide mechanisms for error recovery. In the workshop that will be described in the next paragraph, design teams kept these principles as the main design goals.

2.2 Case-Study: Designing User Interface for an Inhalation Anesthesia Device

The workshop described in this paper aimed to provide students of Graphic Design a methodology to collaborate with medical companies and design user interfaces of a medical device. The workshop held at St Petersburg University from 5th to 11th July 2023 brought together Master's students in Graphic Design to practice designing medical device interfaces. Led by professionals in the field, including Mariia Zolotova, PhD, Assistant Professor of Industrial Design at Xi'an Jiaotong-Liverpool University and an expert in design-research within the medical sphere, Daria Artiukhova, Senior UX/UI Designer at Deutsche Telekom IT Solutions (HU), and Tatiana Aleksandrova, Senior Teaching Fellow of Graphic Design at St Petersburg University. The workshop was conducted in collaboration with the medical company "Krasnogvardeets" JSC. Throughout the workshop, students were guided through a structured methodology to analyze the existing interface of the Orfei-M" – a device for inhalation anesthesia (Fig. 3), – identifying and addressing errors while proposing innovative redesign concepts. This workshop provided an opportunity for students to sharpen their skills in medical device interface design under the guidance of academic and industry professionals and real-world collaboration. A part of the workshop's methodology included a new method developed by the author (Zolotova 2019, 2021), which purpose was to help designers identify errors in existing design and interaction between the users and the device in order to propose a new improved design. Therefore, this workshop represents a tester of this methodology, and in the discussion paragraph we will analyze its efficiency and potential.

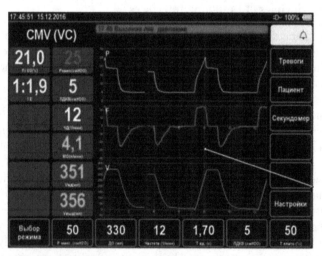

Fig. 3. "Krasnogvardeets" JSC. (2022). User interface of "Orfei-M", inhalation anesthesia device, main screen.

2.3 Pedagogical Methodology

The workshop followed a human-centered design approach, prioritizing the needs and experiences of the end-users, and in case of the inhalation anesthesia device these are medical doctors and nurses. Students were assigned the task of analyzing the interaction with the user interface of the inhalation anesthesia device "Orfei-M", aiming to identify existing errors in the interaction design. The methodology involved several key steps to thoroughly understand the user experience. Firstly, the students familiarized themselves with the device by studying its manual. Next, they conducted eye-tracking tests and generated heat maps to gain insights into users' visual attention and interaction patterns. To further enhance their understanding, the students interviewed the medical company engineer and an experienced user to gather valuable feedback and firsthand experiences. They proceeded to create paper mock-ups, allowing them to ideate and test new design ideas in a low-fidelity format and conduct A/B testing. Every phase of this user research and tests was fixed into a canvas called "Check Tool". This is the method developed specifically for the purpose of analyzing and designing user interfaces. This canvas is built based on the principles of Cognitive Ergonomics (Fig. 4).

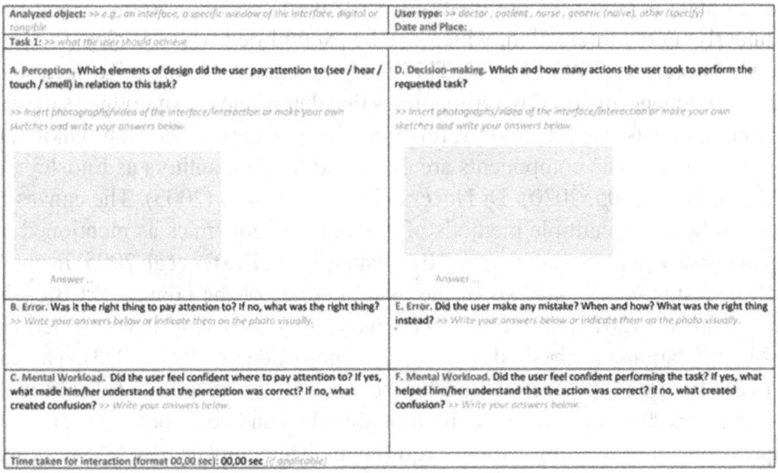

Fig. 4. Zolotova, M. (2023). "Check" tool for analyzing and designing interfaces. Revised.

Medical equipment has become more complex, and the need for interface research has increased. Interaction with such equipment requires high concentration of attention and adaptability to technology from users. Manufacturing companies strive to stand out in the market thanks to their attractive yet reliable design. Therefore, especially in economically developed countries, design research is increasingly involved in the development of medical equipment. Such studies are rare in developing countries (Bitkina et al., 2020).

Designers can improve usability through clear visual communication and consideration of ergonomic factors. However, it is important that new design decisions are made in direct dependence on the actual interaction with the device and take into account the accepted standards. To carry out an ergonomic analysis, the designer needs to determine:

– The type of users (patients, medical staff, caregivers and general profile);
– The conditions in which the device operates;
– The main functions of the device.

The methods of ergonomic analysis are: surveys, interviews, observations, etc., quantitative and qualitative. Usability is usually the main goal of the ergonomic evaluation of medical devices, while UX is not considered, because:

– Safety is a priority;
– The need to use the device strictly for its intended use, while UX studies the unintended use (IEC 62366–1, 2015);
– Key users are experts, not general users.

To contribute to the improvement of usability methods, the author of this paper proposed a new canvas as an auxiliary tool for conducting usability research. The novelty lies in the fact that the template includes a UX component in the analysis and is based on the principles of cognitive ergonomics.

The template is a grid for observations, structured according to the cognitive processes underlying the interaction, which can be exemplified with Endsley's scheme of Situational Awareness (2000) (Fig. 5). This allows researchers to organize notes according to the components of cognitive ergonomics that determine the smoothness of interaction. The components are: subjectivity, functionality, perception, decision-making, mental stress and errors. The components are discussed by such authors as Endsley (1995, 2000, 2015), Tosi (2005, 2020), Di Nocera (2011), Ferlazzo (2005). The canvas is the result of synthesizing multiple methods of Cognitive Ergonomics as mentioned above and (Hazlehurst et al 2008, Kahneman, 2011, Patel, 2010, Baxter et al. 2005) in one. This method was tested on the analysis of the user interface of the Ginveri Srl Bio-Shuttle transport incubator (2019) and, after revisions, in this workshop it was tested on the "Orfei-M" inhalation anesthesia device of "Krasnogvardeets" JSC (2023). The canvas (Fig. 4) visually highlights the relationship between user perception, decision-making, and design errors. It is used to collect high-quality data and describes the user's subjective impressions of interacting with the equipment. The template also allows designers to collect data on the subjective aspects of interaction and unintended use of medical devices. Students were given the canvas without explaining how to use it, just asking them to fill it in intuitively. The reflections on the use of this canvas will be presented in the paragraph Results and Discussions.

After completing the analysis, the students translated their refined concepts into interactive mock-ups using the design tool Figma, enabling them to simulate and validate the proposed interface improvements. This comprehensive methodology allowed students to iteratively analyze, ideate, and validate their design solutions in a user-centered manner.

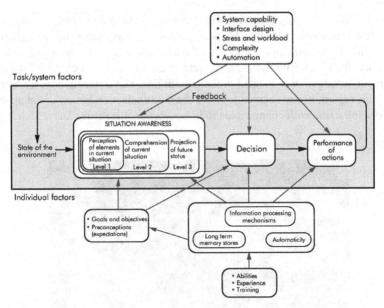

Fig. 5. Endsley, M. (2000). Situational Awareness Model.

3 Results and Discussion

3.1 Redesigning the Interface of the Inhalation Anesthesia Device

Medical equipment and the interaction with it are regulated by the standards, which are important to take into account and integrate into a new design solution. Thus, the design is built around the existing constants and limitations associated with the need to act quickly and accurately in emergency situations.

Based on the experience of this workshop and methodology, the work with medical devices can be summarized in three key aspects:

- A structural analysis, such as when interactive blocks are located in the blind area, availability of the space for visualizing data, interaction and visualization hierarchy;
- Microinteractions design, such feedback and interactivity indicators, use of texts and icons, optimization of the necessary interaction steps;
- Innovations, that can happen only with the close and careful study of the standards and its "rooms for flexibility", addressing ethical concerns, integration of new technologies, implementation of intuitive visualizations.

To illustrate these aspects, below will follow a reflection on the design process shared by the design team leader Angelina Kablova.

"The main design goal of the workshop was not to redesign the aesthetics of the interface, but rather to develop a structure to fit the current system and user needs. The problem of insufficient differentiation of zones on the screen was chosen as the main one after testing interactions with the device and filling in the "Check" tool (Fig. 9). Another important goal was to simplify interaction with the device by adding feedback elements to the interface.

Structural Changes. *A) Relocating key elements* – At the research stage, an eye-tracking test was conducted (Fig. 6), during which it was discovered that the user's main attention falls on the upper and central part of the screen. In the initial version of the interface, the block with the main element of interaction – the choice of the device mode and its settings – was located in the bottom line, and consequently, it was out of sight. In this regard, it was decided to move the mode selection button to the upper-left corner, placing a line with changeable mode parameters there (Fig. 7).

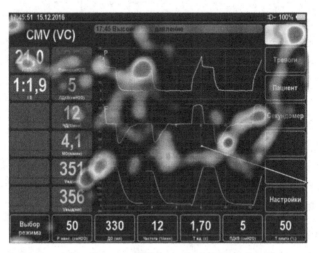

Fig. 6. Generating heat map for the user interface of "Orfei-M", inhalation anesthesia device, main screen. Design team Angelina Lablova, Anastasiia Mareva, Veronika Volkova.

b) Releasing space (Fig. 7) – The settings and timer remained in the rightmost column, but changed their appearance. Instead of text, icons appeared on the "settings" and "timer" buttons - a gear and a stopwatch, respectively. This solution seems acceptable, since such icons are considered standard, are found in many interfaces and have become familiar and understandable to most users. In addition, this made it possible to reduce the column width by half and thereby expand the area with charts and patient indicators. All settings remained hidden in a separate menu, which opens by clicking on the gear icon. This is done in order to maximally unload the main screen with the patient and mode parameters, removing unnecessary information. The settings located inside this menu are not used regularly, but are configured by a specialist only before starting work and entering the data of a new patient.

c) Clarifying the hierarchy (Fig. 7) – From the point of view of the interface hierarchy, it was important to distinguish between the modifiable parameters and patient's condition indicators that the device reads and displays on the screen. At the same time, the difficulty was that the patient's indicators can also be clickable to personalize the interface: the doctor independently chooses which indicators will be displayed on the main screen. To solve the problem, two types of buttons have been developed for these groups of values: buttons with an outline to change the mode parameters and buttons with a transparent fill to select the displayed indicators. Thus, the button has a sense of volume and implies the possibility of interaction, while not distracting attention from working with changeable parameters, the interactivity of which is more obvious.

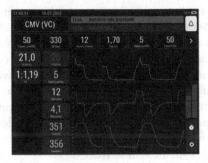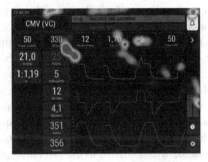

Fig. 7. New interface design and its heat map. Design team Angelina Kablova, Anastasiia Mareva, Veronika Volkova.

Microinteractions. It was important not only to structure the blocks of information on the display, but also to streamline some processes of interaction with the device settings to minimize errors.

One of the steps to improve the user experience was to work on clarifying the confirmation of the parameter changes. For example, the need to save changes was not obvious enough in the original interface: when closing this window without confirmation, the parameter remained the same, and all the steps had to be repeated again, wasting extra time. To optimize this interaction, the following scenario was developed: 1) the specialist clicks on the parameter that needs to be changed; 2) the numeric value blinks, the "+" and "−" buttons appear under it; 3) after making changes, the specialist closes the window and confirms the changes by clicking on the parameter again. This rather simple model allows you to avoid duplicating the parameter change window, as it was before. Now, in the process of making changes, the doctor still controls all the patient's indicators and can take them into account when making adjustments, and the flickering numeric value suggests that it is unstable and prompts you to click on it to approve new data.

The minimum and maximum limits for the variable parameters were also indicated in the interaction. Now, when the upper limit of the numeric value is reached, the "+" button becomes inactive, without color-filling, which clearly indicates that further increase is impossible. In the original version, such a scenario was not taken into account and there was a feeling of error, as if the device simply did not respond to pressing.

Innovations. Immersion in the design process and communication with a specialist from the field of medicine pushed us to think more broadly, after we worked with the main interface problems. For example, we suggested adding a schematic visualization of the patient's breathing to the panel, since for some indicators on the graphs it is important to keep track of the synchronization of curve trends with the patient's breaths. On the screen, this function is not yet obvious and convincing enough, it requires testing and refinement.

Of particular interest was the difficult issue of ethics and respect for the patient in the process of interaction between the doctor and the device. Namely: how does the patient react to the alarms of the device and is it possible to minimize stress for him in such situations without compromising medical activity? What can be done to achieve this?

Our team's proposal was to put the alarms and their log on a separate portable screen (e.g., a mobile phone), which will always be at the doctor's office and signal him about critical situations with an audible alarm and an alarm screen (Fig. 8). The screen will display the patient's data (last name, ward, metrics), as well as the cause of the alarm. The ventilator, instead, will not emit an alarm sound, but will only show a blinking message about it on the screen in the corresponding alarm field. This solution will allow the doctor to respond promptly to the alarm, while maintaining the patient's calmness, because he will not listen to the call and worry until the staff arrives."

These were the reflections on the design process by the design team leader, and in the next paragraph we will discuss the methodology adopted in this workshop and its implications.

Fig. 8. Proposed innovation: the alarms and their log put on a separate portable screen (e.g., a mobile phone), which will always be at the doctor's office and signal him about critical situations with an audible alarm and an alarm screen. Design team Angelina Kablova, Anastasiia Mareva, Veronika Volkova.

3.2 Pedagogy and Necessary Design Skills

Currently, there are many tools available for designers assisting them in their work. In this case-study we applied the Human-Centered Design approach, and used the following tools to empathize the end-user:

- Eye-tracking the interaction with the device;
- Interview with the medical company which produces the device;
- A/B tests conducted on paper mock-ups;
- Figma interactive mock-up to demonstrate the interaction.

Additionally, participants used "Check" tool to synthesize data collected via conducting various tests performed with the tools mentioned above into meaningful insights.

Here is a reflection shared by the design team leader Angelina Kablova: "It was possible to come to the solutions described above thanks to the correct formulation of tasks and the placement of focus, and it was possible to identify and clarify these problems thanks to filling in the canvas ("Check tool") (Fig. 9). Such a tool allows you to separate the emotional and rational components of interaction with the interface, but at the same time take into account both of these aspects by structuring your thoughts.

In the process of filling out the canvas, the researchers are in two states: on the one hand, they fix their feelings at the moment of interaction, on the other hand, they observe their actions after completing the interaction with the device, analyzing their own decisions and establishing cause-and-effect relationships. This exercise can be useful for learning the principles of interaction and finding solutions, as it allows you to identify both general errors and make small changes that will improve the user experience.

Moving into the position of an observer of oneself and engaging in self-reflection can be difficult due to cognitive bias. To solve this, the tool should suggest/allow recording the interaction on video. Video recordings make it possible not to lose sight of the details, the sequence of decisions made, since it is possible to return to this data." The designer mentions the differentiation of the emotional and rational components of interaction. The emotional component is part of the unintended use, as mentioned in the paragraph 2.3. The awareness of user value and added value arises as a result of such use. We may infer that the future of a successful medical device depends on technological and user (emotional) factors. The latter are not well studied in healthcare (Bitkina et al., 2020). Therefore, additional studies of the interaction between the user and the medical device are needed, which will include subjective components in the analysis. To achieve this, designers should be trained to research and design considering the unintended use, including the emotional component, and equip themselves with the necessary skills and tools to address such a goal.

3.3 Collaboration Between Designers and Companies, Conclusions

While the tool demonstrates to be valuable to the designers, how could it become more meaningful to the specific context of designing medical devices? It is commonly recognized that designers can contribute to the improvement of medical devices through visual communication, consideration of ergonomic factors and empathy, thus, humanizing the technology. The methods, mentioned above are quite common and broadly used in the UX/UI field, regardless of the industry. However, medical field is characterized by strict standards that are in place to ensure safe use of the device. In this scenario, further development of the "Check" tool should test the integration of medical standards and other technical requirements into it, so that designers could have a quick reference to the involved restrictions and medical companies could participate by checking and updating the list of requirements and their successful or less implementation by the designers.

As it was mentioned in the introduction paragraph, Design thinking and human-centered design approaches may require a shift in the mindset and culture within medical organizations. And this shift may be tough and tense for the both sides of the collaboration. An example of misunderstanding could be a wrong interpretation of the data collected via user research by designers. Medical companies, if feeling collaborative and trustful towards designers, would willingly help designers get a clear picture. But if there

Subject of analysis: **Display 2 (main menu), "Orpheus" inhalation anaesthesia machine, "Krasnogvardeets"**	Date: 2 November 2022 Place: PJSC "Krasnogvardeets"
Task 2: **Choose the amount and type of trends/curves to be displayed**	
A. Which elements of design did you pay attention to (see / hear / touch / smell) in relation to this task? Centre of the screen, graphics, touch buttons in the pop-up menu. 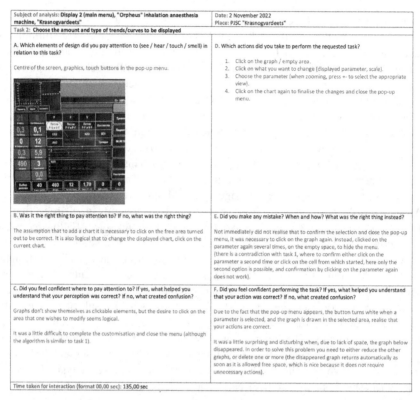	D. Which actions did you take to perform the requested task? 1. Click on the graph / empty area. 2. Click on what you want to change (displayed parameter, scale). 3. Choose the parameter (when zooming, press +- to select the appropriate view). 4. Click on the chart again to finalise the changes and close the pop-up menu.
B. Was it the right thing to pay attention to? If no, what was the right thing? The assumption that to add a chart it is necessary to click on the free area turned out to be correct. It is also logical that to change the displayed chart, click on the current chart.	E. Did you make any mistake? When and how? What was the right thing instead? Not immediately did not realise that to confirm the selection and close the pop-up menu, it was necessary to click on the graph again. Instead, clicked on the parameter again several times, on the empty space, to hide the menu. (there is a contradiction with task 1, where to confirm either click on the parameter a second time or click on the cell from which started, here only the second option is possible, and confirmation by clicking on the parameter again does not work).
C. Did you feel confident where to pay attention to? If yes, what helped you understand that your perception was correct? If no, what created confusion? Graphs don't show themselves as clickable elements, but the desire to click on the area that one wishes to modify seems logical. It was a little difficult to complete the customisation and close the menu (although the algorithm is similar to task 1).	F. Did you feel confident performing the task? If yes, what helped you understand that your action was correct? If no, what created confusion? Due to the fact that the pop-up menu appears, the button turns white when a parameter is selected, and the graph is drawn in the selected area, realise that your actions are correct. It was a little surprising and disturbing when, due to lack of space, the graph below disappeared. In order to solve this problem you need to either reduce the other graphs, or delete one or more (the disappeared graph returns automatically as soon as it is allowed free space, which is nice because it does not require unnecessary actions).
Time taken for interaction (format 00,00 sec): 135,00 sec	

Fig. 9. A fragment of the analysis conducted by the design team during the workshop.

is no trust yet, a single misinterpretation may result in non-productive efforts and weakened confidence between designers and medical companies. In this case, written forms or other ways of structuring and standardizing the communication may be beneficial to create a perceived formality and sense of collaborative efforts and mutual responsibility in the collaboration.

In this paper, we have looked into the process of designing medical interfaces by adopting the HCD approach and the new analytical canvas "Check tool". In particular, we have shared the experience of delving into the specific culture of designing medical interfaces from a perspective of pedagogy and the design team. We have concluded that the UX component is currently understudied and that there is a lot of potential for both designers and medical companies to explore it more. In that sense, "Check" tool offers a methodology for the designers to self-reflect and diversify emotional and rational components of the interaction and structuring them according to principles of cognitive ergonomics. However, due to highly complex nature of the medical equipment, the collaboration between designers and medical companies could be highly innovative yet challenging due to almost opposite cultures: the one empathetic, flexible, and experimental of the design, and a more conservative, hierarchical, and strict culture of medical equipment development. To overcome these challenges, designers need additional support in understanding the standards and other requirements, while medical companies would need a structured communication with an opportunity to check and control the design output at early stages.

Acknowledgments. The author would like to thank the Xi'an Jiaotong-Liverpool University Design School for providing financial support to this project, the medical company "Krasnog-vardeets" JSC for collaboration and providing invaluable opportunity to conduct user research, Daria Artiukhova, Senior UX/UI Designer at Deutsche Telekom IT Solutions (HU), Tatiana Aleksandrova, Senior Teaching Fellow of Graphic Design at St Petersburg University for supporting the workshop with professional expertise, and the research assistant Yao Yongxin for important contributions to this research.

Disclosure of Interests. The authors have no competing interests to declare that are relevant to the content of this article.

References

Bardram, J.E., Frost, M., Szántó, K., Marcilly, R., Houben, S.: Designing interactive technology for crowd experiences in healthcare. Commun. ACM **61**(11), 68–77 (2018)

Bitkina, O., Kim, H.K., Park, J.: Usability and user experience of medical devises: an overview of the current state, analysis methodologies, and future challenges. Int. J. Ind. Ergon. (76) (2020). https://doi.org/10.1016/j.ergon.2020.102932

Borycki, E., Kushniruk, A., Carvalho, C.: Usability and safety in electronic medical records. Stud. Health Technol. Inform. **151**, 356–366 (2010)

Broniatowski, D.A.: Do design decisions depend on "dictators"? Res. Eng. Design **29**, 67–85 (2018). https://doi.org/10.1007/s00163-017-0259-2

Carayon, P., et al.: Incorporating health information technology into workflow redesign—summary report. Agency Healthc. Res. Qual. (2015)

Di Nocera, F. (Ed.). (2011). *Ergonomia cognitiva [Cognitive Ergonomics]*. Carocci editore

Endsley, M.R.: Toward a theory of situation awareness in dynamic systems. Hum. Fact. 9–42 (1995). ISBN 9788843051175. https://doi.org/10.1518/001872095779049543

Endsley, M.R., Garland, D.J.: Theoretical underpinnings of situation awareness: a critical review. Situat. Awaren. Anal. Measur. **1**, 24 (2000)

Endsley, M.R.: Situation awareness misconceptions and misunderstandings. J. Cogn. Eng. Decis. Making 9(1), 4–32 (2015). https://doi.org/10.1177/1555343415572631

Ferlazzo, F.: Metodi in ergonomia cognitive [Methods of Cognitive Ergonomics]. Carocci (2005)

GDPR (General Data Protection Regulation). Regulation (EU) 2016/679 of the European Parliament and of the Council of 27 April 2016 on the protection of natural persons with regard to the processing of personal data and on the free movement of such data

"Ginevri" Srl. https://www.ginevri.com. Accessed 1 Feb 2024

Baxter, G.D., Monk, A.F., Tan, K., Dear, P.R.F., Newell, S.J.: Using cognitive task analysis to facilitate the integration of decision support systems into the neonatal intensive care unit. Artif. Intell. Med. **35**(3), 243–257 (2005). ISSN 0933-3657, https://doi.org/10.1145/3335082.3335094

Hazlehurst, B., Gorman, P.N., McMullen, C.K.: Distributed cognition: an alternative model of cognition for medical informatics. Int. J. Med. Informatics **77**(4), 226–234 (2008)

IEC 62366–1:2015. Medical devices — Part 1: Application of usability engineering to medical devices

ISO 14971:2019. Medical devices — Application of risk management to medical devices

ISO 9241–210:2019, Ergonomics of human-system interaction - Part 210: Human-centred design for interactive systems

Kahneman, D.: Thinking, Fast and Slow. Macmillan (2011)

Kimbell, L.: Rethinking design thinking: Part II. Des. Cult. **3**(2), 129–148 (2011)

"Krasnogvardeets" JSC. https://gvardman.ru/?ysclid=ls2qghama2617822473. Accessed 1 Feb 2024

Kushniruk, A.W., Patel, V.L.: Cognitive and usability engineering methods for the evaluation of clinical information systems. J. Biomed. Inf. **37**(1), 56–76 (2004)

Norman, D.A., Draper, S.W.: User-Centered System Design: New Perspectives on Human-Computer Interaction. CRC Press (1986)

Norman, D.A.: The Design of Everyday Things. Basic Books (2013)

Patel, V.L., et al.: Recovery at the edge of error: debunking the myth of the infallible expert. J. Biomed. Inform. **44**(3), 413–424 (2010)

Roberts, J.P., Fisher, T.R., Trowbridge, M.J., Bent, C.: A design thinking framework for healthcare management and innovation. Healthcare **4**(1), 11–14 (2016). ISSN 2213-0764. https://doi.org/10.1016/j.hjdsi.2015.12.002.

Shneiderman, B., Plaisant, C.: Designing the User Interface: Strategies for Effective Human-Computer Interaction, 4th edn. (2004)

Tosi, F.: Design for ergonomics. In: Tosi, F. (ed.) Design for Ergonomics, Springer Series in Design and Innovation, pp. 31–45 (2020). ISSN 2661-8184. https://doi.org/10.1007/978-3-030-33562-5

Tosi F. (2005). *Ergonomia, progetto, prodotto [Ergonomics, Project, Product]*. Franco Angeli. ISBN 9788846466679

Vincent, C.J., Niezen, G., O'Kane, A.A., Stawarz, K.: Can standards and regulations keep up with health technology? JMIR mHealth Health **3**(2), 64 (2015)

Zolotova, M.: Cognitive ergonomics 'Features' as a tool for designing interaction with medical devices. In: Cotrim, T.P., Serranheira, F., Sousa, P., Hignett, S., Albolino, S., Tartaglia, R. (eds.) Health and Social Care Systems of the Future: Demographic Changes, Digital Age and Human Factors - Proceedings of the Healthcare Ergonomics and Patient Safety, HEPS 2019, vol. 1012, pp. 350–356, 7 p. Advances in Intelligent Systems and Computing. Springer (2019)

Zolotova, M.: "ChECk" the hospital: cognitive ergonomics components for the analysis of a human-system interaction in a hospital environment. Int. J. Des. Objects **15**(1-2), 1–14 14 p. (2021)

Cross-Cultural Product Design

Discussion on Common Audience's Cognitive Differences of Cultural Commodities - Taking Contemporary Lighting Design as an Example

Bin Chen[✉]

Creative Industry Design, National Taiwan University of Arts, 59, Section 1, Daguan Road, Banqiao District, New Taipei City 22058, Taiwan
yeshanhua825@gmail.com

Abstract. Today's products are rich in shapes and categories. In-depth discussions on how to express traditional cultural characteristics and meet users' higher-level spiritual needs through product design have become what contemporary designers need to think about and learn from. With the cultural collision of industrial products, the traditional oriental culture of paper lanterns has begun to promote the development of contemporary cultural product design. However, the current design of traditional paper lantern culture still lacks the emotional connection with users and the expression of relevant cultural connotations behind it.

This study uses literature analysis to deeply explore the product expression of the cultural codes of paper lanterns, establishes a cognitive model of cultural commodity design, collects contemporary paper lantern product design samples, and creates a balanced relationship between contemporary and traditional culture through the participation of designers in the design. Artificial intelligence paper lantern products. By collecting cognitive questionnaires on 12 paper lantern products, based on the relevant attributes of paper lantern cultural codes, as well as product innovation, beauty, audience preference, etc., we investigated the differences in perceptions of product design among general audiences on both sides of the Taiwan Strait. Finally, through statistical analysis such as multidimensional analysis, we sorted out the differences in the general audience's perception of the cultural codes of cultural commodities on both sides of the Taiwan Strait, the differences in the general audience's perception of modern and artificial intelligence products, and the differences in the audience's perception of gender, region, and identity. Influence, et. The research results are basically consistent with expectations. This research will help promote the design of contemporary traditional culture and contemporary lamps, promote the charm of traditional culture while realizing works that are both functional and aesthetic. The designer's subsequent paper lantern products Innovative design, as well as testing the auxiliary role of artificial intelligence in product design and providing substantial help in establishing cognitive models for artificial intelligence product design.

Keywords: Paper lanterns · product design · artificial intelligence · cognitive differences

© The Author(s), under exclusive license to Springer Nature Switzerland AG 2024
P.-L. P. Rau (Ed.): HCII 2024, LNCS 14699, pp. 195–206, 2024.
https://doi.org/10.1007/978-3-031-60898-8_13

1 Introduction

In the globalized market, in view of the fact that people's needs at the material level (function, external representation) are quickly met, their competitiveness and focus have shifted to the improvement and requirements at the spiritual level (emotion, connotation). Today, with rich product shapes and numerous categories, lamps cannot only provide the basic function of lighting, but more importantly, meet the higher-level spiritual needs of users. In addition to integrating with innovation, culture is also a carrier of local culture and global design value, and the basis for shaping cultural brands [1]. With the cultural collision of industrial products, the traditional culture of paper lanterns has begun to promote the development of contemporary cultural product design. However, the current design of traditional paper lantern culture still lacks the emotional connection with users and the expression of cultural connotations. Therefore, designers need to seek more cultural integration and thinking in traditional and modern products. There is a close relationship between cultural commodities and cultural codes. The development of products that emphasize cultural value and local characteristics has become the key to the design process. It is worthy of in-depth discussion on how to apply traditional cultural characteristics to modern product design [2]. Today, artificial intelligence is developing rapidly. The addition of artificial intelligence technology has become a hot topic in the design industry, making artificial intelligence a good assistant for designers to quickly realize design ideas. How assistive artificial intelligence is to designers' product design is currently a topic in design academic circles. One of the hot topics in the field that needs to be discussed urgently.

In the future, artificial intelligence technology will be widely used in all walks of life. Currently, AI technology can help humans with creative conception and image generation in the early stages of product design and research and development. It can also help non-professionals quickly complete product design simulation drawings, thus promoting the development of many industries. Inter-professional cooperation in various fields. The birth of AI products is the perfect fusion of the aesthetics of the times and artificial intelligence technology and is also the aesthetic expression of artists and appreciators. The human audience's perception of contemporary lighting products is essentially an aesthetic experience of life aesthetics, and the resulting difference in perception depends on whether the product's aesthetic expression and style features are liked by the audience.

Two research questions raised in this study:

1. To study the difference in the general public's perception of contemporary paper lantern product design
2. To explore the expression and dissemination of cultural symbols in contemporary cultural commodity design.

2 Theoretical Background and Literature Review

2.1 The Development and Value of Paper Lantern Culture

The famous archaeologist, Wei Cuncheng once pointed out that Chinese lanterns are the earliest portable lighting tools invented in the world. Paper lanterns are a treasure with significant cultural value in the history of the development of lighting fixtures in the world. They have a long history of development and profound cultural origins. The earliest paper lanterns originated in the Han Dynasty of China, and then began to develop and expand, and influenced the lantern culture of other countries. Paper lanterns in various regions have different aesthetic characteristics and cultural connotations. The most used function of paper lanterns in ancient China was night lighting. In the early days, they were the main indoor light source. It has become an indispensable mascot for festival customs. To this day, some areas continue this cultural etiquette. Viewing lanterns during the Lantern Festival is one of China's millennium customs. The custom of enjoying lanterns during the Lantern Festival originated in the early years of the Han Dynasty. In the first year of the Tang Dynasty to celebrate the prosperity of the country, for celebrating the prosperity of the country, the Lantern Festival lanterns were used in the celebration, and the shining lights were used to symbolize the prosperous country and safe society. The atmosphere of enjoying the lanterns has become one of the important activities of the New Year [3]. In the design of modern lighting fixtures, paper lanterns are highly interactive and decorative. In addition to lighting, lanterns are also rich in other symbolic meanings. The symbol of all the world is a universal symbol [4].

As a representative symbol of oriental culture, they have great cultural value and cultural compatibility, reflecting the cultural memory of local folk festivals. The development of traditional paper lantern products to this day, in addition to following the creation ideas of ancient Chinese traditional culture, must be based on mass manufacturing, market orientation, practicality first, and emotional needs as the main characteristics, and pay attention to the interaction and communication between products and people to enhance the use experience. With the passage and progress of the times, the demand for living materials is no longer scarce. The emphasis on personal taste and personalization has become the main axis of contemporary life. With the progress of the times, traditional lanterns have also developed lighting in line with the current life. However, the shape is still a skeleton that continues the tradition. The micro-innovative material makes the traditional lanterns with more folk colors a new modern appearance [5].

2.2 Cultural Commodities and Cultural Codes

The term cultural code is found in Roland Barthes's book ⌈S/Z: An Essay⌋ . It is a functional code that Barthes uses to analyze the structure of narrative works to define five textual meanings - hermeneutic code. One of code), behavioral code (proairetic code), seminal code (semic code), symbolic code (symbolic code) and cultural code [6]. Cultural commodities are to re-examine and reflect on the cultural factors contained in the utensils themselves, to use design to find a new modern look for the cultural factors, and to explore the spiritual satisfaction of using the utensils. This is the difference between cultural commodities and general commodities. The difference is that it has an additional function of cultural identity [7]. As one of the important expression elements of cultural commodities, cultural codes greatly affect the process and results of product design. [8] defined in The Code of Emotional Marketing that cultural codes are people giving objects a meaning subconsciously through the culture in which they grew up. [9] divided codes into three levels to analyze the code applications of cultural commodities. As far as the design of cultural products is concerned, in addition to considering their functionality and basic human needs, designers also consider implicit connotations such as emotional cognition, cultural identity and social value system, which also affect consumers' preferences for products. Cultural goods are the carriers of cultural transformation into tangible concepts. The challenge facing modern people is not only to turn to more ecologically efficient or low-carbon products and systems, but to more sustainable consumption and lifestyles [1]. Integrating cultural codes into the design of cultural products and vigorously promoting cultural revitalization has become one of the design hot spots promoted by cultural policies in various countries in recent years.

2.3 Audience Cognition Model of Cultural Commodities

Audience cognition is closely related to cultural communication theory and cultural aspects. As far as communication theory is concerned, the process by which an artist (addresser) expresses an artistic concept is called encoding, while the way in which an audience (recipient) obtains an intuitive understanding of a work of art is called decoding. In terms of the programmatic school of communication theory [10], there are three levels of communication that must be met for a successful 'artistic creation' to be communicated from the artist (the sender) creating the artwork (the message) to the audience (the recipient). Successful communication needs to meet three levels, namely the technical level, the semantic level, and the effect level [11]. On the technical level, the designer must accurately convey the information he wants to convey, so that the

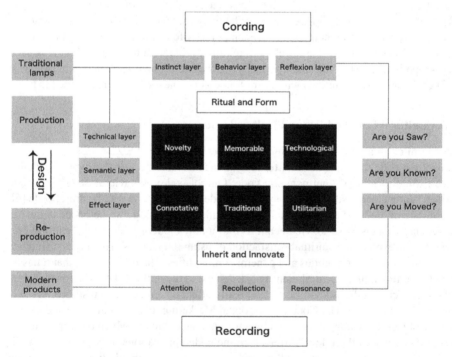

Fig. 1. Cognitive model of contemporary lighting design

audience can fully experience the beauty of the image; on the semantic level, the designer must accurately convey the relevant cultural meaning, so that the audience can deeply experience the beauty of the image; on the effect level, On the one hand, the message needs to influence the recipient in a way that triggers a specific response or behavior, and achieves the effect of the beauty of the audience's thoughts on it. For the listener, there are three key steps to understanding the meaning of a work of art: recognition (attracting attention), awareness (understanding and perception) and reflection (deep emotion). The viewer's aesthetic experience of art is a dynamic process, in which the 'inner feeling' is stimulated by the 'perception of form' of the aesthetic object, resulting in a holistic experience [12]. The designer is the creator of the product form and the coder of information. Whether the product can resonate with the user is guided by the subjective process in the heart and the decoder of the product [1]. Based on the solid literature and theoretical foundation and the content of this study, a preliminary cognitive model of contemporary paper lantern design in this study was constructed (see Fig. 1).

3 Materials and Methods

In order to explore the cognitive differences between general audiences on both sides of the Taiwan Strait, this study focused on the audience's emotional perception of the cultural codes of contemporary paper lanterns. First, we will analyze the cultural codes of ancient and modern paper lanterns to find their differences. Then we will collect cases of existing contemporary paper lantern products. We will creatively conceive products based on paper lanterns and modern aesthetic and functional requirements and use popular artificial intelligence. The image generation website 「Midjourney」 assists in the design of contemporary paper lantern products, integrates 12 research samples and 8 cultural code attributes, conducts sample questionnaire design and online questionnaire survey, and finally conducts statistical analysis of MDS based on the collected data. In this way, we can understand the cultural code recognition and aesthetic preferences of contemporary cross-strait audiences towards paper lantern products.

3.1 The Cultural Codes of Paper Lanterns

For analyzing the cultural codes of paper lanterns and the characteristics of today's paper lantern products, this study conducted an analysis of the cultural codes of ancient and modern products in Modeling, Color, Technique, Function, Cultural meaning. By comparing the cultural codes and design expressions of ancient and modern paper lanterns (see Table 1), we can discover their differences. Combining the above related cultural code attributes with the elements of contemporary successful cultural product design, this study sorted out 8 evaluation attributes: f1 Shape and conception harmony, f2 Appropriate color, f3 Fine workmanship, f4 Functional, f5 Interesting, f6 Strong atmosphere, f7 Local specialties, f8 Cultural connotation, provide beneficial help for subsequent research.

3.2 Case Introduction

The sample design of this study is divided into two categories: existing paper lantern products and artificial intelligence paper lantern products. In the early stage, many

Table 1. The cultural codes of ancient and modern paper lanterns

Cultural codes	Traditional paper lantern	Modern paper lantern
Modeling	Most of the patterns are flowers, totems, and characters, and the shapes are mainly oval, barrel, winter melon, and palace lantern shapes	Various styles, rich and different shapes, multiple shape combinations, fashionable and elegant
Color	Red, yellow, gold, green and other traditional Chinese colors	Mainly white and beige, Color advanced and simple
Technique	Hand-made, bamboo weaving combined with rice paper and oil paper, Cross-bone, boneless and other techniques	Mainly industrial production, combined with different comprehensive materials, focusing on functionality
Function	Festival blessings and other folk activities	Lighting, decoration, viewing
Cultural meaning	Enhance the festive atmosphere and inherit traditional customs and culture	The collision of Chinese and Western cultures embodies aesthetics, individuality, and multi-functional products

paper lantern products were collected. According to the requirements of cultural code attributes, the product was selected based on the appearance, popularity, country, and connotation of the product. Collected in the early stage and conducted the final screening of existing products through expert questionnaires, and finally obtained 6 existing paper lantern product samples. Then, we combined the aesthetic elements, product application scenarios, cultural connotations, etc. of ancient and modern paper lantern products to conceive new product ideas and combined with the artificial intelligence image generation website 「Midjourney」 to generate images for new product designs. Midjourney has become the largest natural language image generation website in the world today. MidJourney-AI works entirely based on a text-to-illustration-based system called "prompt". A particular order and system are built into "prompt" writing for AI to recognise it as a prompt [13]. The application of Vincentian diagrams can include images described according to natural language, or generating corresponding images based on keyword text. It has been widely used in creative industries. The following are some relevant introductions to product samples (see Table 2).

3.3 Questionnaire Design

In order to test the accuracy of the audience's perception of the attributes and the differences in sample perceptions, the strength of the aesthetic attributes of the selected works was questioned. In the questionnaire, the questions are set in a matrix form, and the target audience is the broad audience on both sides of the Taiwan Strait. By allowing them to make intuitive judgments on the 8 cultural code attributes of each of the 12 works, we can quickly see the general audience's recognition of these cultural code attributes and the communication effect of the NFT virtual image.

Table 2. This study cases' Introduction

Existing products Cases	Case Introduction
	Jaime Hayon &Tradition Formakami Suspension Lamp in Rice Paper The designers redesigned it with a modern aesthetic. Seen in an ultra-light rice paper chandelier that echoes ancient lanterns from Asia, Hayon dispensed with cultural formalities and created a series of all-white lanterns. Handcrafted from rice paper, it brings together a variety of sizes and shapes.
	Hong Kong Life & Traditional Taiwanese Lantern These lanterns are handmade in the last traditional workshop in the mountains of Taiwan. Each lamp is hand-painted by local Taiwanese artists. Each painting is unique in color and pattern.
	Sixianfengwu & Revolving Lantern DIY National Trend Lantern It uses the original illustration "Mid-Autumn Garden Picture" with the style of ancient folk paintings of humans, monsters, fairies and other people as the main decorative image, and makes the traditional folk craft toy of the Han Dynasty revolving lantern into a DIY toy gift.
	Ganshunxing & 2021 Hsinchu Art Festival Joint Creative Lantern This art festival selected 20 spaces in the old city of Hsinchu to create lanterns, which serve as guides for walking around the streets to review the past and learn about the new. This work is inspired by the long-established seafood dry goods store "Ganshunxing" and the silhouette of seafood.
	AKARI Japanese paper lantern This series is designed based on traditional Gifu lanterns. At the time of their introduction, ordinary lanterns had a strong image of being used for funerals and were not favored for interior decoration. So, Isamu Noguchi also created lanterns with hand-drawn abstract patterns and calligraphy. Later, rustic, modern white lanterns became highly sought after in Western countries.

(continued)

Table 2. (*continued*)

National Museum of China & Oriental Collection Paper Carving Lamp

This work is one of the oriental collections of paper carving lamps. The material is all paper. It is combined with the picture of returning to the pasture in the autumn suburbs, and each petal is given a pattern. The light and delicate material, exquisite and elegant shape, and strong decorative effect.

AI products Cases	Case Introduction

Comfortable Wood & rice paper lantern aromatherapy lamp

This product combines the elements of aromatherapy and paper lanterns, and is designed in color, pattern, and function to make it rich in oriental aesthetics and meet the daily needs of modern people.

Wake & Paper Lantern Fashion Bedside Clock

Bedside lamps are usually highly used products, and there are certainly very few products that combine human sleep with lanterns. This product combines paper lanterns with the functions of smart alarm clocks in a fashionable and simple shape, giving the work a minimalist aesthetic. Practical and lightweight.

Happy festival & Chinese-style small lantern plate lamp

This product combines a fruit plate with a Spring Festival atmosphere with the shape of a paper lantern, so that it can be used as an ornament, a fruit plate, and a lighting function.

Retro paper lantern potted ornamental lamp

Among indoor decoration ornaments, ornamental value is one of the most important consumption factors. Potted plants with ornamental functions are environmentally friendly while maintaining a natural atmosphere in the room. Therefore, the design is combined with potted plants and paper lanterns to create a multi-functional ornamental experience.

(*continued*)

Table 2. (*continued*)

Retro Sugar & Bluetooth Audio Paper Lantern Lighting Fixture

The retro collision of Bluetooth speakers and traditional Chinese paper lantern elements allows this product to not only have a viewing function, but also meet the music playback preferences of young people nowadays, making it both retro and contemporary traditional and practical.

Bloom & Paper Lantern Holiday Lighting

Paper lanterns are closely related to traditional Chinese festivals and often appear as festival products during the Lantern Festival and Spring Festival. Therefore, the shape of paper lanterns is changed and innovated based on the inspiration of fireworks.

For the fairness of the questionnaire, all subjects were informed of the purpose of the experiment. They were then asked to evaluate the sample of this study based on intuitive questions, which explored the audience's perceptions of this study using a 5-point Likert scale ranging from 1 ("Strongly Disagree") to 5 ("Strongly Agree") Identification of selected cultural codes.

Finally, 107 valid online questionnaires were collected, of which 36.45% were male (39) and 63.55% were female (68). Respondents aged 18–25 accounted for 40.19%, with a total of 43 respondents; In addition, among the respondents, 42.06% have a college (college) degree, and about 55% of the respondents live in mainland China.

4   Results and Discussion

The above literature analysis reflects that the cognitive model and evaluation matrix of the cultural codes of contemporary paper lantern products are reasonable and reflects the process of the general audience's cultural perception of paper lantern products.

Therefore, taking 12 contemporary paper lantern products that embody 8 cultural evaluation attributes as samples, a spatial analysis of the audience's product perception was conducted, and a confusion matrix of contemporary paper lantern products was established (see Table 3). From the MDS statistical analysis Judging from the results, the stress index and absolute coefficient are Kruskal's Stress = .07470 and RSQ = .98588 respectively, which shows that these two vectors are suitable for describing the spatial relationship between the 12 aesthetics.

The following conclusions are drawn from the confusing matrix of this study:

1. p1, p3, p5, p6, p7, p8, p9 and p11 performed in line with the strength of the aesthetic attributes as expected.

Table 3. Contemporary lighting design matrix of aesthetic properties

	p1	p2	p3	p4	p5	p6	p7	p8	p9	p10	p11	p12
f1 Shape and conception harmony	3.73	4.11	3.76	3.82	4.28	3.79	3.92	4.13	3.9	4.33	3.17	3.74
f2 Appropriate color	3.26	4.01	3.8	3.63	4.19	3.82	4.09	3.96	3.95	4.16	2.96	3.7
f3 Fine workmanship	3.61	3.95	3.77	3.91	4.21	3.68	4.07	4.13	3.86	4.25	2.99	3.86
f4 Functional	3.01	3.23	2.99	2.94	3.74	3.4	4.22	3.36	3.62	3.48	2.9	2.79
f5 Interesting	3.13	3.39	3.78	3.51	3.8	3.49	3.95	3.81	3.91	3.99	3.13	3.78
f6 Strong atmosphere	3.29	4.04	3.73	3.86	4.06	3.35	3.66	3.98	3.82	4.01	3.07	3.56
f7 Local specialties	3.08	3.96	3.9	3.88	3.81	3.17	3.26	3.9	3.65	3.79	3.21	3.41
f8 Cultural connotation	3.41	4.13	4.06	3.91	4.02	3.24	3.37	3.73	3.73	3.99	3.07	3.5

2. Among the performance of all attributes of p1, p5, and p10, the attribute f1 (Shape and conception harmony) is strong. Among them, p10 has the highest score for this attribute and the highest score among all attribute scores; P2, p3, and p4 have the best performance of all attributes. Among them, f8 (cultural connotation) attributes are all strong, among which p2 reflects the highest score of this attribute.
3. p1 has the highest score in the f1(Shape and conception harmony) attribute among all attribute performances and has also become the work with the highest attribute scores in f2(Appropriate color) and f6(Strong atmosphere); p10 has the highest score in the f1(Shape and conception harmony) attribute among all attribute performances and has also become the work with the highest attribute scores in f3(Fine workmanship) and f5(Interesting) the highest works.

Based on the results of the confusion matrix (see Fig. 2), a cognitive-spatial analysis of the 12 aesthetic attributes of the viewers in the 12 works was conducted, and the angle between each aesthetic attribute and the three-way axial diagram of the products was analyzed in terms of multiple vectors. This is the conclusion drawn from the multi-directional analysis diagram:

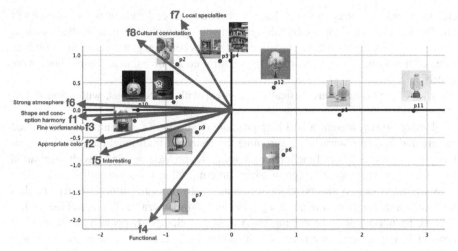

Fig. 2. Multi-dimensional cognitive analysis of Contemporary lighting design

1. f1, f3, f6, f2, and f5 each form a cluster, and these attributes are closely related to each other.
2. p5 and p10 have the strongest correlation with f1, f3, and f6, indicating that they are stronger in attributes such as strong atmosphere, harmonious shape and artistic conception, and skillful materials, art, and craftsmanship.
3. The major attributes of p1, p6, p11 and p12 have weak significance.
4. The local characteristics of p2, p3 and f7 and the cultural connotation of f8 are more significant than others.
5. p7 has the highest significance among all works with f4 in daily practical attributes.
6. The angle between f4 and f8 is close to 90 degrees, indicating that the correlation between cultural connotation and daily practicality is the weakest.

5   Conclusion

In today's world where culture and science and technology emphasize the integrated development, seeking cultural differences and exploring humanized design are one of the hot topics in the field of design. Product designers should make good use of cultural codes to establish potential emotional connections between products and consumers as imprints [8]. The connection between cultural commodities and cultural codes that are recognized and accepted by the audience has become something that designers need to consider when designing products.

This study uses literature analysis to deeply explore the product expression of the cultural codes of paper lanterns and establishes a cognitive model of cultural commodity design. By collecting contemporary paper lantern product design samples, and through designers participating in the design, we create a balance between contemporary and traditional culture. Artificial intelligence paper lantern products, by collecting cognitive questionnaires on 12 paper lantern products, based on the relevant attributes of paper lantern cultural codes, as well as product innovation, aesthetics, audience preference, etc., to investigate the cognitive differences between general audiences on both sides of the Taiwan Strait on their product designs. Finally, through statistical analysis such as multidimensional analysis, the cognitive differences between general audiences on both sides of the Taiwan Strait regarding the cultural codes of cultural commodities were sorted out.

The research results are basically consistent with expectations, with some differences.

Through this research, it will help promote the design of contemporary traditional culture and contemporary lamps, promote the charm of traditional culture while realizing works that are both functional and aesthetic, provide designers with inspiration for subsequent innovative design of paper lantern products, and test artificial Wisdom assists product design and provides substantial help in establishing cognitive models for artificial intelligence product design. In today's digital era, artificial intelligence has become an important force driving innovation and change. Especially in the field of product design, the empowerment of artificial intelligence allows us to break traditional boundaries and create smarter and more personalized products. By fusing human intelligence with technological intelligence, we can open new possibilities and redefine the user experience. Future research will conduct an in-depth analysis of factors such as gender and age in the study from the perspective of user preferences, as well as research on the auxiliary role of artificial intelligence in art design and explore how creators can use artificial intelligence products to better unleash their creativity.

References

1. Cao, J.: Research on innovative styles of local wedding custom product design: Research on innovation model of local marriage custom articles: A case study of ten-mile red dowry. doctoral thesis at National Taiwan University of the Arts (2023)
2. Xu, Q.X., Lin, R.T.: Cultural product design process. J. Des. **16**(40), 1–18 (2011)
3. Guangyuan Lantern Tourism Factory Lighting Celebration Interview (2014)
4. Shen, Q., Rhetoric: Wunan Book Publishing, Taipei, p. 56 (2013)
5. Shao, Y.: The Innovative Design of My Bionic Concept Lantern, Master's Class, Department of Business Design, Master's thesis of National Taichung University of Science and Technology (2016)
6. Barthes, R.: S/Z: An essay. (Trans. Richard Miller). Hill & Wang, New York (1974). (Original work published 1970)
7. He, M.Q., Lin, Q.X., Liu, Y.J.: Conception of cultural commodity development. J. Des. **1**(1), 1–15 (1996)
8. Rapaille, C.: The culture code: An ingenious way to understand why people around the world live and buy as they do. Currency (2007)
9. Lin, M.H.: Symbols and codes in product modeling. J. Des. **5**(2), 73–82 (2000)
10. Fiske, J.: Introduction to Communication Studies, pp. 5–6. Routledg, London (2010)
11. Craig, R.T.: Communication theory as a Field. Commun. Theory **9**(2), 119–161 (1999)
12. Beardsley, M.C.: Aesthetics, Problems in the Philosophy of Criticism. Hackett, Indianapolis, IN, USA (1981)
13. Panicker, S.: AI-Inflected Art/Architecture: Who (or rather, what) is the artist/architect? Blueprint September 2022 **3**(2), 15–36 (2022)

Angular vs. Rounded Perception? The Eye-Tracking Study of Cross-Cultural Differences in Visual Perception of the Relationship Between Product Outline and Its Surface Texture

Tseng-Ping Chiu[(⊠)] and Syu-Wei Chen

Department of Industrial Design, National Cheng Kung University, Tainan, Taiwan
{mattchiu,p36104097}@gs.ncku.edu.tw

Abstract. Eyes are basically the most direct way for human beings to understand the world. Among the visual stimuli we receive, besides the overall outline of the object, we are also stimulated by the material, and the color and surface treatment accompanying the material will bring us different feelings and stimuli. In recent years, the globalization of product design has developed rapidly. Therefore, products designed by different cultures are everywhere in the world. When a product is sold and displayed in the market, people with different cultural backgrounds may have different views and feelings on the product. In this era of paying attention to consumers' feelings, it is bound to consider the differences in cross-cultural perception into product design. However, the past literature shows that there are two different self-construction models between East and West, and self-construction will affect a person's cognition, emotion, and motivation. Therefore, the common "shape" elements in product design have different cognitive differences between East and West consumers. In addition, we have observed in recent years the rise of parametric software, which has led to an increasing application of "shape" elements through the method of "arrangement" in product design. Such as consumer electronics, vehicles, and sportswear, etc. However, how do designers confirm whether the shape arrangement elements produced when applied to product design conform to the aesthetic preferences of East and West consumers? Therefore, this study will explore the visual perception of Eastern consumers on the application of such products through the design application of "form" and "arrangement of angular and rounded shapes" on the surface of the product. Among them, we further use eye tracking equipment to assist in examining the physiological information of Eastern consumers and use scientific methods to study the differences in consumers' visual perception of product outlines and surface textures. These studies provide a prospective insight into cross-cultural product design and provides a reference for designers to apply the "shape" element in products.

Keywords: Cross-cultural self-construction · Cross-cultural aesthetic differences · Visual perception · Shape arrangement products · Eye tracking

© The Author(s), under exclusive license to Springer Nature Switzerland AG 2024
P.-L. P. Rau (Ed.): HCII 2024, LNCS 14699, pp. 207–223, 2024.
https://doi.org/10.1007/978-3-031-60898-8_14

1 Introduction

In recent years, the global development of product design has rapidly shifted towards globalization. This signifies the mutual integration of design philosophies and styles from different cultures, enabling the same product to be marketed and showcased world-wide. However, due to consumers with diverse cultural backgrounds, varying percep-tions and evaluations of the product may arise. Therefore, in this era that emphasizes consumer experience, considering cross-cultural perceptual differences has become an indispensable aspect of product design.

The past literature shows that there are two different self-construction models between Eastern and Western cultures. Eastern cultures emphasize harmony and interde-pendence with others, hence classified as "interdependent self-construction" and "col-lectivism"; In contrast, Western cultures exhibit characteristics of "independent self-construction" and "individualism", emphasizing individual will and independence from others [1]. Furthermore, self-construction can affect one's cognition, emotion, and moti-vation. For example, past research focusing on trademarks found that collectivist cultures tend to prefer round outline, as round shape symbolize harmony and closeness; Con-versely, individualist cultures lean towards angular edges, as angular shape symbolize a sense of conflict and strength, etc. Therefore, it corresponds to the characteristics of aesthetic preference in the context of independent self-construction [2].

However, in recent years, the rise of parametric software has led to an increasing application of "shape" elements through the method of "arrangement" in product design. This trend is evident in various products such as consumer electronics, transportation vehicles, sports equipment, etc. (Fig. 1). The emergence of parametric software allows designers to build upon generative logic. Through a proficient grasp of design concepts and the clarification of the relationships among relevant parameters, designers can more swiftly and accurately control the surface details of products, including shape, arrange-ment, density, compositional rules, and proportions. In general, how to properly use the parametric design application of "shape arrangement" to make the visual perception of products more attractive to consumers of different cultures is the subject of this study.

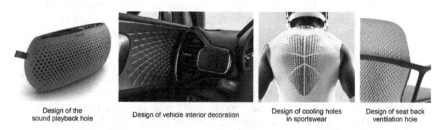

Design of the
sound playback hole   Design of vehicle interior decoration   Design of cooling holes
in sportswear   Design of seat back
ventilation hole

Fig. 1. Application of parametric shape arrangement to surface details of product design.

Therefore, the purpose of this study are: (1) To explore the visual perception dif-ferences among Eastern consumers regarding the design application of "form" and the surface "arrangement of angular and rounded shapes" in products; (2) To explore the physiological information through the eye tracker, and to study the visual perception of

Eastern consumers on products arranged in shape with scientific methods; (3) Finally, the above experimental results will be applied to the shape arrangement design of consumer electronic products, and through the parametric software Grasshopper in the modeling software Rhinoceros (abbreviated as Rhino) constructs a set of parameter databases. The database is placed on a public website, hoping to provide a reference for designers to apply "shape" elements in products.

2 Literature Review

2.1 The Self-construction of "Individualism" and "Collectivism"

"Self-construction" is defined as "the relationship between self and others" [3]. The past literature shows that there are two different self-construction models between East and West. In Eastern culture, individuals often place themselves within the overall group, emphasizing collaboration, tolerance, and the needs of the group. This self-construction model encourages individuals to be more inclined towards harmony and interdependence, and to establish stable interpersonal relationships in society, thus being described as "collective self-construction"; In contrast, in Western culture, individuals place greater emphasis on independence, autonomy, and the pursuit of personal goals. This self-construction model makes individuals more inclined to express their uniqueness, pursue personal achievement, and emphasize personal will and independence from others, thus being described as "individualistic self-construction" [1]. In such a culture, individual success is often seen as the result of individual abilities and efforts, rather than the collective efforts of the group. As shown in "Fig. 2", people with independent are less closely connected with those around them and belong to "individualistic self-construction"; while interdependent people are closely connected with those around them, which is more of a "collectivist self-construction".

In summary, these two self-construction models reflect different cultural values regarding the relationship between self and others. Therefore, understanding these cultural differences contributes to fostering cross-cultural communication and understanding, while also reminding us to adapt to and respect diverse value systems in cross-cultural environments.

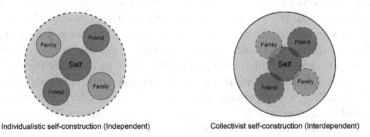

Individualistic self-construction (Independent)   Collectivist self-construction (Interdependent)

Fig. 2. "Individualistic self-construction" and "Collectivist self-construction".

2.2 Aesthetic Preference of "Shape"

"Shape" has a profound impact on people's perceptions and associations. Different shapes often convey different messages and associations. For example: Shapes with sharp edges often give people a symbol of energy, resilience, and strength; while rounded shapes are often seen as a symbol of harmony, and friendliness, and bring a feeling of intimacy. Therefore, the choice of shape in design can often affect people's overall impression and emotional experience of an object, place, or product.

In addition, self-construction affects a person's cognition, emotion, and motivation. For example, when researchers studied trademarks in the past, they found that collectivist culture preferred the "round outline", while individualistic culture preferred "angular edges" [2]. In addition, Tzeng, Trung, and Rieber (1990) found that students in Mexico, Colombia and Japan have different opinions on the same icons and graphics. For example, Japanese students think that circular graphics are powerful and beautiful, while Colombian students think they are ugly and weak [4]. In addition, Simonson, and Schmitt (2009) discussed the building of the "Bank of China Tower in Hong Kong" in the book "Marketing Aesthetics", which is composed of typical angular and triangular elements. They believe that in a culture that values harmony, although this structure symbolizes the display of authority and power, it also symbolizes conflict, conflict and bad luck for them [5].

The above theories and cases reflect the cognitive differences of "shape" in different cultural backgrounds. In individualistic cultures, there is an emphasis on independence, individual expression, and uniqueness. Therefore, angular shapes may be more likely to attract attention and be seen as symbols of individuality and strength; conversely, in collectivistic cultures, there is a focus on group and common harmony. So, the softness and flow of a round shape may be more popular.

2.3 Overview and Practical Application of "Parametric Design"

The most important feature of parametric design is that it can adjust the parameter values between features through dynamic control and repeatedly, so that designers can quickly evaluate the feature parameter rules they set, and process complex parameter operations by computer, which greatly reduces the time of manual processing. Coupled with the advancement of today's digital manufacturing technology, it not only provides a new design method, but also accelerates the overall design process [6]. In addition, parametric design enables the presentation of complex structures that were previously impossible to achieve. By changing some elements of the design into variables of a function, and by changing the variables of a function, or by changing the algorithm to generate new design elements, in addition to enabling the product to display a varied and rich aesthetic feeling, it also promotes the visual presentation effect of the product to be more diversified and can meet the personalized needs of consumers. The most important thing is to make the design very rational [7].

As shown in "Fig. 3" we use the parametric software "Grasshopper" to conduct a demonstration. By adjusting different parameters, we can accurately control the appearance, hole shape and density of the air cleaner, so that the same product can produce hundreds of thousands of possibilities at the same time. And our subsequent experimental samples and research outputs will also be constructed and produced using this parameterized software (Grasshopper).

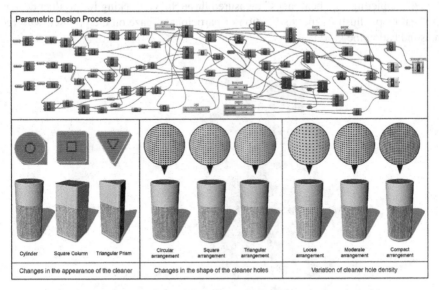

Fig. 3. Parametric software (Grasshopper) applied to air cleaner design.

2.4 Overview of "Eye-Tracker"

Eye-tracker will be used as an auxiliary tool for visual perception measurement in the experimental phase of this study. As a visual observation tool, the eye tracker can detect the subject's pupils through infrared rays and transmit the subject's eye movement data back to the eye tracking instrument for subsequent analysis. However, there are mainly four types of physiological phenomena related to eye movements, namely (1) "Fixations", also known as gaze, which refers to continuous gaze in an area for more than 60 ms, usually observing things; (2) "Saccades" refers to the short and fast movement trajectory of the eyeball between gaze points; (3) "Smooth pursuits" refers to the eyeball looking at moving objects in the picture and keeping the image on the retina still; (4) "Miniature eye movements" refer to phenomena such as drift, tremor, and micro saccades [8, 9].

In addition, there are some common definitions of terms used when analyzing data with eye trackers, namely (1) "Area of interest", which refers to the designated area used to count eye movement behaviors, generally referred to as "AOI"; (2) "Visit" refers to the time when the eye focus enters a certain area and leaves this area, which is regarded as a visit; (3) "Fixation Point" refers to the time when the eye focus is at a certain position. The dwell time is 60 to 600 ms, recorded as a point of fixation [8, 9]. Analyzing the eye-tracking data mentioned above assists in understanding what visual content attracts the attention of consumers or participants. It also helps identify which visual elements may distract consumers' attention or what content fails to engage consumers in interaction [9].

Furthermore, eye-tracking data analysis can be visually presented, as shown in "Fig. 4", depicting the "heat maps" measured through eye-tracking for product design. The heat maps illustrate the distribution of participants' gaze on the product, with red areas indicating the gaze hotspots.

Fig. 4. "Heat maps" of eye trackers in product design.

3   Method

Previous cross-cultural research has shown that different cultural self-constructions will produce differences in aesthetic preferences between angular and round shapes [3]. The differences in visual perceptions and feelings of consumers with different cultural backgrounds will also affect whether a product is loved by others. Therefore, this experiment will use 3D software (Rhinoceros) to build a series of products and use parametric software (Grasshopper) to build the design application of "round and angular shape arrangements" on the product surface. The study aims to investigate the visual perception differences among Eastern consumers regarding this type of product application. Additionally, we will employ eye tracking equipment (Tobii pro nano) to further examine physiological aspects of information, scientifically studying consumers' visual perception differences regarding product outlines and surface textures.

3.1   Participants

In the experiment, a total of 7 participants with Eastern cultural backgrounds participated (4 males and 3 females), with an age range between 20 and 30 years old.

3.2 Procedure

Select Product Experiment Sample Type. In the first part of this experiment procedure, we found three experts in the field of industrial design and asked them to extensively collect products available in the market. Finally, the collected products were divided into six groups of different product types through the KJ method. As shown in "Fig. 5", each group of product types has two products of the same type. These two products are identical in terms of functions, uses, and usage scenarios. The only difference is "outline style of the overall appearance of the product." As shown in "Fig. 5", items labeled A-1, B-1, C-1, D-1, E-1, and F-1 exhibit a presentation of "rounded and soft product outline styles." Conversely, items labeled A-2, B-2, C-2, D-2, E-2, and F-2 showcase "sharp and angular product outline styles."

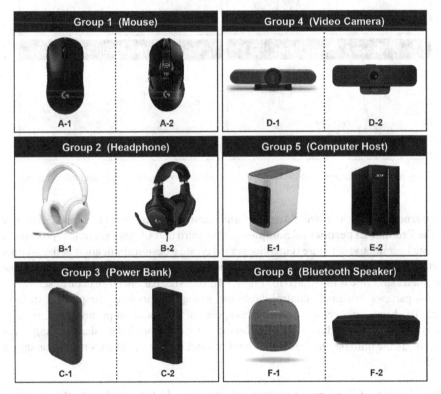

Fig. 5. Product experiment sample selection and classification chart.

Constructing a 3D Appearance Model of Product Experimental Samples. In the second part of this experiment procedure, we used 3D modeling software (Rhinoceros) to construct a 3D appearance model of the product. When constructing a 3D appearance model, the visual impact of brand, color and material will be removed. As shown in "Fig. 6", product samples of the six groups have been construct as 3D models.

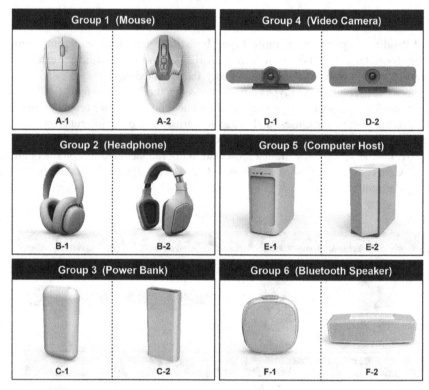

Fig. 6. Classification chart of 3D appearance model for product experimental samples.

Constructing the Surface "Angular and Round Shape Arrangement" Texture of the Product Experimental Samples. In the third part of this experiment procedure, we used parametric software (Grasshopper) to create a design application of the product surface with "arrangement of angular and round shapes." The process of constructing the parameter structure is illustrated in "Fig. 7." Through the parameter structure established in this part, we can easily control the shape arrangement type of the product surface, such as: shape, arrangement, density, composition rules and proportions, etc. Finally, we combined the "product 3D model" in the second part with the "shape arrangement texture" in the third part to become the final product sample of this experiment, as shown in "Fig. 8."

Classification of Product Experimental Samples. In the fourth part of the experimental procedure, we classified the constructed product samples mentioned above and organized them into "Fig. 9." As shown in "Fig. 9", each set of product samples has a surface texture of "arrangement of circular and angular shapes," resulting in a total of 24 experimental product samples.

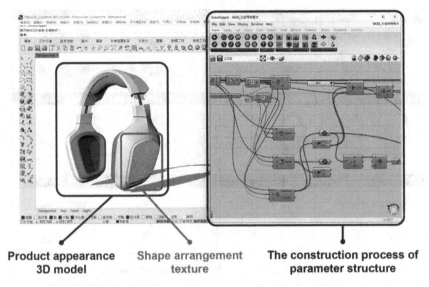

Product appearance   **Shape arrangement**   **The construction process of**
3D model   **texture**   **parameter structure**

Fig. 7. Construction process diagram of parameter structure.

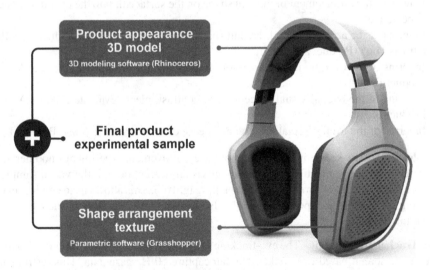

Fig. 8. Final product experimental sample.

Making Experimental Samples for Eye Trackers. In the fifth part of the experimental procedure, we use the product sample in "Fig. 9" as material to make it into a visual sample in the eye tracker experiment. In addition, we also listed a series of questions about visual perception and used them to ask participants' feelings when performing eye movement experiments, such as.

1. How would you evaluate the visual appearance of this product?

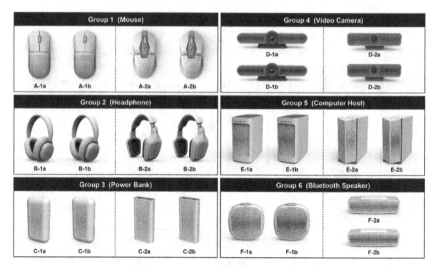

Fig. 9. Overview of product experimental samples.

2. How does the arrangement of the unit shape on the surface fit into the overall product appearance?
3. In terms of the arrangement of the unit shape on the surface, which product visually attracts you? (Product A or Product B)
4. In terms of the overall visual perception of harmony, please evaluate Product A and Product B.
5. In terms of the overall visual perception of contrast, please evaluate Product A and Product B.
6. In terms of the overall visual preference, please evaluate Product A and Product B.

However, to make the overall process of the eye movement experiment smoother, we integrated the above-mentioned issues about visual perception into the visual samples of the eye movement experiment (as shown in "Fig. 10"). This allows us to conduct eye-tracking physiological experiments while also asking participants about their feelings about the product.

Eye Tracker Instrument. The eye-tracking instrument selected was "Tobii Pro Nano", which is a screen-based eye tracker that can capture 60 Hz gaze data. This instrument can be attached to the bottom of the computer screen and is mainly used to observe the movement of sight on the computer screen (as shown in Fig. 11).

Experimental Space Setup. The space for conducting the eye-tracking experiment is a research room of approximately 10 square meters. The setup in the room includes two tables, each equipped with a display screen. One screen is for the experimenter's operation, and the other screen is for the participant to engage in the eye-tracking experiment (as shown in Fig. 12).

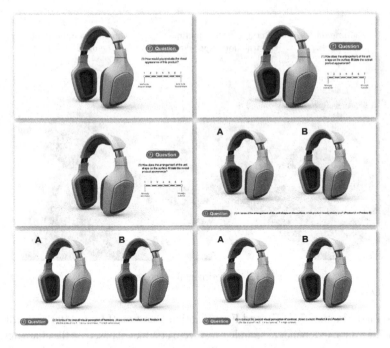

Fig. 10. Schematic diagram of experimental sample of eye tracker.

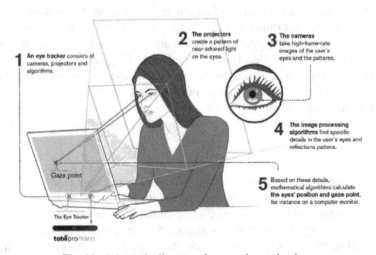

Fig. 11. Schematic diagram of eye tracker technology.

3.3 Measurement

The measurement was divided into two parts: eye-tracking and questionnaire survey. Eye-tracking data indicates the time participants spent observing the product samples in milliseconds (ms). This study applied three eye-tracking metrics: Area of Interest (AOI),

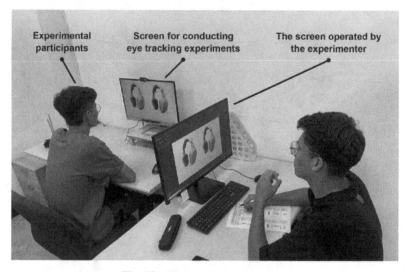

Fig. 12. Experimental space setup.

Time to First Fixation (TTFF), and First Fixation Duration (FFD). After collecting the eye-tracking data, independent sample t-test were conducted based on the characteristics to observe differences in participants' attention time to the product samples and make comparisons.

In addition, we designed a series of questionnaires integrated with the eye-tracking experimental samples (as shown in Fig. 10) for participants to answer simultaneously with the eye-tracking experiment. Psychological questions include "Adaptability of product texture," "Harmony of product texture," "Preference for product texture," etc. Participants responded to these questions using a 7-point Likert scale, where 0 indicates strongly disagree, and 7 indicates strongly agree. Finally, quantitative analysis was conducted using independent sample t-test.

4   Result

This study was divided into two aspects: physiological (eye-tracking) and psychological (questionnaire), primarily aiming to explore the impact of the relationship between product outline and surface texture on Eastern cultural consumers. In the eye-tracking experiment, there were 7 participants (4 males, 3 females), each observing 12 products (as shown in Fig. 9) and providing verbal responses based on the questions displayed on the screen. Each participant collected eye-tracking data for 12 sets, resulting in a total of 84 sets of eye-tracking data in the experiment.

4.1 Physiological Response (Eye-Tracking)

Attraction and Attention on "Products with a round arrangement texture" vs. "Products with an angular arrangement texture." Firstly, an independent samples t-test was conducted using the "Time to First Fixation (TTFF)" and "First Fixation Duration (FFD)" data obtained through eye-tracking, to compare the attention differences among Eastern participants towards products featuring "round arrangement texture" and "angular arrangement texture." Table 1 presents the experimental results. There was a significant difference in "Time to First Fixation (TTFF)" between products with a round arrangement texture (M = 0.419, SD = 0.259) and products with an angular arrangement texture (M = 1.067, SD = 0.802); t (166) = −7.052, p < 0.001. This indicates that Eastern participants, when simultaneously viewing products with "round" and "angular" arrangement textures, were more rapidly drawn to visually attend to products with a "round" arrangement texture. Additionally, there was a significant difference in "First Fixation Duration (FFD)" between products with a round arrangement texture (M = 0.349, SD = 0.325) and products with an angular arrangement texture (M = 0.228, SD = 0.099); t (166) = 3.259, p < 0.03. This indicates that Eastern participants, when fixating on products with a "round" arrangement texture, exhibit a longer duration of fixation compared to products with an "angular" arrangement texture, suggesting a higher level of visual attention.

Table 1. The independent sample *t*-test of TTFF and FFD on product.

	Variable	n.	M	SD	df	*t*	*p*
Time to first fixation (TTFF)	Round	84	0.419	0.259	166	−7.052	.000
	Angular	84	1.067	0.802			
First fixation duration (FFD)	Round	84	0.349	0.325	166	3.259	.003
	Angular	84	0.228	0.099			

Furthermore, we compared the attractiveness of products featuring a "round arrangement texture" and those featuring an "angular arrangement texture." Farnsworth (2022) suggests that higher FFD and shorter TTFF can identify participants' higher attraction to the object [10]. As depicted in "Fig. 13," the time spent on products with a "round arrangement texture" was shorter than that on products with an "angular arrangement texture" (0.419 < 1.067 ms). This indicates that Eastern participants fixated on products with a "round arrangement texture" more quickly and spent more time gazing at those products (0.349 > 0.228 ms). Therefore, compared to products with an "angular arrangement texture," products with a "round arrangement texture" exhibit higher visual attractiveness for Eastern participants.

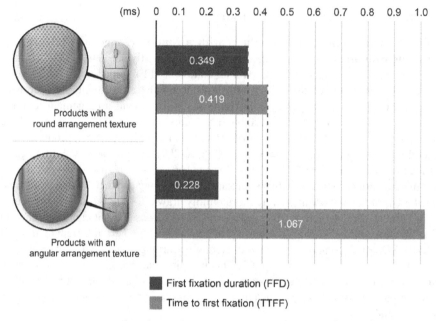

Fig. 13. Attraction comparison on product.

4.2 Psychological Response (Questionnaire)

The Overall Psychological Impact of Shape Arrangement Textures. As shown in Table 2, the results indicate that "products with round arrangement textures" have a positive impact on the psychology of Eastern participants. Firstly, there is a significant difference in product preferences between conditions with products featuring round arrangement textures (M = 5.40, SD = 1.131) and those with angular arrangement textures (M = 4.02, SD = 1.397); t (159.132) = 7.041, p < 0.00. This suggests that "products with round arrangement textures" have a positive influence on the preference level of Eastern participants. Second, there is a significant difference in product adaptability between conditions with products featuring round arrangement textures (M = 4.96, SD = 1.468) and those with angular arrangement textures (M = 3.81, SD = 1.525); t (165.763) = 5.000, p < 0.00. This indicates that, compared to products with angular arrangement textures, Eastern participants perceive products with round arrangement textures to have higher visual adaptability. Finally, there is a significant difference in the visual harmony between products featuring round arrangement textures (M = 5.97, SD = 1.226) and those with angular arrangement textures (M = 3.79, SD = 1.537); t (166) = 8.769, p < 0.00. This suggests that, in comparison to products with angular arrangement textures, Eastern participants believe that products with round arrangement textures have higher visual and aesthetic harmony.

Table 2. The independent sample *t*-test of psychological feelings on product.

	Variable	n.	M	SD	df	t	p
Adaptability	Round	84	4.96	1.468	165.763	5.000	.000
	Angular	84	3.81	1.525			
Harmony	Round	84	5.67	1.226	166	8.769	.000
	Angular	84	3.79	1.537			
Preference	Round	84	5.40	1.131	159.132	7.041	.000
	Angular	84	4.02	1.397			

5   Conclusion and Discussion

In the past, numerous studies have explored the aesthetic preferences between culture and shapes. Our research not only revisits the cultural construction of aesthetic preferences for angular and round forms but also examines the impact of the arrangement of angular and round textures in products on the visual perception differences and aesthetic preferences in the self-construction of Eastern culture (collectivist self-construction). Firstly, by examining eye-tracking data, the results indicate significant differences. Eastern participants, when simultaneously viewing products with both "round" and "angular" arrangements, exhibit a faster attraction of visual attention to products with "round" arrangements and a longer gaze duration, signifying higher visual attention. Secondly, through a questionnaire experiment, significant differences are observed at the psychological level among Eastern participants. From an aesthetic preference perspective, Eastern participants generally prefer incorporating round textures in products compared to angular arrangements. From the perspective of adaptability and harmony, Eastern participants also commonly perceive the inclusion of round textures in products as more suitable, providing an overall more harmonious visual feeling.

In summary, shapes have an impact on the visual perception of self-construction in different cultures. While this study focused on participants with an Eastern cultural background, we have gained insights into the visual differences in physiological attraction and psychological preferences for angular and circular arrangements. This research provides a new perspective for global product designers. In addition to addressing the design aspects of appearance and functionality, careful consideration of shape and arrangement elements on the product surface is crucial to enhance the attention and preference of consumers from diverse cultural backgrounds. This study offers valuable inspiration for product designers worldwide, encouraging them to be more mindful of the visual elements that contribute to the overall appeal of a product.

Finally, this study consolidates the parameter framework developed during the experimental process and constructs a comprehensive parameter database using parametric software Grasshopper within Rhino (short for Rhinoceros), as illustrated in "Fig. 14." This database can be applied to the design of shape arrangements on the surface blocks of various products, such as texture design on headphone surfaces, ventilation hole patterns on computer casings, and arrangement designs for sound-emitting holes on speakers (as shown in Fig. 14). We have made this database accessible on a public website (URL: https://drive.google.com/drive/u/0/folders/16DFJTI2Egkc1C1wuOCZe 7fSO7L-mI-t5), with the hope of providing designers with a reference for incorporating "shape" elements into product design. Additionally, our future research endeavors will extend to more cross-cultural studies on shape arrangements, aiming to contribute valuable insights and data to design practices.

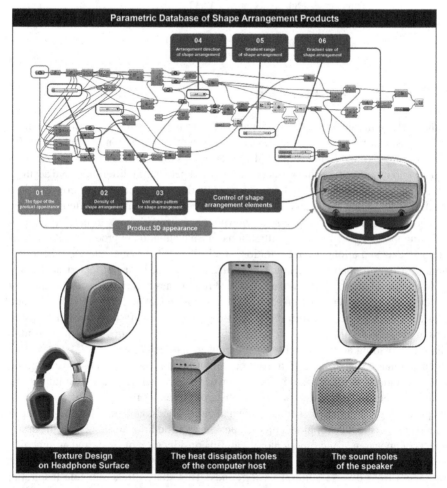

Fig. 14. Parametric database of shape arrangement products.

References

1. Markus, H.R., Kitayama, S.: Culture and the self: Implications for cognition, emotion, and motivation. Psychol. Rev. **98**(2), 224–253 (1991)
2. Henderson, P.W., et al.: Building strong brands in Asia: selecting the visual components of image to maximize brand strength. Int. J. Res. Mark. **20**(4), 297–313 (2003)
3. Zhang, Y., Feick, L., Price, L.J.: The impact of self-construal on aesthetic preference for angular versus rounded shapes. Pers. Soc. Psychol. Bull. **32**(6), 794–805 (2006)
4. Tzeng, O.C., Trung, N.T., Rieber, R.W.: Cross-cultural comparisons on psychosemantics of icons and graphics. Int. J. Psychol. **25**(1), 77–97 (1990)
5. Simonson, A., Schmitt, B.H.: Marketing Aesthetics. Free Press (2009)
6. Li, S.-Y.: 參數式設計應用於產品創作與探討 (2013)
7. 陳秀杏, 參數化建模應用架構研究-以Grasshopper建構樓梯為例 (2019)
8. Du, P., MacDonald, E.: Eye-tracking aids in understanding consumer product evaluations. The Psychology of Design: Creating Consumer Appeal, pp. 301–314 (2015)
9. White. Tobii Eye Tracking An introduction to eye tracking and Tobii Eye Trackers (2010)
10. Farnsworth, B.: 10 Most Used Eye Tracking Metrics and Terms (2022)

The Relationship Between Ming-Style Chair Form Attributes and GenY Emotion by Kansei Engineering in China

Ting Gao[1,2] (ID), Irwan Syah Mohd Yusoff[1,3](✉) (ID), and Ming Gao[4]

[1] Consumer Science, Universiti Putra Malaysia, 43400 Serdang, Malaysia
irwansyah@upm.edu.my
[2] Industrial Design, Wuyi University, Jiangmen 529020, China
[3] MyAgeing, University Putra Malaysia, 43400 Serdang, Malaysia
[4] Architecture, Shanghai University, Shanghai 200444, China

Abstract. With the increasing national self-confidence in China and advancements in artificial intelligence technology, there is a growing emphasis on the country's unique culture and consumer emotions. This study aims to investigate the relationship between the form attributes of Ming-style chairs and the consumption emotions of Generation Y. A total of 198 GenY consumers aged 23–42 participated in the study, providing evaluations of representative Ming-style chair samples using a semantic differential 5-point scale across six groups of Kansei words. The relationship between the shape of Ming-style chairs and consumer emotions was explored using multiple linear regression analysis in SPSS26 to establish innovative design principles for these chairs. The findings reveal a direct correlation between the form attributes of Ming-style chairs and the emotions of Generation Y consumers. Specifically, the Danao section, armrest panel surface, and stretcher style of Ming-style chairs factors significantly influenced the "Simplicity," "Sturdiness," and "Style Spectrum" of consumers' emotions. Consequently, developing new chair forms should be guided by consumer emotions and based on Ming-style chair form merits to meet their needs.

Keywords: Ming-style Chair · GenY Emotion · Kansei Engineering · China

1 Introduction

With Chinese national self-confidence growing, greater attention will be paid to their unique culture [1], which provides an opportunity for Ming-style chairs. Ming-style furniture (MF), as a representative artistic style, serves as a portrayal of a country, offering a glimpse into a facet of its cultural identity. It mirrors the artistic preferences of a nation [2] Ming-style chairs (MC) are the concentrated embodiment of Ming-style furniture culture [3] and are often presented by their visual shapes consumers at first sight [4].

In recent years, artificial intelligence has developed rapidly, and understanding consumers' emotions and emotions has become a top duty and task [5] products with product

P.-L. P. Rau (Ed.): HCII 2024, LNCS 14699, pp. 224–239, 2024.
https://doi.org/10.1007/978-3-031-60898-8_15

experience, emotion, and social value have become more attractive to consumers [6]. Among them, GenY (millennial) consumers show strong shopping patterns, and their greater motivation is to focus on the emotional recognition of brands [7] and a sense of participation [8]. IFirst, many studies only study the MF itself and do not touch on the current consumer lifestyle, resulting in design strategies that cannot adapt to changing needs. Niu & Zhao [9] clarified the key principles of the relevant forms and spatial aspects of Ming-style furniture but lacked a comprehensive understanding of how these principles align with the preferences and lifestyles of younger consumers. Yu [10] also highlighted that the consumption of furniture products has evolved from solely fulfilling functional needs to encompass cultural and emotional preferences as well. Second, the exploration of Ming-style chairs in Kansei Engineering (KE) is still in its preliminary stages, most of the research focused on semiotics and literature analysis, but lacked strong objective quantitative data, resulting in subjective narratives [11–13] Therefore, this study wants to answer the following two research questions (RQ): RQ1: What are the emotional demands of GenY consumers regarding innovation in Ming-style chairs? RQ2: What are the relationships between the form attributes of Ming-style chairs and GenY emotion by KE?

The study was conducted to explore new designs for Ming-style chairs that would appeal to GenY consumers' emotions, particularly by using the semantic difference method to understand their Kansei needs. The significance of the study lies in its ability to provide detailed insights into the design of Ming-style chairs that balance traditional elements with contemporary preferences, while also enhancing the overall consumer experience with innovative designs.

2 Literature Review

2.1 The Concept of Kansei Engineering

"Kansei" is a branch of cognitive science, originally developed as a philosophical term. The term "Kansei" was first used by Japanese philosopher Nishi Amane [14]. In the psychological definition, Kansei refers to the state of mind where knowledge, emotion, and passion are harmonized; "people with rich Kansei" are full of emotion and passion, and able to react adaptively and sensitively to anything [15]. Moreover, at the beginning of the 1970s, the concept of Kansei Engineering (KE) was introduced in Japan [16, 17], KE is a technology that focuses on the consumer for product development, based on the principles of ergonomics, which uses advanced computer technology to translate the consumer's emotions about the product into design elements. The process aims to connect the explicit design parameters with the implicit customer psychology [18]. KE was classified into 6 categories [19] and category classification (TypeI) is used in this study—Identifying the design elements of the product to be developed, translated from consumer's emotions.

2.2 Generation Y Consumers in China

In China, the population of Generation Y is 315 million (RMB), with a consumption scale reaching 6.68 trillion (RMB) [20]. Due to their potential spending power, trendsetting abilities, and adoption of new products, Millennials have distinct decision patterns and emphasize emotional factors, and social influence [21]. However, some consumers with ethnocentric tendencies exhibit stronger intentions to purchase domestic products in the emotional, cognitive and behavioral dimensions compared to foreign products [22]. Generation Y is also increasingly inclined towards design innovation to achieve integration with modern living spaces and aesthetics and inherit Eastern literati aesthetics [23].

2.3 Consumer Emotion

Consumer research has demonstrated that emotions play an important role in decision-making [24] prompting marketers to strategically target consumers' emotions which are the specific emotional responses elicited during product usage or consumption experiences [25]. In consumer behavior, emotions are not a straightforward, easily observable phenomenon [26]. Emotions shape behaviors and perceptions, emotional variables contribute most significantly to the establishment of dedicated and close customer relationships and are significant in distinguishing relationship types within the consumer market [27].

2.4 The Form Attributes of Ming-Style Chair

The exploration of Ming-style furniture intricately weaves considerations of form, spatial aesthetics, and cultural influences. The study [28] begins with a meticulous analysis of the impact of form and space, examining the visual dynamics in both two and three-dimensional spaces and evaluating the position, form, composition, and distance of each furniture element. The integration of Gestalt psychology establishes a connection between furniture and the viewer's emotions influenced by spatial relationships. This connection is a key element in understanding the profound impact of Ming-style furniture on its observers, as it is not merely a utilitarian object but an artistic expression that engages the viewer on a psychological level. Niu [29] further explores how the frame design of Ming-style chairs, as mentioned, influences the perception and associations of viewers, enhancing the overall aesthetic experience. Simultaneously, some researchers [29–32] explore the interdependence of curves and straight lines, the coexistence of squareness and roundness, and the generation of space through emptiness and solidity. This dual perspective provides a comprehensive understanding of Ming-style furniture by integrating both practical considerations and spatial aesthetics. The interplay between curves and straight lines, for instance, is not just a formal design principle but a manifestation of the Ming style's intrinsic beauty, representing a harmonious balance between opposing elements. The design of Ming-style furniture is deeply rooted in traditional Chinese craftsmanship and art, and the appreciation of form is not separated from its historical and cultural context.

2.5 Conceptual Framework

Through the analysis of the research question and the review of the literature, we identified the main issue of the study, which is to explore the experiences of Chinese Generation

Y consumers' emotions under the form of Ming-style chairs. We constructed a conceptual framework (Fig. 1), clarifying the relationships between independent variables (The form attributes of Ming-style chairs) and the dependent variable (Consumer emotion) to comprehensively understand these influencing mechanisms.

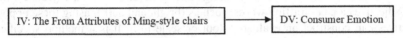

Fig. 1. Conceptual framework

3 Methodology

3.1 Study Design

We will use KE type I which is a mixed-method approach that combines qualitative and quantitative data to conduct a comprehensive analysis of research questions [33]. We have broken down the research process into six steps: (1) Choosing the product domain; (2) Spanning the Semantic space; (3) Spanning the space of Ming-style chair properties; (4) Kansei imagery cognition experiment about the form attributes of Ming-style chair; (5) Test of validity; (6) Model building.

Here, the population is sampled by simple random sampling and primarily conducted in China through snowball data collection by Google form, adopting the birth years of 1981 [34–36] to 2000 [35, 37, 38] for Gen Y. The total number of participants in the survey was 256. After excluding individuals below 23 years old and above 42 years old, there were 198 valid questionnaires. The demographic variables are described in Table 1.

Table 1. Demographic variable description (N = 198)

Variables	Category	Frequency	Percent (%)
Gender	Male	87	43.9
	Female	111	56.1
Age	23–33(years old)	150	75.8
	33–43(years old)	48	24.2
Educational background	Junior high school or below	18	9.0
	Bachelor	90	45.5
	Master	55	27.8
	PhD	35	17.7
Professional field	Engaged in professions related to furniture, art, design, and collecting	98	49.5
	Other fields	100	50.5

3.2 Semantic Difference

Osgood [39] developed a method of measuring the emotional content of a word more objectively, called the 'Semantic Differential Technique'. This technique involves using adjectives to measure subjective feelings toward certain things. This is because people typically express their evaluations of things through oral or written adjectives. Since most adjectives are contrasting words, such as (bright and dark), using these opposing adjectives can construct an evaluative tool or scale [40]. It is a method specifically designed for studying the psychological images of the subjects, serving as the cornerstone of sensory image research and one of the main tools in this study. The questionnaire uses the Osgood Semantic Differential 5-point scale (ranging from −2 to 2), where "−2" represents the negative emotional term, "2" represents the positive emotional term, and "0" indicates neutral emotion, for example (Fig. 2).

Fig. 2. Osgood Semantic Differential 5-point scale

3.3 Quantification I Theory

Quantification I Theory involves studying the relationship between a set of qualitative variables (independent variable x) and a set of quantitative variables (dependent variable y). Through multiple regression analysis, a mathematical model is established to predict the dependent variable y based on the independent variable x, facilitating the prediction of y through mathematical modeling. The perceptual image evaluation scale of Ming-style chairs is translated into an engineering scale. This involves further quantifying the form attributes of representative samples of Ming-style chairs into an editable data format based on qualitative encoding. The specific procedure is as follows: when the mth stylistic element of the kth chair sample is qualitatively encoded as the nth category, it is represented as dk = 1; otherwise, dk = 0. Here, m refers to the stylistic element, n is the category, and dk (m, n) is the reflection of the nth category for the mth stylistic element in the kth sample. For example, if the encoding for the cranial shape of a chair sample is represented as curve a1, the data transformation would be a1 = 1, a2 = 0, a3 = 0, a4 = 0, a5 = 0. Similarly, if the encoding for the side profile of the backrest is S-shape b3, the data would be b1 = 0, b2 = 0, b3 = 1, b4 = 0, and so on.

4 Procedures Design of Ming-Style Chair Based on Kansei Engineering Type I Method

4.1 Choosing the Product Domain

This study categorizes the product field into Ming-style chairs, including round-backed chairs, hanging lamp chairs, official hat chairs (including Northern and Southern official hat chairs, rose chairs, and Zen chairs), and folding armchairs.

4.2 Spanning the Semantic Space

By extensively reviewing relevant literature, books, magazines, websites, and papers in the furniture field, as well as product brochures in the furniture market, and considering the demands, ideas, and visions of experienced users [41]. Ultimately, based on the collection process, the number of Kansei words typically falls within the range of 50 to 600. It is essential to exhaustively gather existing vocabulary to ensure the validity of the results [42]. Through the elimination of synonymous and similar words, a selection of 20 pairs of vocabulary has been filtered (Table 2). Subsequently, 44 consumers ultimately participated in the selection of words, with over one-third of the chosen sensory imagery words considered to represent the consumers' expectations for furniture. Finally, six pairs of representative Kansei word pairs were selected, as shown in Table 3.

Table 2. The average values of emotional words' statistics (N = 44)

Order	Kansei word pairs	Mean
1	Traditional - Modern	0.55
2	Classical - Fashionable	0.64
3	Simple - Gorgeous	0.73
4	Elegant - Vulgar	0.73
5	Natural - Artificial	0.45
6	Low-key - Luxurious	0.45
7	Minimalist - Elaborate	0.64
8	Unified - Varied	0.27
9	Rhythmic - Static	0.55
10	Sturdy - Soft	0.73
11	Fluent - Stagnant	0.45
12	Clumsy—Light	0.64
13	Ethereal - Congested	0.55
14	Fresh - Murky	0.27
15	Practical - Decorative	0.55
16	Lively - Stiff	0.18
17	Affectionate - Indifferent	0
18	Comfortable - Uncomfortable	0.36
19	Curved - Straight	0.55
20	Unique - Ordinary	0.18

Table 3. Representative Kansei word pairs

Order	1	2	3	4	5	6
Kansei words	Classical—Fashionable	Simple—Gorgeous	Elegant—Vulgar	Minimalist—Elaborate	Sturdy—Soft	Clumsy—Light

4.3   Collection of Ming-Style Chair Samples

The spanning of the space of product properties is similar to the semantic space. One underlying idea is that there is an existing vector space depicting the domain's properties. The task in this part is to collect all the attributes representing the domain chosen select those which have the largest impact on the consumer's Kansei, and choose Ming-style chairs representing the chosen properties before the data is compiled for the following synthesis phase [42]. The subjects of this experiment are Ming-style chairs. Sample collection was conducted through various paths, including relevant literature, historical records, image collections, museum websites, Yachang Art Network, on-site investigations at antique furniture stores, and participation in auctions. A systematic collection of Ming-style chairs was carried out through these channels. Through an assessment by three experts, 20 representative samples were selected (Table 4).

Table 4. Representative Ming-style chairs samples

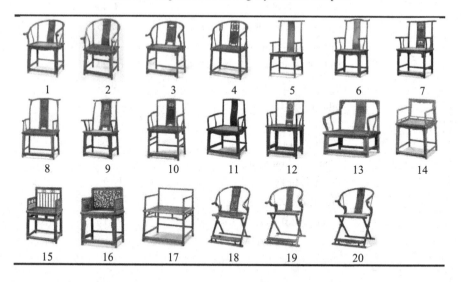

According to the principles of morphological analysis, the explicit chair is deconstructed in terms of its form. The overall form is broken down into several independent components, referred to as design items, including Danao, backrest, armrests, board between legs, and Stretcher. Each design item is further analyzed into various design elements or items based on their distinct forms (Table 5). For instance, the backrest can be categorized into different forms such as no openings, partial openings, and full openings; carving styles like through-carving, relief carving, and plain panels; surface types such as grating and solid panels; and segmented styles like two-section and three-section designs. Utilizing the theory of Quantity I, the final analysis results are systematically coded (Table 6), due to space limitations, not all are listed.

Table 5. Various design elements or items

Element	Project	Items
Danao	Danao Section a	Integrated Type a_1, Segmented Type a_2
	Head Protrusion b	Protruding b_1, Non-Protruding b_2
Backrest	Backrest Section c	Single-section c1, Two-section c2, Three-section c3, Four-section c4
	Backrest Cutout Form d	Partial Cutout d_1, Full Cutout d_2
	Backrest Side Profile e	Curved e_1, Straight e_2
	Backrest Carving Style f	No Carving f_1, Relief Carving f_2, Openwork Carving f_3
	Backrest Surface g	Blank g_1, Grid g_2, Partial Panel g_3, Full Panel g_4
Armrest	Armrest Protrusion h	Protruding h_1, Non-Protruding h_2
	Armrest Side Profile i	Curved i_1, Straight i_2
	Armrest Surface j	Blank j_1, Grid j_2, One Line j_3, Full Panel j_4
Board Between legs	Board Front Profile k	Curved k1, Straight k2
	Board Front Carving Style l	No Carving l_1, Relief Carving l_2
	Board Front Surface m	Grid m_1, Full Panel m_2
Stretcher	Stretcher style n	Step-by-Step High Stretcher n_1, X-Stretcher n_2

The Backrest side profile describes the left-view profile; the Armrest Side Profile describes the top-view profile

4.4 Semantic Difference Experiment About the Form Attributes of Ming-Style Chair

The selected participants were instructed to rate symbols (words) representing objects on a bipolar scale. These scales comprised contrasting adjectives, with participants marking positions that best represented the direction and intensity according to their perspective [33]. A Semantic Difference Experiment was conducted to survey the form attributes of Ming-style chairs through a questionnaire, which garnered evaluations from 198 Gen Y

Table 6. Form attributes elements encoding table of samples

Sample	a1	a2	b1	b2	c1	c2	...	l1	l2	m1	m2	n1	n2
1	1	0	1	0	1	0	...	1	0	0	1	1	0
2	1	0	1	0	1	0	...	0	1	0	1	1	0
3	1	0	1	0	0	0	...	1	0	0	1	1	0
4	1	0	1	0	0	0	...	0	1	0	1	1	0
...	...	...	...	...	...	...	...	...	...	...	...	...	...

consumers for 20 samples. The mean values of Kansei for 20 representative samples of Ming-style chairs were obtained (Table 7).

Table 7. Kansei mean evaluation table of 20 representative samples

Sample	Classical–Fashionable	Simplel–Gorgeous	Elegantl–Vulgar	Minimalistl–Elaborate	Sturdyl–Soft	Clumsyl–Light
1	−0.93	−0.82	−0.84	−0.85	0.38	0.48
2	−1.00	0.01	−0.68	−0.14	0.18	0.10
3	−0.73	−0.65	−0.66	−0.70	0.17	0.38
4	−0.80	−0.35	−0.62	−0.30	0.13	0.32
5	−0.61	−0.80	−0.64	−0.93	−0.36	0.61
6	−0.73	−0.66	−0.61	−0.62	−0.08	0.31
7	−0.81	0.00	−0.60	0.01	−0.50	−0.05
8	−0.82	0.23	−0.43	0.31	−0.21	0.02
9	−0.74	−0.01	−0.33	0.20	−0.35	−0.34
10	−0.65	−0.57	−0.47	−0.46	0.02	0.18
11	−0.37	−0.38	−0.58	−0.52	−0.13	0.14
12	−0.74	−0.10	−0.54	0.01	−0.35	−0.11
13	−0.55	−0.28	−0.40	−0.20	−0.18	−0.28
14	−0.58	−0.42	−0.25	−0.38	−0.15	0.08
15	−0.67	−0.34	−0.24	0.11	−0.39	−0.20
16	−0.84	0.44	−0.29	0.84	−0.25	−0.65
17	−0.24	−0.75	−0.60	−1.00	−0.16	0.79
18	−0.36	0.44	−0.46	0.51	0.36	0.36
19	−0.41	0.17	−0.28	0.27	0.38	0.35
20	−0.37	−0.11	−0.32	−0.02	0.32	0.34

Table 8. Total variance explained

Component	Initial Eigenvalues			Extraction Sums of Squared Loadings			Rotation Sums of Squared Loadings		
	Total	% of Variance	Cumulative %	Total	% of Variance	Cumulative %	Total	% of Variance	Cumulative %
1	3.045	50.747	50.747	3.045	50.747	50.747	2.834	47.229	47.229
2	1.423	23.713	74.460	1.423	23.713	74.460	1.403	23.382	70.611
3	1.054	17.570	92.030	1.054	17.570	92.030	1.285	21.419	92.030
4	0.330	5.503	97.534						
5	0.130	2.168	99.702						
6	0.018	0.298	100.000						

Extraction Method: Principal Component Analysis

Table 9. Rotated component Matrix[a]

	Component		
	1	2	3
Classical—Fashionable			0.957
Simple—Gorgeous	0.951		
Elegant—Vulgar	0.678		0.542
Minimalist—Elaborate	0.987		
Sturdy—Soft		0.960	
Clumsy—Light	−0.698	0.586	

Extraction Method: Principal Component Analysis
Rotation Method: Varimax with Kaiser Normalization
a. Rotation converged in 5 iterations

The data table containing scores for Kansei word pairs was imported into the SPSS software, and factor analysis was utilized to reduce the dimensionality of the Kansei words. Prior to conducting factor analysis, both the Kaiser-Meyer-Olkin (KMO) measure and Bartlett's sphericity test were executed to evaluate the structural validity and interrelationships of the factors. The experimental results revealed a KMO value of 0.505. As KMO is greater than 0.5, the data is deemed suitable for factor analysis. Additionally, Bartlett's sphericity test yielded an approximate chi-square value of 91.364 with 15 degrees of freedom, indicating significant differences ($p < 0.05$). Overall, both the KMO and Bartlett's sphericity test confirmed the suitability of the data for factor analysis (Tables 8 and 9).

In the explanation of total variance (Table 6), it is highlighted that the cumulative contribution rate of the first three indicators was 92.030%, exceeding the threshold of 90%. This indicates that the six groups of emotional vocabulary items could be condensed into three main factors. Using the normalized maximum variance method, the emotional vocabulary items in the measurement table were orthogonally rotated to extract two main factors. The rotated component matrix is presented in Table 7. To enhance clarity and minimize visual interference, blanks were utilized to denote factor loadings with absolute values less than 0.5, while negative values indicated negative correlations between indicators. Within the extracted three main factors, the first factor comprised the indicators "Simple—Gorgeous, Elegant—Vulgar, Minimalist—Elaborate, and Clumsy—Light" and was labeled as the "Simplicity Factor". The second factor encompassed the indicators "Sturdy—Soft" and "Clumsy—Light" and was termed the "Sturdiness Factor". Lastly, the third factor included the indicators "Classical—Fashionable" and "Elegant—Vulgar", designated as the "Style Spectrum Factor". The factor values for the three principal components are provided in Table 10.

Table 10. Factor values for the three principal components

Sample	Simplicity Factor	Sturdiness Factor	Style Spectrum Factor
1	−1.29855	1.42697	−1.70735
2	0.32342	0.99761	−1.87597
3	−0.93158	0.68823	−0.56911
4	−0.27126	0.72857	−0.79468
5	−1.70207	−0.71395	0.23417
6	−0.93565	−0.10787	−0.40126
7	0.14615	−1.035	−0.9094
8	0.92692	−0.18876	−0.63728
9	0.80234	−1.17812	−0.15821
10	−0.46961	−0.02365	0.10866
11	−0.56591	−0.25903	0.85069
12	0.22106	−0.83709	−0.53471
13	0.19446	−0.85899	0.43088
14	−0.08276	−0.7553	0.91527
15	0.40986	−1.50507	0.48629
16	2.02365	−0.80925	−0.73523
17	−1.70589	−0.04271	1.69394
18	1.30172	1.86915	0.92724
19	1.09576	1.48151	1.28998
20	0.51794	1.12276	1.38607

4.5 Test of Validity and Iterations

The results are elucidated using regression analysis, and given that the independent variables are binary categories, there is no necessity to draw a scatter plot. In the table, the model summary serves as a crucial indicator for assessing the linear relationship between the variables, as well as reflecting the regression's fitting degree. With an Adjusted R

Square value of 0.746, it is evident that the "independent variable" explains approximately 74.6% of the variation in the "Simplicity Factor". The Durbin-Watson test result of 1.924 (between 0 and 4) suggests that the data can be considered independent (Table 11).

The distribution state of the standardized residuals is observed through a histogram. It is noted that the residuals conform to a normal distribution. Furthermore, the standardized residual plot from the scatterplot exhibits a distribution around the 0 value, demonstrating symmetry both above and below. This distribution characteristic remains consistent regardless of the increase in predicted values, indicating that the data meet the conditions of homogeneity of variance and independence.

Table 11. Model Summary[b]

Model	R	R Square	Adjusted R Square	Std. Error of the Estimate	Durbin-Watson
1	0.966a	0.933	0.746	0.50425900	1.924

a. Predictors: (Constant), n2, j4, g2, c4, g1, j1, c3, a2, l1, k2, h2, f1, i2, m2
b. Dependent Variable: Simplicity Factor

Since collinearity was observed in the independent variables f2 and f3, Coefficients in Table 12 were generated after filtering them out. The linear relationship among the dependent variables in the Simplicity Factor is represented by f1 and j4, with significance values of 0.05 and 0.067 ($p < 0.1$) respectively, indicating a significant influence. This suggests that whether the chair back is carved and whether the armrests are full panels have a notable impact on the Simplicity Factor.

Since there was collinearity among the independent variables f1 and f3 in the "Sturdiness Factor", Table 13 was obtained after filtering them out. The linear relationship among the dependent variables "Sturdiness Factor" is represented by a2, with the significance values of 0.024 ($p < 0.1$), indicating a significant relationship. Furthermore, in the dependent variable "Style Spectrum Factor", the collinear f1 and f3 were excluded, and the final analysis focused on a2 and n2. The significance values obtained were 0.072 ($p < 0.1$) and 0.013 ($p < 0.1$) respectively, suggesting a significant influence (Table 14).

Table 12. Coefficients about "Simplicity Factor"

Model		Unstandardized Coefficients		Standardized Coefficients	t	Sig.	90.0% Confidence Interval for B		Collinearity Statistics	
		B	Std. Error	Beta			Lower Bound	Upper Bound	Tolerance	VIF
1	(Constant)	0.785	1.237		0.635	0.553	−1.707	3.278		
	a2	0.141	0.407	0.069	0.346	0.743	−0.679	0.960	0.338	2.960
	c3	0.547	0.422	0.275	1.298	0.251	−0.302	1.397	0.298	3.354
	c4	0.117	0.834	0.026	0.140	0.894	−1.564	1.798	0.385	2.599
	f1	−1.333	0.519	−0.627	−2.570	0.050	−2.378	−0.288	0.225	4.442
	g1	−0.208	0.779	−0.064	−0.267	0.800	−1.777	1.361	0.233	4.293
	g2	1.234	1.424	0.276	0.867	0.426	−1.634	4.103	0.132	7.571
	h2	−0.763	0.447	−0.383	−1.708	0.148	−1.663	0.137	0.266	3.765
	i2	0.497	0.685	0.234	0.726	0.500	−0.883	1.877	0.129	7.748
	j1	−0.465	0.691	−0.170	−0.673	0.531	−1.857	0.927	0.209	4.786
	j4	2.107	0.905	0.471	2.328	0.067	0.283	3.932	0.327	3.062
	k2	−0.361	0.438	−0.182	−0.825	0.447	−1.244	0.521	0.276	3.621
	l1	0.209	0.447	0.105	0.467	0.660	−0.691	1.109	0.266	3.765
	m2	−0.745	1.141	−0.229	−0.653	0.543	−3.043	1.554	0.109	9.208
	n2	0.927	0.490	0.340	1.892	0.117	−0.060	1.915	0.415	2.410

a. Dependent Variable: Simplicity Factor

Table 13. Coefficients about "Sturdiness Factor"

Model		Unstandardized Coefficients		Standardized Coefficients	t	Sig.	90.0% Confidence Interval for B		Collinearity Statistics	
		B	Std. Error	Beta			Lower Bound	Upper Bound	Tolerance	VIF
1	(Constant)	1.325	0.930		1.425	0.213	−0.549	3.198		
	a2	−1.248	0.389	−0.611	−3.208	0.024	−2.032	−0.464	0.328	3.051
	c1	0.493	0.373	0.253	1.320	0.244	−0.260	1.245	0.324	3.087
	c4	−0.540	0.640	−0.121	−0.844	0.437	−1.830	0.749	0.580	1.724
	d1	−0.872	0.535	−0.269	−1.630	0.164	−1.951	0.206	0.438	2.284
	h2	0.107	0.405	0.054	0.266	0.801	−0.708	0.923	0.287	3.481
	i2	−0.858	0.637	−0.404	−1.347	0.236	−2.142	0.426	0.132	7.556
	j1	−0.319	0.538	−0.117	−0.593	0.579	−1.404	0.766	0.305	3.274
	j2	−0.416	0.647	−0.128	−0.643	0.548	−1.721	0.888	0.299	3.341
	j4	0.223	0.859	0.050	0.259	0.806	−1.508	1.954	0.322	3.106
	k2	0.458	0.416	0.230	1.102	0.321	−0.380	1.296	0.272	3.677
	l2	−0.181	0.435	−0.088	−0.416	0.695	−1.057	0.695	0.263	3.808
	n2	0.634	0.512	0.232	1.239	0.270	−0.397	1.666	0.338	2.962
	m2	0.203	0.559	0.062	0.363	0.732	−0.924	1.329	0.401	2.493
	f2	−0.360	0.344	−0.181	−1.045	0.344	−1.054	0.334	0.396	2.523

a. Dependent Variable: Sturdiness Factor

Table 14. Coefficients about "Style Spectrum Factor"

Model		Unstandardized Coefficients		Standardized Coefficients	t	Sig.	90.0% Confidence Interval for B		Collinearity Statistics	
		B	Std. Error	Beta			Lower Bound	Upper Bound	Tolerance	VIF
1	(Constant)	−2.107	1.797		−1.173	0.294	−5.727	1.514		
	a2	1.083	0.477	0.530	2.272	0.072	0.122	2.044	0.328	3.051
	c3	−0.231	0.457	−0.116	−0.505	0.635	−1.153	0.691	0.337	2.964
	c4	−0.883	0.926	−0.197	−0.954	0.384	−2.748	0.982	0.417	2.401
	f2	0.051	0.422	0.026	0.122	0.908	−0.799	0.902	0.396	2.523
	g1	0.983	0.911	0.303	1.080	0.330	−0.852	2.818	0.227	4.404
	g2	0.599	1.603	0.134	0.374	0.724	−2.631	3.829	0.139	7.201
	h2	0.635	0.496	0.319	1.280	0.257	−0.364	1.634	0.287	3.481
	i1	0.288	0.781	0.136	0.369	0.727	−1.285	1.862	0.132	7.556
	j1	0.712	0.660	0.261	1.079	0.330	−0.618	2.041	0.305	3.274
	j4	−0.727	1.053	−0.163	−0.691	0.520	−2.849	1.394	0.322	3.106
	k2	0.388	0.510	0.195	0.761	0.481	−0.639	1.415	0.272	3.677
	l1	−0.112	0.533	−0.056	−0.210	0.842	−1.185	0.962	0.249	4.018
	m2	0.381	1.310	0.117	0.291	0.783	−2.259	3.021	0.110	9.113
	n2	2.370	0.628	0.868	3.777	0.013	1.106	3.635	0.338	2.962

a. Dependent Variable: Style Spectrum Factor

4.6 Model Building

When the validity tests give satisfactory results, the data collected from synthesis can be presented as a model. These models are functions that depend on product properties and are used to predict the emotional scores for specific words. In model building, a relationship model is established with Kansei evaluation as the dependent variable and Ming-style chair form attribute as the independent variables:

$$y_{kansei} = x_{Ming-style\ chair\ form\ attribute}$$

So, the models are $y_{Simplicity\ Factor} = -1.333f_1 + 2.107j_4 + 0.78$; $y_{Sturdiness\ Factor} = -1.248a_2 + 1.325$; $y_{Style\ Spectrum\ Factor} = 1.083a_2 + 2.370n_2 - 2.107$.

5 Conclusion

In conclusion, it is evident that the simplicity factor of the Ming-style chair correlates with the carving on the front and back of the chair and whether the armrests are full panels. Meanwhile, the sturdiness factor is associated with whether Danao is segmented, and the style spectrum factor is linked to whether Danao is segmented and the leg shape is X. However, there exists an overarching issue of collinearity, indicating a need for improvement in the independent variables in subsequent stages. Additionally, the limited number of significant independent variables may be attributed to the questionnaire's quality and the model's fit. Based on the results of the Semantic Difference Experiment and the evaluations from Gen Y consumers regarding the form attributes of Ming-style chairs, designers can gain valuable insights into the elements that resonate with consumers' emotions, designers can innovate and create new chair designs that meet the emotional demands of consumers. This finding ensures that the new chair designs not only incorporate the traditional Ming-style elements but also resonate with the emotional preferences of contemporary consumers, thus increasing the likelihood of acceptance and success in the market.

References

1. Wang, Y., Chung, T., Lai, P.C.: Go sustainability—willingness to pay for eco–agricultural innovation: understanding chinese traditional cultural values and label trust using a VAB hierarchy model. Sustainability (Switzerland) 15(1), 751 (2023)
2. Yang, Y.: Ming-Style Furniture Research. China Architecture & Building Press, Beijing (2002)
3. Men, C.: Study on the Aesthetic Characteristics of Chairs in Ming Style Furniture. Furniture Interior Design 11–13 (2018)
4. Jia, T.-Y., Niu, X.-T.: Analysis on the image of Ming-style chair based on eye movement tracking technique. Packag. Eng. 39, (2018)
5. Rust, R.T.: THE FEELING ECONOMY: How Artificial Intelligence Is Creating the Era of Empathy. Palgrave Macmillan (2021)
6. Reyes-Menendez, A., Palos-Sanchez, P., Saura, J.R., et al.: Revisiting the impact of perceived social value on consumer behavior toward luxury brands. Eur. Manag. J. 40, 224–233 (2022)
7. Kang, I., Koo, J., Han, J.H., et al.: Millennial consumers perceptions on luxury goods: capturing antecedents for brand resonance in the emerging market context. J. Int. Consum. Mark. 34, 214–230 (2022)
8. Klein, A., Sharma, V.M.: Consumer decision-making styles, involvement, and the intention to participate in online group buying. J. Retail. Consum. Serv. 64, 102808 (2022)
9. Niu, X., Zhao, Y.: Research on the functional basis, inheritance and innovation of leg and foot modeling of ming-style furniture. Furniture Interior Design 29, 18–22 (2022)
10. Yu, K.: Design of new ming-style furniture from the perspective of regional cultural gene. Packag. Eng. 44, 382–391 (2023)
11. Zuo, W., Wang, N., Zhang, Z.: Study on the design of imagery of Ming-style chair shape based on Kansei Engineering. J. Forestry Eng. 190–197 (2023)
12. Niu, X., Huang, J.: Research on backrest modeling of Ming-style furniture with full carving using the technology of eye tracking. J. Forestry Eng. 7, 200–206 (2022)
13. Jia, T., Niu, X.: Analysis on the image of Ming-style chair based on eye movement. Packag. Eng. 39, 208–214 (2018)
14. Nishi Amane - Wikipedia. https://en.wikipedia.org/wiki/Nishi_Amane. Accessed 10 Feb 20242024/2/10
15. Nagamachi, M., Lokman, A.M.: Innovations of Kansei Engineering. CRC Press (2016)
16. Nagamachi, M.: Kansei engineering in consumer product design. Ergonom. Design 10, 5–9 (2002)
17. Nagamachi, M.: Kansei Engineering: A New Ergonomic Consumer-Oriented Technology for Product Development. (1995)
18. Schütte, S.T.W., Eklund, J., Axelsson, J.R.C., Nagamachi, M.: Concepts, methods and tools in Kansei engineering. Theor. Issues Ergon. Sci. 5, 214–231 (2004)
19. Nagamachi, M.: Kansei engineering and its applications. Jpn. J. Ergonom. 32, 286–289 (1996)
20. National Bureau of Statistics. The Main Data Overview of the Seventh National Population Census. 国家统计局 (stats.gov.cn). Accessed 10 Feb 2024

21. Ordun, G.: Millennial (Gen Y) consumer behavior, their shopping preferences and perceptual maps associated with brand loyalty. Can. Soc. Sci. **11**, 40–55 (2015)
22. Trivedi, S.D., Tapar, A., Dharmani, P.: A systematic literature review of the relationship between consumer ethnocentrism and product evaluation. J. Int. Consum. Mark. (2023)
23. Yao, J., Liu, Z., Yi, X., et al.: Ming-style furniture research status and development trend analysis: a bibliometrics-based study. Furnit. Interior Design **30**, 17–23 (2023)
24. Garg, N., Wansink, B., Inman, J.J.: The influence of incidental effect on consumers' food intake. J. Mark. **71**, 194–206 (2007)
25. Westbrook, R.A., Oliver, R.L.: The dimensionality of consumption emotion patterns and consumer satisfaction. J. Consum. Res. **18**, 84 (1991)
26. Bondi, L.: Emotional Geographies. Routledge (2016)
27. Fernandes, T., Proença, J.: Reassessing relationships in consumer markets: emotion, cognition, and consumer relationship intention. J. Relationship Market. **12**, 41–58 (2013)
28. Song, Y.: Research of Space Composition Modality on Chairs of the Ming-style chair. Northeast Forestry University, Harbin (2010)
29. Niu, X.: Seeking the Roots of Craftsmanship: Analysis and Reflection on the Ontology Beauty of Ming-style furniture. Art Design Res. 81–86 (2022)
30. Sun, M.: The research on the traditional aesthetic connotations of the Ming-style furniture. Northeast Forestry University, Harbin (2008)
31. Guan, J. & Wu, Z.: The structural aesthetics and cultural images of Chinese Ming-style furniture. Furniture Interior Design 16–19 (2012)
32. Zhang, Y., Wang, W.: Application of moulding type in modeling of ming style furniture. China Wood Indust. **15**, 17–18 (2001)
33. Schütte, S.T.W., Eklund, J., Axelsson, J.R.C., et al.: Concepts, methods and tools in Kansei engineering. Theor. Issues Ergonom. Sci. **5**, 214–231 (2007). https://doi.org/10.1080/146392 2021000049980
34. Fornell, C., Larcker, D.F.: Evaluating structural equation models with unobservable variables and measurement error. J. Mark. Res. **18**, 39–50 (1981)
35. Gursoy, D., Maier, T.A., Chi, C.G.: Generational differences: an examination of work values and generational gaps in the hospitality workforce. Int. J. Hosp. Manag. **27**, 448–458 (2008)
36. Loughlin, C., Barling, J.: Young workers' work values, attitudes, and behaviours. J. Occup. Organ. Psychol. **74**, 543–558 (2001)
37. Brown, E.A., Thomas, N.J., Bosselman, R.H.: Are they leaving or staying: a qualitative analysis of turnover issues for Generation Y hospitality employees with a hospitality education. Int. J. Hosp. Manag. **46**, 130–137 (2015)
38. Lu, A.C.C., Gursoy, D.: Impact of job Burnout on satisfaction and turnover intention: do generational differences matter? J. Hosp. Tourism Res. **40**, 210–235 (2016)
39. Osgood, C.E., Snider, J.G.: Semantic Differential Technique: A Sourcebook. Aldine Publishing Company (1969)
40. Neuman, W.: Basics of Social Research: Qualitative and Quantitative Approaches (2006)
41. Schütte, S., Eklund, J.: An Approach to Kansei Engineering - Methods and a Case Study on Design Identity. In: Conference on Human Affective Design, Singapore June, 27–29 (2001)
42. Nagamachi, M.: Kansei engineering: a new ergonomic consumer-oriented technology for product development. Int. J. Ind. Ergon. **15**, 3–11 (1995)

Investigation Into the Elderly's Appraisal of Visual-Tactile Association Imagery Perception Design in Smart Product

Kuo-Liang Huang[✉], Yi-chen Liu, and Hua-Jieh Sun

Department of Industrial Design, Design Academy, Sichuan Fine Arts Institute,
Chongqing, China
shashi@scfai.edu.cn

Abstract. As global aging accelerates, older adults increasingly become a critical focus in smart product design. This research centered on older adults' evaluations of visual and tactile combined imagery perception design in smart products, aiming to investigate their perceptual challenges and requirements, and how these elements affect their user experience and satisfaction with smart products.

Using the Evaluation Grid Method (EGM) and survey techniques, the study engaged in comprehensive interviews and surveys with a group of older adults between 55 and 75 years of age. These methods enabled an exploration into older adults' preferences for certain features and design imagery associated with visual and tactile combined perception in smart products.

The findings revealed that older adults prefer smart products that offer comfort, aesthetic appeal, and practical reliability. They exhibit distinct preferences for tactile design elements, such as materials, textures, and shapes, which significantly affect their user experience and satisfaction. The study's outcomes highlight the criticality of addressing the sensory needs of older adults in the design of smart products, providing valuable insights to improve product accessibility and inclusivity. Furthermore, the research advocates for designers to integrate interdisciplinary knowledge to better cater to the unique needs of older adults, thus enhancing their acceptance and satisfaction with smart products.

Keywords: Elderly · Smart product · Visual-tactile Association · Imagery Perception · Evaluation Grid Method

1 Introduction

With the accelerated aging of the global population, the elderly have increasingly become a key demographic of social interest. In the realm of intelligent product design, the requirements and experiences of the elderly are receiving heightened attention [1]. These investigations focus on the elderly's adaptability to smart products and on enhancing their usage experience [2, 3]. Yet, the exploration of how the elderly evaluate the design of visual and tactile imagery perception in smart products is still under-researched [4, 5].

P.-L. P. Rau (Ed.): HCII 2024, LNCS 14699, pp. 240–255, 2024.
https://doi.org/10.1007/978-3-031-60898-8_16

Visual perception encompasses not just the identification and comprehension of colors, shapes, and layouts but also tactile perception, which conveys details about materials, temperature, and weight [6]. The concept of design imagery involves users' subjective impressions and emotional reactions to the design of a product, often reflected in their intuitive assessments of its appearance and tactile feel [7, 8]. Given the possible decrease in visual acuity and tactile sensitivity among older adults, how smart products address their unique needs through integrated visual and tactile design - and how this impacts their user experience and satisfaction - represents a subject meriting thorough exploration [9–12].

While research on smart product usage among the elderly has expanded, the majority of studies primarily focus on universal usability and functionality issues, like interface accessibility and clarity of information. However, research is relatively scarce in the area of the elderly's visual and tactile perception.

Options, particularly concerning design aesthetics [13]. This suggests that the perceptual obstacles and emotional requirements of the elderly in using smart products may not be comprehensively understood or addressed. Furthermore, there is a notable absence of multidisciplinary methodologies in existing research, such as the combination of psychology, gerontology, and design theory, to craft thorough and nuanced design strategies for the elderly [14, 15]. Consequently, this research endeavors to bridge this gap by examining the elderly's perceptions of the aesthetic elements in smart product design and its consequent influence on their product assessments.

This study is driven by an attention to the specific needs and experiences of the elderly in smart product design, with a special focus on visual and tactile perceptions. Acknowledging the limitations in current research, this study seeks to investigate the elderly's appraisal methods of smart product design aesthetics and their correlation with user experience and satisfaction. We aim to provide targeted design recommendations that enhance the sensory and interaction experiences of the elderly and to encourage the adoption of interdisciplinary methodologies. By amalgamating insights from design, psychology, and gerontology, we aspire to more effectively comprehend and fulfill the distinct needs of the elderly.

This research addresses crucial queries: How do older adults appraise the visual and tactile imagery perception design in smart products? The specific sub-questions are as follows: What are the challenges and requirements of older adults regarding the combined visual and tactile perception? How do they interpret and assess the design imagery in smart products? And how do these assessments influence their acceptance and satisfaction levels with the products? This study holds substantial importance in the realm of smart product design, especially in designing for older adults. Delving into the elderly's perceptions and evaluations of visual and tactile imagery in design offers essential insights for designers, helping them address the requirements of this increasingly significant user demographic.

2   Literature Review

2.1   The Intersection of Smart Product Design and the Elderly

With the accelerating trend of global population aging, smart products have become increasingly vital in improving the elderly's quality of life. Technologies like smartphones, smart home devices, and health monitoring tools are integral to the elderly's daily living and health management [16, 17]. However, the elderly's acceptance of technology is often hindered by complexities in operation, unfamiliarity with new technologies, and a decline in cognitive and sensory capabilities [18, 19].

The importance of designing smart products that consider the elderly's perceptual and cognitive needs cannot be overstated [20]. The elderly have unique emotional requirements for smart product design, which can be addressed through interfaces that are more intuitive and empathetic [21]. By enhancing the design's imagery perception, designers can aid the elderly in better understanding and utilizing these products [21]. This approach not only bolsters the independence of the elderly in using smart products but also boosts their sense of security in daily life. The design of imagery perception in smart products should focus on functionality as well as catering to the emotional and psychological needs of the elderly [21]. For instance, interfaces that fulfill imagery perception and evoke positive memories can offer emotional satisfaction and psychological comfort to the elderly while using these products.

In essence, for the elderly population, the imagery perception design of smart products is crucial not just for intuitive understanding and use efficiency, but also for enhancing overall life quality, sustaining psychological health, and meeting emotional needs.

2.2   The Role of Visual and Tactile Imagery Perception in Product Design

In the realm of product design, elements like appearance, shape, color, material, and surface treatment processes, when perceived through the integration of visual and tactile senses, shape not just a composite perception but are intimately linked with users' emotional experiences and cognitive judgments, influencing their emotional reactions and cognitive evaluations of the products [7].

The perception through a combination of visual and tactile senses – perceiving attributes of smart products like materials, textures, and shapes using sight and touch – is vital for users' intuitive understanding, emotional experience, and cognitive assessment. In smart product design, effective integration of visual and tactile elements can amplify product attractiveness, enhance user experience, and increase satisfaction [22]. By selecting suitable materials, designing surface textures, and determining product forms, designers can craft products that are both visually attractive and functional, fulfilling the users' needs for integrated visual and tactile perception.

As people age, a decrease in visual and tactile sensitivities can profoundly affect the use of smart products. This is particularly significant for older users, whose diminished vision leads to a greater reliance on tactile sensations, a factor that should be incorporated into smart product design [23]. For instance, materials that are soft and warm can stimulate feelings of comfort and joy among the elderly [12]. Designers should prioritize the positive emotional experiences that appeal to older demographics, making adaptive changes in their designs to ensure the products are approachable and easy to use for all ages [21].

2.3   The Concept of Design Imagery and Its Implementation in Smart Products

Design imagery, as a psychological characteristic, is a pivotal concept in the realm of product design. It encompasses sensory perception, perceptual recognition, and cognitive processes, and is instrumental in the design of products [7]. Design imagery not only imparts the conceptual essence of objects but also evolves with shifts in societal cultures and values [24]. In the context of smart product design, the utilization of imagery significantly impacts the user experience and the usability of the product. Design imagery indirectly affects users' evaluations and experiences of a product by influencing their perceptions. For example, a product that is aesthetically appealing and meets user aesthetic standards may be perceived as more user-friendly, regardless of its actual operational complexity [25]. Moreover, design imagery can intensify the emotional bond between the user and the product by eliciting emotional responses [26].

The application of design imagery is especially crucial for older users. With advancing age, users may experience a decline in sensory capacities, such as a decrease in vision and tactile sensitivity [12]. Consequently, smart product design should prioritize intuitiveness and ease of use. In this context, design imagery is key, offering clear visual indicators and tactile feedback to assist older users in more easily understanding and using products [11]. For instance, large text and strong color contrasts can help visually impaired elderly users to read information with greater ease.

Overall, design imagery is fundamental in smart product design. It influences not just user perception and product usability but is also vitally important for specific demographics, like older users. As the societal focus on the needs of the elderly intensifies, the application of design imagery will become an essential aspect of smart product design.

2.4   Utilizing the Evaluation Grid Method (EGM) in Design Research

The Evaluation Grid Method (EGM) is a qualitative research approach specifically tailored for deep analysis of how users evaluate product designs. At its core, EGM focuses on uncovering users' inner evaluations and preferences concerning product attributes through structured interviews and analytical processes [27, 28]. This technique involves detailed interviews, meticulously mapping the relationship between users' subjective feelings and the tangible aspects of products, thereby delineating the factors and their interconnections considered in evaluating products.

In design research, EGM is applied to comprehend users' perceptions of product features and to formulate evaluative criteria based on these perceptions. It is especially effective for probing into users' latent needs and preferences, revealing the more profound, often unarticulated factors in the evaluation process [29, 30]. EGM, through its interview-based and network analysis methods, offers insights more nuanced than those obtained from conventional surveys or questionnaires, highlighting the subtle differences in users' perceptions of design elements and their impact on product evaluations [31].

The adoption of EGM as a research instrument is particularly aimed at capturing the intricate evaluations of the elderly regarding smart product designs [32]. It enables researchers to gain a deeper understanding of the multitude of factors that affect the elderly's product selections and experiences. In evaluating the elderly's perspectives on smart product design, EGM elucidates their requirements and preferences in terms of visual, tactile, and functional features [28]. The evaluative network created by EGM not only mirrors direct assessments but also exposes the underlying psychological and emotional considerations, which are vital for crafting products tailored to the elderly.

Overall, EGM stands as a robust tool in analyzing, particularly among older adults, the evaluations of smart product designs. It transcends beyond surface-level evaluations to excavate hidden needs and preferences, offering crucial insights for designing products that align with user demands.

3   Method

This research, grounded in the EGM, unfolds across five phases. Initially, in the first phase, sample cards required for the experiment were gathered, and those aligning with the tactile perception design elements of smart products were identified through focus group interviews. In the second phase, deep interviews using EGM were conducted to delve into older users' perception of the appealing elements of tactile sensation in smart products, establishing a qualitative link between tactile perception in these products and the preferences of specific users. Moving to the third phase, the KJ method was utilized to categorize, organize, and distill the findings from the in-depth interviews, extracting distinct appealing traits of tactile perception in smart products and creating a comprehensive tactile imagery perception evaluation grid for these products. In the fourth phase, a survey was carried out with older users, employing the abstract semantic categories refined from the evaluation grid. The detailed research methodology is depicted in Fig. 1.

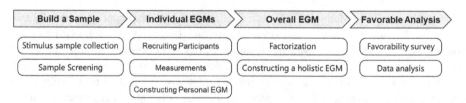

Fig. 1. Research flow chart Research Technical Route.

3.1 Study Subjects and Sample Collection for Assessment of Visual-Tactile Associations

This study targeted older adults between the ages of 55 and 75 who regularly purchase and frequently use smart products as the subjects of the research. Through detailed interviews, we delved into their perspectives and feedback regarding preferences in tactile perception, cognitive aspects, habitual use, and the extent to which their needs align with the features of smart products.

To gather representative smart product samples, we conducted a broad search for product images on platforms such as Pinterest and Behance. Our initial screening focused on products where the tactile perception aspect was more prominent than functionality, resulting in a collection of 279 sample images. These images were standardized into 10 * 15 cm colored pictures with logos removed and white backgrounds. To facilitate the experiments, we conducted focus group interviews with 6 product design experts to discuss and categorize these images. Based on our preliminary literature review, we classified the images into three categories of tactile design elements: materials, textures, and shapes, eventually selecting 182 most representative samples. Post-discussion, we refined these sample images, emphasizing the tactile design elements to enable clear and direct observation by participants of the key features influencing tactile perception. The experimental samples are illustrated in Fig. 2.

Fig. 2. Examples of stimulus samples from interviews.

3.2 Gathering and Structuring Data via EGM

In a quiet indoor setting, we engaged in individual interviews with 7 participants, thoroughly documenting the process with both text summaries and audio recordings. The interview procedure was as follows:

Initially, the participants sorted the 182 experimental samples into 5 to 7 groups based on their preferences and arranged them accordingly. Subsequently, a separate EGM gathering was conducted, wherein participants were asked to articulate their visual and tactile impressions of the different samples. To deepen our understanding, we encouraged participants to expound on their grouping rationale and reasons and to perform comparative analyses between sample groups. This approach was aimed at uncovering the tactile allure characteristics of each group. Following this, based on participants' inputs, we probed into the psychological impacts or abstract notions each group elicited, categorizing these as the upper-tier elements in EGM structuring. Concurrently, we identified the specific conditions and characteristics that underpinned these initial impressions, categorizing these as the lower-tier elements in EGM structuring. Finally, we synthesized individual evaluation grid charts for each participant from the interview data. Using the KJ method, we converted the upper, middle, and lower tier factors from individual EGMs into card-based factors, starting with "initial evaluations," and then moving to the upper and lower tiers. The final step involved creating a comprehensive evaluation grid chart from these factors.

3.3   Analysis of Favorable Factors

During this stage of our research, our objective was to investigate the elements that make tactile perception in smart products attractive and to ascertain how these elements impact the overall image of the products. We transformed the upper-level concepts (encompassing abstract ideas and psychological impressions) identified through the KJ method in the preceding phase into six key dimensions for the survey. Additionally, by integrating elements from the middle layer (initial evaluations) and the lower layer (specific conditions and detailed characteristics), we crafted tailored categories and questions. This approach aimed to gain insights into the tactile perception preferences of the elderly demographic towards smart products.

4   Results

4.1   Compilation and Construction of Individual EGMs

We meticulously compiled the interview data to create distinct visual and tactile imagery perception evaluation grids for each of the 7 participants, as illustrated in Fig. 3:

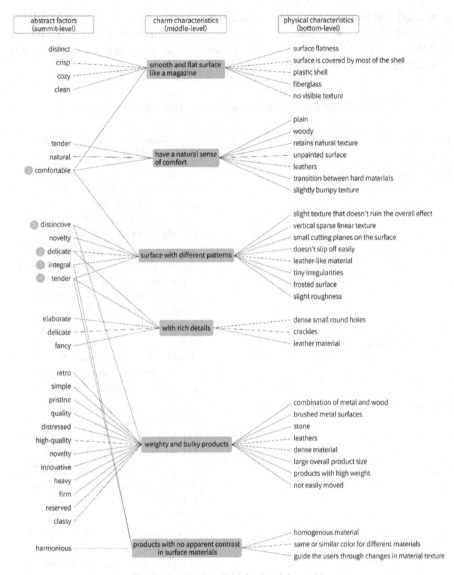

Fig. 3. Evaluation Grid for Participant 03.

4.2 Overall Visual-Tactile-Associative-Imagery Perception EGM

Having developed individual evaluation grids for the tactile imagery perception of smart products for 7 elderly participants, we applied the KJ method to aggregate and integrate similar elements within the upper-level abstract concepts. This led to a reduction in the number of categories to 14, and each was given a specific name while the total mentions were recorded. The mean number of mentions was 14.57, which we rounded to 15. In this phase, the abstract concepts that stood out, surpassing the average, included terms such as "relaxed and comfortable," "sleek and artful," "practical and reassuring," "delicate and refined," "firm," and "pristine." Ultimately, we documented the most frequently cited phrases in each category, representing their core semantics, and presented these in a streamlined format, as depicted in Table 1.

Table 1. Product imagery and mentions after attribution simplification.

Type	Total Number of Times	Formulation Before Simplification (Number of References)
Relaxed And Comfortable	32	comfortable (6), soft (6), warm (4), cozy (4), tactile (2), relaxing (2), pliable (2), soothing (1), decompressing (1), relaxing (1), pleasurable (1), joyful (1), gentle (1)
Sleek And Artful	25	aesthetically pleasing (5), artistic (4), stylish (3), contemporary (3), beautiful (1), attractive (1), beautiful (1), design (1), technological (1), decorative (1), elegant (1), strong (1), bold (1), impactful (1)
Practical And Reassuring	22	safe (6), practical, (4) visual (3), durable (2), peace of mind (2), controllable (1), convenient (1), intuitive (1), trusted (1), reliable (1)
Delicate And Refined	21	sophisticated (5), quality feel 3(), delicate (3), fine (2), elegant (2), subtle (1), quality (1), well-crafted (1), quality (1), premium feel (1), textured (1)
Firm	16	sturdy 3 (), solid (2), calm (2), hard (1), forceful (1), hard (1), stiff (1), heavy (1), solid (1), thick (1), steady (1), stable (1)
pristine	15	back to basics (2), rough (3), natural (2), plain (2), real (1), simple (1), environmentally friendly (1), organic (1), harmonious (1)

Drawing from the interviews conducted with 7 elderly participants, we sorted and amalgamated the upper-level concepts related to tactile perception in smart products. By linking abstract concepts with corresponding initial evaluation items and detailed descriptions, we developed an evaluation grid chart for the tactile imagery perception of smart products (illustrated in Fig. 4). This chart explicitly delineates the significance of each element within the evaluation framework.

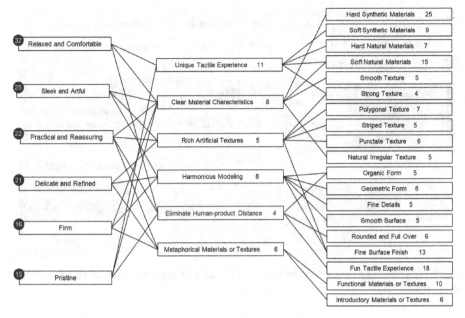

Fig. 4. Tactile Imagery Perception Evaluation Construct for Smart Products.

4.3 Analysis of Favorable Factors

The survey was disseminated online, resulting in the distribution of 227 questionnaires, from which 199 valid responses were collected. The respondents were exclusively older adults aged between 55 and 75 years, encompassing both genders. From the demographic information, it was noted that females accounted for 59% and males for 41%.

After processing the survey data for visualization, the results were depicted in percentages, illustrating the relative significance of various attributes in the initial evaluations of product imagery among the elderly demographic. As illustrated in Fig. 5, using the tactile imagery perception evaluation grid for smart products, it is evident that "relaxed and comfortable," "sleek and artful," and "practical and reassuring" are the tactile imagery aspects most preferred by older users in smart products.

Data analysis on the elderly's perception of "relaxed and comfortable" in the tactile experience of smart products indicates that "unique tactile experience" ranks high among their considerations when evaluating these products. Within this category, older adults favor "soft synthetic materials" (45.23%) and "soft natural materials" (30.15%) for creating a sense of comfort and ease, over "hard natural materials" (10.55%) and "strong texture" (14.07%). Regarding the primary evaluation of "clear material characteristics," the data shows a lower preference among older adults for "hard synthetic materials" (10.05%). This indicates that smart product design should increasingly focus on incorporating soft and natural materials and mild textures, along with engaging tactile interactions, to cultivate a perception of relaxation and comfort, thus making them more attractive to the elderly demographic.

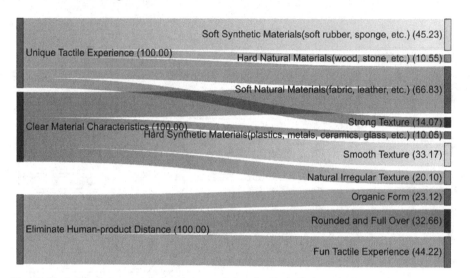

Fig. 5. Evaluation of seniors' perceptions of the visual-tactile association of "relaxation and comfort".

In the evaluation of "sleek and artful" tactile perception in smart products by older adults, data analysis reveals varying preferences for material features under the middle-level original evaluation of "clear material characteristics," as illustrated in Fig. 6.

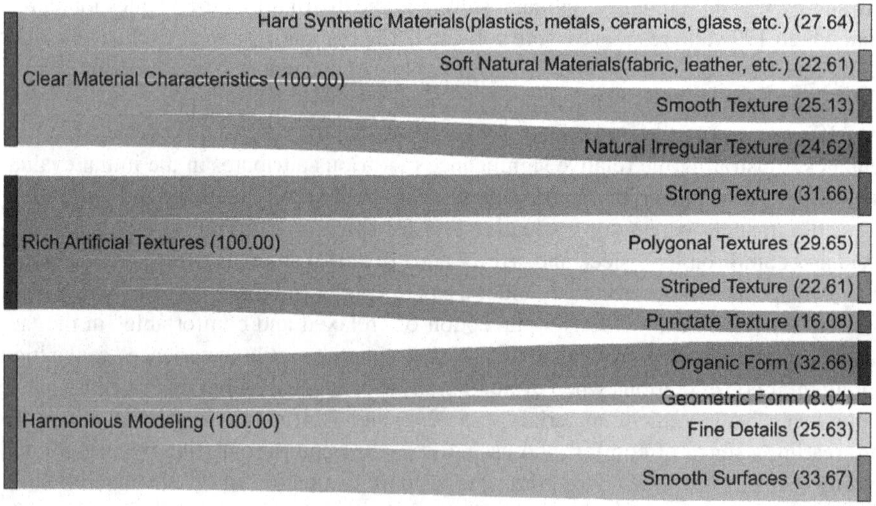

Fig. 6. Evaluation of seniors' perceptions of visual and tactile associations of "sleek and artful".

Participants identified "hard synthetic materials" as significantly important (27.64%), followed by preferences for "smooth textures" (25.13%) and "natural irregular textures" (24.62%), whereas "soft natural materials" were deemed less important

(22.61%). Regarding "rich artificial textures," the analysis showed that older adults find "strong textures" more impactful in conveying a sense of fashion and art (31.66%). In the "harmonious modeling" category, there was a clear preference for artistic and stylish designs, like "organic form" (32.66%) and "smooth surfaces" (33.67%), showcasing distinct styles.

Analysis of the evaluation data from older adults on the "practical and reassuring" aspect of visual and tactile perception in smart products, as depicted in Fig. 7, demonstrates their distinct preferences for different material features. Specifically, soft natural materials garnered the highest preference score (35.68%), suggesting that older adults find these materials more effective in providing a practical and reassuring visual and tactile experience. Furthermore, the data indicates a strong preference among older adults for "rounded and full over" (50.25%), as they help diminish the perceived distance between the product and the user, thereby enhancing the image of "practical and reassuring" in the combined visual and tactile perception of smart products.

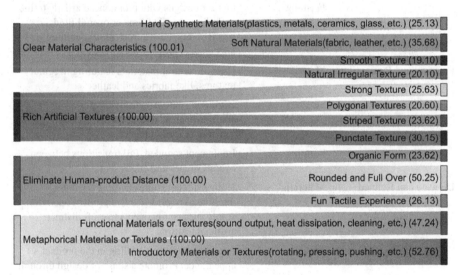

Fig. 7. Evaluation of seniors' perceptions of visual and tactile associations of "practical and reassuring".

Furthermore, the interviews uncovered that older adults also express high levels of satisfaction with tactile imagery that is "delicate and refined," "form," and "pristine." Given that older adults demonstrate diverse interests in tactile perceptions related to various styled smart products, designers can consider the six categories of images preferred by this consumer group, along with their respective visual and tactile combined design features, when developing or enhancing smart products. Drawing from the survey findings, we have formulated design suggestions tailored to smart products reflecting different images, as elaborated in Table 2.

Table 2. Design elements of visual-haptic-associative perception for different types of smart products.

Types	Design Elements	Design Recommendations
Relaxed and Comfortable	Materials	It is made of soft synthetic or natural materials (fabric, leather, soft rubber, sponge, etc.)
	Texture	It is gently textured
	Forming	Rounded transitions are used for the overall shape and between turning surfaces; Eliminating the sense of distance with interesting tactile interactions
Sleek and Artful	Materials	Employ hard synthetic materials like plastic, metal, ceramics, glass, etc.
	Texture	Create strong, polygonal, or striped textures
	Forming	Opt for designs with pronounced artistic traits, including organic forms or overall fluid surfaces; emphasize meticulous detailing in appearance
Practical and Reassuring	Materials	Use soft natural materials featuring irregular textures, like fabrics and leather
	Texture	Highlight subtly suggestive materials or textures in areas relevant to the product's function or user guidance
	Forming	Implement rounded, full transitions between overall shapes and edges
Delicate and Refined	Materials	Utilize subtle textures and materials for intuitive user guidance and product operation. Apply surface treatments to craft distinct artificial textures
	Texture	Prioritize intricate detailing in the product's appearance. Promote a sense of design through smooth surfaces and incorporate simple, clean transitions in the shape
Firm	Materials	Choose hard synthetic materials like plastic, metal, ceramics, glass, etc.
	Texture	Focus on subtle textural or material elements in the appearance, especially for user guidance
	Forming	Emphasize geometric forms and the sense of solidity in the product's shape

(continued)

Table 2. (*continued*)

Types	Design Elements	Design Recommendations
Pristine	Materials	Combine soft natural materials (like fabric and leather) with hard natural materials (such as wood and stone) Use composites mainly made of natural materials
	Texture	Maintain the gentle, irregular textures inherent to natural materials

5 Conclusions and Suggestions

The main outcomes of this study reveal that older adults have definitive preferences for visual and tactile combined perception in smart products, significantly impacting the affective qualities and user experience of these products. It was observed that older adults favor features that offer comfort, artistic appeal, and practical reassurance, closely linked to their perception of smart products' visual and tactile combined imagery.

From the discussion centered around our research questions, it is evident that older users show a preference for soft synthetic or natural materials, corresponding with their desire for tactile and visual comfort. This aligns with theories regarding the importance of sensory experiences in the interaction between users and technology, particularly in the context of sensory decline associated with aging.

When comparing our study's findings with existing literature, both similarities and differences are notable. While Norman (2007) [7] highlighted the significance of design in enhancing user experience, our study identifies specific preferences of older adults in terms of visual and tactile combined perception, an area not extensively covered in prior research.

Theoretically, these findings underscore the necessity to revisit design thinking processes, emphasizing sensory aspects in creating smart products tailored for older users. Practically, this research provides valuable guidance for developing products that are not only functionally fitting but also emotionally engaging for elderly users.

Nevertheless, this study faces limitations, including the sample size and cultural context. Future research should therefore broaden these insights across more varied cultural settings and larger groups of participants. Delving deeper into the convergence of visual and tactile combined perception with cognitive ergonomics in product design could offer further insights for refining design approaches tailored to this demographic.

Acknowledgments. This study was supported by the Science and Technology Research Program of Chongqing Municipal Education Commission [Grant No. KJZD-M202201001], Major Project Cultivation Project of Sichuan Academy of Fine Arts [22BSQD010] and Chongqing Municipal University Innovation Research Group "Research on Aging-Ready Design in Smart Recreation Scenarios" [CXQT20021].

References

1. Tian, M., Zhang, J., Cai, Y., Dong, X.: Design of smart products for the elderly based on affordance. In: Human Interaction & Emerging Technologies (IHIET-AI 2022): Artificial Intelligence & Future Applications, vol. 23 (2022)
2. Wang, L.: Functional visualization design of medical products based on user perception analysis under the aging background. In: 2021 13th International Conference on Measuring Technology and Mechatronics Automation (ICMTMA), pp. 59–62. IEEE (2021)
3. Johnson, J., Finn, K.: Designing User Interfaces for an Aging Population: Towards Universal Design. Elsevier Science, Cambridge, MA (2017)
4. Li, Y.: Design visual elements and brand-based equity: mediating role of green concept. Front. Psychol. 13, 888164 (2022)
5. Yuan, J., Zhang, L., Kim, C.-S.: Multimodal interaction evaluation and optimization design of smart landscape devices for elderly people in seaside parks. Electronics 12, 3822 (2023)
6. Charness, N., Boot, W.R.: Aging and information technology use: potential and barriers. Curr. Dir. Psychol. Sci. 18, 253–258 (2009)
7. Norman, D.: Emotional Design: Why We Love (Or Hate) Everyday Things. Basic Books (2007)
8. Kaushik, V.: Impact of the visual design language of social media advertisements on consumer perceptions. Inf. Technol. Ind. 9, 810–817 (2021)
9. Wang, Y., Liang, W.: Design of intelligent medicine box for visually impaired people based on QFD and TRIZ theory. In: 2022 International Conference on Culture-Oriented Science and Technology (CoST), pp. 64–68. IEEE (2022)
10. Fa, W., Soo, K.C.: Research on smart phone interfaces for the elderly based on ergonomics. J. Phys. Conf. Ser., 012011 (2018)
11. Zajicek, M.: Interface design for older adults. In: Proceedings of the 2001 EC/NSF Workshop on Universal Accessibility of Ubiquitous Computing: Providing for the Elderly, pp. 60–65 (2001)
12. Fisk, A.D., Czaja, S.J., Rogers, W.A., Charness, N., Sharit, J.: Designing for Older Adults: Principles and Creative Human Factors Approaches. CRC Press (2020)
13. Pérez, I.G.: The effect of the images depicted on food packaging on consumer perception and response. Universidad de Zaragoza (2018)
14. Bowen, J.P., Giannini, T., Polmeer, G.: Coded communication: digital senses and aesthetics, merging art and life. In: Electronic Visualisation and the Arts (EVA 2017), pp. 1–8 (2017)
15. Triggs, T.: Research notes: communication design. Commun. Des. 3, 1–5 (2015)
16. Liu, L., Stroulia, E., Nikolaidis, I., Miguel-Cruz, A., Rincon, A.R.: Smart homes and home health monitoring technologies for older adults: a systematic review. Int. J. Med. Informatics 91, 44–59 (2016)
17. Montague, E., Perchonok, J.: Health and wellness technology use by historically underserved health consumers: systematic review. J. Med. Internet Res. 14, e2095 (2012)
18. Peek, S.T., et al.: Older adults' reasons for using technology while aging in place. Gerontology 62, 226–237 (2016)
19. Vaportzis, E., Giatsi Clausen, M., Gow, A.J.: Older adults perceptions of technology and barriers to interacting with tablet computers: a focus group study. Front. Psychol. 8, 1687 (2017)
20. Docampo, R.M.: Technology generations handling complex user interfaces (2003)
21. Czaja, S.J., Lee, C.C.: The impact of aging on access to technology. Univ. Access Inf. Soc. 5, 341–349 (2007)
22. Hekkert, P.: Design aesthetics: principles of pleasure in design. Psychol. Sci. 48, 157 (2006)
23. Charness, N.: Aging and human performance. Hum. Factors 50, 548–555 (2008)

24. Crilly, N., Moultrie, J., Clarkson, P.J.: Seeing things: consumer response to the visual domain in product design. Des. Stud. **25**, 547–577 (2004)
25. Tractinsky, N., Katz, A.S., Ikar, D.: What is beautiful is usable. Interact. Comput. **13**, 127–145 (2000)
26. Desmet, P., Hekkert, P.: Framework of product experience. Int. J. Des. **1**, 57–66 (2007)
27. Hsiao, S.-W., Chen, C.-H.: A semantic and shape grammar based approach for product design. Des. Stud. **18**, 275–296 (1997)
28. Lu, P., Hsiao, S.-W.: Research on product design education based on evaluation grid method. In: 2019 International Joint Conference on Information, Media and Engineering (IJCIME), pp. 267–271. IEEE (2019)
29. Kawakita, J.: The KJ method–a scientific approach to problem solving. Kawakita Res. Inst. **2** (1975)
30. Kang, X., Yang, M., Wu, Y., Ni, B.: Integrating evaluation grid method and fuzzy quality function deployment to new product development. Math. Prob. Eng. **2018** (2018)
31. Nagai, Y., Noguchi, H.: An experimental study on the design thinking process started from difficult keywords: modeling the thinking process of creative design. J. Eng. Des. **14**, 429–437 (2003)
32. Chen, J.-C., Chen, C.-C., Shen, C.-H., Chen, H.-W.: User integration in two IoT sustainable services by evaluation grid method. IEEE Internet Things J. **9**, 2242–2252 (2021)

Research on Cross-Cultural Product and Service Design Dynamics in a Global Perspective

Weiqi Jiang[✉]

Beijing Normal University, Beijing, People's Republic of China
1371281520@qq.com

Abstract. With the accelerated development of the global economic pattern, the exchanges between countries gradually form a diversified trend, transnational trade such as the emergence of a spring, in this economic context, cultural exchanges between countries also presents a prosperous scene, but cultural diversity will inevitably bring cross-cultural contradictions and conflicts.

From the perspective of design thinking to look at cross-cultural issues, design products as an important carrier of trade exchanges, the diversity of cultures makes the product creation of a constant source of inspiration. Compared with the distinctive traditional art of each country, cross-cultural integration is more capable of stimulating the acceptance of local culture to foreign propaganda, thus opening the door to the country and benignly promoting the world's cultural exchanges. Some scholars divide the process of cross-cultural design into three stages, i.e. quotation, simulation and transformation. Especially in the field of brand visual design, the cultural packaging of a product is undoubtedly the first element of product sales. Through the external extraction of cultural factors, such as patterns, colours, ways of use and other information presented to visual elements to show the national culture. It can make it have the significance of symbolic communication and stimulate consumers' desire to buy.

In terms of product design, some scholars have proposed design techniques for product imagery. Different cultures have different cultural backgrounds, which can express different cultural imagery. Different cultures have different cultural backgrounds, which can express different cultural imagery. By exploring the imagery behind a particular culture, the modelling design of products can be generated based on this approach. This is especially represented by handmade artefacts. Such as porcelain, gold and silverware and other daily necessities, they are closely related to human life, and most of them have played a role in history as a collection of religious beliefs, life concepts and philosophical ideas. We can see from their shapes, colours and materials the level and state of people's lives at that time. This can also be applied to today's design world, fusing cultures and adding modern colours to traditional shapes to cater for modern cross-cultural design.

In terms of service design, we can start with the local culture of the service object and conduct cultural research on the user group. According to their growing environment and living habits, we should analyse their functional needs, psychological needs, spatial perception and other multi-dimensional experiences. We can collaborate with multiple stakeholders, such as operators and customers, to achieve systematic innovation in service provision, service processes and service contacts, and to improve the comfort of service design.

P.-L. P. Rau (Ed.): HCII 2024, LNCS 14699, pp. 256–263, 2024.
https://doi.org/10.1007/978-3-031-60898-8_17

In addition, in terms of design talent cultivation, with the optimisation and expansion of higher education in society, design majors within universities have gradually developed cross-cultural design courses. Teachers and international students with multicultural backgrounds have also been introduced, which makes the courses more international. However, most of the universities are still limited by the local environment in the teaching design of the course, and the traditional way of teaching in large classrooms and students submitting assignments cannot achieve the goal of flexible globalisation. This has led to the gradual emergence of an educational model of interdisciplinary communication in such an environment.

The concept of intercultural design is an important theoretical basis for the development of the contemporary market. Under the role of the whole market, cross-cultural product design should reasonably collect many aspects of culture. And understand the background of culture and contemporary cultural development. From the creation of cultural products to the cultivation of design talents, the preparatory force to adapt to multiple cultures should be developed. We should formulate feasible strategic objectives for the industry and integrate the essence of world civilisation to better face the cultural fusion under the trend of globalisation.

Keywords: Cross-cultural communication · Cultural products · Service design · Talent cultivation

1   Introduction

Under the wave of globalisation, cross-cultural product and service design is no longer confined to a single geographical and cultural context, but has gradually become an important bridge connecting people around the world. This design trend not only reflects the diversified needs of the market, but also the human desire for understanding of different cultures. Cross-cultural product and service design is not only an emerging field, but also a field with both challenges and opportunities. How to maintain the cultural uniqueness and sustainability of design while meeting consumer needs is a common theme for designers and researchers.

2   Methods and Ways of Realising Cross-Cultural Design

In the era of globalisation, cross-cultural design is not only the key to achieving business success, but also an important means of connecting different cultures and promoting cultural exchange. As the global market continues to expand and deepen, cross-cultural product and service design has become an important area of competition for enterprises. In order to succeed in the global market, companies need to fully understand the needs and expectations of users in different cultures, as well as the impact of cultural differences on product design and services.

Firstly, the trend of globalisation has had a profound impact on cross-cultural product and service design. On the one hand, globalisation has enabled businesses and organisations to access a wider range of markets and face challenges from competitors from different cultural backgrounds. In order to stand out from the fierce competition, enterprises need to design and provide products and services that are culturally adapted to meet the expectations and preferences of users from different cultural backgrounds, thus enhancing their competitiveness.

On the other hand, globalisation also brings about cultural exchange and integration. The mutual influence and intermingling of different cultures provide enterprises with more creativity and inspiration. Designers can learn from them and skillfully integrate elements of different cultures into products and services to create designs with unique charms. This kind of cross-cultural design not only meets the diversified needs of the global market, but also helps to enhance the brand image and influence of enterprises.

In the practice of cross-cultural product and service design, designers need to focus on several key factors. Firstly, cultural adaptation and localisation are crucial. When entering a different cultural market, companies need to undertake in-depth cultural adaptation and localisation to ensure that their products and services are compatible with the local culture. This includes understanding local aesthetics, values, customs and social behaviours in order to gain recognition and acceptance in the local market. Designers also need to be aware of language differences to ensure that product information is accurately communicated and understood. This may involve designing for multilingual interfaces, localised translations and culturally sensitive communication methods.

Secondly, designers need to be highly culturally literate and sensitive. Understanding the differences between cultures is key to cross-cultural product and service design. Designers should study in depth the characteristics and commonalities of different cultures and look for themes and emotional expressions that can resonate widely. For example, a successful cross-cultural product may emphasise themes of common human concern, such as environmental protection, health and family. These themes can cross cultural boundaries and elicit empathy and emotional connections from users.

In order to achieve effective cross-cultural design, designers also need to build a design team with multicultural backgrounds and perspectives. Such a team can provide more comprehensive insights and innovative thinking, helping designers to better understand the needs and characteristics of different cultures. It is also beneficial to build collaborative relationships with partners who have experience in local cultures and markets. They can provide valuable local knowledge and professional advice to help designers better adapt to the culture and needs of their target markets.

In a global perspective, cross-cultural product and service design is a field full of challenges and opportunities, and an inevitable trend in the era of globalisation. Through an in-depth understanding of the needs and cultural differences of the global market, as well as the skilful use of cross-cultural elements and creativity, designers and enterprises can create competitive products and services that meet the expectations and needs of users around the world. This will help promote cultural exchange and integration, and facilitate the expansion and deepening of the global market.

3   Differences in User Needs and Cultural Contexts

People from different cultures have different expectations, needs and preferences for products and services. Cultural differences are one of the most obvious differences between different countries and regions. Differences in language, values, beliefs, social practices, etc. all affect the needs and acceptance of products and services. Understanding and respecting these differences is essential to designing products and services that have a global impact. This requires designers to go through extensive market research and user studies, including the history, values, social customs, traditions, and symbolic systems of the target culture, in order to gain valuable information about the needs of users in different cultural contexts.

Take language and national symbols as an example: language serves as the core of cultural communication. Designers need to pay attention to the linguistic characteristics of their target markets to ensure that the message of their products and services is accurately conveyed. This includes understanding the particular meanings, idioms and contexts of the local language, as well as ensuring that instructions, tips and guidance for the use of products and services are easy to understand and follow. There is also a need to avoid using words and expressions that may cause misunderstanding or offence.

Secondly, national symbols are an important part of culture. Different cultures may have different ways of understanding and interpreting symbols and graphics. Designers need to pay attention to these differences and avoid using symbols and graphics that may cause misunderstanding or conflict. At the same time, local cultural traditions and values should be respected and local cultural elements should be incorporated as much as possible. For special groups such as ethnic minorities, regardless of their cultural background, we need to maintain an open and tolerant attitude in order to enhance the cultural identity and affinity of the product.

In addition, cross-cultural product and service design also needs to take into account the value beliefs, social etiquette and aesthetic preferences of some people. These different beliefs and social rituals will determine the preferences of different peoples' needs for products and services. For example, some cultures may pay more attention to the practicality of a product, while other cultures may pay more attention to the appearance and aesthetic value of a product. Designers need to understand these different needs and preferences and tailor their designs to the characteristics of the target market. This involves developing an in-depth understanding of the users in the target market and providing design solutions that meet local market needs and habits. Through culturally sensitive user experience testing, potential cultural difference issues can be identified and optimised and improved in a timely manner. At the same time, cooperation with local market research institutes, consumer associations and other professional organisations is also an effective way to gain localised insights.

4 The Expression of National Culture Image in Design

In cross-cultural products, national culture image design plays a crucial role. It is not only the outer packaging of a brand or product, but also the embodiment of its inner culture and values. A good national culture image design can effectively convey the core value and uniqueness of the brand, and at the same time attract the attention and recognition of the target market.

Firstly, national symbols are indispensable elements in national culture image design. Each ethnic group has its unique symbols and signs that represent the history, culture and values of that ethnic group. These symbols often have deep cultural connotations and broad social identity. Appropriate use of these symbols in design can effectively convey the national characteristics and cultural heritage of the brand. For example, the traditional patterns of China, the Taj Mahal of India, and the tribal totems of Africa are all representatives of their national cultures.

However, when using ethnic symbols, it is crucial to respect and avoid misuse. Designers need to have a deep understanding of and respect for the cultural background and values of these symbols, and avoid using them simply as decoration or in a casual manner. Ethnic symbols need to be used appropriately to express respect and recognition of the culture in question, rather than simply for imitation or commercial exploitation.

For better understanding and cultural resonance, designers need to probe deeply into the cultural background and aesthetic preferences of the target market. In terms of graphic design, traditional elements such as totemic art can be borrowed, but they need to be appropriately simplified and innovated to suit modern aesthetics and design language. At the same time, choosing symbols of universal significance can enable products to convey emotions across cultures and minimise the risk of causing misunderstanding and confusion.

Apart from graphic elements, colour is also one of the indispensable elements in design. The symbolism and preferences of colours vary greatly from culture to culture. For example, in Chinese culture, the colour red symbolises joy, prosperity and happiness, while in Western culture, it is often associated with passion, power and danger. Therefore, it is best to use colours with broad acceptance and positive meaning in your design, and to understand a particular culture's understanding and interpretation of colour before designing.

In addition, brand storytelling is an integral part of national cultural identity design. A good story can bring users into that culture and convey the emotional value of cultural symbols in a more immersive experience. For example, the brand design of a Mexican coffee shop could start with the national characteristics of Mexico, such as sundials, Mayan totems and other traditional motifs. These motifs can show the importance of Mexican culture and apply them to the packaging and logo design. Therefore, the brand story can be told from the coffee planting and roasting process inherited from generations of Mexican farming families, echoing the brand pattern, so that consumers can better understand and experience the culture and values of Mexico. Such uniquely national brand packaging can differentiate the brand from competitors in the global marketplace and provide consumers with an emotional experience related to the brand story and culture.

Finally, in the promotion of the brand, it is equally important to focus on educating and explaining the design elements to help the target audience understand the meaning and symbolism of the signs and elements. This can be done through packaging instructions, the brand's website, promotional materials, social media, and more. The enhancement of promotion can even determine the level of trust consumers have in the brand, thus increasing the user loyalty of the product.

5 Design Talent Cultivation and Sustainable Development

The designer's personal aesthetic, perceptual and cultural experiential skills as a creator who transmits intercultural communication have a decisive influence on the form and meaning of the final product. In today's education field, a systematic education model has also begun to form. And they are all being further improved and experimented with in order to adapt to the changes in the market.

As designers of intercultural products, designers are required to have a wide range of knowledge and skills, including cultural studies, anthropology, psychology, sociology and so on. Such a background has created an interdisciplinary model of education in modern universities. Combining design with knowledge from other fields fosters cultural sensitivity and global perspective, arousing designers' curiosity and interest in different cultures. In addition, where possible, the ability of talents to communicate and co-operate across cultures should be strengthened. This includes language proficiency, cultural understanding, and cross-cultural communication skills. Designers need to be able to work with people from different cultural backgrounds, understand their needs and perspectives, as well as co-ordinate and communicate effectively in cross-cultural teams.

In the era of big data, the cultural elements of different regions will directly or indirectly influence the culture of other regions with the development of the Internet. Cultural sharability should be the goal of teaching in colleges and universities. The school curriculum should be based on small groups, so that students from different regions can communicate with each other, and then the group as a unit for inter-class communication. Since culture has the uniqueness of individual behavioural cognition, and college students as the future preparation for the design field, it is more important to cultivate their ability to actively communicate with different cultures and improve their cross-cultural awareness, so as to enhance ability to independently learn different cultures. At the same time, the students' backgrounds and cultural traditions should be utilised in order to promote the potential of cross-cultural design by enabling them to communicate and collaborate with each other.

Balancing the requirements of innovation and sustainability in the context of sustainable development is an important task for design talent. Designers should consider sustainability as a core value and goal of design, not just an additional requirement. Incorporating sustainability into the early stages of the design process helps to consider sustainability factors alongside innovation. Of course, this means that we need to think about sustainability from the very beginning of the design process in terms of the life cycle of the product or service, choice of materials, energy efficiency, circular economy, and so on.

Among other things, the adoption of a systems thinking approach is necessary to balance the requirements of innovation and sustainability. The impacts of a product or service are considered in an integrated way throughout its life cycle, including raw material acquisition, manufacture, use, maintenance and termination. Through this integrated perspective, designers can find the balance between innovation and sustainability and find the best solutions.

User-centred design principles also provide opportunities for sustainable design. Designers can incorporate sustainability principles into products or services by co-creation with users to make them aware of the importance of sustainability. And provide relevant information and resources to help them make sustainable decisions when choosing and using products or services.

Additionally, adopting circular economy thinking is an important way to drive a balance between innovation and sustainability. Not only designers, but producers as a whole need to explore circular economy models such as reuse of materials, remanufacturing of products, and recycling of resources in order to reduce the consumption of resources and the burden on the environment.

6 Summary

Under the global perspective, the future of cross-cultural product and service design is full of infinite possibilities. As technology advances and cultures intermingle, the boundaries of design will be further blurred, providing a broader stage for designers. However, at the same time, we also need to pay attention to the challenges posed by cultural differences, and ensure that design is not only a tool for commercial interests, but also a powerful weapon to promote cultural exchange, understanding and symbiosis. It is hoped that through continuous research and practice, we can better grasp the dynamics of cross-cultural product and service design. Under the trend of sustainable development, we will contribute to building a more harmonious and diversified world.

References

1. Beveridge, I.: Intercultural Marketing: Theory and Practice. Taylor and Francis, 1 January 2020. https://doi.org/10.4324/9781003025344
2. Gao, Y., Xu, X.: Service design: a new concept of contemporary design. Lit. Art Res. (06), 140–147 (2014). (in Chinese)
3. Chui, H., Lichtenstein, D.: Cross-cultural design: considerations for successfully entering global markets. Interactions 17(3), 36–41 (2010)
4. Gucciardi, L.: Cross-cultural design: a literature review. Des. Cult. 6(3), 285–300 (2014)
5. Guo, Q., Teng, L.: Seeking consensus across cultures-revisiting the way of communicating Chinese culture to the world from the perspective of culture and cognition. Int. J. 33(04), 30–36 (2011). https://doi.org/10.13495/j.cnki.cjjc.2011.04.003. (in Chinese)
6. Hong, J., Chang, Y.: Cross-cultural design in the age of globalization: a critical review. Des. Stud. 39(2), 185–205 (2018)
7. Hwang, G., de Jong, M.: Cross-cultural design methods for global products and services. J. Bus. Res. 68(7), 1494–1503 (2015)
8. Ying, J., Linghao, Z.: Exploration of the evolution and design principles of service design system diagram. Decoration (06), 79–81 (2017). https://doi.org/10.16272/j.cnki.cn11-1392/j.2017.06.013. (in Chinese)
9. Lisa, D., Katrina, H., Joseph, W., et al.: Designing interculturally: adopting a social justice research framework for "Seeing Difference". J. Tech. Writ. Commun. 53(1), 33–49 (2023)
10. Luo, S., Hu, Y.: Service design-driven model innovation. Packag. Eng. 36(12), 1–4+28 (2015). https://doi.org/10.19554/j.cnki.1001-3563.2015.12.002. (in Chinese)
11. Meng, X.: The use and communication of cultural symbols in the construction of China's national image. Shanghai International Studies University (2014). (in Chinese)
12. Nan, Q., Patrick, L.P.R.: Design of cross-cultural communication supporting system: the appropriate level to provide cultural information. Int. J. Hum.-Comput. Interact. 38(5), 406–418 (2022)

13. Xiao, T.: Research on Social Innovation under the Perspective of Participatory Design. Hunan University (2017). (in Chinese)
14. Tuan, Y.-F., Gale, B.: Cross-cultural design for global markets: an examination of Taiwanese and Anglo-American cultural differences in user preferences for web design attributes. J. Glob. Mark. **17**(2), 73–94 (2004)
15. Xie, S.: Research on Cross-Cultural Product Design. Nanjing University of Aeronautics and Astronautics (2012). (in Chinese)
16. Xu, L., Liu, J.: Value flux in cross-cultural communication: cultural discount and cultural value-added. China Publishing **08**, 8–12 (2014). (in Chinese)
17. Xu, X., Gao, Y.: Research on availability evaluation system and its application in service design. Decoration **02**, 108–110 (2015). https://doi.org/10.16272/j.cnki.cn11-1392/j.2015. 02.030.(inChinese)
18. Yang, Q.H., 양해경, et al.: A study on the fused-innovation method of cross-cultural design through analyzing the Guangdong-Hong Kong-Macao Greater Bay Area Design Activities. 한국과학예술융합학회39(3) (2021)
19. Sikao, Z.: Research on the strategy of Chinese culture going to the world under the perspective of intercultural communication. Hebei Normal Univ. (2016). (in Chinese)

Research on Modular Experience Based Design of Wearable Products for Scuba Diving

Zhilin Jiang[✉] and Hanling Zhang

Hunan University, Changsha, China
zhilin@hnu.edu.cn

Abstract. With economic development and an improved quality of life, China's sports and health industry is continuously expanding. In particular, water sports, with scuba diving as a prime example, have emerged as promising avenues for growth. This study delves into the demands and behaviors of "Generation Z" youth in the realm of scuba diving to explore opportunities for the development of intelligent sports products.

To provide a comprehensive understanding, we commence with an analysis of the research background and current status. Subsequently, we propose key design trends, including scene digitization, product light-weighting, and integrated services, with a focus on enhancing multimodal interactive experiences and intelligent features.

Conducting a comparative analysis of scuba diving and other water sports products, we uncover their respective strengths and weaknesses in terms of user engagement, entertainment value, usability, portability, interactivity, social aspects, and professionalism. Drawing from these results, we identify pivotal opportunities and delineate directions for future research.

Employing both qualitative and quantitative research methods, we conducted user surveys, resulting in the identification of 11 critical user needs and functional levels. Building upon this foundation, we introduce five distinct features for scuba diving scenarios: modular assembly and disassembly, multifunctionality for sports assistance, comprehensive representation of sports health data, gamification of skill mastery, and scuba emergency prompts and responses.

Central to this study are the design principles and strategies that shift the focus from entertainment experiences to scuba diving skill mastery and cognition. This approach caters to the needs of "Generation Z" youth who possess curiosity but lack experience in scuba diving. In light of the anticipated trends in artificial intelligence and water sports, we expect that scuba diving will gain increased attention and become an integral component of healthy physical activities.

Keywords: Modular experience · Scuba diving · Generation Z · Intelligent sports products · Sports health

P.-L. P. Rau (Ed.): HCII 2024, LNCS 14699, pp. 264–277, 2024.
https://doi.org/10.1007/978-3-031-60898-8_18

1 Introduction

1.1 The Demand for Nationwide Physical Activities

In August 2021, in the "National Fitness Plan (2021–2025)" policy, the government emphasizes promoting high-level development, integrating sports with various sectors, including tourism and the healthcare industry. It aims to achieve technological and practical reforms, constructing a smart and healthy lifestyle for the national sports. Nowadays, during the preparation of major sports events such as the 2022 Beijing Winter Olympics, various projects are exploring towards intelligence under the influence of factors like policy, economy, society, and technology, utilizing artificial intelligence and internet technologies. For instance, in the Winter Olympics, sleep pods equipped with multiple sensors ensure athletes' healthy rest, while super high-speed 4K track cameras are installed on the field for precise capture of athletes' movements, enhancing the audience experience. In the realm of internet enterprises, the transformation is underway from simple hardware products to a combined smart ecosystem. For example, Peloton, with data indicating over 3 million users within its entire system, including 2 million in fitness and nearly 900,000 in online subscriptions. Peloton integrates hardware, software, media, retail, logistics, etc., to create an immersive experience for users. In summary, the development of the intelligent sports and health industry shows a promising trend. In the future, intelligent sports will integrate algorithms, new scenarios, and new ecosystems to create a more specialized and personalized system, optimizing the user's sports experience.

Over the past decade, China's diving industry has experienced an annual growth rate exceeding one-third, notably in Sanya City, Hainan Province. Since 2010, close to 1.5 million tourists annually have visited this region to experience diving [1]. Diving has long been considered as an auxiliary service, and in the minds of many, it was perceived merely as a high-end, niche product, facing challenges for substantial development. Nowadays, diving is gradually becoming a popular trend, expanding from a subsidiary activity in island tourism to independent diving, gradually capturing a larger market share. Figures indicate that in 2023, the revenue of the diving experience industry will approach 640 billion USD, marking an emerging blue ocean [2]. Encouraged by national policies and driven by the marketing environment for water sports, there has been a significant shift in perception, particularly among different age groups, especially the Z-generation youth. They now view diving more as an adventure and novelty. Propelled by the younger generation, diving is gradually evolving into a trend, showcasing the optimistic attitude towards life and the boundless spirit of exploration among the youth.

1.2 Concept of Product Modularization

The concept of modular design was initially applied in the field of computer programming. Unlike the traditional programming mindset of entering statements line by line, the modularization concept involves first constructing the program framework with a main program and subprograms, and then programming by gradually filling them in. This hierarchical approach not only reduces the complexity of the program but also proves more conducive to modifications. Gradually, the idea of breaking down the whole into various components has been widely applied across diverse fields [3].

Until the 1950s, some Western countries officially introduced the "modular design concept." Modularization then became a distinct design approach formally applied in the field of product design. In academic terms, its definition mainly falls into two categories: first, within a fixed scope, components with similar functions but different characteristics are combined through standardization and serialization to broaden their functional and environmental attributes. Second, within a specific scope, individual modules with identical functions and forms are overlaid or nested, enhancing their combined functional attributes and applicability. As one of the most representative categories in green design, the modular design concept not only influences the appearance of products but also plays a decisive role in their functional attributes and usage. Additionally, modular products, with their unique connection methods and external features, offer advantages compared to similar competitors: (1) Versatile usage: Unlike the generally singular functionality and applicability of common products, modular products can enhance their attributes by assembling accessories, thereby expanding their scope and functionality [4]. (2) Standardization of structural assembly: Modular products commonly adopt standardized components in their structural design, relieving users from the need to learn complex assembly methods and significantly reducing the burden of use. Similarly, in case of damage to sensory equipment, repairs can be made by replacing damaged components, greatly extending the overall lifespan of the equipment. (3) Manufacturing and processing advantages: Modular products mostly employ relatively simple forms as their basic units, later achieving the construction of complex forms through combination. This simplification of basic units effectively reduces the difficulty of product processing, achieving the control of production costs and shortening processing cycles.

2 Research on Diving Sports Product Demand Among Generation Z

2.1 Methods for User Research

By conducting research and discussions with users, analyze the attitudes, perceptions, behaviors, and even expectations of Generation Z youth towards diving sports. Study the specific processes of the target users in diving or other sports, analyze pain points and potential opportunities, and uncover their needs.

2.2 Characteristics and Basic Needs of Generation Z

Key Characteristics of Generation Z Population. Based on preliminary results from online surveys, a comprehensive analysis was conducted regarding the characteristics of Generation Z in terms of consumption patterns, sports environments, motivations, and product demands. In terms of consumption patterns and sports environments, Generation Z exhibits diverse features. In daily consumption, they demonstrate a strong pursuit of individualized needs in areas such as "eating," "drinking," "wearing," and "using," reflecting a focus on convenience, aesthetics, and personalization. Particularly in the aspect of "using," Generation Z is predominantly inclined towards pursuing sophistication, quality, and convenience. Simultaneously, they exhibit characteristics of being "lazy," which doesn't strictly imply laziness in the literal sense but rather reflects a desire for a smart lifestyle in the era of the internet [5].

Regarding sports environments, Generation Z tends to lean towards exercising at home or outdoors, enjoying the advantage of having control over their exercise time. Particularly in terms of exercise choices, aerobic activities like running have become mainstream, with relatively lower interest in professional places such as gyms. They prioritize the freedom and privacy of their workouts [6].

In terms of exercise motivation, Generation Z's motivations include both external factors (such as improving physique, socializing, and showcasing unique self) and internal factors (such as maintaining a healthy and disciplined lifestyle, alleviating life stress, and boosting confidence). External factors are somewhat influenced by the "aesthetic economy," making confidence enhancement and stress relief the primary internal motivations.

Generation Z demonstrates a strong interest in smart sports products and their expectations. Emerging devices, particularly those representing gamified sports products, are gaining popularity, especially in home environments, where people's interest in such products is steadily growing. For products like smart wristbands and watches, data visualization and sharing take center stage, with a simultaneous emphasis on product safety. Furthermore, the expectations of Generation Z regarding products are gradually evolving, seeking not only the fulfillment of basic functionalities but also placing a greater emphasis on higher-level requirements, such as the usage experience of new devices like "gamification," "VR," and "AR."

The brief usage cycle of existing sports products prompts further in-depth research on the potential for utilizing these products in various situations [7]. The prominent presence of technology and its sensible integration with ergonomics will be crucial factors to consider in product design. A thorough investigation into these features holds significant guiding implications for understanding and meeting the demands of Generation Z in terms of consumption and sports.

Survey and Interview Research on Generation Z. Amid the trend of the gradual dominance of the smart sports market today, scuba diving, as a prominently watched emerging sports sector, is gradually revealing its market potential. In this context, the Generation Z youth, with their explorative and knowledge-seeking traits, are evolving into a primary driving force for scuba diving, opening up new prospects for the further development of this field.

In order to gain a more profound insight into the attitudes, behaviors, needs, and preferences of Generation Z in scuba diving, the author conducted a comprehensive survey and in-depth interviews. The main data from the survey are illustrated in the graph (Fig. 1). The survey results indicate that, although some respondents have limited knowledge of scuba diving, the majority expressed a willingness to actively try it. However, compared to other water sports, the perceived complexity of scuba diving equipment becomes a constraint, leading to a strong preference for lightweight sports accessories among this demographic.

In the era of fragmented internet use, Generation Z seeks autonomy in learning scuba diving skills, intending to broaden their perspectives through online tools, reflecting their independent information-seeking nature. To effectively promote comprehensive scuba diving development among Generation Z, there is a pressing need for in-depth popularization of scuba-related knowledge. Exploring flexible strategies for scuba diving learning that transcend geographical and temporal limitations, emphasizing personalized and lightweight features, is necessary to meet this demographic's unique needs. By addressing common concerns, more individuals can be encouraged to actively participate in scuba diving. Future research should focus on refining effective ways to convey scuba diving information to Generation Z and further integrating scuba diving into the health domain for widespread adoption and sustainable development among young people.

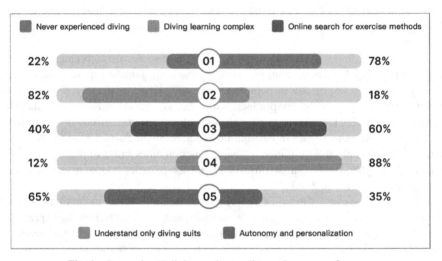

Fig. 1. Generation Z diving understanding and sports preferences

Analysis of Scuba Diving Demand among Generation Z. By observing, conducting interviews, and leveraging big data to gather information on user behaviors throughout the process, the user model (Fig. 2) and the user journey map (Fig. 3) for scuba diving are integrated as follows.

The current state of the scuba diving experience mainly involves four key stages: arrival preparation, journey to the site, daily diving, and post-departure check. During the arrival preparation stage, users perform various actions, including payment and form filling. They then learn basic safety precautions, don equipment, dive, and finally organize before leaving. However, in the early preparation stage, users face issues such as complex and time-consuming equipment preparation, carrying numerous items, leading to fatigue during the journey. During the journey, safety measures are not emphasized timely, the equipment is complex, and the diving process lacks interactivity and immersion. Upon leaving the dive, there is a lack of well-matched and visualized data. To enhance the scuba diving experience, there are opportunities, including lightweight scuba-assist health equipment, providing a more comprehensive diving experience, and establishing a community to facilitate interaction and integration among divers, diving equipment, and social connections [8].

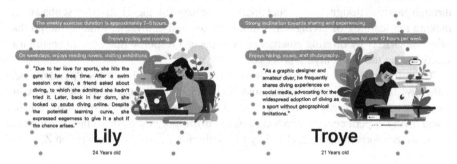

Fig. 2. User Model

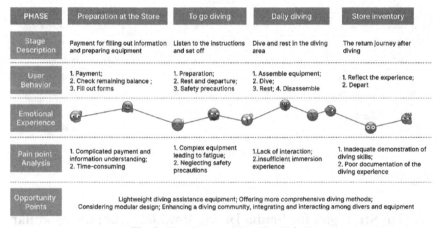

Fig. 3. User Journey Map (For diving)

2.3 Demands and Functional Transformation in Scuba Diving

Following a thorough analysis of user needs, the product design primarily focuses on aspects such as fragmented information acquisition, assistive devices, sports learning, and exercise assistance. To meet user expectations, the product design encompasses 14 key features, evaluated through a comprehensive assessment across four dimensions: user demand, user expectations, product innovation, and business expansion. This process ultimately identifies distinctive features (Fig. 4).

Among them, the distinctive features of the product include modular combination and disassembly, aiming to allow users to freely combine and disassemble product modules according to the needs of different diving stages, thereby overcoming the sense of weight and fatigue. Additionally, the product's exercise assistance function is not limited to scuba diving itself but extends to regular exercise to enhance user engagement and physical fitness. Emphasizing the representation of exercise health data, the product utilizes data visualization to provide users with a deeper understanding of the status of scuba diving, surpassing the functionality of traditional fitness trackers. Moreover, through gamified design, the product breaks down psychological barriers to scuba diving, making the learning of diving skills more relaxed and enjoyable. Finally, the product prioritizes safety by offering emergency prompts and response functions to ensure user safety during the scuba diving process.

Overall, the design of these distinctive features aims to lower the "psychological difficulty" threshold of scuba diving, making it not only a singular sport but also encompassing a more comprehensive experience and learning process. By providing a better scuba diving experience, the product aims to attract more users, drive the development of the water sports industry, and satisfy the exploratory desires of Generation Z.

Functions	Intensity of demands	Intensity of desires	Innovativeness of features	Market expansiveness	Comprehensive assessment
Modular equipment assembly and disassembly	5	5	4	5	19
Gamification of skill learning	5	4	5	4	18
Simultaneous Entertainment Diving and Exercise	4	5	4	4	17
Diving history and data recording	4	4	3	4	15
Wireless connectivity with other devices	4	4	3	4	15
Five-senses experience	4	4	3	4	15
Emergency rescue device	4	4	3	4	15
Diverse operations	3	3	3	4	13
Scuba diving community interaction	3	3	3	2	11

Fig. 4. Function prioritization

3 Design Strategies for Scuba Diving Products from the Modular Experience Perspective

3.1 Design Requirements

Comfort and Maneuverability. Sports products, as the name implies, involve users engaging in real operations and control of the product to mobilize specific body parts for exercise, aiming to achieve physical fitness or entertainment purposes. The comfort and maneuverability of use have always been highlights of such products. Therefore, while emphasizing modularity in sports product design, equal attention should be given to the ergonomics of the product. Factors such as the comfort of dimensions, durability of materials, and the adaptability of proportions in the design process need careful consideration [9].

Scenario Compatibility. From market research on sports products and analysis of some similar products, it can be understood that the biggest drawback of scuba diving products is the limited audience for individual products, influenced by both the user base and the scuba diving method itself. The integration of the modular design concept can broaden the product's scenario compatibility through the interconnection of individual components. The characteristics of scuba diving involve coordinated limb movements with scuba products, and users need to warm up before engaging in scuba diving, requiring a certain level of physical activity. At the design level, consideration can be given to the portability of the product, incorporating the modular design concept while contemplating compatibility with multiple scenarios. In the context of the future "experience economy" era, smart scuba diving products should be designed with a multi-sensory interactive approach, emphasizing the humanization and emotional aspects of the product [10].

Convenience of Use and Assembly. One major highlight of modular design is the uniformity of connection methods and component dimensions. This standardization not only saves costs in manufacturing but also brings a lot of convenience at the user level. The combination of different components can be more of a user's exploration. Figuring out how to assemble suitable exercise equipment is an inherently interesting and exploratory activity for users. The convenient and universal connection structure design makes all of this possible. Users, in their exploration, discover new product shapes and apply functionalities to exercise. In certain situations, the novelty of the new operational experience can even surpass the enjoyment derived from the exercise itself, showcasing one of the unique charms of modular design.

3.2 Design Strategies

Summarizing the Features of Diving Equipment. After observing and summarizing the types of diving sports products, it is found that the currently high-usage types include: diving watches, underwater propulsion devices, surfboards, and entertainment float boards. Therefore, they cover a wide range of functions, such as speed adjustment, data acquisition, emergency display, and sports recording. By classifying and comparing the usage of these products and then designing the functional areas through the modular design concept. Comprehensive analysis of existing products reveals that the market is mostly dominated by diving watches and visual screens, emphasizing data display in front of users. However, there is a significant problem of homogeneity, especially in the wristband or watch category. As for the underwater propulsion device category, due to technological innovations, new underwater diving modes are becoming more prevalent, with multi-mode experiences becoming a mainstream trend. However, in terms of skill mastery, there is less involvement, and it is not suitable to detach the hands from the equipment during the diving process. Combining skill mastery cycles is a new development trend. Power float boards are a type of entertainment product that has risen in recent years. They are mostly targeted at family activities, especially for children's entertainment in water. However, their target audience is limited to different age groups and is mostly suitable for novice divers.

Lowering the Barrier to Entry and Enhancing the Diving Experience. Traditional scuba diving products have a limited user base and high operational complexity. Observation reveals that users require extensive specialized learning and training to engage in scuba diving, along with the need for proficient equipment operation. These intricate procedures significantly elevate the threshold of scuba diving and adversely impact the user's sports experience. Modular equipment effectively mitigates such challenges. With uniform connection structures and assembly methods among modules, users can effort-lessly replace and match external devices by simply assembling or disassembling product modules without the need for reconnection. This swift and natural transformation not only significantly reduces preparation time beyond scuba diving but also provides users with the pleasure and immersive experience of hands-on assembly.

Enhancing the Versatility of Scuba Diving Equipment for Use in Various Sporting Scenarios. Market and user research reveal that scuba diving, in terms of both equip-ment and user numbers, has a relatively low share in the overall sports industry. This phenomenon is primarily attributed to the high entry barriers and limitations in product usage scenarios. Modular design, by dividing components of traditional scuba diving equipment into multiple parts, can serve different purposes before, during, and after diving. This design philosophy not only meets the operational requirements of scuba diving but also enables control in other sports after disassembly, thus breaking down the hardware barriers between scuba diving and traditional sports.

4 Practical Application of Modular Experience in Scuba Diving Product Design

4.1 Product Design Philosophy

Guided by design principles such as "Balancing Sport and Health," "Staged Learn-ing," and "Balancing Other Sports with Diving," we incorporate user demands for "Lightweight Diving Equipment," "Multi-mode Learning and Recording," and "Sen-sory Interaction" into our design practices. Through user research, we found that the Z-generation youth exhibit a phased understanding of diving. Currently, diving is mostly considered as an auxiliary activity, but it is expected to evolve into a mainstream sport in the future. Therefore, our product design aims to balance with other sports, breaking away from traditional concepts, shifting from "professionalism" toward "experiential learning," making diving more accessible to the public.

The ideal diving experience doesn't require complex equipment and paid services; instead, it involves enjoying a conversation with the sea when your body touches the water. The product's design philosophy emphasizes a moderate combination with other sports, enhancing its versatility and ultimately evolving towards a health-oriented direc-tion [11]. The core values for users include a "lightweight and convenient" learning method, an "immersive and worry-free" diving experience, and an "adaptable and diverse" bridge to other sports.

After analyzing innovation, feasibility, acceptability, and business viability, we ulti-mately decided to focus on the design and implementation of an underwater propulsion device. The underwater propulsion device exhibits innovation in its usage, sporting activities, and learning aspects compared to other products. In terms of feasibility, the underwater propulsion device integrates smart features and utilizes online applications or apps for data analysis and matching, leveraging relatively mature technology. Regarding user acceptance, the characteristics of the Z generation make them willing to try novel things; the compact size and wide applicability of the underwater propulsion device con-tribute to its high user acceptance. From a business perspective, with the rapid growth of the water sports industry and the increasing popularity of smart sports products, the underwater propulsion device is poised to secure a place in the market [12].

4.2 Product Design Practice

Based on the product design positioning and functional framework, several initial design proposals were generated using brainstorming and mind mapping techniques. These proposals primarily focus on modular assembly and disassembly, as well as expanding the scope of sports assistance beyond diving, encompassing both handheld and wearable dimensions (Fig. 5).

Fig. 5. Sketches

Firstly, the modular design considers the replacement of the handle and strap to meet the diverse speed adjustment requirements for handheld auxiliary equipment during diving. Additionally, attaching the propeller to the feet introduces a new recreational experience for users, enhancing the product's entertainment value and interactivity.

Secondly, the second proposal involves the disassembly and combination of various components, including the handle, health data detection module, equipment movement module, and entertainment photography device, catering to diverse user needs. The arched design of the handle enables wearable use even when not diving, meeting additional sporting requirements and emphasizing the product's multifunctionality.

Lastly, the third proposal integrates auxiliary equipment with other products such as wristwatches and water float boards to enable users to explore new experiences while engaging in healthy activities. This integrated design allows users to flexibly use the product in various sporting scenarios, enhancing its versatility and multifunctionality, further satisfying the explorative desires of the Z generation. These proposals aim to break the tradition of singular functionality in diving equipment, offering users a more personalized and comprehensive intelligent diving experience.

4.3 Product Design Description

X-DIVING is a series of diving sports products designed specifically for the Z generation, consisting of underwater propellers and handle modules. As a diving sports device,
it prioritizes simple operational performance, aiding users in receiving timely feedback
during the learning process, combining sports and entertainment (Fig. 6). The design
caters to three experiential levels to meet users' usage needs. At the instinctive level,
the product image emphasizes a bright, immersive, and lightweight style. The design
is inspired by sharks, exuding a sense of dynamic aesthetics, aligning with the external
characteristics of sports equipment. In terms of material selection, the metal coating
imparts a modern feel and a degree of strength to the propeller, while the handle uses
frosted silicone for a comfortable grip. The color palette, predominantly blue and black,
echoes the themes of diving speed and power, creating a cool and distinctive visual
experience. At the behavioral level, the diving equipment achieves multifunctionality
through modular design, lowering the learning threshold for diving. The equipment
includes two types of gear for different sports. During diving, users can adjust speeds in
multiple levels by combining the propeller with the handle to meet varying user needs in
different stages. In leisure moments, the handle can be used for basic exercise training,
such as jumping rope and push-ups. During the diving process, the equipment informs
users of information such as water temperature and diving depth through interface data
and sensor vibration feedback, allowing users to stay focused. On a reflective level,
the design of this product primarily focuses on how to introduce users to diving and
facilitate low-threshold learning. Firstly, establish a feedback mechanism where all user
exercise results are visualized on the app, providing users with a sense of achievement.
Secondly, create a social mechanism through the mobile app's social features (offline
friend connections or online communities), forming a social circle for users of diving
sports products. This helps users avoid feeling lonely during the process of achieving
fitness goals, aligning with the psychological preferences of the Z generation. Additionally, transforming professional and challenging exercise activities into entertaining and
progressively structured behaviors can alleviate users' psychological burden, facilitating
long-term adherence and habit formation.

4.4 Product Use Mode

Through exploration and analysis of hardware products and online interaction design,
the "X-DIVING" underwater propeller and the "X-SPORTS" online app have completed the corresponding design practices under the guidance of design strategies such
as lightweight and convenient, versatile fitness, and immersive experience, essentially
achieving the design goals. The product includes two types of sports equipment: an
underwater propeller and a wireless handle, serving different purposes for sports training. The underwater propeller is used to perform diving movements. Before engaging
in diving, connect the app with the device to create a personalized sports learning plan.
Diving enthusiasts might worry about whether this small propeller can withstand the
pressure of deep diving. However, experiments have shown that it can meet the needs
of deep diving enthusiasts in deeper underwater depths. Moreover, the underwater propeller is also suitable for use in swimming pools and can be used by novices or children

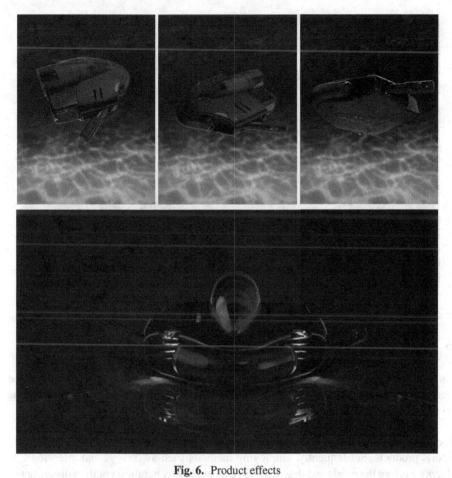

Fig. 6. Product effects

for underwater play or learning swimming movements. There is no need to worry about the propeller being too dangerous; the propeller is equipped with a double-layer protective net to prevent users from being accidentally pinched. The research and development design incorporates a quick assembly/disassembly system and a finger-worn remote control. The X-DIVING underwater propeller can be mounted on the arm, leg, or air cylinder. By wearing the finger-worn remote control on the index finger and long-pressing it for 15 s, the X-DIVING underwater propeller enters a constant speed cruising mode. At this point, the diver can free up their hands, move freely underwater, and achieve underwater filming, garbage collection, or underwater operations (Fig. 7).

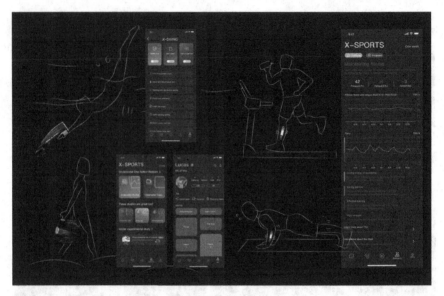

Fig. 7. Usage diagram

5 Conclusion and Future Work

This research is grounded in the context of marine diving activities, applying modular design theory, and focusing on the Z generation youth as the research subjects, aiming to delve into intelligent sports and health products.

Initially, providing a clear definition of the concept of intelligent sports, while also focusing on the development trends of artificial intelligence and IoT technologies in sports products. Subsequently, employing methods such as surveys and interviews, to deeply explore the needs and design highlights of the Z generation youth in diving activities. Simultaneously utilizing the user journey analysis method to comprehensively understand user behaviors and emotional experiences, facilitating the identification of pain points and the synthesis of requirements. During the design phase of health equipment based on marine diving activities, the study transforms user needs into specific functions, conducts a quantitative assessment of these functions, and specifies their priorities.

Emphasizing the design of the "X-DIVING" underwater propeller, this product not only meets the needs of users at different stages but also accomplishes various functions, including underwater environmental perception, data acquisition and analysis, and speed adjustment. On the system level, multiple systems are employed, including data analysis systems, diving safety systems, and power propulsion systems, highlighting the integration of hardware and software. In terms of interaction, the integration of hardware and software achieves a user experience characterized by seamless immersion and diverse adaptability.

During the practical implementation, the author encountered technical limitations, particularly in the conceptual validation of machine learning and interaction modules.

Simultaneously, further refinement of the diving skill mastery cycle is an area of future focus. Ultimately, the author envisions that this academic conceptual design will make a substantive contribution to the health and lifestyle of the future sports field.

Acknowledgments. This work was supported in part by Key R&D Program of Hunan (2022SK2104), in part by Leading plan for scientific and technological innovation of high-tech industries of Hunan (2022GK4010), in part by Keeson Technology Corporation Limited.

References

1. Chen, Y.W.: A discussion on the exercise value and development of recreational scuba diving. Talent **35**, 70 (2019)
2. Shi, H.E.: Diving as an emerging blue industry. Glory, 48–50 (2020)
3. Wu, Q., Jia, K., Liu, Y.: Sustainable research design based on modularity. Packag. Eng., 140–144 (2019)
4. Deng, W.B., Liu, Y., Liu, H.M., Wang, C.: Design research of sensory devices based on indoor sports decompression. Popular Lit. Art, 77–78 (2021)
5. Research Report on China's Intelligent Sports and Fitness Industry. https://report.iresearch.cn/report/202110/3857.shtml. Accessed 1 Feb 2024
6. Zhang, R.: Analysis of the business logic of beauty economy in the "internet+" era. Bus. Econ. Res., 41–43 (2022)
7. Yang, X.F., Guo, Y.P.: Research on the development trends of wearable sports devices. Fujian Sports Sci. Technol. **37**(03), 17–19+37 (2018)
8. Yu, C.Y.: Research on product design service mode under the background of internet+. China Market, 179–183 (2020)
9. Xu, R.Y.: Research on user experience design methods for intelligent wearable products. Design, 102–103 (2015)
10. Design in the Era of Experience Economy. Design **35**(07), 7 (2022)
11. Han, X.: Research on intelligent product design based on emotional experience. Jiangnan Univ. (2021)
12. Liu, X.H., Xi, Y.F., You, W.T., Jiang, H., Sun, L.Y.: Data-driven sustainable design. Packag. Eng.. Eng. **42**(18), 1–10 (2021)

Design Thinking and Cognitive Patterns in Corporate Image Shaping: A Case Study of Formosa Plastics Group's Corporate Identity System (CIS)

Jhih-Ling Jiang[1], Yikang Sun[2][✉], and Yen-Yu Kang[3][✉]

[1] Graduate School of Creative Industry Design, National Taiwan University of Arts, New Taipei City 220307, Taiwan
jausten@ntua.edu.tw

[2] College of Art and Design, Nanjing Forestry University, Nanjing 210037, China
sunyikang120110@hotmail.com

[3] Department of Industrial Design, National Kaohsiung Normal University, Kaohsiung, Taiwan
yenyu@mail.nknu.edu.tw

Abstract. The Corporate identity systems play an important role in establishing corporate image. These systems include brand positioning, product design and overall packaging, among which "Visual Identity (VI)" is the first impression that leads consumers to understand the company. A perfect VI can highlight the brand spirit and establish visual distinction in the market. Therefore, among the three major concepts of modern corporate identity system (CIS), the importance of VI has gradually been strengthened, and "Mind Identity (MI)" and "Behavior Identity (BI)" is relatively downplayed. Formosa Plastics Group was the first company in Taiwan to introduce a corporate identification system. This was due to Mr. Yong-Qing, Wang, inviting Shux-Xiong, Guo, to design the CIS corporate trademark for Formosa Plastics Group, thus starting the trend of industrial design in Taiwan. What is even more commendable is that Formosa Plastics launched the CIS manual half a century ago. Its unique and innovative act was the first of its kind in the industry at the time. This article takes the Formosa Plastics corporate identity system as an example, uses the method of qualitative data analysis, and uses private communication with Shux-Xiong, Guo, to learn more about the creativity and ingenuity of the Formosa Plastics corporate identity system back then. At the same time, a set of CIS design, evaluation and recognition models are proposed to understand the general audience's perception and preferences of CIS systems. Research has found that corporate identity systems play an important role in establishing brand image, forming market competitive advantages, improving customer experience, strengthening social responsibility, and consolidating corporate culture. This study explores the value of Formosa Plastics' corporate identity system in Taiwan's design history, and explores the future trend of CIS design through the model proposed in this study.

Keywords: Corporate Identity System · Brand Image · Creative Thinking · Cognitive Model · Formosa Plastics Group

P.-L. P. Rau (Ed.): HCII 2024, LNCS 14699, pp. 278–292, 2024.
https://doi.org/10.1007/978-3-031-60898-8_19

1 Introduction

A Corporate Identity System, CIS, also known as Corporate Image Design System, is a comprehensive system adopted by businesses to highlight uniqueness, product differentiation, or image in competitive markets [22]. This system aims to effectively convey the company's philosophy and cultural spirit to relevant stakeholders or groups through well-developed visual and cultural elements while ensuring consistent identification and values alignment with the company. In essence, the Corporate Identity System combines modern design concepts with considerations of corporate management theories to portray the company's personality, highlighting its corporate spirit. This fosters consumer identification with the company and leaves a lasting impression, thus achieving promotional goals through design systems [1, 14, 16, 36–40, 42]. Therefore, the role of the Corporate Identity System can be summarized into two main aspects: (1) Internal Function - Value Cohesion: The internal function focuses on the cohesion within the company, influencing internal employees and stakeholders through visual communication methods, fostering consensus, deepening corporate culture, and strengthening corporate spirit. (2) External Function - Identification and Promotion: The external function concentrates on consumer identification, serving as an outward centrifugal force. It highlights the company's uniqueness through CIS's visual identity, deepening its image from visual appearance to trust in product quality, building brand loyalty, enhancing corporate competitiveness, and ultimately achieving the goal of promoting products.

According to the provisions of company law, companies exist for profit-making purposes in the form of organized, registered, and established legal entities. Therefore, enhancing the profitability of enterprises is the primary rule for their survival. Establishing an effective Corporate Identity System (CIS) is the best way to enhance a company's profitability.

Looking at the internal and external effects of the CIS mentioned above, it is easy to understand the needs of the enterprise. The CIS has become an important visual symbol in modern business operations. It serves not only as the business card for the public to recognize the company but also as a means for the company to showcase its internal values through professional design. In other words, the system is an integral part of modern business marketing strategies and plays a crucial role. It can be said that good design leads to good marketing, resulting in quality profitability, and ultimately leading to business success. Therefore, the Corporate Identity System has become an indispensable tool in modern business marketing management.

Simply put, the "Corporate Identity System" is a unified design plan that embodies a company's intangible business philosophy across all media channels accessible to the public, including products, buildings, advertisements, business cards, stationery, and even the attitudes of employees. The ultimate goal is to instill confidence in consumers regarding the company and its products, thereby establishing a unified corporate image.

The concept of a unified corporate image originated from AEG, a nationwide electrical appliance company in Germany before World War I, which fully adopted the trademark designed by the German designer Peter Behrens (1868–1940). After World War II, with the prosperity of the international economy, various industries expanded their operations, moving towards diversification and internationalization. Business operators felt that their existing image could not keep up with rapid developments. Therefore, major European and American companies began adopting Corporate Identity Systems to convey their unique styles.

This study aims to use the Formosa Plastics Group's Corporate Identity System as an example to explore its origin and trace the creative ideas behind its design, especially observing the significant role and contributions of the Formosa Plastics Group's Corporate Identity System in the history of design in Taiwan. The design of the Formosa Plastics Group's Corporate Identity System can be traced back to the 1970s when the group was undergoing restructuring and expansion. In order to enhance the company's image, the Formosa Plastics Group decided to introduce a new Corporate Identity System. The design of this identity system was entrusted to the Ming Chi Industrial Design Center, including the design of logos, fonts, colors, advertisements, etc. Using the Formosa Plastics Group as an example, its Corporate Identity System not only attracted widespread attention at the time but is still considered a successful case today. This study intends to explore the development of CIS in Taiwan through the design team responsible for designing it, mainly led by Shou-Xiong, Guo.

2 Literature Review

2.1 Enterprise Identity System: Value and Typical Cases

In the mid-20th century, the Corporate Identity System (CIS) began to receive significant attention from businesses. Subsequently, driven by the economic prosperity of the 1960s to 1980s in Europe and America, numerous enterprises embarked on constructing corporate identity systems. This period witnessed the emergence of many globally renowned cases, including the International Business Machines Corporation (IBM) in 1955, Radio Company of America (RCA) in 1969, Coca-Cola in 1970, and Minnesota Mining and Manufacturing Company (3M). Additionally, three American enterprises, namely CBS Corporation, IBM, and Westinghouse Electric Corporation, adopted CI design during this period, with IBM's logo design being the most famous. Thus, some regard IBM's adoption of the CI program at that time as a landmark event in CI establishment. The introduction of CIS significantly boosted the revenue of many enterprises; for instance, Chrysler's market share increased by 18% in the early 1960s, and Coca-Cola's global CIS transformation sparked a CIS trend worldwide.

In contrast, Japan began embracing the concept of corporate identity design influenced by Japanese aesthetics, catalyzed by the post-war economic miracle, only in the 1970s. Japan introduced the concept of enterprise identity design in 1970 and gradually promoted it within the corporate sector. Among them, Nakanishi Motoo emerged as a prominent figure, and his leadership of Paos Corporation became a significant case. The company boasted several influential examples of Japanese-style CI, including Mazda Motor Corporation in 1975, DAIEI Department Store, Matsuya Department Store in 1977, Kirin Brewery in 1980, Kenwood Corporation in 1982, NTT in 1985, and INAX in the ceramic industry, all of which became well-known and influential examples of Japanese CI.

The prototype of corporate identity design in Taiwan can be traced back to the mid-1960s when Yan Shui-long (1903–1997) designed logos, signs, packaging, and mosaic murals for Taichung Sun Cake. In 1967, the Formosa Plastics Group, under the guidance of Shou-Xiong, Guo, proposed a corporate design policy and initiated the use of a wave-type integrated logo. Since the late 1980s, influenced by the concept of Japanese corporate identity system planning, corporate identity design in Taiwan has gradually become popular and entered a mature stage. Especially in the past decade, due to increasingly fierce market competition, corporate image has been receiving more attention in market marketing.

It's worth noting that Corporate Identity Systems (CIS) are not limited by the size or scale of a business; they can be implemented by companies of any industry, businesses, or individual organizations to create their unique CIS. But why is it necessary to design a CIS? Corporate image is a crucial and valuable concept for businesses as it directly correlates with the company's image and reputation [7, 33]. However, corporate image is influenced by various factors, and to the public, it's often an abstract concept. If companies want the public to have a tangible perception of their corporate image, thus fostering identification and support, they must systemize and organize their corporate image to achieve unity and integration. In today's fiercely competitive business environment, if companies can make their image understood by the public, win brand reputation, and garner support, corporate image will become one of their most valuable assets [1, 2, 8, 27].

Corporate Identity Systems (CIS) play a crucial role in modern brand management, aiming to establish a unique brand image for companies, enhance brand recognition, and effectively communicate the core values of the company. Designers play an important role in creating visual symbols that are unique and representative of a company's brand, culture, and spirit within the corporate identity system. Renowned graphic designers such as Paul Rand (1914–1996), Saul Bass (1920–1996), Massimo Vignelli (1931-), Michael Bierut (1957-), and Stefan Sagmeister (1962-), among others, have significantly contributed to this field. Many well-known CIS designers have created distinctive identity systems for globally recognized companies. The works of these famous graphic designers hold a significant position in the field of corporate identity system design and have a profound impact on subsequent brand design and visual communication.

These internationally renowned CIS cases underscore the pivotal role of corporate identity systems in brand construction and communication, while also showcasing the outstanding achievements of these famous designers in the field of modern graphic design. Their design works are not only elegant in design aesthetics but also achieve remarkable success in brand positioning and market communication, making them successful paradigms in brand design and visual communication.

2.2 Design Thinking and Cognitive Patterns in Corporate Identity Systems

Corporate identity systems consist of several essential elements, including the following key components [40]:

Mission Identity (MI): Mission Identity serves as the cornerstone of the corporate identity system, conceptualizing the company's mission and values into ideals and goals pursued collectively by members of the organization. This encompasses the company's creed, motto, and core values, expressing its fundamental principles.

Behavior Identity (BI): Behavior Identity translates the company's mission identity into organizational behaviors and activities to garner recognition and response from employees and consumers. Internal activities encompass employee training, incentive mechanisms, work environment, and research and development strategies, while external activities include public relations, promotional events, philanthropic activities, market research, and product development.

Visual Identity (VI): Visual Identity externalizes the company's internal mission through visual elements and graphic designs, achieving concretization, visualization, uniformity, and systematization effects. This enables immediate visual recognition and conveys the company's message. Basic elements of visual identity include the company name, brand logo, corporate standard colors, proprietary fonts, slogans, and exclusive images or designs. Applications encompass advertising, communication, product packaging, signage, and banners.

These elements intertwine to form the overall framework of a corporate identity system. Corporate identity systems not only help establish a unique corporate image but also enhance brand awareness and loyalty in the competitive market, strengthen the company's social image, and further promote sales and profitability. Therefore, companies should prioritize and construct their identity systems effectively to realize the shaping and continuous development of their corporate image.

The designers of corporate identity systems communicate a company's culture through design, and the audience, in observing these systems, is essentially engaging in a dialogue with the designers. This dialogue relationship can be explained using communication theory, which identifies three levels of requirements in the communication process between designers and audiences:

Technical Level for Visual Identity (VI): Designers must accurately convey the intended message and capture the audience's attention, allowing them to see, touch, and feel the designer's creativity. Semantic Level for Behavior Identity (BI): Audiences need to accurately understand the conveyed message's meaning to correctly interpret the content expressed by the corporate identity system.

Effect Level for Mission Identity (MI): The visual message of the identity system must evoke psychological resonance in the audience, eliciting emotional responses and creating a profound impression of the company.

A corporate identity system mainly consists of three parts: the company's mission identity (MI), which transforms ideas into consistent communication patterns (BI), and the visual experience (VI) that aligns with the company's personality. Designers need to first understand the company's mission identity, then translate these ideas into behavior identity, and finally transform them into visual identity through design elements. This is a top-down visual thinking process, where understanding of behavior identity is derived from visual identity design, leading to the realization of mission identity. The communication process and cognitive model between designers and audiences can be illustrated using a conceptual model, as shown in Fig. 1.

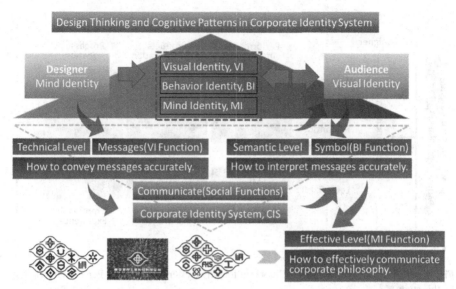

Fig. 1. Design Thinking and Cognitive Patterns in Corporate Identity System. (Redraw from [20].)

3 Research Methodology

3.1 Construction of Evaluation Criteria

To validate the design of the Formosa Plastics Corporation's Corporate Identity System (CIS) against the general audience's perception, this study utilized the research framework outlined above and referenced relevant communication theories and principles of symbol communication [2, 3, 9, 15, 17–20, 41]. Following the structure depicted in Fig. 2, which illustrates how designers proceed from conceptual identification through behavioral identification to visual identification in creating a perfect CIS, the study segmented the process into three stages: "Creative Expression," "Creative Process," and "Creative Presentation." These stages were further encoded to correspond with the three phases of CIS design: "Visual Identification," "Behavioral Identification," and "Conceptual Identification." This preliminary encoding framework was used to construct the assessment framework for CIS design and perception, as illustrated in Fig. 2.

The principle and operational thinking mode of this framework are as follows:

Based on the premise of "creative expression, creative process, and creative presentation," this study suggests that the three aspects of visual identity, behavioral identity, and ideological identity can each be further divided into three stages of cognitive processes:

1. Three Stages of Visual Identity

Conceptualization Stage of Visual Identity (Creative Expression): Designers or teams brainstorm and sketch various possibilities and creative ideas for visual identity. They engage in brainstorming sessions, sketching, and creating samples to find the most suitable visual identity solution.

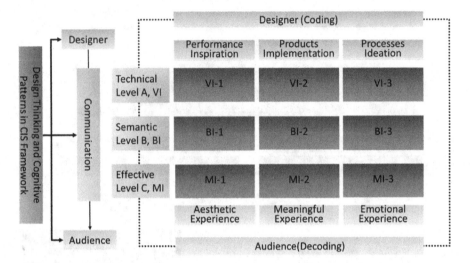

Fig. 2. "Conceptual Framework of Corporate Identity System Design and Perception." (Drawn by this study)

Design Stage of Visual Identity (Creative Process): Once the conceptualization stage defines a general direction, the next step is to enter the concrete design stage. Designers will detail the elements of visual identity, such as logo design, color selection, and font usage. This is a crucial stage in the creative process that considers brand values, target audience, and market positioning.

Implementation Stage of Visual Identity (Creative Presentation): After the design stage is completed, visual identity moves into the implementation phase. This includes applying the design to various media and platforms, such as the company's website, business cards, advertisements, and packaging. Creative presentation brings visual identity into reality, ensuring consistency and recognizability across different platforms.

2. Three Stages of Behavioral Identity

Conceptualization Stage of Behavioral Identity: During this stage, individuals or teams brainstorm various possibilities and creative ideas for behavioral identity. This involves designing behavioral identity plans or strategies to determine the goals, scope, and methods of behavioral identity.

Design Stage of Behavioral Identity: Once the conceptualization stage defines a general direction, the next step is to enter the concrete design stage. In this stage, people will design the steps, procedures, and methods required to implement behavioral identity.

Implementation Stage of Behavioral Identity: After the design stage, behavioral identity moves into the implementation phase. This includes applying behavioral identity to practical situations, such as implementing organizational procedures or individual behaviors. In this stage, people need to execute behavioral identity strategies, follow up on actions, and evaluate their impact and effectiveness.

3. Three Stages of Ideological Identity

Conceptualization Stage of Ideological Identity: During this stage, relevant individuals or teams brainstorm various possibilities and creative ideas for ideological identity. They discuss different directions for ideological identity and evaluate the strengths and limitations of each idea.

Design Stage of Ideological Identity: Once the conceptualization stage defines a general direction, the next step is to enter the concrete design stage. In this stage, relevant individuals will design the steps and methods needed to implement ideological identity.

Implementation Stage of Ideological Identity: After the design stage, ideological identity moves into the implementation phase. This includes applying ideological identity to practical situations, such as launching promotional activities and interacting with target audiences. In this stage, relevant individuals need to execute ideological identity strategies, follow up, and evaluate their impact and effectiveness.

In conclusion, the visual identity, behavioral identity, and ideological identity of CIS are all aimed at ensuring that the company presents a consistent image, values, and behavioral attitudes internally and externally. These efforts transform creative results into the company's identity system, helping to establish a strong brand image and market position. Based on the aforementioned CIS design and evaluation model (see Fig. 2), the research team, through private discussions with Shu-Xiong, Guo, comprehended the entire process of designing the CIS for Formosa Plastics Corporation and combined literature discussions to finally construct the criteria for assessment (see Fig. 3).

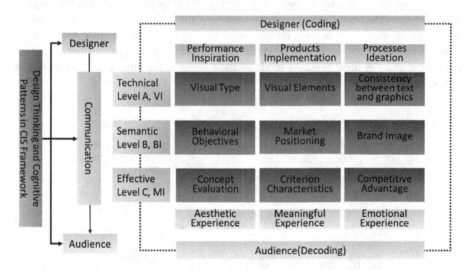

Fig. 3. Evaluation Criteria of the Study. (Illustrated by the Study)

3.2 The Selection of Case Studies

The research focuses on Taiwan's first CIS implementation in the Formosa Plastics Corporation (FPC). During its restructuring and expansion in the 1970s, FPC recognized the crucial importance of enhancing its corporate image, leading to the introduction of a new corporate identity system. This system, including elements such as logo, typography, color, and advertising, was designed by the Ming-Chi Industrial Design Center. It garnered widespread attention at the time and continues to be regarded as a successful case in design history. A corporate identity system encompasses a unified set of brand elements designed by a company to shape its brand image. A successful corporate identity system not only effectively shapes the corporate image but also enhances brand recognition and acceptance. FPC was the first company in Taiwan to introduce a corporate identity system, designed by the Ming-Chi Industrial Design Center under the leadership of Mr. Shou-Xiong, Kuo. Through their professional and exquisite design, they created a unique and successful brand image for FPC, making it one of the pioneers in corporate identity design at the time.

4 Theoretical Framework and Application Examples: Enterprise Identity System of Formosa Plastics Corporation

According to communication theory, if designers can successfully utilize encoding to transmit messages to the audience, and if the audience can successfully decode and understand these messages, then the requirements on three levels are met: accurate transmission on the technical level (Did you see it?), correct understanding on the semantic level (Did you understand it?), and emotional response effectiveness on the efficacy level (Did it move you?). Audiences need to go through three steps to understand the significance of the enterprise identity system: capturing the audience's attention (acknowledgment), generating correct cognition (understanding), and encouraging audiences to generate profound emotional responses (reflection). These three steps together constitute the design and cognitive thinking mode of the enterprise identity system, as shown in Fig. 4.

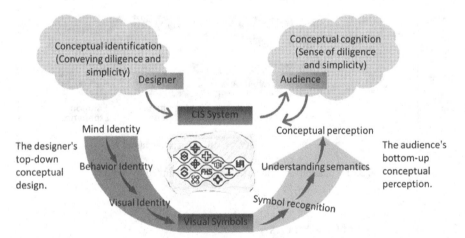

Fig. 4. "Design Creativity and Audience Perception Model of Corporate Identity System" (Illustrated in this Study)

Based on the aforementioned research framework, our research team engaged in private discussions with Shou-Xiong, Guo, who was leading the design at the time, to understand his design thinking. Utilizing the structure depicted in Fig. 4, we elucidate how designers, through conceptual identification, behavioral identification, and visual identification, developed an outstanding CIS. The design thinking and process will be explained from the following three aspects.

4.1 Conceptual Identification

In addition to unclear conceptual understanding, many domestic companies in our country have been hesitant to establish CI systems due to the significant financial investment required. Moreover, the larger the company and the longer the delay, the harder it becomes to make changes, and the greater the expense involved. Shou-Xiong, Guo believes, "In fact, from the inception of a company, there should be a long-term vision and the concept of CIS. However, unifying the logo is just the first step of CIS. To successfully implement CIS, the most important condition is to be 'consistent inside and out.' It's not just about changing the appearance of the trademark; it's about starting from internal reforms so that all employees can identify with the company's management philosophy and characteristics. Then, we can further promote the company's image to the general public."

4.2 Behavioral Identification

Through the business aspects of Formosa Plastics, we can understand the various behaviors of its business operations. Through design inspiration and ideas, we have a specific design for Formosa Plastics' corporate identity system. The design intent of Formosa Plastics' corporate identity system can be briefly described as follows [34]:

1. Each company is represented by the most appropriate Chinese characters of the company. Chinese characters are my country's inherent traditional culture. They not only have excellent national character, but are also unmatched by other characters in terms of pictography, structure and symmetry. For example, Taiwan Chemical Fiber - the upper half of the character "糸" also resembles the character "台"; the hexagon is the basic code for the chemical structural formula, and the overlapping of two hexagons means that this is a company with chemical properties.
2. Use the chain pattern as the common trademark of the entire enterprise. It can be used alone or in combination, and it can continue to be developed in the future. Complete and developmental. That is to say, it follows the design concept of unifying and integrating components. The advantage of this design structure is that the units in the graphics can be increased or decreased. Finally, we chose a wavy shape as the outer frame, with individual trademarks of each company inside, as the overall LOGO design. The separate logos of each company are formed between waves, and together they become the corporate logo. If the corporate body continues to increase, it can be expanded without limit (see Fig. 5).

Fig. 5. Formosa Plastics Group Corporate Branding (Image Source: Formosa Plastics Corporation Official Website)

4.3 Visual Identification

The design of the corporate identity system for Formosa Plastics Group originated in 1966 when Shou-Xiong, Guo recognized that there were numerous related enterprises under the Formosa Plastics Group, each with its own name and logo, seemingly unrelated to each other. This lack of coherence made it difficult for outsiders to identify these enterprises as part of the Formosa Plastics Group, and it also hindered the sense of unity and cohesion among the employees. Consequently, Shou-Xiong, Guo proposed to Mr. Yung-Ching, Wang the idea of designing a unified corporate logo for the Formosa Plastics Group, which was adopted. Subsequently, Shou-Xiong, Guo established a design center at Ming Chi Institute of Technology to begin the design of the Formosa Plastics Group corporate identity system.

The central idea of the design was to unify and integrate the components as the foundation of the design concept, treating it as a structure of conjoined twins. Initially, the design center selected a combination of circles from the many components available as the basic structure of the conjoined twins. Its characteristic is that it is a single unit, but it can be expanded infinitely or selected without losing its relevance.

In summary, the distinctive features of the Formosa Plastics corporate identity system can be summarized as follows, along with an analysis of the design characteristics and meanings of the images:

1. Integration of Individuality and Unity

The most significant feature of the Formosa Plastics corporate identity system, which sets it apart from other corporate identity systems, lies in the combination of individual representations of each company and the unity of the group enterprises. When separated, each component serves as the individual emblem of a specific company within the group. However, when these individual emblems are combined, they form the collective emblem of the Formosa Plastics Group. The overall image within the wave framework allows for flexible adjustments based on the needs of the enterprises. During periods of economic prosperity, when expansion of the group membership is necessary, new member emblems can be added within the wave structure. Conversely, during economic downturns or when changes in membership are required, adjustments can be made or emblems of specific companies can be reduced without necessitating a redesign of the group emblem. This flexibility reflects the company's adaptability to changing societal circumstances and demonstrates its agile and responsive philosophy and values.

2. Minimalist Design Style

The logo design of the Formosa Plastics Group is characterized by simplicity, clear imagery, and easy recognition. The wave-like outline adds a sense of depth, and the combination of individual emblems enhances the visual impact of the overall logo. The dynamic nature expressed by the wave-like outline signifies the company's adaptability to societal demands, showcasing its core principles and values.

Flexible Use of Colors: The Formosa Plastics Group employs colors with precision and flexibility. The overall color scheme is unified, yet different color tones such as red, purple, and blue are utilized according to the interface presented. These color variations represent the company's professionalism and contribute to the uniqueness of its brand image.

5 Conclusions and Recommendations

5.1 Conclusions

The research findings suggest that corporate identity systems play a significant role in establishing brand image, forming competitive advantages in the market, enhancing customer experiences, strengthening social responsibility, and consolidating corporate culture. Taiwan's Formosa Plastics Corporation introduced Taiwan's first corporate identity system in the 1970s during its restructuring and expansion phase, recognizing the importance of enhancing company image. Through innovative design approaches, this study explores how corporate identity systems shape corporate image and elevate brand value. Analyzing the creative design and application of Formosa Plastics Corporation's identity system, the study concludes that the creative ingenuity of corporate identity systems plays a crucial role in various aspects, including brand image, market advantages, customer experiences, social responsibility, and corporate culture.

5.2 Recommendations

Over the years, Formosa Plastics Corporation's identity system has deeply embedded itself in society and gained widespread trust. However, looking ahead, as times evolve, Formosa Plastics Corporation may consider potential directions and strategies for improving or adjusting its design or identity system. The following suggestions are proposed:

1. Simplification of the corporate identity system

With the advancement of technology and widespread access to information via smartphones, tablets, computers, and other electronic devices, capturing the audience's attention amidst the overwhelming amount of information becomes increasingly challenging. In response to this information explosion, there is a trend towards simplifying corporate identity systems. For instance, conglomerates like Fubon Financial Holding Co., Ltd. and Hon Hai Precision Industry Co., Ltd., present a simple logo despite having numerous subsidiaries. While Formosa Plastics Corporation's wave-inspired logo is distinctive, amidst this trend towards simplification, it may appear visually complex. Therefore, reconsideration of simplification may be warranted based on the current landscape.

2. Strengthening corporate visual identity systems (CVIS)

In the era of information explosion, there is a trend towards enhancing the visual elements of corporate identity systems to stand out amidst the sea of information. This includes selecting appropriate fonts, using vibrant colors, and employing 3D effects to attract attention and make the brand more valuable and competitive.

3. Similar cases can further validate the findings and recommendations of this study, providing insights for future research. Melewar et al. (2017) argue that implementing high-standard CVIS strategies helps multinational corporations effectively enhance global marketing amidst the competitive environment. Therefore, if Formosa Plastics Corporation plans to adjust its corporate identity system in the future, it may consider strengthening its corporate visual identity system, aligning with evolving trends and consumer preferences.

4. Furthermore, an essential element of corporate identity systems includes the brand story, which serves as the narrative context of the corporate identity system, conveying the company's history, values, mission, and vision to consumers, fostering emotional connections, and building brand loyalty and perceived brand value. Therefore, in addition to emphasizing visual elements such as logos, standard fonts, and colors, corporations should focus on crafting compelling brand stories to resonate with consumers, establish unique brand personalities, and gain a competitive edge in the market.

5.3 Future Research Directions

Due to time constraints, this study only utilized informal discussions to understand the design thinking behind the CIS of Formosa Plastics Corporation (FPC). In-depth interviews and analysis with the CIS design team of FPC will be conducted in future research. Another direction for future research is to integrate the perspective and theory of Corporate Identity Management (CIM) [4, 5, 11, 16, 29, 30] and contemplate how to highlight brand characteristics through the design and communication of "corporate image" in the era of globalization, thereby enhancing the role of CIS in corporate marketing.

Furthermore, with the increasing maturity of Artificial Intelligence (AI) technology, further application of AI to assist in CIS design becomes feasible. As with other fields facing AI integration, such as how to highlight human creativity in this process and leverage AI's advanced algorithms and abundant big data to provide more inspiration and possibilities for CIS design, it is worth further consideration and exploration.

References

1. Balmer, J.M.: Identity based views of the corporation. Eur. J. Market. **42**(9/10), 879–906. https://doi.org/10.1108/03090560810891055 (2008)
2. Balmer, J.M.T., Wilson, A.: Corporate identity: there is more to it than meets the eye. Int. Stud. Manag. Organ. **28**(3), 12–31 (1998)
3. Barthes, R.: Elements of Semiology. Jonathan Cape, London, UK (1967)
4. Bick, G., Jacobson, M.C., Abratt, R.: The corporate identity management process revisited. J. Market. Manag. **19**(7–8), 835–855 (2003). https://doi.org/10.1080/0267257x.2003.9728239
5. Bravo, R., Matute, J., Pina, J.M.: Corporate identity management and employees' responses. J. Strateg. Market. **25**(1), 1–13 (2015). https://doi.org/10.1080/0965254x.2015.1076876
6. Comrey, A.L.: Factor-analytic methods of scale development in personality and clinical psychology. J. Consult. Clin. Psychol. **56**(5), 754–761 (1988). https://doi.org/10.1037/0022-006x.56.5.754
7. Cornelissen, J.: Corporate Communication: A Guide to Theory and Practice, 3rd edn. Sage, London, UK (2011)
8. Downey, S.M.: The relationship between corporate culture and corporate identity. Pub. Relat. Q., 7–12 (1986)
9. Fiske, J.: Introduction to Communication Studies. Routledge, London, UK (2010)
10. Fletcher, R., Melewar, T.: The complexities of communicating to customers in emerging markets. J. Commun. Manag. **6**(1), 9–23 (2001). https://doi.org/10.1108/13632540210806900
11. Foroudi, P., Melewar, T.C.: Corporate brand signature management. Corp. Brand Des., 43–65 (2021). https://doi.org/10.4324/9781003054153-6
12. Foroudi, P., Foroudi, M.M., Ageeva, E.: Corporate brand website design, image, identification, and loyalty. Corp. Brand Des., 168–179 (2021). https://doi.org/10.4324/9781003054153-14
13. Hartigan, M.F.: Organizing for global identity. J. Bus. Ind. Market. **2**(3), 65–73 (1987). https://doi.org/10.1108/eb006037
14. Harwood, J.: The Interface: IBM and the Transformation of Corporate Design, 1945–1976. University of Minnesota Press, Minneapolis, MN (2011)
15. Jakobson, R.: Language in Literature. Harvard University Press, Cambridge, MA (1987)
16. Lee, C.W.: Corporate identity as strategic management communication: a working framework. In: Melewar, T.C., Karaosmanoğlu, E. (eds.) Contemporary Thoughts on Corporate Branding and Corporate Identity Management, pp. 138–149. Palgrave Macmillan UK, London (2008). https://doi.org/10.1057/9780230583221_8
17. Lin, C.L., Chen, J.L., Chen, S.J., Lin, R.: The cognition of turning poetry into painting. US-China Educ. Rev. B **5**(8) (2015). https://doi.org/10.17265/2161-6248/2015.08b.001
18. Lin, R.T.: Transforming Taiwan aboriginal cultural features into modern product design: a case study of a cross-cultural product design model. Int. J. Des. **1**(2), 45–53 (2007)
19. Lin, R., Hsieh, H.-Y., Sun, M.-X., Gao, Y.-J.: From ideality to reality- a case study of Mondrian style. In: Rau, P.P. (ed.) Cross-Cultural Design. LNCS, vol. 9741, pp. 365–376. Springer, Cham (2016). https://doi.org/10.1007/978-3-319-40093-8_37
20. Lin, R., Qian, F., Wu, J., Fang, W.-T., Jin, Y.: A pilot study of communication matrix for evaluating artworks. In: Rau, P.-L.P. (ed.) Cross-Cultural Design. LNCS, vol. 10281, pp. 356–368. Springer, Cham (2017). https://doi.org/10.1007/978-3-319-57931-3_29
21. Melewar, T.: Determinants of the corporate identity construct: a review of the literature. J. Market. Commun. **9**(4), 195–220 (2003). https://doi.org/10.1080/1352726032000119161
22. Melewar, T.C., Jenkins, E.: Defining the corporate identity construct. Corp. Reputation Rev. **5**(1), 76–90 (2002). https://doi.org/10.1057/palgrave.crr.1540166

23. Melewar, T., Karaosmanoglu, E.: Seven dimensions of corporate identity. Eur. J. Market. **40**(7/8), 846–869 (2006). https://doi.org/10.1108/03090560610670025
24. Melewar, T., Saunders, J.: Global corporate visual identity systems. Int. Market. Rev. **15**(4), 291–308 (1998). https://doi.org/10.1108/02651339810227560
25. Melewar, T., Wooldridge, A.R.: The dynamics of corporate identity: a review of a process model. J. Commun. Manag. **5**(4), 327–340 (2001). https://doi.org/10.1108/136325401108 06866
26. Melewar, T., Foroudi, P., Gupta, S., Kitchen, P.J., Foroudi, M.M.: Integrating identity, strategy and communications for trust, loyalty and commitment. Eur. J. Market. **51**(3), 572–604 (2017). https://doi.org/10.1108/ejm-08-2015-0616
27. Moingeon, B.: From corporate culture to corporate identity. Corp. Reputation Rev. **2**(4), 352–360 (1999). https://doi.org/10.1057/palgrave.crr.1540091
28. Sands, S.: Can you standardize international marketing strategy? J. Acad. Market. Sci. **7**(1–2), 117–134 (1979). https://doi.org/10.1007/bf02721919
29. Schmitt, B.H., Pan, Y.: Managing corporate and brand identities in the Asia-Pacific region. Calif. Manag. Rev. **36**(4), 32–48 (1994). https://doi.org/10.2307/41165765
30. Simoes, C.: Managing corporate identity: an internal perspective. J. Acad. Market. Sci. **33**(2), 153–168 (2005). https://doi.org/10.1177/0092070304268920
31. Stuart, H.: Towards a definitive model of the corporate identity management process. Corp. Commun. Int. J. **4**(4), 200–207 (1999). https://doi.org/10.1108/13563289910299328
32. Tinsley, H.E., Tinsley, D.J.: Uses of factor analysis in counseling psychology research. J. Couns. Psychol. **34**(4), 414–424 (1987). https://doi.org/10.1037/0022-0167.34.4.414
33. Williams, L.S.: The mission statement: a corporate reporting tool with a past, present, and future. J. Bus. Commun. **45**(2), 94–119 (2008). https://doi.org/10.1177/0021943607313989
34. Wang, Y.: Corporate Design Policy of Formosa Plastics Corporation. Mingzhi Design Center, New Taipei City (1967)
35. Wang, M.H., Huang, W.S.: A study on the contribution of Formosa Plastics Corporation founder Wang Yung-ching to the development of design in Taiwan. J. Arts **91**, 85–103 (2012)
36. Li, X.F.: Research on corporate image and its communication issues. J. Nat. Taichung Univ. Sci. Technol. **4**, 323–342 (2003)
37. Lin, D.H., Chang, L.C.: Corporate Identity System. New Image Publishing, Taipei (1993)
38. Lin, P.S.: Advancing together, creating the future—a comparison of CIS development across the Taiwan Strait. Decor **4**, 6–8 (1994)
39. Lin, P.S.: The development and case analysis of CIS in Taiwan. Mon. Aesthetic Educ. **90**, 17–26 (1997)
40. Lin, P.S.: Corporate Identity System, 3rd edn. Art Wind Press, Taipei (2018)
41. Sun, H.M.: How to win hearts? Exploring the impact of psychological distance on consumer cognition in corporate social responsibility initiatives. Unpublished doctoral dissertation, Feng Chia University, Taichung, Taiwan (2018). https://hdl.handle.net/11296/48ce9v
42. Gao, Y.J., Yan, H.Y., Lin, R.T.: A study on the transformation of artwork into interior design patterns: taking the "Poetic and Pictorial" series as an example. J. Arts **101**, 107–134 (2017)
43. Chen, D.Y.: The significance of constructing corporate image in marketing structure with CIS. Hum. J. Kuanghua Univ. **9**, 243–259 (2000)
44. Deng, C.L.: A study on the design strategy of corporate internal design activities. J. Des. **6**(2), 101–111 (2002)

Research on the APP Design of "Time Tea" Tea Drinking Brand Under Service Design

XiaoFang Lin[✉], Feng He, and XinRen Miao

Guangxi Normal University, Guilin 541006, China
1376353135@qq.com

Abstract. To investigate and analyze the drinking and selling methods of traditional Guangdong herbal tea, and to propose the use of service design thinking and methods to improve the adaptability of various types of users to the taste of Guangdong herbal tea and the need for the emotionalization of the non-heritage culture, and to establish a set of systematic and youthful service strategies for Guangdong herbal tea. On the basis of literature survey, user interviews and sample study, we put forward the idea and strategy of service design and constructed the design prototype of "Time Tea" tea brand APP through the establishment of character role cards, storyboards, user itinerary maps, and service blueprints to realize the multi-functions of product management, order management, and after-sale service, and to demonstrate the design orientation and strategy implementation. The design prototype "Time Tea" is constructed to realize product management, order management, after-sales service, and other functions. The user-centered Guangdong herbal tea experiential service design combines the elements of geographic environment and human history, and at the same time analyzes the user behavior, user emotions, pain points and opportunity points, to understand the users more intuitively and objectively. Through the establishment of tangible entities and intangible service concepts, service priority considerations are utilized to provide a more comfortable and interesting service for drinking herbal tea, helping to show all the contents of the brand and product, improving the management efficiency and service quality of Time Tea Herbal Tea brand, and facilitating the rejuvenation of Guangdong herbal tea.

Keywords: Guangdong herbal tea · service design · user experience · APP design

1 Introduction

With the continuous development of society, Guangdong Herbal Tea, as one of the traditional drinks in China, still occupies a vital position in contemporary life. However, when facing the needs of the younger generation, the traditional drinking and selling methods may face certain challenges. In order to better adapt to different user tastes, satisfy the emotional needs of Guangdong herbal tea culture, and enhance brand awareness and popularity among young people, "Time Tea" tea brand applies the thinking and methods of service design to the design of tea brand APP, and carries out a systematic and youthful

© The Author(s), under exclusive license to Springer Nature Switzerland AG 2024
P.-L. P. Rau (Ed.): HCII 2024, LNCS 14699, pp. 293–308, 2024.
https://doi.org/10.1007/978-3-031-60898-8_20

Guangdong herbal tea service strategy design and research. Through in-depth literature survey, user interviews and sample research, a series of innovative thinking strategies with service design concept will be put forward. These strategies will be implemented in the prototype "Time Tea" App by creating role cards, storyboards, user journey maps and service blueprints.

In this paper, the geographical environment and human and historical factors will be deeply integrated, and the user's behavior, emotions, pain points and opportunity will be analyzed to understand user's needs in a more intuitive and objective manner. Through the ingenious combination of tangible entities and intangible service concepts and careful consideration of service focus, the aim is to provide a more comfortable and interesting tea brand APP, improve the management efficiency and service quality of "Time Tea" herbal tea brand, and realize the younger development of Guangdong herbal tea. In this study, the primary features of the design prototype are discussed in detail to prove the practical necessity of Guangdong herbal tea brand service design, and to provide useful insights for the future development of the industry.

2   Research Background

2.1   Research on Guangdong Herbal Tea Cultural Resources

Guangdong herbal tea culture has a long history, which is rooted in the unique climate and long history of the Lingnan area. Influenced by the miasma in the south, the people of Lingnan have long been facing the threat of influenza, fever, pneumonia and other "heat diseases". It was against this background that the people of Lingnan wisely invented a unique drink - "Herbal Tea", which clears away heat and tox-ins, removes heat and dampness, and quenches thirst, and has become an effective weapon for the local people to fight against heat illnesses [1]. Since Ge Hong, a Taoist priest of the Eastern Jin Dynasty, discovered miasma in Lingnan in 306 A.D., he has been devoted to the research of medical technology to treat "fever", which laid the foundation for Lingnan herbal tea culture. In his monograph *"The Handbook of Prescriptions for Emergencies"*, he recorded in detail various preventive remedies and techniques for the treatment of heat poisoning and herbal tea, in order to "cut off warm diseases so that they do not get infected", thus forming the evidence of the deep Lingnan herbal tea culture. During the Ming and Qing Dynasties, *"Yi bian (Medical Bank Stone) "* the book "Moistening Dryness and Nourishing Glory Soup" and "Qingling Drink" and other medicinal tea formulas further proved the gradual maturity of "medicinal tea" made of medicines in Chinese tea drinks. Traditional herbal tea has experienced the development from a mature teahouse to water bowls and then to individual stalls, but today's herbal tea has formed a brand of herbal tea under the good development of commercial economy.

Guangdong herbal tea is rooted in Lingnan culture, which is not only folk culture, but also food culture, medicinal culture, decoction culture and market culture. It not only contains China's unique health-preserving culture, but also is the first batch of national intangible cultural heritage, which shows its unique charm in China folk customs and is favored by consumers with its unique product functions.

Tea Drinking and Food Culture. Compared with other cultures, drinking tea is a major characteristic of Lingnan culture. Different from the thirst-quenching effect of northern big bowl tea, Guangdong herbal tea favors health care and prevention, and drinking tea is called "drinking tea" in Cantonese dialect, and Cantonese people love "drinking tea", and Guangdong herbal tea constitutes the unique "tea culture" in Lingnan. The formation of herbal tea culture is closely related to Lingnan's unique climate and food culture, which is both folk culture and food culture as well.

Medicine and Food Culture and Health Preservation Culture. Medicated diet is the organic unity of traditional medicine and food culture. It is "medicine in food", with the nature of taking medicine, uses the taste of food and the power of medicine to achieve the purpose of treatment and health care, while the herbal tea in Lingnan medicated diet is influenced by Lingnan's special geographical and humanistic environment. Guided by the concept of health care in traditional Chinese medicine and based on Chinese herbal medicine, it is a kind of beverage with the functions of clearing away heat and toxic materials and quenching thirst. In addition, many taboos about drinking herbal tea also reflect its health care methods. First of all, it is necessary to drink herbal tea according to the time. Herbal tea is recommended to be drunk after meals and in the afternoon, so as to avoid gastrointestinal discomfort. Secondly, herbal tea needs to suit the remedy to the case. Because the herbal tea itself has medicinal properties, you need to choose herbal tea according to your physical condition and taste preferences in the selection process. In the process of purchasing herbal tea, the owner will also carry out simple "consultation service" and recommend the herbal tea according to the physical condition of the customer. Third, the herbal tea should be drunk while it is hot. In ancient times, people needed to drink it while it was hot to ensure its medicinal properties. Fourth, herbal tea also needs to be avoided. As a part of food culture, you should pay attention to the dietary taboos when drinking herbal tea, to avoid eating food that are incompatible with the medicinal properties.

Marketplace Culture and Decoction Culture. The marketplace culture and decoction culture of Guangdong herbal tea culture coexist. Guangdong herbal tea market culture is a kind of life-oriented, natural, and unorganized culture, which is produced in the streets with commercial tendency. The decoction culture of Guangdong herbal tea is its traditional dietary processing technology. The complete production process is usually divided into seven steps, which are, in order, cutting and grinding of herbs, weighing, soaking, boiling, adding water, simmering, and storing.

2.2 Overview of Tea Drink Brands

The domestic tea beverage market is showing a trend of diversification, and the rapid development of new tea beverages is showing a prosperous trend. Various types of new beverage offline stores have blossomed everywhere, especially coffee, milk tea drinks and carbonated drinks. At present, on the help of Internet economy, tea brands in the market have gradually become a consumption fashion, and many brands from online celebrity have emerged, such as Modern China Tea Shop and Modern China Tea Shop. As a leading company in the tea industry, it has quickly made a circle on social media platforms with its personalization, youthfulness, and minimalist style. Coupled with brand marketing, IP circle-breaking linkage, multi-platform grass planting and other mechanism, the brand economy will play its greatest role. Nowadays, there is fierce competition in the domestic tea and beverage market, and Guangdong herbal tea needs to compete with the sea of drinks in addition to facing the industry leader. The development of brand economy has become an important way to promote the innovative development of new-style tea drinks and has a crucial role in realizing the economic benefits of the brand.

At present, the domestic new-style tea drinks industry for consumers mainly focuses on the pursuit of trend culture and likes to express the individuality of the crowd, so the new-style tea drinks brand is also in pursuit of personalized features. For Guangdong herbal tea also has a certain reference significance.

2.3 Design Logic Study of Service Design for Tea Drinking Brand APP

The importance of service design in tea brand APP is self-evident. Service design is a combination of theories and methods from multiple disciplines such as design, marketing and management, and is the consideration and design of a specific dynamic service process at a specific time [2]. It is committed to improving the ease of use and efficiency of services, and its goal is to improve user satisfaction and loyalty by providing users with a better experience and create common value for service providers and service recipients. In addition, the interactive logic of service design used in the design of tea APP involves service contact points including physical, digital, and emotional contact points, so as to provide a pleasant, intuitive and efficient user experience. The logic of interactive design mainly considers the following aspects.

Focus on User Experience. In-depth understanding of users' needs, habits and preferences provides a foundation for functional design and optimization. It is necessary to subdivide the target users, such as according to age, gender, consumption habits and other factors, to better understand the needs and preferences of different user groups. At the same time, it is necessary to consider the characteristics of the user group, for example, young people are more inclined to social interaction. An APP can add functions such as sharing and evaluation. To improve the user experience, the interface design should be simple and clear, and the operation process should be smooth and natural. Through service design, the tea brand APP can better meet the needs of users, enhance brand awareness and loyalty, and achieve commercial value.

Visualization of Intangible Services. Visualization of intangible services can arouse customers' memory of services through these tangible objects, extend the service to the post-service stage, and improve customer 'loyalty. Tea drinking APP through interesting interactive ways, such as animation, sound effects and other forms, to enhance the user's sense of participation and experience. At the same time, it provides personalized feedback and tips, so that users can feel the care and attention of the brand and provide special services by linking offline stores. By providing physical goods and services, customers can feel the attention and care during the brand in the process of waiting and consuming, thus generating a positive emotional experience, alleviating customers' waiting anxiety and bad emotions, and enhancing interaction and communication with customers. At the same time, by applying the peak-to-end law in psychology, some well-intentioned gestures are transformed into a service experience that customers can clearly perceive by designing a standardized service performance. In this way, customers can be made to have a positive emotional experience during the service process, thus amplifying the emotional experience of consumers.

Integration of Service Design. Considering the usage requirements in different scenarios, such as ordering, payment, membership activities, etc., it provides a smooth and natural user experience. In addition, a clear and concise information architecture helps users to find the required functions quickly and improve the efficiency. Finally, the APP will collect and analyzes user behavior data to continuously optimize products and services and enhance user satisfaction and loyalty. Although it is obviously impractical to consider every aspect of the service, it is still necessary to consider its wholeness. In the case that personal contact points and service behaviors intersect, changes in the service process need to be constantly evaluated in many aspects to ensure that customers have a high-quality consumer experience and a good emotional experience. Through the service-oriented concept design, the tea beverage brand APP can better meet the needs of users and enhance brand value and market competitiveness. Using service design, the user, and the brand contact to get a better service experience. Guangdong herbal tea brand will carry out systematic, orderly, and global design from the perspective of service design, to seek design breakthroughs for its brand.

3 Analysis of "Time Tea" APP User Requirements

3.1 Existing Tea Drinking Brand APP Market Research

Both tea and coffee have a long history and a large consumer base, but coffee is significantly more mature in terms of globalization, branding, and popularity. Therefore, we can draw on the mature coffee industry and the new tea beverage industry, which is sought after by young consumers, to provide a research path for the Guangdong herbal tea in this paper. Today's tea drink brand APP market according to the different nature of different beverage brands, product positioning, functionality, users, interaction, visual aspects and so on there are many differences in the use of the APP, functionality, users, interaction, visual diversity will also make the APP in the process of the consumer market presents differences (Table 1).

3.2 "Time Tea" User Profile Construction and Demand Analysis

With the post-90s and post-00s becoming the new engine of consumption, the FMCG culture enables brands to be good at capturing social trends, satisfying established re-demand and shaping potential demand, and enables consumers to quickly generate cultural identity and group resonance. The prototype, that is, the portrait of the user, interviewed more than 30 audience groups through the research interview method, sorted out their opinions and classified them into various groups with common interests, as shown in Table 2. And then establish the character traits that can be applied, the character archetype constructed after an exhaustive observation of the potential users, the different groups of customers are categorized into easily recognizable archetypes, and their goals, pain points, needs to find the opportunity point design, and finally draw a user profile, (see Fig. 1).

User stratification is an important means of refined operation. In the increasingly diversified and personalized shopping scene, more and more platforms are carrying out

Table 1. Visual, functional, user orientation, interaction, and extraction analysis of beverage apps

TEA DRINKS APP	Product Positioning	User Positioning	Functionality	Visual Analysis	Interaction Forms
HEYTEA (new style tea drink)	Medium and high-end milk tea, mostly located in the core of shopping districts, high quality, minimalist Target users are young people, mostly students, focusing on the pursuit of quality of life and personalized expression Pick up at the store	Target users are young people, mostly students, focusing on the pursuit of quality life and personalized expression	Pick-up in store Take-out delivery, Group meal service, Cultural and creative neighborhood, Department store, Membership Level	The color is black and white, the UI interface is displayed in the form of cards, the ICON is mainly linear and faceted icons, and the overall style is minimalist, new Chinese style, and Zen	Drink Together" when ordering is the main feature of the store, which is in line with the social attributes of the brand's positioning. When placing an order, there will be a prompt for the production time, which will prompt or alleviate the waiting time of consumers
MIXUE (new style tea drink)	Low-end milk tea, situated in three or four tier cities on the street, low price, price is more affordable	Target users are consumers who seek affordable and cost-effective products, focusing on the mass market	Pick up at the store, Take-out delivery, Welfare shopping, Order selection, Membership Level System	The color is pink and white, supplemented by yellow and blue. The UI interface is displayed in the form of cards, ICONs are face icons, illustrations and C4D design, the overall style is cartoon	When ordering automatically pop-up map of the current store address, to prevent automatic positioning leads to consumers to choose the wrong address. Single order is based on the brand positioning launched in line with the form of

(continued)

Table 1. (*continued*)

TEA DRINKS APP	Product Positioning	User Positioning	Functionality	Visual Analysis	Interaction Forms
Starbucks (coffee category)	The main boutique coffee shop boutique, the location is mostly in the core of the business district or office buildings, high quality, exquisite	The target users are middle and high-end consumers who focus on leisure and enjoyment, white-collar workers with higher consumption levels	Pick up at the store, Take-out delivery, Welfare Purchase, Activity membership card, User Membership System Brand Creative Self-pickup, Delivery, Couponing, Trends, Collecting badges, E-commerce and co-branding	The color is green, the UI interface is displayed in the form of cards, the ICON is linear icons, illustration design, and the homepage has dynamic effects	Banner product images on the home page have dynamic effects, provoking consumers to click on the desire to add the purchase of goods will appear on the vibration effect of the cell phone
Luckin Coffee (coffee category)	Mainly engaged in coffee drinks, "coffee sector of the convenience store", focusing on convenience, site selection for the software park, office buildings, relative to the Starbucks distribution of the core of the business district is less	The target users are consumers who are looking for affordable and high-quality products, mostly students and people starting their careers	Self-pickup, Delivery, Couponing, Trends, Collecting badges, E-commerce and co-branding	The color is blue purple, supplemented by orange red. The UI interface is displayed in the form of cards, ICONs in the form of linear icons, illustrations based on the overall style is clean and simple	After ordering with production video live, no video live after delivery, clear shopping cart with floating tips after ordering

(*continued*)

Table 1. (*continued*)

TEA DRINKS APP	Product Positioning	User Positioning	Functionality	Visual Analysis	Interaction Forms
Hongfutang (Herbal Tea Category)	Mainly engaged in herbal tea drinks, the main ordering and delivery, the location is mostly near the street residential buildings	The target user is the user group of the health care category, the mass family category of consumers	Appointment Registration, Purchase interface, Delivery interface	The color is dominated by the red color, and the style is more old-fashioned	None

Table 2. Summary of user classification and needs

User Type	key feature	user interface	Pain Point Design/Requirements Design	Design Strategies/Opportunity Points
Health and wellness users	Focus on the impact of tea drinking on health, focus on the quality and efficacy of the tea, and obtain knowledge of herbal tea related to health care	Maintaining health and regulating bodily functions Access to relevant health and wellness knowledge Customized health and wellness programs	Provide knowledge of herbal tea and tea drinking suggestions to help users understand the benefits of different herbal teas to the body Add health management functions, such as recording tea drinking habits, physical condition, etc., to provide users with personalized health solutions	Personal health management page. Relevant opinion leaders' health tips are shared and recommended on the community page
Quality of life users	Pursuing the taste and quality of tea, focusing on the experience of tea culture. Enjoy the pleasure of drinking tea	The quest for quality, personalized recommendations, and customized experiences	Provide multiple types of high-quality herbal tea to meet users' needs Provide high-quality tea sets, tea snacks and other peripheral products to enhance the user's tea drinking experience Add a cultural exchange platform for users to share tea culture and exchange tea tasting experience	E-commerce interface related peripheral product design. Regular sharing of new herbal tea products on the homepage. Sharing of tea pictures and videos on the personal homepage to the community page

(*continued*)

Table 2. (*continued*)

User Type	key feature	user interface	Pain Point Design/Requirements Design	Design Strategies/Opportunity Points
Busy working users	Convenient and quick tea service. More focused on the quickness and convenience of tea, with low requirements for tea quality and taste	Convenient and fast tea service	Provide fast and convenient online ordering service to simplify the purchasing process Provide ready-to-drink and portable tea bag products to meet users' tea drinking needs during busy work breaks Provide customized services, such as regular home delivery and tea reminders, to help users develop good tea drinking habits	Pick up at the store, takeaway delivery, interface homepage design Reminders of drinking tea, welfare purchase, activity membership cards and other activities to stimulate consumption, increase user stickiness
Price-sensitive users	More concerned about the price of tea, focusing on value for money	high quality-price ratio	Providing affordable and consistent quality tea products Provide promotions and favorable benefits to attract users to buy Simplifying the purchasing process and improving value for money	Welfare shopping, collocation options, Membership level system banner interface design. Personal load, team meal, family load and other herbal tea product design

Fig. 1. Time Tea user profile.

various user stratification attempts, which are quietly affecting users' behaviors at both the algorithm level and the operation level. After determining the type of hierarchical users, it is necessary to sort out the logic of crowd matching first. The background algorithm will identify and classify users, and the foreground will match different display styles according to the user identification. At the same time, in this process, we need to consider some unusual situations, such as: when the user is not logged in, or when the user data can not be obtained, the default style is displayed.

Conventional activity venue page content is uniform, all people see the same products, brands, coupons, and user layering design ideas, is based on layered user characteristics to derive the design goals, and then develop specific program strategy, from the content of the precise hit. Take the tea brand category APP campaign as an example. According to the AIPL model, the users will be stratified into price-sensitive (cognitive), quality of life type (interest), busy work type (purchase), health and wellness type (loyalty), and the content layer will be matched so as to carry out the design, (see Fig. 2).

Fig. 2. The four user types are intrinsically linked to AIPL and their representation in online shopping

3.3 "Time Tea" Storyboards

A storyboard is a series of sketches or pictures that describe the process of a particular event, including the situation in which a particular service occurs or a virtual scenario in which a new service is envisioned [3]. It is essentially a film script that is used to bring the user service experience into the design process from the service user's perspective, as well as to materialize and simulate the concept of the new service and to envision and plan the behavior of the Time Tea App, introducing the storyboard and placing the target users into the scenario, (see Fig. 3). The storyboard is shown in Fig. 3, in which, according to the development of the story, the user will focus on the pairing waiting time affecting the taste of the herbal tea and the fear of illness caused by the first-time use of the herbal tea, as well as the change of the user's emotional feelings during the use of the app, which will provide a reference for the subsequent design.

Fig. 3. Time Tea Storyboards

4 Construction of "Time Tea" Service System

4.1 "Time Tea" User Travel Chart

By recording and observing service conditions through field surveys, we can understand the common needs and common problems of customers and improve our understanding of service quality. Second, insight into service touch points. Insight into the service process of a specific scenario, through the insight of user needs and user behavior to obtain the whole process of service contact points. Understand the target user's behavioral habits and feedback, as well as the mutual constraints and connections of the entire internal and external links. Through the user demand analysis of "Shun Shi Drinking Tea", the journey map of target users is constructed, and the travel process of target users in the scenario is decomposed into three stages of pre-service, in-service, and post-service according to the timeline, and the main demand line of target users is known through the research of the journey map of target users. Usually, the contact points of consumers' interaction with the service are constructed as a journey, and the overall story is constructed with the most content of consumers' experience, so that we can clearly observe the details of the service interaction and the ensuing emotions, and concretize the overall service process, (see Fig. 4).

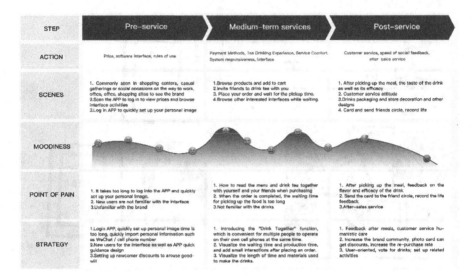

Fig. 4. "Time Tea" User Travel Chart

4.2 Service Blueprint of "Time Tea"

A service blueprint is a method for all aspects of service, and it is recommended to use visual diagrams to show the service system and service process, identifying the roles of users, service providers and other service-related parties, and explaining in detail the process behind the scenes when consumers come into contact with the service. Take the five principles of service innovation thinking as a benchmark to determine user experience needs. Human-centeredness is the core of service design, and the essence of service design is to design for people, so the first task of good service design is to identify human needs and innovate for user needs to enhance user experience. Co-innovation means "co-creation", which refers to considering participants as user resources in the service system, including knowledge and creativity, etc., while global thinking refers to environmental resources in the service system, which represents the scenarios constituted by the service. "Ordered" means that service design is about transforming intangible services into tangible interactions through service touchpoints, creating a unified and coherent user experience journey for users. Based on service design thinking, accurate positioning of consumers after the creation of the brand, reverse-driven supply chain with consumers as the core and promote the transformation of Guangdong herbal tea culture from commodity trading to brand service. It helps to establish clear guidelines and instructions for the service work of "Time Tea" and stipulates all the levels and participants related to providing service, so as to achieve the purpose of checking, realizing and maintaining service, (see Fig. 5).

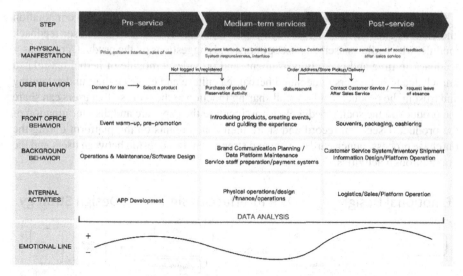

Fig. 5. Service blueprint of "Time Tea"

5   Tea Drinking Brand Service System Application Design–"Time Tea" APP Prototype Design

5.1   Information Architecture of Tea Brand Service Application Design Based on Emotionalization

The famous American cognitive psychologist Donald A. Norman proposed emotional design, for the instinctive layer, behavioral layer, reflection level [4]. The "Time Tea" APP is guided by the theory of emotional design, and according to the design purpose and related research work, it mainly meets the user's functional and experiential needs in three aspects: visual design, interaction design and functional design, as shown in Fig. 6.

Instinctive Layer–Visual Design. Instinct layer is the visual design part of the APP interface design, such as the start page, homepage, color scheme, etc. The visual design part of APP determines the tone of the brand when the user enters the "Time Tea" APP, so it is necessary to meet the needs of consumer according to the current aesthetic style and humanistic elements of the brand. Users can upload their own taste preferences and needs, and purchase products through the system, and the application can provide a basis for functional design and optimization according to the in-depth understanding of users' needs, habits and preferences.

Behavioral Layer - Information Framework. On the other hand, the behavior layer is content-based and incorporates humanistic elements to attract users' attention. Using brand culture or major holiday design to enhance user experience and retain emotional memory points as the design focus. At the same time, a simple and clear interactive process is designed, so that users can easily complete operations such as registration, login and purchase, and appropriate animation effects are added in the process to enhance the user experience.

Reflection layer - interaction design. The reflection layer is based on connotation and ensures customer loyalty through positive guidance. APP designs a user feedback module, which allows users to post opinions and suggestions on the product, collect user feedback in time and make improvement, and provides a module of herbal tea-related knowledge to help users understand herbal tea culture and enhance their understanding and trust in the product. Add a social sharing function to the APP, so that users can share the product on the social media platform, increase the exposure and dis - termination of the product. Users can record and share their touch points on the platform during the purchase process, punch card service and strengthen the adhesion between users and the brand through activities.

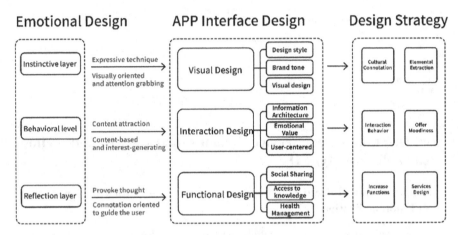

Fig. 6. Emotion Design and App Interface Design Logic Map

5.2   APP Client-Based Service Application Design - "Time Tea" APP Interface Design

The achievement of the service requires the direct participation of the users, so the interactive interface in the service process must be friendly and easy to understand, and the APP icon, brand logo design and interface belong to the visual symbols. In the design process of "Time Tea", we should dig deeply into the herbal tea culture and design the visual image according to the needs of user and the actual situation of the brand. The color tone adopts green and yellow as the main colors, and other auxiliary colors are extracted according to the Lingnan culture, the colors are harmonious and full of sense of hierarchy. The interface design is conducted based on rationality. The color of the social function page of the interface design is consistent with that of the APP as a whole, and the theme color is mainly a combination of cold and warm, which conveys a healthy life and positive feeling to users, and ensures that the tea brand APP has a laid-back and relaxed atmosphere, accessible social characteristics and profound cultural heritage. Minimalist patterns related to herbal tea elements can be used in visual design [5]. Interaction design focuses on emotionality, integrates the brand through service design, promotes brand communication, uses the product to impact the emotional experience of consumers directly or indirectly, and uses appropriate emotions to evoke the deep-seated identity of consumers, and adapts to and changes the psychology of consumers. The overall interface design of "Time Tea" APP is simple and clear, which is easy to arouse the interest of users to achieve the communication effect, (see Fig. 7).

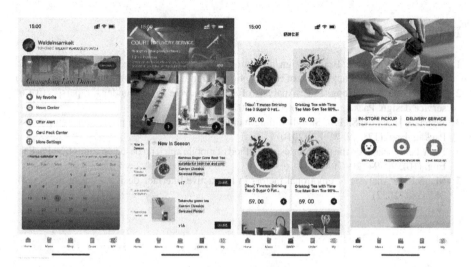

Fig. 7. Time Tea APP Interface Design

6 Conclusion

The current pursuit of health and quality of life has stimulated the rapid development and change of the tea market. In this context, "Shun Shi Drinking Tea" tea brand, as a health tea brand dedicated to providing and spreading the culture of Guangdong herbal tea, needs to improve user experience and satisfy users' needs through the APP design, to stand out in the highly competitive market. Through the study of user profiling, storyboarding and user journey mapping and other methods of reference drawing, user emotions and behaviors, pain points and opportunity points are organically combined, and solutions are proposed to help the service system continue to develop and improve. From the user's point of view, changing the mode of selling herbal tea offline and combining it with online greatly improves the user's purchasing experience and makes it more convenient for the user. From the perspective of commercial value, the online and offline mode creates more economic value, diversifies the single form of selling Guangdong herbal tea, and broadens the sales and consumption scenarios. From the point of view of social value, the appearance of the tea APP not only helps to generate income but also can change the predicament of Guangdong herbal tea dissemination. In terms of social value, the emergence of tea drink APP not only helps to generate income but also changes the predicament of Guangdong herbal tea dissemination, promotes local culture dissemination, and shapes a good social image and sense of social responsibility for the brand.

Acknowledgments. This study was funded by Guangxi Philosophy and Social Science Program (grant number 20BMZ016).

References

1. Yang, M.F., Tan, P.J.S.: Brand design innovation strategy of Guangdong, Hong Kong and Macao old brands under the background of consumption upgrading. Market. Forum (07), 18–24 (2021)
2. Liu Y.F., Li, K.S., Hong, R.T.: Analysis of shared bicycle system under the perspective of service design. Packag. Eng. (10), 11–18 (2017)
3. Wang, X.W.F., Li, S.G.S.: Storyboarding method and application in product design process. Packag. Eng. (12), 69–71+83 (2010)
4. Fu, Y.F.: Research on the graphic design method of mobile app icon based on semiotics. Packag. Eng. (10), 90–94 (2017)
5. Ma, S.F.F.: Analysis of emotional factors in interactive interface design. Packag. Eng. (12), 355–358 (2022)

The Influence of Souvenirs on Establishing the Brand Image of Film Festivals: The Audience's Perception and Preference for Souvenirs

De-Hong Tsai[✉] [iD] and Po-Hsien Lin

Graduate School of Creative Industry Design, National Taiwan University of Arts,
New Taipei City, Taiwan
`cs820827@gmail.com, t0131@ntua.edu.tw`

Abstract. In the diverse and rich contemporary landscape of the film and television culture industry, besides turning on the TV, using mobile phones, or seeing films in theaters, there are different themed film festivals taking the stage around the world every month and year. Each film festival has different communication missions, and the crucial task for curatorial teams is how to convey the information about the film festival to a wider audience range, ensuring a continuous and sustainable viewership. In order to broaden the reach of film festivals, the brand image of the festival becomes a critical consideration for curatorial teams. Thus, the visual identity (VI) extends to the creation of souvenirs, which have also gained attention. The progression from the space of a film festival to the whole participation makes moving experience, and ultimately creates the desire to bring sensory products of related memories -, imbuing the designed items with value. This value gives "souvenirs" a spirit and significance distinct from "merchandise." From a practical and psychological perspective, souvenirs serve as important tangible products linking the film festival image and the audience. This study attempts to analyze, from the perspective of souvenirs, how they become elements attracting potential audiences and explore the relationship between audiences and the film festival image and whether souvenirs, as a mediator between both, possessing influence. The research project will focus on some selected film festivals in Taiwan, collecting souvenir items and designing relevant market research questionnaires. By statistically analyzing the survey results, the study aims to understand audience perceptions and preferences regarding souvenirs. Furthermore, it seeks to identify the potential impact of souvenirs on previously unknown audience segments, influencing their participation in film festival activities. The intention of this research is to uncover potential audience segments, emphasize the importance of souvenirs in film festivals, and provide curatorial teams of various film festivals with a reference basis for cultural product development.

Keywords: Film festival · Souvenir · Brand image · Potential audience groups

P.-L. P. Rau (Ed.): HCII 2024, LNCS 14699, pp. 309–326, 2024.
https://doi.org/10.1007/978-3-031-60898-8_21

1 Introduction

In the thriving global landscape of the film and television industry, in addition to television programs, short films, live broadcasts, series, and theatrical films, there is a unique path known as film festival. Film festivals typically involve the selective screening of well-produced works that align with the spirit of the festivals from numerous submissions within a specified timeframe. These films are often not profit driven but by meaning (or semantics). While some films may successfully encompass both aspects, they are not the typical fare at film festivals. The origin of film festivals can be traced back to Venice International Film Festival in 1932. Obscurely, the earliest edition of the Venice International Film Festival was not "competitive festivals," and their awards were categorized as "Most Amusing Film" and "Most Touching Film." Initially organized to promote tourism, the festival lacked a formal jury and awards, so Best Director and Best Film were determined by audience votes. Looking at this historical context, it seems that film festivals were initially positioned in the "tourism industry" rather than the film and television industry. Regardless of the industry's evolution, film festivals have ultimately developed their own unique identity.

The oldest and most representative film festival in Taiwan history is the Taipei Golden Horse Film Festival, which was held in 1980.At that time, there were no other film festivals, and the Golden Horse Film Festival was the sole channel for film enthusiasts to experience "art films" [10]. Although the Golden Horse Awards were established in 1962, it was purely awards for films and not a complete film festival. It took nearly half century (48 years) from the Venice International Film Festival in 1932 to the Taipei Golden Horse Film Festival in 1980 for such an event to occur in Taiwan [8]. This highlights the difficulty of replicating the industry's success and cannot be achieved overnight.

When film festival first emerged in Taiwan, digital development was not yet widespread. Within the available historical records, it is known that selling tickets manually was in early 1980. Until 1987, with the inauguration of the National Kai-shek Cultural Center's computerized ticketing system (later known as the National Theater & Concert Hall Ticketing System), the era of "computerized ticketing" began. In 1990, Qiu Fu Sheng's interest in ticketing services was spurred after witnessing the manual ticket sales queue at the Taipei Golden Horse Film Festival, and the "Era Ticket" was born [2].

However, Wu mentioned in the book "Film ○ Film Festival" that in 1995, when he was a student in the Department of Film at National Taiwan University of Arts, he had to queue overnight to buy the tickets for the Taipei Golden Horse Film Festival. That was his earliest experience in attending a film festival [10]. In the era of computerized ticketing, due to the continued existence of semi-manual ticket purchasing behavior, the Taipei Golden Horse Film Festival also went through a period of overwhelming crowds. As awareness of film festivals grew among the Chinese-speaking population and numerous film festivals sprouted up in Taiwan, coupled with the dual influence of the Taiwanese New Wave in cinema, art films became dependent on participation in international film festivals for supporting film workers economically. Local audiences' evaluations of these films increasingly trended towards a "rarefied appeal," and the promotion and marketing of film festivals faced frequent setbacks in the local scene.

Nevertheless, the rapid development of technology, from the advent of "online ticketing systems" and "ticket sales at convenience stores" to the rise of "mobile devices and cloud-based ticketing," has taken just more than a decade. In this relatively short period of ticketing development, film festivals have become a certain industry in Taiwan. From the major government-sponsored events like the Taipei Golden Horse Film Festival, Taipei Film Festival, and Kaohsiung Film Festival, to smaller privately-initiated ones such as Women Make Waves International Film Festival and South Taiwan Film Festival, these film festivals now have established a certain scale. However, as the convenience of information access in the era of cloud computing makes it challenging for audiences to physically attend film festivals, curatorial teams must explore alternative marketing channels. Consequently, souvenirs have emerged as a new path for tapping into potential audience segments.

Swanson defines souvenirs as items that serve as mementos of special events or memories [9]. Although film festival souvenirs are a purposeful strategy, a noteworthy example surfaced during the 54th Golden Horse Awards in 2017 when a souvenir, a "rice cooker," was introduced exclusively for the participating filmmakers. This unconventional choice sparked resonant discussions among cinephiles and netizens, establishing the rice cooker as an iconic symbol of film festival memorabilia. In subsequent film festivals, it was gradually opened up the opportunity for audiences to exchange their tickets for the rice cooker upon reaching a specified quota, creating a stable flow of attendees and commercial opportunities for the festival.

Following the debut of the Golden Horse rice cooker, many figures in the film industry hinted that being nominated was simply a means to acquire the coveted item. This seemingly casual remark concealed a driving force pushing forward Taiwan's soft power in the film and television industry. The influence of a souvenir and its ability to indirectly enhance the iconic image of a film festival are aspects worthy of reflection for various cultural events.

In summary, the purpose of this study is to examine several film festivals held in Taiwan in recent years, considering factors such as their scale, target audience, geographic location, and key vision elements. The objective is to assess whether the film festival image is attractive to audiences and to analyze, through questionnaire surveys, whether souvenirs can contribute to the festival's sustainability and uncover potential audience segments.

2 Literature Review

2.1 Film Festival Image

From the perspective of the film festival's industry nature, it possesses characteristics of the cultural and creative industries, offering an experiential service tailored to visual and auditory senses. The cultural and creative industries are based on existing industries, and built on the application of cultural life, aesthetics, and creativity. Through creative life design, they provide high-quality life experiences, developing integrated service innovation designs as a business model [7]. Therefore, the film festival as "an industry that creatively integrates with the lifestyle industry provides with deep experiences and high aesthetic sensibilities." The film festival's curatorial team (hereinafter referred to as the curatorial team) must take the social responsibility of cultivating public aesthetics. In addition to having aesthetic taste, the festival's image representation must not decline the quality of the nominated films. Therefore, the festival's image must achieve an aesthetic dimension that builds on the past and paves the way for the future.

Based on recent observations of the festival's image, it is noted that the curatorial team prefers to have key visual design and related promotional materials for each edition made by the director who received major awards in the last year or the design studios that have won awards both domestically and internationally. This choice highlights the curatorial team's recognition of creators who have previously been acknowledged for their taste and accomplishments.

Among the three world-renowned film festivals, the Cannes Film Festival adopted a unique approach to build its image between 1952 and 1967 through a program called "Reflets de Cannes." This program utilized the fame of film actors as a promotional tool for the festival's image. The program involved side-shooting the nominated film stars, providing viewers with the opportunity to see these stars attending the receptions on the same day. When the stars' images appeared on screen, the host mentioned their names and quickly described their personality traits, attire, or reasons for being in Cannes. This created a win-win situation for both of the film festival and the stars [6]. The festival's value was elevated, and the stars gained visibility and accumulated fame through this platform. This approach shares similarities to the red carpet events at the Golden Horse Awards, strategically enhancing the exposure of the film festival.

However, the actual image of a film festival encompasses more than just these increasing promotion methods. From the conceptual inspiration for the main visual t the design techniques employed, all aspects contribute to the overall festival image. For example, in the 54th Golden Horse Awards, the key visual and related graphic designs were created by the renowned designer Fang Xu Zhong. Taking inspiration from Hong Kong director Wong Kar-Wai, who won the Best Director at Cannes 20 years prior for "Happy Together [3]," Fang incorporated the concept of a draped fabric into the design of standard fonts and the imagery short film. This draped fabric metaphorically represented Taiwan's early open-air cinemas. The fabric in the night presented a metaphor of the beginning of film culture in Taiwan. This nostalgic yet innovative approach elevated the level of the Taiwan film festival to pay homage to the three major film festivals and received positive feedback from the audience.

In this holistic planning approach, from the initial theme to visual design and subsequent marketing and promotional strategies, each aspect is interconnected. In such comprehensive planning, the development of souvenirs becomes a unique point for exploring potential audience segments. The impact of souvenirs extends beyond "audience" to include a broader category of "user."

2.2 From the Image of Film Festivals to the Cultural Value Added of Souvenirs

Similar to other art festivals or cultural events, film festivals serve as cultural symbols for a city or a country. The purpose of these cultural events extends beyond serving the local population; they aim to establish the cultural image of the country or city and even become one of its distinctive features, attracting tourists from elsewhere to come [10]. Therefore, the local culture of the venue where a film festival is held can be integrated into the planning of its image, creating a new cultural landscape for the city. It is evident that the development of souvenirs can also be infused with new cultural value, serving as a link between the film festival and its audience.

Audiences attending world expos are definitely curious about the world beyond the Western. The nature of these souvenir-like publications serves as a means for visitors to bring back what they have seen and learned [5]. From this, we can infer that the precursor of souvenirs refers to printed publications such as exhibition catalogs, similar to guidebooks. In the context of film festivals, there is typically a festival brochure, traditionally seen as merely providing information about the films in competition or for screening, along with, at most, an introductory essay about the festival. However, in recent years, festival brochures have evolved to include articles from the film festival president, senior film critics, and film festival judges, providing insights into global societal issues based on the trends seen in the submitted films for that year. This has added informational value to the festival brochure.

Furthermore, festival brochures also feature a catalog of souvenirs and related events. The appearance of these brochures often apply with higher-quality paper and advanced finishing techniques (such as embossing, spot gloss, and foil stamping) to enhance their collectible value, effectively becoming an integral part of the film festival's souvenir.

Since the key visual design of a film festival can draw inspiration from history, it can naturally combine early products and local cultural customs into the conceptual development of souvenirs. This cultural value not only invokes memories for the older and middle generations but also allows the younger generation to experience historical culture. It brings audiences of different age groups together and serves as a platform to deepen the roots of local culture, expanding it into international cultural marketing.

2.3 Audience Perception and Preferences for Souvenirs

Firstly, among the audience, we can distinguish between two categories: cinephiles and actors. In this study, cinephiles are defined as individuals with regular attendance habits, extensive years of movie-watching experience, or a background in the field of film and arts. Actors, on the other hand, include those who have never participated in a film festival and are part of the general public outside the film and arts domain. From the perspective of perceived value, cinephiles, due to their extensive viewing experience, possess a high level of experiential perception of film festivals. Therefore, their level of engagement is less likely to be influenced by souvenirs. However, participants are different; they need various sensory connections to serve as incentives.

Scholar Dong pointed out that consumers' motivation for purchasing souvenirs can be categorized into intrinsic needs and external stimuli. Intrinsic needs involve using souvenirs as tangible expressions to record life, participate in activities, or prove travel experiences. External stimuli, on the other hand, reinforce consumer purchasing motivation through factors such as the functionality, visual aesthetics, gift considerations, and collectible value of souvenirs [4]. The uniqueness of a film festival, distinct from general exhibition events, introduces an additional opportunity for "close contact with movie stars or directors" as an external stimulus part. In a study by Chen, et al. titled "Factors influencing baseball fans' intention to purchase team merchandise," it was pointed out that the "team identity" has a direct relationship with fans' willingness to purchase peripheral products. Such recognition contributes positively to the overall perceived value. The survey results indicate that most on-site baseball fans can accept the prices of supported team's peripheral products and believe in their good quality [1]. This level of identification is similarly observed among participants in film festivals.

Moreover, fans believe that purchasing peripheral products can increase opportunities for interaction with other fans. The results of the impact of team identity on perceived value suggest that the higher the fans' identification with the supported team, the more it contributes to the enhancement of their perceived value of peripheral products. However, the attributes of film festivals do differ from those of baseball. Based on the author's experience of attending film festivals, sessions with post-screening discussions tend to have more attendees than simple screening sessions. Providing souvenirs during Q&A sessions makes it easier for the audience to engage in and ask questions. When the souvenirs are a set of a complete visual planning system, participants who receive only one item during the Q&A session are more likely to have a willingness to purchase additional sessions to increase their chances of getting more souvenirs, or to increase their willingness to purchase. Therefore, film festivals aim to broaden their range of audience by leaning towards increasing external stimuli, enhancing the participants' willingness to watch films through functionality, visual aesthetics, and interactive opportunities.

3   Methodology

This study employs a mixed-methods approach, combining qualitative and quantitative research. It conducts a literature review based on the research objectives, establishes a research framework, and proposes research hypotheses. Data collection is carried out through a questionnaire survey, and the analysis is performed using the SPSS statistical software. Finally, recommendations are made based on the results of the analysis (Fig. 1).

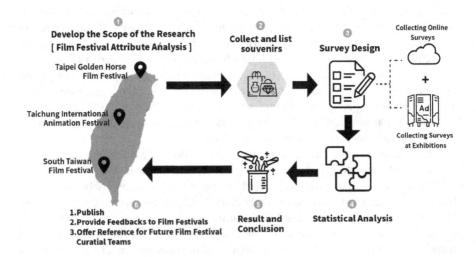

Fig. 1. Research flow chart (drawn in this study)

3.1 Research Scope

This study initially focuses on three film festivals within Taiwan as its scope. The selection of these film festivals is based on geographical locations—north, central, and south Taiwan (Fig. 2)—as well as factors such as type, attributes, and scale. From these three film festivals, the types of memorabilia developed in recent years are listed, and then several memorabilia with common attributes are well-chosen as reference items for questionnaire design (Table 1).

Table 1. Reasons for choosing the film festivals

Film festival name	Location of Taiwan	Age	Film festival attribute
Taipei Golden Horse Film Festival	Taipei (North)	60	International Film Festival
Taichung International Animation Festival	Taichung (Central)	9	International Film Festival (Animation Only)
South Taiwan Film Festival	Tainan (South)	21	Independent Film Festival

Fig. 2. LOGO of film festivals (from the left: the Taipei Golden Horse Film Festival, the Taichung International Animation Festival, and the South Taiwan Film Festival)

This study selected the Taipei Golden Horse Film Festival, the Taichung International Animation Festival, and the South Taiwan Film Festival. The names of these festivals include the regional terms of north (Taipei), central (Taichung), and south, with the South Taiwan Film Festival being the only one named from the perspective of the entire southern region rather than a specific location. Taipei Golden Horse Film Festival was chosen due to its long history and comprehensive development, making it the most prestigious film festival in Taiwan and regarded as the pinnacle of film awards in the Chinese-speaking world. It holds the reputation of the "Oscars of Chinese-Language Cinema" and has significant influence and an international perspective. The choice of the Taichung International Animation Festival is based on its geographical location in the center of Taiwan and its commitment to promoting an international animation festival as a means of cultural development for the city. It is one of the few animation-focused film festivals in Taiwan. Despite its relatively young history, it has become one of the fastest-growing film festivals in recent years in terms of submission numbers and scale. By analyzing the different genre, it can contribute insights of the attractiveness of its souvenirs. The

South Taiwan Film Festival, chosen for its southern location, represents independence and a transition from student-led to private organization. Despite limitations in image and souvenirs planning due to its independent nature, it has thrived for over two decades, overcoming urban-rural disparities and resource constraints. With the titles of "Golden Horse Outpost" and "Wind Vane," it has become a noteworthy reference.

3.2 Research Tools

This study employs an online survey method by using a questionnaire to ensure a smooth and efficient response process. The questionnaire consists mainly of single-choice questions or 5-point scales, with two multiple-choice questions that respondents can fill in their own answers, providing respondents with more intuitive choices, aligning with the research goal of understanding the audience's perceptions and preferences for souvenirs.

The questionnaire comprises two parts. The first part is "Respondent Background and Perception of Souvenirs," aiming to quickly understand the age distribution, educational background, financial capability, relevance to the field, film festival experience, memorabilia awareness, and shopping habits of the respondents (Table 2).

The second part is "Factors Influencing well-chosen from Various Categories of Souvenirs." In this section, the study will collect information on souvenirs categories from the selected film festivals and choose the most distinctive or commonly mass-produced souvenirs as survey items. Each item was accompanied by an illustrative image, and the survey will be conducted using a 5-point scale. Evaluation criteria for each item will include satisfaction, preference, acceptance, significance and intensity, with 1 being the lowest and 5 being the highest.

Table 2. Survey Design

Question Type	First Part: Respondents' Background and Perception of Souvenirs
Single Select	Age: under 20 years old / 21–30 years old / 31–40 years old/ 41–50 years old/ 51–60 years old/ over 61 years old
Single Select	Education Level (including currently studying): High school/vocational school and below / University / Graduate school and above
Single Select	Monthly income: below NT$20,000 / NT$20,000–29,999 / NT$30,000–39,999/ NT$40,000–59,999/ NT$60,000–89,999/ NT$90,000–99,999/ over NT$100,000
Single Select	Are you graduated from the department related to film and arts major? (including film and television, acting, culture, design, animation, art administration): Yes / No
Single Select	Have you been to any film festival? Yes / No
Single Select	Would you visit a film festival or activity because of souvenirs? Yes / No
Single Select	Would the key vision of film festivals affect your intention to purchase souvenirs? Yes / No

(continued)

Table 2. (*continued*)

Question Type	First Part: Respondents' Background and Perception of Souvenirs
Single Select	Would you wear or use the souvenir obtained from film festival based on its function? Always / Never / Depends on the situation
Likert Scale	Self-evaluation: resistance to a "limited edition" souvenir. 1–5
Likert Scale	Is the reputation of co-branded souvenirs a key consideration for you? 1–5
Multi Select	Please choose the reason(s) why you would buy souvenirs: 1. As a memory of participating in an activity or sightseeing tour 2. Attracted by the practicality/functionality of the souvenirs 3. Collected due to the image of key vision 4. Personal collecting habit 5. Others…(free response)
Multi Select	What kind(s) of occasion would make you purchase/obtain souvenirs? 1. Exhibitions (including film festival, museum, book fair and other places that can be called as an exhibition) 2. Sightseeing/Tourism 3. Festivals 4. Cultural and Creative Markets 5. Others…(free response)
Matrix Table	Preference for the way to obtain souvenirs: (like/not bad/dislike) 1. Purchase 2. Lucky draws 3. Redeem Points
Matrix Table	Preference for following categories of souvenirs: (totally dislike/dislike/normal/like/really like) 1. Daily Consumables 2. Foods 3. Tickets 4. Memorabilia 5. Products

3.3 Research Subjects

The second part of this questionnaire (Table 3) will focus on respondents' perceptions and understanding of souvenirs. A total of 15 items, representing five major categories (three items per category), have been well selected to investigate the audience's preferences. These items will be assessed based on seven attributes, and each attribute will be rated on a 5-point scale.

Table 3. A selection of souvenirs and pictures

Category	Picture of Souvenirs		
Daily consumables	Fragrances	Bath Products	Masking Tapes
Food	Chocolate	Boxed Coffee	Liquor
Tickets	Accommodation Vouchers	Air Tickets	Discount Coupons
Memorabilia	Desk Calendars	Keychains	Postcards
Products	Canvas Bags	T-Shirts	Rice Cookers
Seven attributes: product functionality, improtance of appearance, product significance, brand influence, purchase intention on price, presentation of film festival image, commemorative/collectible value (1-5)			

4   Results and Analyses

Through preliminary data collection and questionnaire design, a total of 135 valid questionnaires were collected after online and physical exhibition promotions. In the first part, statistical data from online questionnaire forms were cross-analyzed and presented, while the second part involved importing the data into SPSS for multidimensional analysis.

4.1   Part One: Respondents' Background and Perception of Souvenirs

The collected 135 valid questionnaires were organized and cross-analyzed to illustrate respondents' basic information and their understanding of souvenirs in three tables and one chart. Table 4 presents a cross-analysis of monthly income and age. Due to limited online reach, options for those under 20 without financial capacity were excluded. Although there is a lack of samples in high-income brackets for the middle and younger age group and low-income brackets for the older age group, this table indicates that respondents' average age is concentrated between 21 and 40, with monthly income centered around NT30,000 to NT59,999 (Table 4).

Table 4. Age group and economic ability distribution of respondents

Monthly income	Under age 20	21–30	31–40	41–50	51–60	Over age 61
Below NT$19,999	8	18	2	0	0	0
NT$20,000–29,999	0	4	5	2	0	0
NT$30,000–39,999	0	20	16	1	2	0
NT$40,000–59,999	0	14	13	3	2	3
NT$60,000–89,999	0	1	7	4	2	0
NT$90,000–99,999	0	2	0	0	0	0
Over NT$100,000	0	1	1	2	2	0

Table 5 cross-analyzes educational background with a background in the arts and film industry (Table 5). A background in arts and film-related disciplines is primarily aimed at exploring whether respondents have had exposure or overlap with film festivals during their past educational experiences. Relevant backgrounds include fields such as film, television, broadcasting, mass communication, graphic communication, multimedia design, animation, arts administration, film criticism, documentary, visual communication design, new media, etc. Those with educational experiences outside these categories are considered as not having a relevant background. Table 5, regarding educational levels, presents a relatively balanced distribution after excluding those with education levels below high school. There is a slight difference of only three individuals between respondents with a university education and those with postgraduate education. Among the respondents, 60 respondents have a background in the arts and film industry, while 75 ones do not, indicating that the survey's target audience is slightly higher than the students with the arts and film industry background. It has reference value in objectively exploring potential customer groups.

Table 5. Education and Educational Background Related to Film and Art Filed

	Film and art background	Not related background	Percentage
High school /vocational school and below	0	2	1.5%
University	30	35	48.1%
Graduate school and above	30	38	50.4%
Percentage	44.4%	55.6%	

Table 6 cosolidates the single-choice questions in similar attributes and presents in the percentages (Table 6). It can be observed that 55% of the respondents have participated in film festivals, but not exactly because of the appeal of souvenirs; rather, it is the influence of the film festival itself. Furthermore, by further analyses, it was found that a staggering 84.4% believe that the success or failure of the main visual design is a crucial factor in determining their willingness to purchase souvenirs.

Table 6. Film festival experience and willingness to buy souvenirs

Questions	Yes (%)	No (%)
Have you been to any film festival?	75 (55.6%)	60 (44.4%)
Would you visit a film festival or activity because of souvenirs?	60 (44.4%)	75 (55.6%)
Would the key vision of film festivals affect your intention to purchase souvenirs?	114 (84.4%)	21 (15.6%)

The preference for various categories of souvenirs is presented in a percentage bar chart, ranging from the left "totally dislike," "dislike," "neutral," "like," to "strongly like" (Fig. 3). From this chart, it can be observed that the preference for product-related and commemorative items is relatively high, daily consumables have a moderate acceptance, while ticket-related and food-related items generally have lower acceptance. The chart indicates that the overall acceptance of commemorative items falls into the moderate range, even when categorized by type, with relatively low proportions for " totally dislike " and " dislike."

Here is a List of Souvenirs in Each Category

- **Daily Consumables:** Fragrance candles, commemorative sticky notes, bath products, bottles of mosquito repellent/alcohol spray, masks, skincare products, masking tapes, notebooks.
- **Food Items:** Candy (milk candy/gummies/chewing gum/cotton candy/chocolate, etc.), boxed instant beverages, delicacies (both Eastern and Western-style cakes and pastries), alcoholic beverages, starch (rice/noodles, etc.), small farmer-produced items.
- **Ticket Items:** Amusement park tickets, hotel accommodation vouchers, merchandise pickup vouchers, travel tickets, special store discount vouchers.
- **Memorabilia:** Exhibition-themed figurines, keychains, badges, posters, postcards, exhibition specials, iron-on embroidered patches, bookmarks/commemorative tickets, calendars/desk calendars, stickers, postage stamps, fans, puzzles.
- **Products:** EasyCard (contactless smart card), canvas bags/tote bags/cosmetic bags/insulated bags/shopping bags, picnic mats, umbrellas, thermos cups, mugs, rice cookers, T-shirts, socks, ID holders/sports towels/coasters.

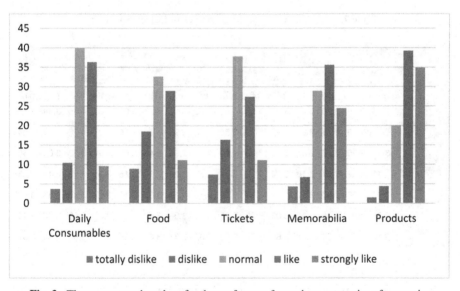

Fig. 3. The percentage bar chart for the preference for various categories of souvenirs

4.2 Part Two: Factors Influencing Audience Preferences for Various Categories of Souvenirs

This section involves listing average or uniquely featured souvenirs available for purchase from the film festivals of this study. Three items were chosen from each category, totaling 15 souvenirs as follows: Fragrance products (p1), bath products (p2), masking tapes (p3), chocolate (p4), boxed coffee (p5), liquor (p6), accommodation vouchers (p7), air tickets (p8), discount vouchers (p9), desk calendars (p10), keychains (p11), postcards (p12), canvas bags (p13), T-Shirts (p14), and rice cookers (p15). Respondents were provided with a 5-point scale to evaluate these items based on seven attributes: Product functionality (f1), importance of appearance (f2), meaningfulness of the product (f3), brand influence (f4), willingness to purchase at market price (f5), exhibition image presentation (f6), and commemorative/collectible value (f7). The scale ranged from 1 (lowest) to 5 (highest), with the criteria for high and low determined by satisfaction, preference, acceptance, attention, and strength/weakness of the respective items. The collected data was then imported into SPSS for multidimensional data analysis, and the results were presented in one table and one chart.

Table 7 illustrates that appearance and functionality are the primary considerations for the audience across various product categories (Table 7). The souvenirs with the highest consideration for functionality include bath products, chocolate, boxed coffee, accommodation vouchers, air tickets, discount vouchers, and rice cookers. On the other hand, items with the highest consideration for appearance are fragrance products, masking tapes, liquor, desk calendars, keychains, postcards, canvas bags, and T-Shirts.

Table 7. Average Scores of the Attributes of Fifteen Souvenirs

	Fragrances p1	Bath Products p2	Masking Tapes p3	Chocolate p4	Boxed Coffee p5	Liquor p6	Accommodation Vouchers p7	Air Tickets p8	Discount Coupons p9	Desk Calendars p10	Keychains p11	Postcards p12	Canvas Bags p13	T-Shirts p14	Rice Cookers p15
f1 Functionality	3.47	3.99	3.10	3.26	3.47	3.38	3.83	3.95	3.57	3.70	3.04	3.08	4.05	3.84	4.33
f2 Appearance	3.61	3.19	3.75	3.25	3.25	3.75	2.54	2.73	2.95	3.98	4.15	3.88	4.06	4.21	3.84
f3 Significance	3.16	2.90	3.17	2.86	2.95	3.39	2.80	3.07	2.96	3.46	3.89	3.64	3.52	3.65	3.46
f4 Brand Influence	3.11	3.39	2.61	3.16	3.22	3.52	3.44	3.32	3.24	2.72	3.15	2.84	3.13	3.44	3.65
f5 Purchase Intent	3.05	3.30	2.87	3.02	3.14	3.13	3.27	3.33	3.13	3.02	3.17	3.13	3.35	3.33	3.48
f6 Film Festival image	3.26	3.04	3.35	2.95	3.03	3.36	2.95	3.16	3.08	3.47	3.91	3.66	3.69	3.70	3.49
f7 Collectible value	3.14	2.61	3.31	2.38	2.69	3.70	2.55	3.05	2.81	3.45	3.96	3.78	3.64	3.64	3.37

After inputting the data from Table 7 into MDS (Multidimensional Scaling) for analysis, the multidimensional cognitive difference structure is presented (Fig. 4). As shown in the table above, p1 to p15 represent various categories of souvenirs, and f1 to f7 represent seven evaluation attributes. As depicted in Fig. 4, the 15 souvenirs are divided into four quadrants. p3, p10, p11, and p12 form one group (Quadrant I), p1, p4, p5, and p9 form another group (Quadrant II), p2, p7, and p8 form a third group (Quadrant III), and p6, p13, p14, and p15 form the fourth group (Quadrant IV). These four quadrants reveal the distribution of souvenirs among various evaluation attributes. Observing these four quadrants, it can be noted that attributes of f2, f3, f6, and f7 tend to represent "Film Connectivity," while attributes of f1, f4, and f5 indicate "Inherent Value of the souvenirs." Therefore, p6, p13, p14, p15 possess both attributes is falling in Quadrant IV Items in Quadrant I lean towards film connectivity but lack prominence in the functional aspect (p3, p10, p11, p12). Items in Quadrant III have functionality exceeding film connectivity (p2, p7, p8), and items in Quadrant II do not strongly align with either attribute (p1, p4, p5, p9).

It can be observed that liquor, canvas bags, T-Shirts, and rice cookers possess both functionality and film festival visualization, while chocolate, boxed coffee, discount vouchers, etc., are less preferred by attendees and have less value on demonstrating the functionality and meaning of souvenirs.

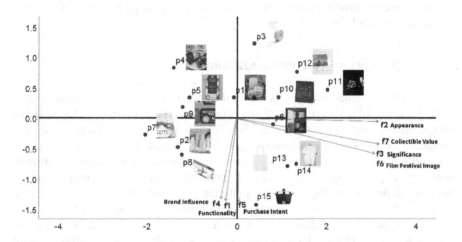

Fig. 4. Four Quadrants analysis of MDS

4.3 Summary

This study aims to analyze the degree of influence on potential audiences through souvenirs. Based on the results of the two parts above, regardless of whether participants have experienced a film festival, a significant 84.4% of respondents indicated that their willingness to purchase souvenirs are influenced by the main visual of the film festival. Although aesthetic preferences tend to be subjective, the popularity of souvenirs can be a reliable indicator of the success of the festival's key vision.

For the group without film festival experience (60 respondents), the observed data is described in textual form. Respondents' education level, monthly income, and occasions for purchasing souvenirs did not have a direct impact. In terms of the art background, 80% of individuals did not attend film festival due to the lack of relevant education, and 50% would not participate in events solely for souvenirs. However, an impressive 80% of respondents believe that the key vision would influence their willingness to purchase souvenirs. Regarding the perception of souvenirs, in the multiple-choice question about purchasing intent, 72.7% of respondents stated they buy souvenirs for practicality, 52%

for the key vision, and 35% for memory and nostalgia. In terms of acquisition methods, both purchasing and through lucky draws were observed a high level of acceptance, with the highest percentage 58.5% preferring the purchase method, while point redemption was less favored. The preference for souvenirs categories ranked from high to low is as follows: product category, memorabilia category, daily consumables category, foods category, and tickets category.

Summarizing the data analysis above, potential audiences without film festival experience are indeed influenced by souvenirs, increasing the likelihood of participating in festivals. Preferences for souvenirs prioritize practicality, followed by the key vision and memory. The preferred method of obtaining souvenirs is through purchase, with the favorite category being products ones. Looking at the preference order for souvenirs, most respondents favor items that can be used "for an extended period," with a lower preference for "single-use" items.

5 Conclusions and Recommendations

To align with the objectives of this study, insights from the literature reveal that to develop a potential audience through souvenirs, it is crucial to broaden the audience from cinephiles to a more general user base. The film festival should be perceived as a foundation for a new culture, incorporating the city's characteristics and traditional cultural customs into the development of souvenirs, and enhancing their rarity and creating memorable experiences. Finally, by utilizing promotional strategies associated with the film festival and introducing external stimuli, the perceived value of souvenirs can be elevated, establishing a sense of identity between the festival and its audience. Thus, this study illustrates the relationship between the film festival image and the audience (Fig. 5), with souvenirs serving as a tangible means to enhance the perceived value of this relationship. When souvenirs become iconic symbols, they can unearth potential customer bases and contribute to the sustainability of the festival.

The study was selected three film festivals in Taiwan that are still in development as the scope, providing detailed reasons for their selection. The objective is to analyze whether souvenirs contribute to the sustainability of these festivals. Specific categories of souvenirs from these festivals were chosen, and a questionnaire was applied to collect relevant data from online communities regarding the festivals and souvenirs. This analysis aims to examine the potential appeal of each souvenir to the audience and provide curatorial teams of these film festivals with reference for future souvenir development.

The research results indicate that out of 135 respondents, 75 have experience participating in film festivals, while 60 have not. Regardless of festival attendance experience, it does not directly impact their perception and preferences for souvenirs. Although the number of individuals influenced by souvenir to attend festivals is only 44.4% of the total (60 people), half of them belong to the group without film festival experience. With an increase in the sample size of respondents, the variability in these results may become more apparent.

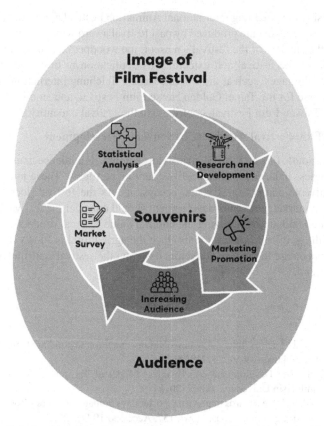

Fig. 5. Relationship of the film festival's image and audience (drawn in this study)

5.1 Study Recommendations

- **Strengthen the Practicality and Aesthetic Importance of Souvenirs**

Based on the multidimensional data analysis results from SPSS, practicality and aesthetic importance are the highest indicators for physical souvenirs, excluding ticket-related items. Souvenirs should focus on the fusion of local culture and visual memory. Taking the Golden Horse rice cooker as an example, it created a souvenir craze due to the strong collaboration between the Taipei Golden Horse Film Festival and Tatung rice cookers. The former represents the daily life of Chinese entertainment, while the latter symbolizes the daily life of Chinese households. Many cookers last for decades, just like movies that can accompany audiences for many years.

- **Optimize and Apply Brand Visual Image**

The visual representation of the film festival's image should embody an aesthetic dimension that carries forward traditions. The brand's visual distinctiveness needs to be more refined, especially in its application to enhance its performance in audio-visual promotion. Using the Taichung International Animation Festival as an example, the promotional videos each year are produced by past festival award winners. The festival logo incorporates the shadow of the festival's mascot, the woodpecker, enhancing the visual distinctiveness of the festival and extending its application to trophy production and VIP gifts. Actual images, such as the woodpecker for Taichung International Animation Festival, the horse for the Taipei Golden Horse Film Festival, and small camera chariot for the South Taiwan Film Festival, contribute to the festival's identity.

- **Consider Film Festival Attributes in Souvenirs Development**

Taking the South Taiwan Film Festival as an example, its audience mainly focuses on social peripheries, independent perspectives, and niche topics. These niche audiences showcase a diverse and complex social ecosystem. As the festival does not cater to the mainstream market, souvenirs development should consider the festival's attributes. Within a limited budget, maximizing the cultural value of local products, such as collaborating with local fruit farmers to introduce the agricultural products by using local ingredients, can create distinctive souvenirs based on the festival's attributes, leading a new cultural trend.

References

1. Chen, Q. F., et al.: Factors influencing baseball fans' intention to purchase team merchandise. J. Sport Leisure Manage. **9**(1), 55–72 (2012)
2. Chiang, C.-S.: The Development and Business Model of Taiwanese Pop Music Concert Ticketing. Shih Hsin University, Taipei (2018)
3. The 54th Golden Horse Awards main visual poster pays homage to "Happy Together". https://www.shoppingdesign.com.tw/post/view/2137. Accessed 19 Dec 2023
4. Dong, S.-J.: The Taste of Souvenirs: An Investigation into Consumer Purchase Decisions for Cultural Event Souvenirs. National Chung Cheng University, Chayi (2012)
5. Farrington, L.: Souvenirs of the past: ephemera from world's fairs and expositions. Expedition **57**(1), 48 (2015)
6. Jennifer, D.C.: La star de Reflets de Cannes: l'image publique du Festival de Cannes. Contemp. Fr. Francophone Stud. **19**(1), 29–37 (2015)
7. Lin, R.-T.: Sensory spaces, moving experiences, qualia products, shaping Taipei into the world's design capital. Taipei Econ. Q. **7**(4), 14–21 (2011)
8. What is the distinctive feature of the longest-running Golden Horse Film Festival? https://www.thenewslens.com/feature/golden-horse-film-festival-2022/176497. Accessed 19 Dec 2023
9. Swanson, K.K.: Souvenir marketing in tourism retailing: Shopper and retailer perception. Dissertation, Texas Tech University, Lubbock (1994)
10. Wu, F.: Film & Film Festival. Bookman Books. (2009)

Research on the Efficiency of Visual Guidance Recognition for Tilt Tray Sorter

Jiangmin Tuo[✉], Chengsheng Tang, Qing Xie, and Yi Ye

The Second Research Institute of CAAC, Civil Aviation Logistics Technology Co., Ltd.,
Chengdu, People's Republic of China
tuojiangmin@caacetc.com

Abstract. The tilt tray sorter is a core product for achieving high-speed automatic sorting of luggage in medium and large airports. The product has a relatively large volume, and it represents a substantial task for personnel during maintenance, repair, and upgrade iterations. The visibility of the equipment's conveyance direction of luggage is crucial for the maintenance and upgrade iteration of the system. Therefore, research on visual recognition markers on tilt tray sorter is necessary. This paper designs a virtual simulation experiment environment in which different-sided graphical markers are created on the outer protective panels on both sides of the tilt tray sorter. Through physical data and subjective evaluation scales, the paper compares the efficiency of different graphical markers in terms of their recognition by participants. The study summarizes the impact of graphical markers on the visual guidance of conveyance. The experimental results indicate that triangular and octagonal graphical markers with fixed sharp angles exhibit better recognition efficiency, providing references and suggestions for the design of equipment orientation markers in the field of large-scale logistics equipment.

Keywords: Baggage handling system · Tilt tray sorter · Visual orientation · Identification efficiency

1 Introduction

On September 25, 2019, during the commissioning ceremony of the Beijing megahub airport, the general secretary Jinping Xi personally attended and provided significant guidance on the civil aviation work. He mandated the construction of an "four-type airport" with a core focus on "safety, green environment, intelligence, and humanistic" aspects, which signaled the future development direction of airports in China [1]. A green airport integrates the "green" ethos throughout the entire lifecycle of the airport, from site selection, planning, design, construction, operation, to decommissioning. The Baggage Handling System (BHS) is a logistics processing system widely utilized in the civil aviation industry. It integrates civil aviation airport technology, modern logistics technology, electromechanical automatic control technology, and information technology. It is one of the core systems in civil aviation and has extensive applications in airports and the civil aviation industry both domestically and internationally [2]. The Baggage

P.-L. P. Rau (Ed.): HCII 2024, LNCS 14699, pp. 327–340, 2024.
https://doi.org/10.1007/978-3-031-60898-8_22

Handling System (BHS) in airports mainly includes baggage check-in and consignment, baggage conveyance and sorting, and arrival baggage processing. It is generally divided into four parts: domestic arrivals, domestic departures, international arrivals, and international departures [3]. The automatic baggage handling systems in airports primarily include equipment such as pusharm baggage sorting systems, crossbelt high-speed automatic sorting systems, ICS (Individual Carrier System) automatic sorting systems, and tray-based high-speed automatic sorting systems [4]. The high-speed automatic sorting system is the most widely applied automatic baggage handling system in large and medium-sized hub airports. It uses tilt tray sorter as the core component, focusing on the sorting of passenger baggage.

The main components of the tray-based high-speed automatic baggage sorting system include tilt tray sorter, conveyors, chutes, carousels, and departure check-in systems. The main working principle of the tilt tray sorter is that the luggage is conveyed to the sorting machine carrier cart through a high-speed injection system. When the carrier cart reaches the corresponding exit position of the luggage, the tray automatically tilts, thereby achieving automatic sorting of the luggage. Each carrier cart is equipped with an electric tilting device and a tray assembly. Under the drive of the electric tilting device, the tray assembly can tilt to any side of the sorter [5]. The equipment integrates mechanical, electrical, and information technologies, featuring a large scale, complex systems, advanced technology, and high reliability and stability. It is one of the largest individual pieces of equipment within the terminal building and is a core product for achieving high-speed automatic sorting of luggage in large and medium-sized airports. The tilt tray sorter was designed with post-maintenance and iterative design in mind from the outset, ensuring the system's efficient operation, which is a core aspect of green airport construction. Currently, there are many tilt tray sorter products both domestically and internationally. However, with the increasing domestic production, there is still a lack of focus on the visual guidance design aspect.

Under the intense market competition for tilt tray sorter products, many enterprises both domestically and internationally have realized the need to enhance market competitiveness through diverse appearance designs, and one of the important roles in this is played by pattern design. Excellent pattern design provides users with a positive visual and psychological experience in the working environment, enhancing the product's quality and image, overcoming product homogenization, and offering a good platform for the market of tilt tray sorter products. Patterns are an important medium for conveying visual information. Beyond expressing emotional needs, they can also possess certain functional attributes. On tilt tray sorter, patterns can prominently highlight the directional functionality of luggage conveyance, distinguishing it from other functional areas of the product. Currently, within the industry, there are no specific standards requirements for the directional identification of sorter. The arrow directional symbols are also set based on individual experience. In actual production, it is frequently encountered that operators are unable to understand the symbol indications in a timely manner to determine the direction of operation, which leads to low maintenance efficiency. Therefore, it is necessary to research the directional identification marks of tilt tray sorter and analyze their recognition efficacy.

2 Research on the Visual Guidance Design of Tilt Tray Sorter Conveyance

Standard ISO 9241–210 defines "people's cognitive impression and response to the use or anticipated use of products, systems, or services" as user experience [6]. With the development of mechanical equipment technology, user experience, which is widely applicable in other industries, is also applicable to tilt tray sorter. Although some mechanical products have begun to focus on user experience, the concept of user experience has not yet been fully formed. Allowing users to understand their own behavior habits, physiological and psychological responses, and various needs is the core of the user experience. User experience is characterized by interactivity and interplay, therefore, designing directive graphic symbols on tilt tray sorter to enhance the user experience brings a high level of sensory experience and usage experience to the practitioners. At present, the combination of user experience and multi fields is a part of serving the product, providing users with experience services [7]. Tray sorter integrates various technologies and design fields, but improving the user experience in appearance design undoubtedly improves the work efficiency of employees. Visual guidance design is widely used in the field of space design. Generally, it guides tourists to the destination through the sign design of signs and road signs [8]. So how to play a guiding role in graphic design? On the basis of taking into account the principle of perceptual vision, the designer reasonably arranges the design elements of graphic design, so as to make users' eyes follow the designer's design ideas, guide users to follow the designer's aesthetic order in aesthetic activities, and transmit information to users in a maximized way [9]. This visual guidance design can also be applied to tray sorters, guiding employees to determine the running direction of the equipment in the fastest time, and then know the baggage conveying direction. In order to ensure that the baggage is intact and transported efficiently, during the operation of the tilt tray sorter, the baggage is carried out in the space with two side guards. When the human body looks at the conveying situation from the outside, such as the visual unguided design, the running direction of the equipment cannot be distinguished. Therefore, the visual guidance design for the appearance of the tilt tray sorter is very important.

The visual guidance design for luggage handling on tilt tray sorter is a category within service design. To enhance the user experience and better serve the workforce, the design of graphic identifiers must possess certain intentionality, not only creativity but also functionality. The graphics should provide information intuitively, be easily recognizable for the direction of operation, and be simple to understand. The communication of graphic information should be concise, in line with the design, thereby ensuring that users receive information accurately [10]. To better design product exterior visual guidance graphic identifiers, the following research will examine the recognition efficiency of different geometric shapes as graphic identifiers.

3 Study on the Efficiency of Visual Cognitive Guidance Graphics for Tilt Tray Sorter

This experiment observed and recorded the changes in the efficiency of visual guidance recognition among participants when different geometric shape indicators are used as directional cues on tilt tray sorter, taking into account the contrast factors arising from variations in angles. The objective is to explore which geometric shape results in a higher level of recognition efficiency.

3.1 Experimental Design

To enhance the efficiency, economy, and realism of the experiment, it was conducted within an enclosed and spacious lighted room. To authenticity simulate the experimental experience, a 360° virtual reality environment was constructed for the study, utilizing PICO 4 VR devices for demonstration. The resolution was set at 4320 × 2160 pixels for both eyes and 2160 × 2160 pixels for a single eye, with a refresh rate of 72 Hz, IPD adjustment ranging from 62-72 mm, and integrated environmental surround sound speakers integrated within the VR devices. Within this virtual environment, a life-sized model of a tilt tray sorter was created, consisting of three segments, each measuring 4500 mm, 1300 mm, and 1350 mm in length, respectively. The distance at which participants observed the machine was set at 5 m, with a field of view of 105° and a viewing height of 170 cm. The environment was simulated to resemble a factory warehouse, with indoor lighting and the addition of mechanical operation sounds typical of tilt tray sorter in operation. The study invited 30 participants with normal vision, hearing, intelligence, judgment, and language abilities. These participants were instructed to stand in the center of the laboratory and wear the VR device for the test.

Within the virtual environment, the simulation depicted operators activating a tilt tray sorter, with the direction of operation randomly set as either clockwise or counter-clockwise horizontally for each experimental group. The operational speed was set at 2 m per second, and all trays were unloaded. The orientation of the icons corresponded to the direction of the sorting machine's operation. The experimental setup is illustrated in Fig. 1. The entire sorting machine stood at a height of 950 mm, with a consistent external color scheme in RAL7035 light gray. Arrow directional indicators were affixed to the protective panel of the tilt tray sorter using lines, triangles, quadrilaterals, hexagons, and octagons. These indicators were crafted as five different images, with the line being a 180° horizontal line, the triangle an equilateral triangle with three angles of 60° each, the quadrilateral having angles of 60°, 90°, 90°, and 120°, the hexagon with angles of 60°, 150°, 120°, 120°, 120°, and 150°, and the octagon with angles of 60°, 150°, 150°, 150°, 120°, 150°, 150°, and 150°, respectively. All graphics have the same height, as shown in Fig. 2.

3.2 Experimental Content

Five groups of experiments were conducted in random order, each group lasted for 30s, and each subject only performed one experiment in each group. Before the experiment,

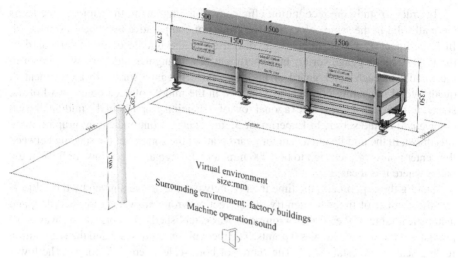

Fig. 1. Experimental design

Experiment 1

Experiment 2 Experiment 3 Experiment 4 Experiment 5

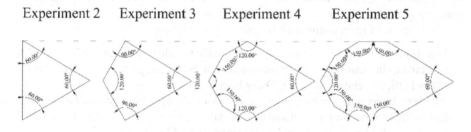

Fig. 2. Graphic identification design

each subject was informed to watch the identifications of the 5 tray sorters under the same virtual environment in 5 sections. By observing the icons on the outer fender shield of the tilt tray sorter, the internal structure of the tilt tray sorter for 5 groups of experiments was identified, and the specific operation direction of the sorter was not informed. At the beginning of the experiment, the subjects were required to quickly inform the experimenters of the identified direction through language. At the beginning of the experiment, the subject shall sit still for 30 s to ensure peace of mind. The virtual environment shall be changed from black screen to the first group of experimental scenes. Before switching to the next group of experiments, the virtual environment shall be changed into black screen for 10 s, and then enter the next group of experiments again. Each subject only conducts one experiment per group, and the experiment timing is s, accurate to 0.01 s.

In order to study the recognition efficiency of the figures to the subjects, the icons were all solid in the same color, and five groups of comparative tests were established. In Experiment 1, a straight line was drawn on in the middle of the outer guard of the three-stage baggage sorter; In Experiment 2, a triangular indicator was drawn in the middle of each outer guard of the three-stage baggage sorter; In Experiment 3, quadrilateral indicating graphics were drawn in the middle of each outer guard of the sorter; Experiment 4: draw a hexagonal row of indication graphics in the middle of each outer guard of the sorter; In Experiment 5, an octagonal line indicating graphic mark was drawn in the middle of each outer guard plate of the sorter. Set the spacing between the center points of each sign to be 1000 mm, and the sign area accounts for 30% of the baffle where it is located.

During the experiment, the time interval between the answers given by the subjects and the number of times to identify the correct or wrong answers were recorded, and a statistical table of the correct/wrong rate was established. The correct rate was + 10 points, and the wrong rate was 0 points. The recognition score scale and the recognition feeling scale were established. The scores of both scales were 1–9 points. The lower the score, the more negative the evaluation result, and the higher the score, the more positive the evaluation result. The subjects were asked to fill in the form immediately after the end of each group of experiments. Identify the subjective rating scale, and ask the subjects to fill it out immediately after each group of experiments. At the end of the experiment, each subject conducted an experimental interview with some ideas, reactions or evaluations generated in the experiment.

The content of the recognition rating scale is as follows:

1. Direction Discrimination Difficulty Scale, which evaluates the difficulty level for participants in identifying the operational direction of tilt tray sorter, with 1 indicating "Very Difficult" and 9 indicating "Very Easy."
2. Auxiliary Recognition Enhancement Scale, which assesses the effectiveness of graphical indicators in aiding participants in recognizing the operational direction, with 1 indicating "No Effect at All" and 9 indicating "Very Obvious Effect."
3. Graphical Simplicity Scale, which rates the perceived simplicity of the graphical indicators by participants, with 1 indicating "Very Complex" and 9 indicating "Very Simple."
4. Graphical Comprehension Scale, which evaluates the ease of understanding of the graphical indicators as perceived by participants, with 1 indicating "Completely Unable to Understand the Direction Indicated by the Icon" and 9 indicating "Very Intuitive Understanding of the Direction Indicated by the Icon."
5. Necessity Scale, which judges the perceived necessity of graphical indicators installed on luggage sorting machines by participants, with 1 indicating "Completely Unnecessary" and 9 indicating "Very Necessary."

Aesthetics Scale, which combines mechanical aspects and graphical indicators to assess the overall aesthetic appeal as perceived by participants, with 1 indicating "Ugly" and 9 indicating "Very Attractive."

The content of the recognition perception scale is as follows:

Confidence Scale, which assesses the confidence level of participants in identifying directions during the experiment, with 1 indicating "No Confidence at All in Direction Identification" and 9 indicating "Very Confident in Direction Identification."

Satisfaction Scale, which evaluates the level of satisfaction of participants with the way various iconographic indicators assist in identifying the machine's direction during the experiment, with 1 indicating "Very Unsatisfied with This Method of Direction Indication" and 9 indicating "Very Satisfied with This Method of Direction Indication."

4 Experimental Analysis

The identification response time for each experimental group was statistically compiled and plotted on a scale, as shown in Fig. 3. Overall, the results indicate that the reaction time difference for the linear experimental group was the longest with the largest variance, while the reaction time differences and variances for the other experimental groups were relatively smaller. Among them, the octagon exhibited the smallest average reaction time difference reaction time difference. This suggests that directional identification using linear markers requires more time during the experiment and has led to greater discrepancies in opinions. In the interview phase, the majority of participants reported that in the linear experimental group, visually there was only a single line with no directional cue, and aurally, no direction could be determined from the sound transmission. Consequently, the method of directional identification was primarily based on guessing. For triangles, quadrilaterals, and octagons, after being labeled on the sorter, a clear directional nature was noticeable. Some participants believed that the 60° equilateral triangle was easily identifiable for horizontal left or right directions, possibly due to cognitive bias. A few participants mentioned that the other two angles of the equilateral triangle might point to the upper left, lower left, upper right, or lower right, which could lead to misunderstandings for those who are not fully aware of the sorting machine's operational direction. Additionally, some participants found that the octagon icon could also be easily identified, while the evaluation of the recognition of quadrilaterals and hexagons was relatively lower compared to triangles and octagons.

Figure 4 illustrates the statistical analysis of scores for correct and incorrect identifications. It was found that the linear experimental group achieved low scores, which, in conjunction with Fig. 3, suggests that the accuracy and efficiency of identifying linear markers are both low. In the quadrilateral experimental group, there were a few instances of incorrect identifications, which may be attributed to individual differences in participants' cognition during the experiment, resulting in slight biases. Overall, the recognition efficiency of triangles, quadrilaterals, hexagons, and octagons was relatively high. To determine if there are any other specific differences, further analysis is required.

As shown in Fig. 5, the radar chart based on the score statistics of the recognition scale is compared with the subjective cognitive differences of the five groups of experiments from six dimensions. The positive feedback of the straight line in the evaluation scales of item 1, 2, 4, 5 and 6 is significantly lower than that of other marks. The other groups are generally in the positive evaluation, which also shows that the directivity of the straight line in the environment combined with the sorter is very weak, and can be used as a reference group for the results of other groups of experiments. Judging from the evaluation results of the difficulty in identifying directions, the score is trilateral > octagonal > quadrilateral > hexagon. Combined with the interview content, the triangles still have a high degree of identification. For octagons, from the visual point of view,

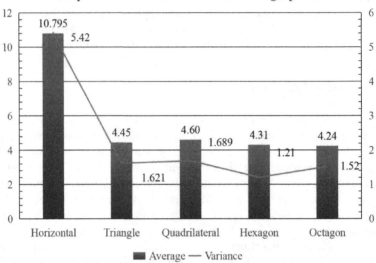

Fig. 3. Response time difference for different graphics

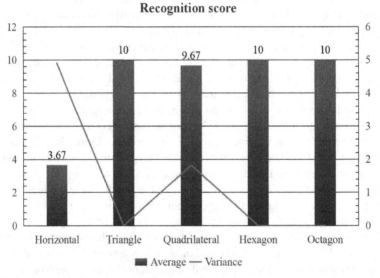

Fig. 4. Recognition score

most subjects believe that the sharp angle shape on one side can clearly distinguish the sharp and mild feelings from the approximate semicircular shape on the other side, so the octagonal group also has a high degree of identification. From the evaluation results of auxiliary lifting degree, the evaluation of quadrangle is slightly lower. Some subjects believe that although quadrangle has a sharp 60° sharp edge, the shape difference between

The radar chart based on the score statistics of the recognition scale

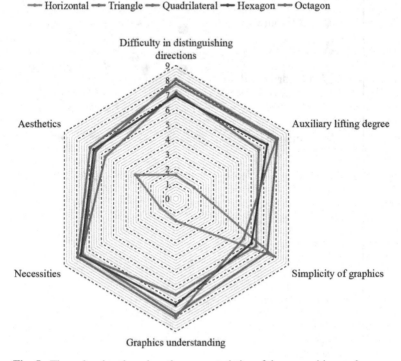

Fig. 5. The radar chart based on the score statistics of the recognition scale

the two sides is small compared with the obtuse edge on the other side. Therefore, in the process of experiment, the time from recognition to thinking to judgment will be increased, and some subjects also have such cognitive results for hexagon. From the perspective of graph simplicity, the score of straight line is the highest, and the score of octagon is the lowest. The number of graph edges may have a certain impact on visual cognitive load. The more the number of edges, the more complex the subjects think the graph is. From the perspective of figure comprehension, both trigonals and octagons are in high evaluation. Combined with Figs. 3 and 4, it is easier for subjects to understand the directivity of trigonals and octagons. From the perspective of necessity, the subjects' cognitive scores are relatively uniform, and they think it is necessary to install directional icons. From the perspective of aesthetics, the overall evaluation of octagons is slightly high, the score difference between triangles and hexagons is small, and the score difference between quadrangles is low. Under the influence of the weak directivity of quadrangles, in the overall effect of combining with sorters, more subjects think it is not beautiful enough, or the effect after combining is not good.

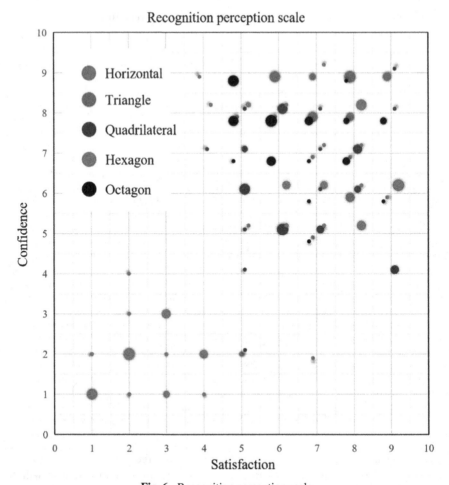

Fig. 6. Recognition perception scale

As shown in Fig. 6, in order to facilitate the complete display of the five groups of data, after processing the data, the scale evaluation results of each group of experiments of all people are displayed in the form of dots on an evaluation scale chart. The larger the dot, the more people with the same evaluation results.

The graph clearly illustrates that the points centered at nodes with horizontal and vertical axes each scoring 5 are dispersed towards the upper right and lower left directions. The confidence and satisfaction levels for the linear group are very low. The confidence and satisfaction levels for the other groups are highly evaluated and exhibit a certain trend, indicating an overall positive experience. To verify whether the evaluation results are influenced by the increase in the number of edges in the graphics, a variance homogeneity test for confidence and satisfaction was conducted first on the data from the four experiments excluding the linear group, using Levene's test. The null hypothesis assumes that the variances of confidence and satisfaction scores are equal across the four experimental groups, while the alternative hypothesis suggests that at least three groups have unequal variances. The results, as presented in Table 1, reveal that the homogeneity of variances for confidence scores is valid, whereas the variances for satisfaction scores are unequal. Consequently, appropriate analysis of variance methods is required for further analysis.

The Shapiro-Wilk test was employed to examine the normality of the confidence scores, with the null hypothesis stating that the confidence scores follow a normal distribution and the alternative hypothesis suggesting non-normal distribution. The results, as presented in Table 2, indicate that the P-value is less than 0.05, and the W-value is close to 1, allowing us to conclude that the confidence scores do indeed follow a normal distribution. Subsequent post-hoc analysis using the Tukey's HSD test revealed significant differences in the confidence scores between the triangular and quadrilateral groups. Although the P-values for the other groups exceeded 0.05, it would be incorrect to assert the absence of differences. Instead, it can be inferred that at least one pair of groups exhibit a significant difference in their mean scores that is not due to random variation but is directly attributable to the manipulation of the grouping variable in the experiment. Therefore, the change in the number of graphical edges is a determinant of confidence scores (Table 3).

A one-way analysis of variance (ANOVA) was conducted on the satisfaction scores using a non-parametric approach. The null hypothesis posited that the variances of satisfaction scores across the four experimental groups were equal, while the alternative hypothesis suggested that at least one group's variance was different from the others. The results, as presented in Table 4, reveal a P-value less than 0.001, leading to the rejection of the null hypothesis. This indicates that there are significant differences in the satisfaction scores among at least one pair of experimental groups. Subsequently, a pairwise comparison was conducted using the Dixon-Sparks-Conover-Fletch-Yates method on the four groups, as shown in Table 5. Statistically significant differences in satisfaction scores were found between the triangular and quadrilateral groups, the triangular and hexagonal groups, the quadrilateral and octagonal groups, and the hexagonal and octagonal groups. These results corroborate that the change in the number of graphical edges is also a determinant of satisfaction scores.

Table 1. Homogeneity of variance (Leven's)

	F	Freedom1	Freedom2	P
Confidence level	1.70	3	116	0.170
Satisfaction level	4.09	3	116	0.008

Table 2. Normality test for confidence score (Shapiro-Wilk)

	W	P
Freedom	0.972	0.013

Table 3. Post test method of confidence score (Tukey)

	Triangle	Quadrilateral	Hexagon	Octagon
Triangle Mean difference	—	1.13 *	0.700	0.233
t	—	3.18	1.96	0.655
Freedom	—	116	116	116
p	—	0.010	0.208	0.914
Quadrilateral Mean difference			−0.433	−0.900
t			−1.22	−2.525
Freedom			116	116
p			0.618	0.061
Hexagon Mean difference			—	−0.467
t			—	−1.309
Freedom			—	116
p			—	0.559
Octagon Mean difference				
t				
Freedom				
p				

Explanatory note. * p <0.05, ** p <0.01, *** p <0.001

Table 4. Single factor analysis of satisfaction score (Kruskal-Wallis)

	χ^2	Freedom	p值	ε^2
Satisfaction level	23.3	3	< 0.001	0.196

Therefore, a further examination of the distribution in Fig. 6 reveals that the triangular evaluations overall cluster in a relatively more positive range of scores. When combined with the analysis of Figs. 3, 4, and 5, this suggests that the triangular shape evokes a strong sense of directionality and mental set, which collectively, along with factors such as shorter response times in graphical recognition, greater simplicity, and easier understandability, contribute to a very positive outcome. The octagonal evaluations, on the other hand, are more inclined towards confidence levels, with participants more readily perceiving a sense of frustration and forming evaluations that are easier and more aesthetically pleasing. This may have led to the observed ratings. Speculatively, as the number of obtuse angles in a shape increases, it approaches a circular form, which may result in a more pronounced sense of frustration on the sides, potentially increasing recognition efficiency and enhancing aesthetics. The overall positive evaluations for

Table 5. Comparison of satisfaction scores (Dixon-Sparks-Conover-Fletch-Yates)

		W	p
Triangle	Quadrilateral	−4.576	0.007
Triangle	Hexagon	−5.022	0.002
Triangle	Octagon	−1.198	0.832
Quadrilateral	Hexagon	−0.809	0.941
Quadrilateral	Octagon	4.529	0.007
Hexagon	Octagon	5.004	0.002

quadrilaterals and hexagons are relatively lower, as indicated by the interviews with participants. This may be attributed to less noticeable frustration, slightly lower difficulty in directional discrimination, lower graphical simplicity, lower aesthetic appeal, or other factors. Future research requires more refined investigation to address these observations.

5 Conclusion

This experiment utilized a virtual simulation environment to select fixed acute-angled polygons as directional indicators and collected physical response data and subjective evaluation scales from participants, which were cross-verified for a comprehensive assessment. The evaluation was conducted from three perspectives: temporal differences, recognition scales, and subjective feelings. The results indicate that polygons with fixed acute angles, such as the triangle and octagon, exhibit better directionality and recognition efficiency. Under unknown conditional constraints, equilateral triangles may evoke a sense of directional ambiguity. Dividing the indicator symbol into two equal parts, it was found that the greater the overall number of sides, the more pronounced the contrast between the fewer-sided and the more-sided ends, thereby enhancing the clarity of directionality. The experimental findings offer insights and suggestions for the field of equipment manufacturing regarding visual recognition efficiency. In the design of directional indicators for large mechanical equipment in the future, a more efficient graphical symbol can be created by considering a combination of factors such as recognition efficiency, recognition, aesthetics, and other factors, which may enhance the recognition efficiency of relevant personnel. However, it is noted that since the scale evaluation primarily stems from subjective scoring, individual factors may influence the evaluation results. Future research can leverage more physiological detection equipment, a larger number of experimental groups, and more refined experimental content to conduct detailed exploration.

References

1. The Civil Aviation Administration: Guidelines for the Construction of Four Types of Airports. Civil Aviation Management (2020)
2. Smith, Z.: Application of RFID technology in automated baggage handling sorting systems in civil aviation airports. Traffic Transp. **38**(6), 248–250 (2023)
3. Tao, L., Tie, C., Zhang, P.: Innovative design concepts of the luggage handling system at Beijing Daxing International Airport. Intelligent Building **09**, 26–27 (2019)
4. Wang, C., Tang, C., Su, F.: Energy-saving analysis of the tray sorting machine in airport luggage handling systems. Logistics Technol. Appl. **28**(2), 142–145 (2023)
5. Huang, R.: Key technology research and prototype development of high-speed automatic luggage sorting equipment for large terminal airports. Unpublished article (2014)
6. ISO 9241–210–2010. Humancentred design for interac-tive systems
7. Zhang, N., Li, X.: Application practice of user experience service model in library: a case study of the digital library experience area in the national library. Libr. Inf. Knowl. **02**, 33–41 (2017)
8. Gao, Z.: Research on icon design of visual guide systems. Master's thesis, Beijing Printing Academy (2023)
9. Ma, Q.: On the visual guidance design in book binding. Popular Art **10**, 80 (2013)
10. Lü, C., Pei, X.: Research on the design of guidance system of Luoyang science and technology library. J. Des. **34**(5), 47–49 (2021)

Research on Interactive Design of Urban Furniture from the Perspective of Smart City

Kan Wang[1,2]([⊠]) and Oleksandra Shmelova-Nesterenko[1]

[1] Kyiv National University of Technologies and Design, Kyiv 01011, Ukraine
wangkan@zwu.edu.cn
[2] Shaanxi University of Science and Technology, Xi'an 710021, People's Republic of China

Abstract. This paper addresses the lack of interaction between urban furniture and users in street spaces and explores the possibility of digital transformation in urban furniture design within the context of smart cities. Historical review, theoretical review, and typological research methods are employed in this study to investigate the development, classification, and digital transformation of urban furniture in the context of smart cities. Theoretical research and practical applications of traditional urban furniture are relatively abundant. However, research on the transformation of urban furniture interaction design within the perspective of smart cities, which serve as a new theoretical foundation for urban development, is relatively limited, and classification remains ambiguous. By summarizing and categorizing the characteristics of urban furniture in the context of smart cities, this study provides a new perspective for the future development of urban furniture in digital transformation, enabling the release of more functional forms and human-machine interaction designs in technologies such as automated driving and intelligent monitoring.

Keywords: Urban Furniture · Smart City · Interaction Design · Street Design · Environmental Design · Furniture Design · Public Space

1 Introduction

Urban street spaces are integral components of the urban public space system, serving as the backbone of urban spatial morphology and essential locales for residents to perceive the city's personality and vitality. Scholars, architects, planners, and artists from various fields engage in practical or theoretical research to explore strategies for sustaining urban spatial vitality and endeavor to identify mechanisms for creating pedestrian-friendly street spaces. Installation art, as a significant means of shaping the artistic quality of urban public spaces, serves as an important avenue for residents to participate in public activities and experience the cultural essence of the city's locality. This paper aims to classify and summarize different types of urban furniture with digital characteristics in street spaces, followed by delineating their interactive features, presentation methods, and design strategies.

P.-L. P. Rau (Ed.): HCII 2024, LNCS 14699, pp. 341–353, 2024.
https://doi.org/10.1007/978-3-031-60898-8_23

2   Background

2.1   Urban Furniture

Urban furniture, as the compound term suggests, comprises elements from both "urban" and "furniture," indicating its functional characteristic of providing services related to people's mobility and interaction in urban public spaces. However, within academic circles, there is still a lack of a unified definition for the concept of urban furniture.

From a conceptual standpoint, urban furniture traces its origins to the notion of public facilities. This material category, encompassing urban furniture or public facilities, was widely utilized in urban public spaces as early as the beginning of the 19th century, although it was not recognized as a distinct concept or spatial element by academia at that time. In 1938, Austrian sculptor and architect Rob Krier proposed a definition for public facilities, indicating them as open facilities in the city, perceived by the public, and serving outdoor activities. These facilities were characterized by geometric forms and aesthetic qualities, including both public and semi-public facilities for internal use [1]. Subsequently, the meanings of public facilities and urban furniture in various countries have generally been synonymous and have evolved with the characteristics of the times. In the 1960s, French designer Jean-Claude Decaux employed the concept of urban furniture (Urbane meuble) to promote his products, marking the first instance of this concept being introduced in the public sphere.

In terms of the scope of research covered by urban furniture, its definition can be interpreted broadly or narrowly. In a broader sense, all material elements observed in urban spaces are referred to as elements [2], with urban furniture being an important category among them. Broadly speaking, some scholars consider urban furniture as a collective term for various elements and facilities in urban public spaces, encompassing visual material entities characterized by product elements in streets and providing different functions and services to the public. This includes three main types: urban sculptures, installations, and street furniture [3], as well as objects such as public green spaces, public squares, and public transportation routes in some studies. In a narrower sense, urban furniture refers to public facilities with product characteristics in public spaces, possessing distinct product functional attributes [4]. Allan B. Jacobs, an American landscape designer and urban planner, proposed in his 1993 book "Great Streets" that "details are not trivial for great streets: various entrances, fountains, benches, gazebos, paving, lighting, signs, and awnings can all be crucial elements, sometimes even decisively affecting the overall street."[5] Narrowly defined urban furniture is closer to the concept of street furniture, encompassing material landscape elements distinct from architecture and landscaping, including public garbage bins, benches, bus shelters, traffic signs, pedestrian direction signs, public bicycle facilities, streetlights, pavement, tree pits, green belts, public sculptures, various lighting fixtures, and even different types of public installation art.

The emergence of the academic concept of urban furniture dates back to the 1960s. It is accompanied by various English terms, including "Urban Furniture," "Landscape Furniture," "Sight Furniture," "City Furniture," and "Public Facilities." In France, it is often referred to as "Mobilier Urbain" in French. In some European countries like Spain, it is called "Urban Elements," directly translated as "Urban Accessories" in Chinese. In the

United States, it is known as "Urban Street Furniture," while in the UK, the narrower definition "Street Furniture" is commonly used. In East Asia, different interpretations exist; Japan often refers to it as "Street Equipment" or "Furniture for Pedestrian Roads."[6] In China, it has been historically termed as "Environmental Facilities" or "Public Facilities," but it is now more commonly referred to as "Urban Furniture." This is because the inception and development of urban public spaces in China differ from those in other Western developed countries, leading to distinctions in urban construction concepts and spatial characteristics [7].

2.2 Smart City

With the development of fields such as Internet Plus, cloud computing, big data, and artificial intelligence, the digital transformation in urban design and the creation of public spaces continues to evolve through interdisciplinary approaches. Smart Cities have emerged as a new concept in the disciplines of design, architecture, and urban planning in recent years, accompanying this transformation and upgrade. The overall framework of Smart Cities is still being continuously explored and extended in engineering practices and academic research. However, due to the lack of unified definitions and understandings within academia and industry, there is still no single definition or systematic research framework for Smart Cities. Generally, it is believed that the concept of Smart Cities gradually evolved from Digital Cities. According to the development and evolution of the concept over time, it can be divided into two stages: the late 20th century to around 2008 was the period of development of Digital Cities in various countries, while from 2008 to the present, it has been the period of application and development of Smart City concepts in various countries [8].

In 2008, IBM first proposed the concept of a "Smart Earth," marking a new research stage for Smart Cities. From an industrial perspective, the American company IBM defines Smart Cities as cities that fully utilize computer technology in their local industrial development, urban services, public utilities, and environment. Through intelligent means, they perceive, integrate, analyze, and respond to the relevant behaviors and needs of local governments in exercising market regulation, public services, economic regulation, and social management. This aims to create more efficient and comfortable working, living, and recreational environments for residents [9].

In the global digital transformation, IBM applies information technology to various elements such as roads, railways, power grids, tunnels, and bridges, helping local governments interconnect important public places in cities such as schools, hospitals, shopping centers, airports, stations, ports, and exhibition centers. This facilitates more convenient and efficient operation of resources, thereby upgrading urban management and operations towards intelligence.

In the United States, Smart Communities advocate for practical technology to change people's lives, aiming to provide residents with more autonomy and convenience in their work and lifestyles, ultimately achieving sustainable development goals. Meanwhile, the European Union aims to establish twenty-five to thirty Smart Cities in Europe according to its strategic energy technology draft, gradually developing urban operating systems centered around Smart Cities. This involves the development of grid systems, new types of buildings, and future transportation vehicles, serving as benchmarks for further promotion.

American scholar Roger Caves believes that Smart Cities, driven by digital transformation, are reinvigorating urban development. This includes providing more public service measures and promoting urban economic development through technological innovations such as remote education and telemedicine. He argues that Smart Cities are not just a single technology but a composite technology under the framework of information technology, integrating and solving various problems in urban development.

The US organization IDC believes that Smart Cities should provide online, high-speed broadband systems in every corner and a complete wireless environment, facilitating communication and connectivity through efficient network devices and managed through a central control center. This ensures that all residents, tourists, etc., can access effective information in their surroundings at any time and place. Remote management is considered a core challenge within the entire information technology framework [10].

In the academic field studying Smart Cities, there are different scholarly viewpoints from those in the practical domain. According to Li Deren, Smart Cities are established on the basis of global urban digital transformation, representing a quantifiable and visualized intelligent urban operation and management model, also referred to as the combination of the Internet of Things and Digital Cities [11].

On the other hand, Wang Jiayao's perspective suggests that the purpose of Smart Cities is to make cities smarter, empowering residents as the main subjects of the city. Smart Cities interconnect sensors placed in urban spaces through networks to form the Internet of Things, enabling comprehensive perception of urban real-world problems. By utilizing cloud computing, the sensed information is processed and analyzed intelligently, achieving seamless integration between physical and digital urban spaces. This facilitates intelligent responses and decision-making support for various urban production and life elements, including the environment, livelihoods, governance, business activities, city services, and public safety [12].

Zhang Yongmin's viewpoint indicates that Smart Cities represent a new development model characterized by the combination of broadband networks, the Internet of Things, telecommunications networks, the internet, and wireless broadband networks. This model integrates intelligent technology, fosters rapid development of smart industries, and promotes efficient and convenient smart services. Smartization represents a new breakthrough following industrialization, electrification, and informatization, marking another revolution in world technological advancement. Constructing Smart Cities using intelligent technology is the trend and characteristic of urban development in today's world [13].

3 Design Transformation of Urban Furniture Under Smart City

3.1 Spatial Characteristics of Traditional Urban Furniture

Traditional urban furniture typically starts from people's emotional needs in street environments, allowing individuals to perceive the narrative expression, humanistic care, and emotional experiences conveyed by street space. This perception maps various behaviors, making narrative-sensing-cognition-action a vital element in urban furniture design.

Therefore, traditional urban furniture exhibits several characteristics in interaction with human behavior in street spaces.

Urban Furniture Serves as a Medium for Disseminating Spatial Information. As an important trait of public media in public spaces, urban furniture is a crucial carrier for conveying spatial messages, with three levels of information delivery. The first level includes basic information related to the inherent functional attributes of urban furniture, such as bus stop signs indicating vehicle routes, schedules, and real-time travel status, meeting basic functional needs. The second level involves expressing and conveying specific historical, cultural, and local characteristics of the entire spatial environment through the artistic design of urban sensory furniture. The third level involves creating a special atmosphere in the space, such as fashion, nostalgia, and leisure, guiding users sensibly and reinforcing cognitive and emotional connections between people and spaces.

Using Urban Furniture as a Carrier to Activate Spatial Cultural Value. A crucial role of urban furniture is to "activate" the cultural value of space. Through the design of furniture shapes and the addition of spatial elements containing cultural information, urban furniture's vividness is increased, helping participants deepen their understanding of the cultural spirit of the furniture. This emphasizes the "activation" of spatial cultural value, enabling resonance between the artistic sense expressed by furniture and participants, allowing participants to perceive and appreciate the conveyed cultural value clearly, fostering a better understanding of local culture, and generating cultural pride among local residents.

Urban Furniture Creates Specific Places to Enhance Interactive Experiences. By utilizing the fun and artistic experiences brought by such interactive experiences, urban furniture attracts more participants, strengthening emotional connections between people and spaces. Ultimately, this enhances people's sense of experience and satisfaction with the space, improving satisfaction with space experience while providing basic functional usage.

3.2 Characteristics of Urban Furniture Upgrading and Transformation Under Smart City

Traditional urban furniture has been studied systematically around the triad of "people-machine-environment". With the advancement of technology and the evolution of urban design concepts, coupled with the integration of the smart city concept into street design, the design elements of urban furniture are gradually shifting towards a digitized approach characterized by the triad of "people-technology-environment". In this process of smart transformation, urban furniture should consider its connection with street public spaces and digital interactions. For instance, in the collaborative development of urban street public spaces, attention should be paid to systematically considering the layout and characteristics of urban furniture when constructing urban public spaces. The narrative and design of space should be harmonized to integrate the two seamlessly. People, as the main actors in public spaces, should be the focus when creating urban furniture to enhance collaboration with public spaces. Moreover, in the application and development combined with digital design, the development of urban furniture should adapt to the trends of the times. New technologies such as technological innovation, artificial intelligence, big data, and the Internet of Things should be effectively integrated. For example, introducing smart guidance in directional systems to provide more convenient guidance services, integrating intelligent features into resting seats to monitor users' physical changes in real-time, thus providing better services. The integration of urban furniture with technology can lead technological advancement and elevate the manufacturing level of the entire public furniture industry.

With the deepening of the digital transformation under the smart city paradigm, pedestrian travel modes, street space forms, etc., will change with the development of technologies such as autonomous driving and public transportation algorithms. These significant changes in public spaces pose both opportunities and challenges for the future design of urban furniture.As smart cities develop further into urban neighborhoods, the number and scale of TOD (Transit-oriented Development) districts are rapidly increasing, and new fields such as vehicle networks and autonomous driving technology are continually being explored. It can be foreseen that the travel frequency of traditional private motor vehicles and non-motor vehicles may decrease significantly. The development of unmanned rail transit systems, bus systems, and tram systems is being continuously improved, while new bicycle lanes and pedestrian paths are gradually receiving attention in urban design, incorporating digital and interactive designs into spatial experiences. With the deepening of the sharing economy in various sectors, shared transportation facilities such as shared cars, shared electric bicycles (Shared Pedelec), and shared bicycles are penetrating into residents' production and life with a "point-to-point" public transportation service model. Therefore, changes in pedestrian activities in future urban spaces are foreseeable. The following points are based on the development of smart cities, and the digitization of travel methods has an impact on street blocks.

The Functional Transformation of Street Space from Single to Complex. Through Maslow's hierarchy of needs, it can be seen that the third level of emotional and belonging needs (Love/Belonging), also known as social needs, is the important public space where people communicate and connect. Currently, in most urban streets, the rights of motor vehicles far outweigh those of pedestrians. However, under the influence of new transportation systems such as autonomous driving technology and intelligent traffic signals, the efficiency of motor vehicle models has greatly improved. Street planning and design can save more space for motor vehicle travel and be transformed into spaces for pedestrians, such as bicycle lanes, roadside green spaces, tactile paving, and recreational facilities. It can be observed that there are many new street design cases and street design guidelines in various regions that have begun to promote and implement sports facilities and recreational urban furniture on the streets. With the intelligent transformation of motor vehicle lanes, more smart interactive urban furniture that promotes community interaction will continue to appear to enhance the service experience for cities and communities. For example, the information visualization of public transportation systems is presented through station or roadside guide signs, allowing residents to have access to transportation information within a fifteen-minute walking radius. Additionally, interactive service facilities for unmanned public transportation, where residents can complete travel pick-ups, deliveries, and other tasks at any time through roadside unmanned transportation service stations.

The Transformation of Pedestrian and Vehicular Travel Behaviors from Chaos to Harmony. Public facilities such as parking spaces occupy a large amount of public space on streets. In the future scenario of smart transportation, shared motor vehicles will operate in real-time in cities, and scenes such as roadside parking may gradually disappear. Moreover, through current experiments, it can be seen that the safety of pedestrian spaces will be greatly improved in the future smart transportation. In conjunction with the current promotion of complete streets advocating for reduced turning radii for motor vehicles to reduce pedestrian crossing obstacles, pedestrian-friendly and harmonious public spaces with mixed pedestrian and vehicular traffic become possible. In this scenario, urban furniture such as crosswalks and traffic signals will automatically adjust crossing times based on pedestrian flow, age, and physical condition to achieve better interaction experiences with urban furniture for transportation.

The Transformation of Outdoor Interactive Experiences for Pedestrians from Lack to Abundance. With the deeper development of digital technologies, various shared, smart, unmanned, and robotic urban furniture with different functions will provide residents with more new public services and interactive experiences in urban public spaces. Future new types of urban furniture equipped with unmanned driving functions or intelligent service functions, such as mobile cafes, mobile newsstands, mobile public toilets, mobile rest stations, unmanned logistics vehicles, and unmanned convenience stores, will provide more convenient scenes for residents' urban public space life. Furthermore, according to different business scenarios, detachable unmanned vehicles can carry different compartments to provide different service functions, adding more digital interaction scenes.

3.3   Transformation of the Spatial Form of Streets

In the current transition from traditional transportation modes to smart transportation modes such as autonomous driving, the traditional urban planning concept of prioritizing cars is also shifting towards a people-centric urban design concept. While maintaining the basic layout of roads, the space vacated by roads will be used to create more humanized street spaces, with street spaces being reorganized to a more pleasant scale. Firstly, sidewalks are widened to better accommodate pedestrians, and street space planning gradually shifts from the scale of vehicles to the scale of people, thereby creating safer, more convenient, and comfortable high-quality street spaces. For example, the "New York City Street Design Manual" [14] emphasizes that streets are an important part of urban public spaces and encourages users of all ages to linger and enjoy the environment by widening sidewalks. Secondly, surplus space is utilized through the addition of greenery and green spaces to create comfortable and pleasant public environments. The expansion of sidewalks facilitates the planting of street trees, which serve to separate and connect pedestrian and vehicular spaces. By improving the quality of streets, roadside green spaces enhance the comfort of pedestrian activities and contribute to reducing noise and air pollution. Thirdly, wider sidewalks, more green spaces, public activity areas, and richer pedestrian spaces facilitate spontaneous and social activities such as walking, strolling, sightseeing, and shopping, effectively stimulating the vitality of streets. Lastly, more pedestrian space also facilitates the installation of more sophisticated urban furniture to meet the public's daily fitness and leisure needs.

4 Classification of Smart Urban Furniture

Regarding the classification of smart urban furniture, Bao S. et al. proposed six major systems for urban furniture in public street spaces based on the current development status of Chinese cities. These systems include public services, public transportation, public lighting, information services, traffic management, and road pavement [6].

In March 2021, relevant departments in Hangzhou organized the compilation of the "Hangzhou Urban Furniture Setting Management Guidelines," which explicitly delineate the design standards, management requirements, and long-term management mechanisms for urban furniture. The guidelines roughly classify urban furniture into six categories and twenty-seven subcategories: public transportation facilities, road traffic facilities, environmental sanitation facilities, cultural landscape facilities, urban lighting facilities, and other public facilities. Road traffic facilities can be further subdivided into traffic facility poles, public management cameras, road signs, pedestrian guidance signs, traffic signs, comprehensive service kiosks, comprehensive facilities, and traffic control boxes. The category of public transportation facilities can be further divided into bus stops, bus shelters, and public bicycle service point facilities. The urban lighting facilities category includes both landscape lighting facilities and functional lighting facilities. Cultural landscape facilities include postal kiosks, mailboxes, telephone booths, public seats, landscape sculptures, kiosks, and volunteer service kiosks. Environmental sanitation facilities include toilet direction signs and litter bins. The category of other public facilities includes other street supporting facilities such as transformer boxes, distribution boxes, weak current boxes, warning signs, and other kiosks [15].

In 2023, China classified urban public facilities and urban furniture at the national level, proposing principles and systems for classification. The principles include system coordination, compatibility and expansion, and full utilization. The system coordination principle emphasizes the interrelationship between individual urban furniture units and between the same hierarchy, forming a hierarchical and coherent whole. The compatibility and expansion principle advocates leaving room for expansion in the classification structure based on urban development, infrastructure updates, and actual use of urban furniture. The full utilization principle aims to classify urban furniture from multiple dimensions based on specific attributes to serve citizens, optimize urban appearance and environment, ensure urban safety and order, and optimize urban management.

This classification method classifies urban furniture from two dimensions: functional application and priority setting. Functional application dimension focuses on the common characteristics and functions of individual units of urban furniture, while priority setting dimension emphasizes the importance in the urban construction process. Based on this classification standard, urban furniture is divided into six primary categories: urban transportation system, urban lighting system, public information system, road pavement system, public service system, and urban public art appreciation system.

Through the perspectives of Bao Shidu et al., the Hangzhou Urban Furniture Guidelines, and the Chinese urban furniture classification method, it can be observed that these methods classify urban furniture in a traditional manner and assume the singular functionality of urban furniture. However, in the context of the digital transformation of urban construction, the development of smart urban furniture may lead to functional changes over time and space. Therefore, a more detailed classification of composite urban furniture is worthy of further attention in the context of smart cities (Fig. 1).

(a) Bao Shidu et al. proposed a categorization chart for urban furniture.
(Source: https://mp.weixin.qq.com /s/tsFwHZrMwCYoyrCPdFGENg)

(b) Classification criteria in the Hangzhou urban furniture setting management guidelines
(Source:http://cgw.hangzhou.gov.cn/art/20 22/5/11/art_1229482813_1815725.html)

Fig. 1. Mainstream urban furniture classification methods proposed by Chinese scholars and government agencies

5 Smart City Furniture in Practice

In the aforementioned context, urban furniture with smart attributes often breaks the traditional classification rules of urban furniture. These types of urban furniture utilize technologies such as computer information, artificial intelligence, and big data, interacting with sites and pedestrians. In this digital transformation background, urban furniture exhibits multifunctional service characteristics, vividly and diversely interpreting the urban context and the spirit of the place.

5.1 Smart City Furniture for Public Transportation and Public Lighting Integration Functions

The "Warde" installation, featuring blooming flowers, is located in Vallero Square on a pedestrian pathway in the downtown area of Jerusalem. Designed by the team at HQ

Architects, this installation consists of four giant poppy-shaped parasols. In regions with sparse street trees typical of Mediterranean climates, these four large, brightly colored sunshades have become a beautiful sight on the street and even the entire city. They not only provide a comfortable resting place for passersby but also alter the spatial spirit of the entire street and square, illuminating the cultural narrative of the city. However, "Warde" is not just traditional urban furniture with sunshade functionality; in fact, it is a smart digital flower that changes its function based on observations of the surrounding environment [16].

The "Warde" installation consists of four inflatable flowers, each standing nine meters tall. The base support portion is cast from dark brown stainless steel, while the top is made of soft two-layered red inflatable fabric. During the daytime, these flower installations provide shade for pedestrians passing by. At night, the flowers transform into lighting fixtures, with three LED lights hidden in the center of each flower. The light emitted by the four flowers illuminates the nearby streets and squares, reflecting off the red petals to create a soft and ethereal glow, becoming a fun light source in public spaces. This also attracts people to gather for singing, dancing, sports, chatting, and other public activities (Fig. 2). The "Warde" installation not only adjusts its brightness based on sensitivity to light but also autonomously controls the blooming and withering of its petals. Equipped with traffic flow sensors inside, the installation also has an internal air circulation system. When the air is full, the petals naturally open. If there is frequent pedestrian or vehicle traffic, the installation slowly opens its petals to bloom; conversely, if there is less traffic, the flowers gradually wither."Warde" is an interactive digital art installation designed for human-computer interaction. Through intelligent sensing devices, it serves as a multifunctional urban furniture in street spaces, providing diverse services for residents' activities at different times.

Fig. 2. "Wared", street-side smart urban furniture in Jerusalem (Source: http://www.landscape.cn/article/64148.html)

5.2 Smart City Furniture for Public Services and Public Lighting Integration Functions

With the future development plans for the Boston Convention Center, there is an urgent need for the development and utilization of the large vacant space on the side of the building known as the D Avenue Block. The relevant departments hope to create a vibrant urban block in this area with temporary characteristics, providing possibilities for future spatial transformations. With assistance from the Sasaki urban design team and through integrating community feedback and discussions with governing bodies, the design team behind "The Lawn on D" created a landscape project on this temporary lawn plaza. The D-Avenue Block is located at the central intersection of several important areas in South Boston, including the Innovation District, the Seaport, the North Canal, and the Channel Center community. The management department has ambitious goals, aiming to establish a new neighborhood full of art and activity in this interactive, flexible, and high-tech street block, where local residents, workers, participants, or visitors can find places they enjoy. The limited space of just 2.7 acres needs to accommodate numerous activities and possibilities, posing significant challenges to the team's design capabilities and imagination. "The Lawn on D" plaza serves as a creative platform and a vibrant event venue. From the outset of the design process, the team considered the flexibility of the site and the ease of spatial transformation. Considering that "The Lawn on D" plaza is only a temporary open space during the transition period, both the owners and the designers aimed to maximize the spatial appeal while keeping the budget low. The construction budget for the entire project is only $1.5 million.

The main space of "The Lawn on D" plaza is divided into two parts: the hard plaza area and the lawn area. On the plaza, a variety of activities attract a continuous stream of people. Long orange walkways connect the street with the side entrance of the convention center, and a unique lighting system appropriately scales the gathering place. Vibrant and whimsical movable furniture invites everyone to unleash their imagination and create exclusive small spaces [17].

One particularly popular urban furniture installation is the Swing Time swing set, which has been warmly welcomed by many local residents and tourists alike. Designed by artists Eric Howeler and Meejin Yoon, there are a total of 20 swing installations on the lawn, each made of polypropylene material and designed in three different scales to accommodate various people. Moreover, these swings have digital features such as inter-activity. They emit purple lighting beams at night, controlled by specially customized microprocessors, and the swings are equipped with accelerometers to measure swing acceleration. When the swings are stationary, the LED lighting emits white light; as they swing, the white light gradually transforms into purple, creating a romantic atmosphere. This interactive feature is highly contagious, quickly activating the urban space and providing a new sensory experience (Fig. 3).

5.3 Smart City Furniture for Public Transportation and Information Services Integration Functions

Public transit shelters have always played a role in conveying transit information, evolving from handwritten texts to printed metal signs and now to interactive smart shelters, becoming increasingly intelligent. One such innovation is a new type of minimalist "information display" bus shelter designed by Hikvision (Fig. 4). Unlike traditional single-column shelters with a single content presentation format, the diversified information display shelter is a versatile multifunctional digital display unit. Its information system is housed on an aluminum alloy steel frame that blends into the urban color scheme, with the central OLED screen nested in a black polycarbonate panel within the

Fig. 3. Boston's temporary lawn urban furniture "the Lawn on D" (Source: https://www.sasaki. com/zh/projects/the-lawn-on-d/)

aluminum alloy profile frame, providing high durability and glossiness, ensuring information readability even under direct sunlight. This LCD display can be connected to a smart city platform and a transit dispatch platform to obtain real-time vehicle location information, calculate it into arrival time and distance, and display it on the electronic shelter screen in real time, supporting voice broadcasting as well. Additionally, while waiting for the bus, passengers can browse through bus transfer guides, transit operation information, government news, etc., and view route guides. Future public transit systems may even integrate weather, entertainment, advertising, and other related information to form visual information service points [18]. Furthermore, to maximize walkability on streets, when used as pedestrian crosswalk signals, these smart shelters may not require dedicated pedestrian buttons; instead, they can use cameras to automatically sense waiting pedestrians, replacing traffic signal devices.

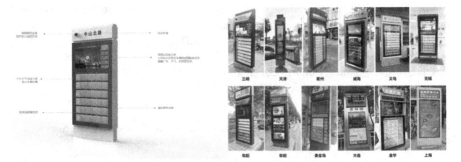

Fig. 4. Intelligent interactive bus stop signs designed by Hikvision are used in smart city construction in various cities in China (Source: https://mp.weixin.qq.com/s/orMnMccIx1uSUggLcb EbSA)

6   Conclusion

This article addresses the issues of urban furniture in street spaces being stuck in single-functionality, lacking human-centric design, neglecting user interaction, and not adequately addressing the daily needs of citizens. These furniture pieces often appear monotonous and lack fun. With the development of technologies such as artificial intelligence, autonomous driving, and augmented reality, urban furniture, as an important element reflecting the narrative and spirit of urban spaces, has begun to undergo functional diversification in design as part of a new round of smart city construction. Consequently, the interaction design of urban furniture is evolving from singularity towards interactive, flexible, and high-tech composite service functions. This developmental trend, propelled by the richer technological advancements of the future, opens up more possibilities. Therefore, further subdivision and reorganization of the types, interactive features, and spatial forms of urban furniture under digital transformation are necessary.

References

1. Zhang, D., Pei, X.: Design of urban public facilities from the perspective of industrial design. Urban Issues **03**, 21–24 (2003)
2. Fan, W.: Research on Organic Integration of Contemporary Urban Elements from the Perspective of Urban Designpp, pp. 71–76. Tongji University (2008)
3. Barbeau, S.: Urban Vignettes. Liaoning Science and Technology Press, Shenyang (2010)
4. Liang Y.: Research on Urban Furniture System Planning and Design. China Academy of Art, pp.68–73 (2015)
5. Alain, B.: Great Streets. China Construction Industry Press, Beijing (2008)
6. Bao, S., Shi, H.: A theoretical study of urban furniture in China. Decoration **07**, 12–16 (2019)
7. Bao, S.: Basic Concepts of Urban Furniture in China, pp.12–13. China Building Industry Press, Beijing (2019)
8. Luo, W.: A new approach to the management of urban diseases: from digital cities to smart cities. Sci. Technol. Innov. Appl. **26**, 75–76 (2019)
9. IBM. Smart Cities in China. https://doc.mbalib.com/view/b0dc42f99579a972ed7f12dc13d a3d55.html. Accessed 19 Nov 2023
10. Wu, Y., Ai, H.: The Way of Modern City Construction in the Context of Smart City Internet of Things. Electronic Industry Press, Beijing (2011)
11. Li, D.: Digital city + internet of things + cloud computing = smart city. China Surveying Mapp. **20**, 46 (2011)
12. Wang, J.Y.: Wisdom makes cities better. Nat. Mag. **34**(03), 139–142 (2012)
13. Zhang, Y., Du, Z.: Current situation and thoughts on the construction of smart cities in China. China Inf. Commun. **02**, 28–32 (2011)
14. New York Department of Transportation: New York Street Design Manual. Zhengzhou University Press, Zhengzhou (2017)
15. Hangzhou urban furniture setting management guidelines. http://cgw.hangzhou.gov.cn/art/ 2022/5/11/art_1229482813_1815725.html. Accessed Dec 2023
16. Can art revitalize a dead urban space? http://www.landscape.cn/article/64148.html. Accessed Jun 2015
17. Put to Test: Lawn on D. https://www.sasaki.com/zh/projects/the-lawn-on-d/. Accessed 19 Dec 2023
18. Hikvision's electronic bus stop signs make traveling more convenient. https://mp.weixin.qq. com/s/orMnMccIx1uSUggLcbEbSA. Accessed 11 Dec 2023

Application of Experience Design in the Design of Home Medical Products: A Case Study of QUINOVARE Needle-Free Injector Products

Ji Xu[1,2], Danlan Ye[3(✉)] [iD], Ding-Bang Luh[1], and Hao Tan[3] [iD]

[1] School of Art and Design, Guangdong University of Technology, Guangzhou 510000, China
[2] Industrial Culture Development Center of MIIT, Beijing 100846, China
[3] School of Design, Hunan University, Changsha 410000, China
yedanlan@hnu.edu.cn

Abstract. In recent years, the escalating prominence of health issues has heightened public awareness regarding healthcare. Consequently, there has been a discernible surge in the utilization of home medical products. In this paper, we will delve into how to enhance the user experience related to medical products, with a particular focus on the application of experience design in home medical products. Needle-free syringes are a relevant example for a comprehensive exploration. To lay a robust foundation for our research and to understand the current status of research development, this paper provides a systematic review of the relevant literature on home medical products and needleless syringe experience design including both domestically and internationally. In this paper, Comprising Comparative Testing, Experiential Research, and Design Case Studies were used to scrutinize and analyze the research object. By integrating these methods and analyses, we endeavor to proffer design guidance and contemplation premised on the imperative tenets of experience design: Experiences require active interaction between the individual and products; Recognize the need for experience-oriented design requirements; Asserting that experience should manifest intervention and care to amplify inclusiveness; and Recognize that other factors may diminish the experience and trigger paradoxes in the logic of consumption. This scholarly research aims to provide insights into the current state of affairs, offer nuanced understanding, and provide valuable references for subsequent research endeavors. Furthermore, the constraints of medical products themselves are discussed in the paper. The overarching objective of this research is to contribute substantively to the exploration and subsequent application of experience design in the domain of medical product design. By continuously optimizing and refining the experiential design of healthcare products, this study aspires to ensure that healthcare products become safer, more effective, and user-friendly. The ultimate goal is to offer consumers high-quality healthcare products and services, thereby enhancing the overall healthcare experience.

Keywords: Experience design · Medical products · Needleless syringe · Product design

P.-L. P. Rau (Ed.): HCII 2024, LNCS 14699, pp. 354–367, 2024.
https://doi.org/10.1007/978-3-031-60898-8_24

1 Introduction

In recent years, with the impact of the pandemic, there has been an increasing focus on healthcare. Issues such as the aging of society, sub-health status showing a youthful trend, and the rising incidence of chronic diseases have become more pronounced. The demand for products related to home healthcare services continues to grow. According to statistics, there are approximately 463 million diabetes patients globally, with around 116 million in China, and the incidence of diabetes in adults is around 10% [1]. Chronic diseases have lengthy durations, complex etiologies, significant health implications, and are challenging to cure, placing a substantial long-term economic burden on families [2]. Consequently, people are exploring solutions within home healthcare products.

The progress in drug therapy has brought about improvements in the lives of many patients facing chronic diseases. Statistical data reveals that globally, there are at least 16 billion preventive and therapeutic injections administered annually [3]. However, needle phobia and the pain associated with injections remain significant challenges leading to treatment non-compliance and interruptions for both physicians and patients relying on self-injection therapies [4–6]. Approximately 3% to 4% of people worldwide suffer from severe needle phobia, with 20% to 50% of adolescents exhibiting needle fear [7]. The high prevalence of needle phobia poses serious health risks; during the COVID-19 pandemic, fear of needles may contribute to vaccine avoidance, increasing the risk of infection [8]. Furthermore, the use of needles and injection devices increases the risk of needlestick injuries, and specialized handling of needles requires substantial economic and manpower investments [9].

In past research, needle-free injection technology has been developed and utilized to address challenges related to injection pain and needle phobia. The origins of needle-free drug delivery technology can be traced back to the early 19th century, with one of the key patents submitted by Lockhart in 1930 [10]. The early needle-free injection systems emerged in the 1940s and 1950s, taking the form of air-powered devices. Needle-Free Injection Technology (NFIT) involves the generation of high pressure using a pressure source, which instantly propels the drug through a nozzle, forming a high-speed, high-pressure jet. This jet penetrates the outer layer of the skin and reaches the appropriate depth, facilitating drug absorption and therapeutic effectiveness. As illustrated in Fig. 1 (see Fig. 1), comparing needle-free injection with needle injection for the distribution of subcutaneous tissue fluids, needle-free injection technology excels in achieving intradermal, subcutaneous, and intramuscular injections. Its advantages include the ability to deliver drugs locally or systemically, improved drug delivery efficiency, precise dosing, and faster absorption [11]. Applied in home healthcare products, needle-free injection technology is characterized by its compact size, portability, simple and safe operation, meeting daily user needs with broad applications and research significance.

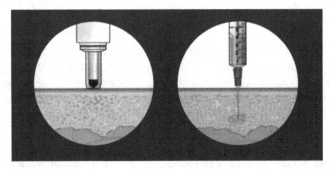

Fig. 1. Schematic diagram of drug distribution into the subcutaneous tissue by needleless injection and needle injection

2 Literature Review

2.1 Research on Experience Design of Home Healthcare Products

Home healthcare products constitute a vital component of home healthcare engineering, primarily referring to medical devices suitable for public use outside the hospital setting. These devices are characterized by their small size, portability, ease of use, and safety. Their purpose includes monitoring, treatment, health maintenance, and rehabilitation [12]. Home Healthcare Engineering (HHCE) is an emerging interdisciplinary field that integrates medicine and technology. It aims to extend medical care to every household by designing and introducing advanced home healthcare products and devices. The goal is to facilitate patient diagnosis, treatment, and rehabilitation, providing more convenient and personalized services to patients [13]. Experience Design is a design methodology centered around delving into users' emotions and perceptions to create meaningful, enjoyable, and efficient user experiences. Emphasizing a profound understanding of user needs, expectations, and behaviors, Experience Design seeks to optimize interactions between users and designed entities, such as products, services, or systems. The objective is to craft comprehensive, emotionally rich, and user-centric design solutions [14, 15]. Applying experience design to home healthcare products is a crucial aspect of healthcare innovation.

Liu Xinyu et al. [16] conducted research on theories such as interaction design, human-centered design, universal design, and experience design, providing guidance for the design of home healthcare products. Wu Xinxin [17] explored the current state of design for domestic mobile medical products, principles of experience design, and methods based on user experience for designing mobile medical products, offering valuable insights for the development of this field. Ma Jiefan [18] applied sensory engineering methods to the study of Color, Material, and Finish (CMF) design in home healthcare products, constructing a CMF design process based on sensory engineering methods. Lü Ke et al. [19] analyzed the prospects of medical equipment demand and the current application status of industrial design, discussing key issues and innovative trends influencing the integration of industrial design and medical equipment development. Liu Jianjun et al. [20], from the perspective of user experience, compared traditional rehabilitation methods with immersive experience-based rehabilitation methods, elaborating on the advantages of applying immersive experiences in the design of medical rehabilitation products. Zhang Junjia [21] dissected the application of five user experience methods – sensory experience, interactive experience, emotional experience, virtual role simulation, and experimental testing – in the design of rehabilitation medical products. Han Yue et al. [22], using a questionnaire survey, summarized the design elements of home healthcare products for the elderly. Through the Analytic Hierarchy Process (AHP) and scoring, they ranked the importance of design elements, enhancing the evaluation system for the design of home healthcare products for the elderly and providing guidance for design optimization and improvement. These studies collectively contribute to a comprehensive field of experience design for home healthcare products, providing a solid theoretical and practical foundation for optimizing the user experience of medical products and meeting user needs.

2.2 Research on Needle-Free Injectors

Self-injection therapy plays a crucial role in home healthcare, and subcutaneous drug delivery technology is driving innovation in global healthcare systems [23, 24]. Advances in technology and the innovative design of home medical devices provide patients with the ability to self-treat at home. This not only avoids the inconvenience and costs associated with frequent hospital visits but also reduces medical expenses, alleviating the burden on families and society. Marco Boeri et al. [25] found that patients' confident ability to self-inject can improve their overall experience, helping them feel more autonomous, mitigating the psychological impact of chronic diseases on their lives, and enhancing their overall quality of life related to health. Yan Wei et al. [26], through a discrete choice experiment conducted in China, demonstrated that attributes of self-injection devices, such as injection pain, operational steps, size, needle visibility, needle protection, and feedback indicators, significantly influence patients' choices and preferences for injection devices. The research highlights the essential value of developing self-injection devices to enhance patient treatment adherence and promote patient-centered care for autoimmune diseases. Bart J. F. van den Bemt et al. [27] found that involving patients in medical device development, device selection, and patient support programs can enhance their sense of control over the treatment process. Autonomously designed injection devices, based on patient needs, contribute to improving the patient experience, subsequently enhancing treatment adherence and improving the outcomes of long-term treatments.

The development of self-injection devices heavily relies on the preferences and human factors of actual users to ensure optimal design, usability, safety, and effectiveness. Placing expected users at the core of the design process helps designers better understand user preferences and limitations that impact device usability. Continuously refining device design through iterative improvements, incorporating feedback from actual users and human factors research, can enhance the user experience and treatment adherence of self-injection devices. Currently, regulatory bodies including the European Medicines Agency, Japanese Ministry of Health, Labour and Welfare, and the US Food and Drug Administration recognize the importance of human factors research in the development of medical devices. They mandate effective usability assessment and usability testing validation during product design and development stages [28].

3 Method

The fundamental requirements for medical device products are safety and effectiveness, ensuring that products can pass tests to meet certain standards and possess the necessary performance. With the continuous integration of design thinking, the usability and user-friendliness of medical device products have gradually become areas of focus. In the field of needle-based injections, research continues to explore ways to improve their usability, such as optimizing needle fineness while considering length and flexibility. Needle-free injectors, classified as Class III medical devices, are closely related to user interaction and usage. They stand out among similar products, and current research focuses on addressing challenges in needle-free scenarios. This study employs user comparative testing, experiential research, and design case analysis to explore the application of experience design in the design of needle-free injectors and similar medical products, providing better guidance for design decisions.

3.1 Comparative Testing

The design concept of needle-free injectors originates from an innovative drug delivery technology that utilizes the principle of pressure jet streams to precisely deliver medication to subcutaneous tissue through extremely small openings. The entire injection process takes only 0.3 s, and patients hardly feel any discomfort, experiencing only mild vibrations. The figure (see Fig. 2) shows a schematic diagram of the user-friendly operation of the needle-free injector.

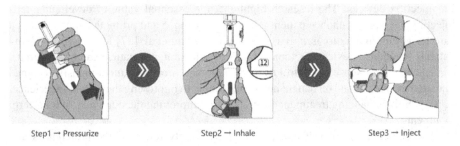

Step1 → Pressurize   Step2 → Inhale   Step3 → Inject

Fig. 2. Schematic diagram of the easy-to-use operation of a needleless syringe

To explore the effectiveness of user interactions with needle-free injectors and needle-based injectors and to delve into detailed consumer demands, two comparative tests were conducted. Test one focused on users' pain perception scores when using needle-based and needle-free injections. A ten-point scale was employed to score pain intensity, where 0–3 points represented mild pain, 4–6 points indicated moderate pain, and 7–10 points indicated severe pain. The goal was to understand the impact of different injection methods on user experience and perception. Test two concentrated on postprandial physiological indicators after using needle-based and needle-free injections. Comparative measurements were taken for users' postprandial plasma insulin concentration and postprandial blood glucose concentration. Concentrations of various indicators were measured every half hour, aiming to gain an in-depth understanding of the physiological effects of user usage and to provide objective and accurate data support for designing products that better align with user needs.

3.2 Experiential Research

Experiential research refers to the method of conducting research and studies through direct participation and firsthand experience. This approach is quite common in user experience design and typically involves on-site observation, participatory interviews, experiential activities, and the like. Experiential research aids researchers in gaining a better understanding of the behaviors and contexts of the subjects under study, thereby providing more insightful research outcomes. Inspired by experiential research, team members, during a business trip, visited the emergency department due to a sudden illness. Seeking a deeper understanding of users' real experiences and needs, they assumed the role of patients, personally experiencing the process and meticulously documenting the obtained experiential insights.

3.3 Design Case Studies

This paper, based on theories and methods from design disciplines such as product design, interaction design, and user experience, focuses on the analysis and exposition of the case of needle-free injectors. It delves into the current state and developmental trends of user experience research in medical products, aiming to distill relevant guidelines for the application of experience design in the design of home medical products.

4 Results

4.1 Test Analysis

The chart (see Fig. 3) shows the specific pain perception scores of users after using needle-based and needle-free injections. The data indicates a significant reduction in pain in the needle-free group, particularly for moderate to severe pain.

The chart (see Fig. 4) presents the specific postprandial insulin concentration and blood glucose concentration of users after using needle-based and needle-free injections. The data suggests that needle-free injections closely mimic the physiological insulin secretion pattern, resulting in better postprandial blood glucose control.

The data results from both tests visually demonstrate that needle-free injection is more effective than needle-based injection. Using this as a starting point, the discussion delves into design issues related to the product and continuously extends knowledge and refines consumer demands based on these findings.

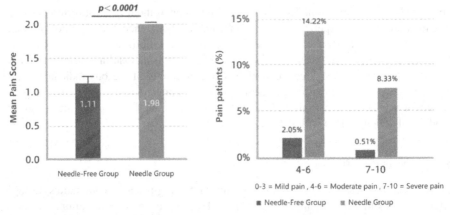

Fig. 3. Experimental data showing that the needle-free group significantly reduced pain, especially moderate to severe pain

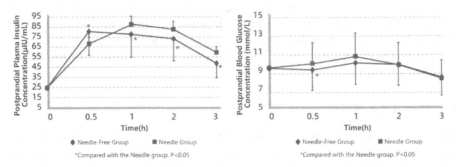

Fig. 4. Experimental data show that needle-free injections are closer to the physiologic insulin secretion pattern and result in better postprandial glycemic control

4.2   Experiences Require Active Interaction Between the Individual and Products

In medical product design, user experience is a crucial influencing factor. Through experiential research, we studied and analyzed the use of infusion needles (see Fig. 5). During the infusion process, nurses offer two choices: a regular needle and a soft needle. The latter has the advantage of moving smoothly in the blood vessels, reducing the risk of bleeding for users but comes at a higher cost.

From a design perspective, the simplicity of the product is crucial. Designers strive to make users grasp the operational methods intuitively through product semantics, without relying on instructions. This design philosophy reflects the principle of "less is more," aiming to provide an intuitive and user-friendly product experience. However, from the consumer's standpoint, the experience gained from a more complex product tends to be more positive. Consumers often perceive that a more complex product implies higher value. Excessive simplicity may lead to a psychological expectation gap for users, while products with rich experiences are more likely to be seen as worthwhile. In the context of infusion scenarios, the traditional single-puncture method with a rigid

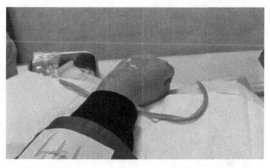

Fig. 5. One of the authors' experiences with soft needle infusion in a hospital emergency department

needle often provides a stiff experience. In contrast, the design of a paid soft needle involves the interweaving connection of various small parts, sealing tightly after puncture and minimizing the occurrence of needle rolling. Although the soft needle requires an additional fee and cannot be taken away, users generally believe that the experience has service value.

Experience is the relationship between people and products, whether it be the interface or the user. When a product introduces new features, its complexity increases exponentially. The introduction of new features also multiplies the likelihood of problems and adds to the cost of user learning and the probability of mis-operation. Medical products should strive to avoid this situation, prioritizing the efficient treatment of patients as a primary goal, ensuring simplicity and the absence of sudden issues, rather than pursuing a multitude of features. On a legal and regulatory level, the more functions a product has, the higher the risk cost during testing. Therefore, excessive design integration in pursuit of multiple functionalities should be avoided. Instead, a people-centric approach should be taken to design medical products that better align with user needs.

4.3 Experience Driven Design Requirements

In the design of medical products, user experience is an indispensable factor. Taking the needle-free injection device as an example, it incorporates a spring structure internally, requiring the application of a relative rotational force during use. Users need to hold the product tightly during the injection process, which puts new demands on the user experience of products. First, the product should facilitate smooth rotational operation to achieve pressurization and drug inhalation. Second, the injection action needs to be perpendicular to the direction of rotation. Undoubtedly, this places explicit requirements on the user experience of the product. The initial design of the first-generation product opted for a circular appearance. However, during user experience testing, it was found that the circular design made the handle slippery, compromising efficiency. Therefore, the design team made functional adjustments, changing the circular design to a square one with certain chamfers to enhance stability during the gripping process. Additionally, to optimize the user experience, at the conclusion of the spring pressurization and energy storage operation, for safety and functional limitations, the product incorporated the emergence of two buttons (safety lock and injection button) as clear visual and tactile cues, indicating the current status of the product to the user.

Fig. 6. QUINOVARE Needle-Free Syringe Products

Taking the QUINOVARE needle-free syringe products as an example (see Fig. 6), during usage, the drug enters the drug storage device through the adapter and is then propelled out by the pressure released from the spring. When drawing in medication, there is a noticeable pause with each rotation, and each pause represents a dose of 0.01 ml, which is the minimum unit for insulin injection. This design detail takes into full consideration the usage experience of the elderly population. Given that some elderly users may have poor eyesight, counting the rotations can assist them in determining the dosage drawn. Additionally, to further accommodate elderly users, the product incorporates a magnifying glass module for easy reading confirmation, and the product's angle of use was adjusted for ease of use.

The Color, Material, and Finish (CMF) design also has a certain impact on the user experience. Taking the adult version of the needle-free injection device as an example, the CMF design of the product is considerate of the user experience. The product adopts white, a color associated with hygiene commonly chosen for instruments and devices in hospitals. The public has an inherent cognitive connection between white color and medical equipment, representing easy cleanliness. This association not only influences the user acceptance of the product but also, to some extent, affects its market performance. Surface treatment is another crucial factor affecting user experience. To enhance the product's durability and resistance to dirt, the surface is coated with antibacterial paint and anti-dirty paint, filling in scratches and abrasions that may occur during the manufacturing process. The antibacterial function, in reality, has a psychological market demand greater than its functional aspect. The primary function of needleless injection equipment is therapeutic, and adding value increases costs when the product functions to the required standard. Therefore, the design needs to strike a balance between meeting user needs, ensuring functionality, and controlling costs.

4.4 Experience Should Manifest Intervention and Care to Amplify Inclusiveness

User experience not only concerns the appearance and tactile sensations of a product but also involves the psychological feelings and emotional needs of the user. The sharp form of injection needles induces a sense of fear at the perceptual level, stemming from bio-logical instincts. Pain and fear are natural reactions when humans face sharp objects, and sometimes, this fear can significantly impact a patient's willingness to accept the proce-dure. Which demographic experiences a stronger fear of injection needles? One group includes those without injection medical experience or exposure, and the other comprises individuals with poor self-protection and defense abilities, such as children. Insulin is a common injectable medication, serving as a hormone to regulate the body's blood sugar levels. There are also insulin analogs that perform similar functions to insulin. These medications require special attention to dosage and injection methods to ensure effective treatment. For example, growth hormones require an increase in dosage cor-responding to the child's weight gain. Additionally, children frequently receive vaccine injections, especially during the infancy and toddler stages with frequent vaccinations. Since the methods for administering the aforementioned medications and vaccines are similar, requiring long-term adherence and having a high frequency, needle-free injec-tion technology can also be considered for broader application in the field of vaccine administration.

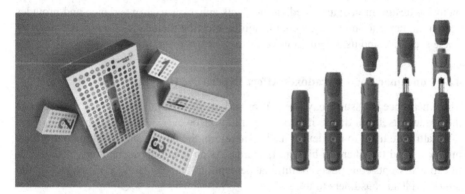

Fig. 7. QUINOVARE Needle-Free Injector Pediatric Model

Taking the child-friendly product as an example (see Fig. 7), during the trial pro-duction process, some parents suggested designing the product in the shape of a toy or a bird-like structure. The designers expressed disagreement, emphasizing that medical devices should not be treated as toys, and their safety should not diminish or fade away with the affinity of toys. Such products pose risks even if used for activities as innocent as spraying clear water into the eyes. However, the product can be designed to incor-porate the curiosity associated with toy-like features. A plug-in building block concept was adopted (see Fig. 8) in Children's products, creating various relationships between the components, allowing for separation, rotation, resembling the modularity of build-ing blocks. Multiple color schemes were chosen to achieve modularity, catering to the color preferences of children of different genders. To avoid the risk of mis-operation, noticeable visual changes were designed around crucial buttons to alert the user.

In the early stages, universal design primarily focused on individuals with disabilities. With societal progress, an increasing number of scholars have shifted their attention

Fig. 8. Internal structure of a QUINOVARE needleless syringe product

towards inclusive design. The aim is to broaden the coverage of products to serve a more diverse range of consumers and users. It is a challenge to introduce design theories and perspectives to guide the realization of the complete chain in the practical aspects of production, manufacturing and distribution. Consumers provide feedback at all stages of production and marketing. During the trial production process, testing user experiences and interactions can further optimize and refine the product's usage. The application of inclusive design in pediatric medical products enhances user experience and provides design guidance to improve product usability, meeting the needs of a broader range of usage scenarios and user demographics.

4.5   Consumer Logic Paradoxes Affect Experience Design

The emergence of issues may stem from various factors, potentially not as defects in the product itself but due to improper operation. However, when problems arise, users often attribute them to the device itself. Therefore, the design and development of new products need to adhere to higher standards. As an emerging technology, needle-free injection disrupts consumers' traditional perceptions and habits. A good product should guide and lead consumers to use it.

In the current stage of societal development, traditional injection needles are widely accepted and inexpensive. When consumers are required to make a one-time expenditure of several thousand yuan to purchase needle-free injection products, they may resist or have higher expectations. There is a segment of consumers who use these products on a daily basis, so a deeper understanding and insight into the market is critical to the development of such products. Their expectation is for new products that are both economical, safe, and practical, rather than every consumer meticulously calculating costs.

There is a compromise between design and consumers. As a commercial product, home medical products have commercial attributes that require profits to support further research and development. To find a balance point that incorporates design thinking, designers need to coordinate material selection, reduce manufacturing process complexity, and control costs. Consumers desire an increased injection dose, but this requires greater propulsive force during product use, leading to a corresponding increase in the volume of the spring, resulting in the overall size and weight of the product also increasing. At this point, consumers may reduce purchases due to the increased volume and weight, forcing the product to shift toward lightweight design. This presents a logical paradox. To avoid such problems, a new design order needs to be established, breaking free from existing product theories, establishing new causal relationships, and constructing new design logic. This includes exploring new power methods, structural approaches, design proportions, and more. It involves reconstructing user relationships, clarifying user profiles through market feedback, making them increasingly clear.

5 Discussion

Both domestic and international medical device products place a high emphasis on industrial design and user experience. The increase in market competitors and the continuous refinement of product functionalities at the market level compel enterprises to enhance their product competitiveness for acquiring market shares. At the regulatory level, governments have enacted a series of laws, regulations, and standards to standardize such products. The introduction of relevant regulations and standards has led to a more complete and standardized framework for the industry, as well as increasingly stringent requirements for products. Some national standards have mandatory access requirements for medical device products, which need to be tested by professional testing centers for stability and safety in terms of frequency of use. Additionally, standards are subject to continuous updates and improvements. For instance, the coupling of syringes and injectors is due to the close correlation between internal spring dynamics and fluid flow, and this connection should not be arbitrarily separated. Diverging from the traditional consumer goods industry and the electronic information industry's product update plans for light industry, textiles, clothing, and household appliances, the successful market entry of medical products is constrained by the following factors: First, medical device products are subject to national standards, and they can only be launched after meeting these standards, with the introduction of new products not solely driven by market demand. Second, these products face certain technological barriers, necessitating a longer research and development cycle, along with substantial time and technical support investments. Third, monitoring adverse reactions from consumers requires recording and tracking user experience feedback samples in the market. These factors, acting as reactive forces, compel enterprises to passively accept and make appropriate adjustments.

6 Conclusion

It is important to apply experience design in the development of medical products. As a unique category of products that directly impacting human health, the design of medical products must be user-centric, taking into account the consumer needs and the user convenience. Medical products are charged with the responsibility of ensuring safety, efficacy, and enhanced usability, and these responsibilities should also implicitly influence the professional ethics of practitioners. On the one hand, safety is the paramount consideration in medical product design, requiring designers to ensure that the product does not cause harm to consumers and users during usage. On the other hand, effectiveness is a crucial consideration, as products need to efficiently assist users in addressing health issues. Given that medical products cater to diverse user groups, including the elderly, children, and individuals with disabilities, these special populations often require more assistance and guidance. Therefore, in order to reduce the difficulty of use and improve the user experience, it is necessary to fully consider the needs of these users in the design and improve the usability of the product through human-centered design. Positive user-product interaction experiences can better meet user needs, improve product usage and experience, and generate favorable design demands that drive technological innovation. This, in turn, provides better services for consumers and users. Intervention and care-focused design can assist users in improving their quality of life and enjoyment while ensuring safety. This approach can provide users with a way to better cope with diseases and health issues, ultimately enhancing their overall quality of life and enjoyment. The design of home medical products necessitates a comprehensive consideration of these factors to deliver an improved product experience and service.

References

1. Zhou, B., Carrillo-Larco, R.M., Danaei, G., et al.: Worldwide trends in hypertension prevalence and progress in treatment and control from 1990 to 2019: a pooled analysis of 1201 population-representative studies with 104 million participants. The Lancet **398**(10304), 957–980 (2021)
2. LV, W.T., Zhong, Y.S., Qi, R.J.: The development trend and current situation of household medical equipment industry. China Med. Device Inf. **24**(12), 153–156 (2018)
3. Simonsen, L., Kane, A., Lloyd, J., et al.: Unsafe injections in the developing world and transmission of bloodborne pathogens: a review. Bull. World Health Organ. **77**, 789–800 (1999)
4. Deacon, B., Abramowitz, J.: Fear of needles and vasovagal reactions among phlebotomy patients. J. Anxiety Disord. **20**(7), 946–960 (2006)
5. Devonshire, V., Lapierre, Y., Macdonell, R., et al.: The global adherence project (GAP): a multicenter observational study on adherence to disease-modifying therapies in patients with relapsing-remitting multiple sclerosis. Eur. J. Neurol. **18**(1), 69–77 (2011)
6. Orenius, T., LicPsych, Säilä, H., et al.: Fear of injections and needle phobia among children and adolescents: an overview of psychological, behavioral, and contextual factors. SAGE Open Nursing **4**, 2377960818759442 (2018)
7. McLenon, J., Rogers, M.A.M.: The fear of needles: a systematic review and meta-analysis. J. Adv. Nurs. **75**(1), 30–42 (2019). https://doi.org/10.1111/jan.13818
8. Love, A.S., Love, R.J.: Considering needle phobia among adult patients during mass COVID-19 vaccinations. J. Prim. Care Community Health **12**, 21501327211007390 (2021)
9. Pepin, J., Abou Chakra, C.N., Pepin, E., et al.: Evolution of the global use of unsafe medical injections, 2000–2010. PLoS ONE **8**(12), e80948 (2013)
10. Patwekar, S.L., Gattani, S.G., Pande, M.M.: Needle free injection system: a review. Int J Pharm Pharm Sci **5**(4), 14–19 (2013)
11. Zhang, H., Cheng, Y., Wang, Z.M., et al.: Research progress of needle-free injection technology. Acta Pharmaceutica Sinica 1–21 (2024) https://doi.org/10.16438/j.0513-4870.2023-0853
12. Yang, X.: Humanized Design of Family healthcare products. Qilu University of Technology (2013)
13. de Bono, E.: Lateral Thinking: Creativity Step by Step (e-book). (2015)
14. Carbone, L.P., Haeckel, S.H.: Engineering customer experiences. Mark. Manage. **3**(3), 8–19 (1994)
15. Pullman, M.E., Gross, M.A.: Ability of experience design elements to elicit emotions and loyalty behaviors. Decis. Sci. **35**(3), 551–578 (2004)

16. Jiefan, M.: Research on CMF design of home medical products. China Univ. Min. Technol. (2021)https://doi.org/10.27623/d.cnki.gzkyu.2021.001321

17. Ke, L., Yaxin, Z., Dong, W.: Research on the application of industrial design in medical devices. Mach. China **2023**(14), 19–22 (2023)

18. Xinyu, L., Xiaoying, Z., Jianwei, M.: The application of modern design concepts and design methods in the design of home medical products. Design **2018**(12), 127–129 (2018)

19. Jianjun, L., Zhang, X., Wei, W.: Design and research of flow experience in medical rehabilitation products. Art and Design 2(12), 109–111 (2022)

20. Xinxin, W.: Research on the experience design of mobile medical products under the environment of "Internet+." Art Sci. Technol. **32**(12), 54 (2019)

21. Junjia, Z.: Application research on user experience method in the design of medical rehabilitation product. Ind. Des. **2018**(11), 136–137 (2018)

22. Yue, H., Zhu, T.L., Zhou, Z.J., Zhou, T.: Improvement of evaluation method of elderly family medical product design based on AHP. Math. Prob. Eng. **2022**, 1–8 (2022). https://doi.org/10.1155/2022/4036030

23. Kim, H., Park, H., Lee, S.J.: Effective method for drug injection into subcutaneous tissue. Sci. Rep. **7**(1), 1–11 (2017)

24. Jones, G.B., Collins, D.S., Harrison, M.W., Thyagarajapuram, N.R., Wright, J.M.: Subcutaneous drug delivery: an evolving enterprise. Sci. Transl. Med. **9**(405), eaaf9166 (2017). https://doi.org/10.1126/scitranslmed.aaf9166

25. Boeri, M., et al.: From drug-delivery device to disease management tool: a study of preferences for enhanced features in next-generation self-injection devices. Patient Prefer. Adherence **13**, 1093–1110 (2019). https://doi.org/10.2147/PPA.S203775

26. Wei, Y., Zhao, J., Ming, J., Zhang, X., Chen, Y.: Patient preference for self-injection devices in rheumatoid arthritis: a discrete choice experiment in China. Patient Prefer. Adherence **16**, 2387–2398 (2022). https://doi.org/10.2147/PPA.S375938

27. van den Bemt, B.J.F., Gettings, L., Domańska, B., et al.: A portfolio of biologic self-injection devices in rheumatology: how patient involvement in device design can improve treatment experience. Drug Deliv. **26**(1), 384–392 (2019)

28. Berman, K., Moss, S., Holden-Theunissen, B., et al.: Design development of the SMARTCLIC®/CLICWISE® injection device for self-administered subcutaneous therapies: findings from usability and human factor studies. Adv. Ther. **40**(7), 3070–3086 (2023)

The Influence of Anthropomorphism on the User Experience of Digital Products

Ruining Yang[1,2] and Yue Qi[1,2(✉)] (iD)

[1] The Department of Psychology, Renmin University of China, Beijing 100872, China
qiy@ruc.edu.cn
[2] The Laboratory of the Department of Psychology, Renmin University of China,
Beijing 100872, China

Abstract. Nowadays, the user experience of products is very important, and anthropomorphism is widely used in product design, but it may also cause negative effects if used improperly. From the perspective of human-computer interaction, this paper constructs a moderated mediation model, designs and implements two studies, discusses the impact of anthropomorphism on the user experience of digital products, and analyzes its internal psychological mechanism and applicable conditions. The research results show that: In general, anthropomorphism can improve the user experience of digital products, and psychological distance plays a mediating role. Product type and belongingness need moderate this relationship, but there are some differences in 4 dimensions of user experience. The conclusion of this paper can help designers use anthropomorphism more pertinently.

Keywords: anthropomorphism · user experience · psychological distance · the need to belong · digital product

1 Introduction

1.1 Research Background

The rapid development of the digital economy has brought about comprehensive and profound changes in people's production and lifestyle. In the context of fierce external competition and dynamic changes in the market environment, digital product developers face great challenges as well as new opportunities (Xu et al., 2023). More and more attention is paid to user experience, and digital products with excellent user experience should not only provide users with functional value, but also provide users with emotional value.

An effective means of providing emotional value is the anthropomorphism of the product. The application of anthropomorphic means in the field of digital products conforms to the transformation of China's consumption trend from usefulness to beneficial consumption. Anthropomorphism is also important in the field of human-computer interaction because it provides a reference for how people interact with non-human subjects and the psychological mechanisms that illuminate this relationship, such as triggering emotions (Shank et al., 2019), and protecting privacy (Ha et al., 2020). Most studies have shown that anthropomorphism can have positive results, but anthropomorphism can also play a negative role in some fields and conditions (Velasco et al., 2021). For example, when asked to undress and undergo a physical examination in front of an anthropomorphic robot, people will be more embarrassed than in front of a mechanical box (Bartneck et al., 2010), and when interacting with a highly anthropomorphic virtual assistant, people tend to have more privacy issues (Ha et al., 2020; Xie et al., 2020).

The "digital product" discussed in this article refers to "interactive digital products" (Kidultoo, 2020), such digital products are programmable, can be transmitted, used, exchanged, consumed through the network, it can run on different hardware platforms - computers, mobile phones, watches, cars, glasses, etc. Compared with traditional phys-ical products, digital products have their particularities, such as focusing on experience and rapid iteration (Zhang, 2022), so it is necessary to conduct targeted research.

According to the three-factor theory of anthropomorphism (Epley et al., 2007), social motivation is an important intrinsic motivation in the process of anthropomorphism, so this paper examines the mechanism of users' psychological distance from products. Indi-vidual differences will moderate the role played by anthropomorphism, belonging-need plays a moderating role in the influence of anthropomorphism on brand attachment and brand experience, and high belonging-need enhances the positive influence of anthro-pomorphism on brand attitude (Chen & Lin, 2021). Therefore, whether there will be a similar rule in digital products remains to be studied.

1.2 Research Hypothesis

Anthropomorphism and User Experience of Digital Products. Anthropomorphism generates positive emotional (Delbaere et al., 2011), attachment to products (Yuan & Dennis, 2019), and trust in autonomous vehicles (Waytz et al., 2014), as well as the joy of interacting with AI assistants (Kim et al., 2019) and the likability of robots (Yam et al., 2021). In the widely used user experience measurement tool SUPR-Q, user experience is accurately divided into four dimensions, namely usability, credibility, loyalty and appearance (Sauro, 2015). Given the anthropomorphic can affect the emotion, trust and attachment of users, it is proposed that:

H1: The anthropomorphism of digital products enhances the user experience.

Anthropomorphism and Psychological Distance. The perceptual similarity generated by anthropomorphism is one of the dimensions of psychological distance (Liviatan et al., 2008), and social motivation is an important determinant of anthropomorphism (Maeng & Aggarwal, 2018). Social motivation is the motivation to seek social contact, social bonding and social support (Waytz & Epley, 2012). It promotes anthropomorphic tendencies by improving the availability of social cues (Zong & Wang, 2016).

Anthropomorphism can increase the sense of self-brand connection (Fazli-Salehi et al., 2022), and studies have shown that psychological distance mediates the relationship between anthropomorphism and users' attitude towards products (Li & Sung, 2021; Du Jiangang et al., 2022), thus proposing:

H2: The anthropomorphism of digital products will reduce the psychological distance of users from the product.

H3: Psychological distance mediates the impact of anthropomorphism of digital products on user experience.

The Moderating Effect of Belongingness Needs. Belonging-need theory points out that people want to establish and maintain psychological and emotional connection with others (Baumeister & Leary, 1995), which is a basic human need (Allen et al., 2022), and anthropomorphizing non-human subjects can satisfy people's need for social connection. Compared with subjects with sufficient social connections, subjects with a long-term lack of social connections showed a closer social response to anthropomorphic non-human subjects (Baddoura & Venture, 2013) and a higher evaluation of supportive anthropomorphic individuals (Epley et al., 2008).

Users with low belongingness need usually seek a sense of autonomy and want to keep a distance from others, while users with high belongingness need want to narrow the distance between themselves and others, so anthropomorphism enables users with high belongingness need to reduce their psychological distance from products to a greater extent (Chen & Yang, 2017). Belongingness need play a moderating role in the influence of anthropomorphism on brand attitudes (Chen & Lin, 2021), which suggests that:

H4: Belongingness needs moderate the influence of anthropomorphism of digital products on psychological distance. Compared with users with low belongingness needs, anthropomorphism can reduce psychological distance to a greater extent for users with high belongingness needs.

The Moderating Effect of Product Type. Digital products are a category of products, which can be divided into hedonic and practical products, and users' evaluation of products often depends on their satisfaction with hedonic and practical motives (Choi et al., 2020). Hedonic products refer to the products that bring positive emotional valence to users, which enables users to obtain emotional value as much as possible. Practical products refer to products that satisfy functional and instrumental purposes (Voss et al., 2003) and enable users to obtain as much functional value as possible (Dugan et al., 2021). In the hedonic scenario, individuals are more inclined to choose anthropomorphic products; In practical scenarios, this tendency is weakened (Meng Linghao, 2021). For hedonic products, under the condition of anthropomorphic design, more products were used after purchase; For practical products, the post-purchase usage of products is higher under the condition of non-anthropomorphic design (Du et al., 2022).

In addition, for the anthropomorphic effect of practical products, cognitive need, information processing fluency and other mediating variables related to efficacy motivation have stronger explanatory power (Chen & Lin, 2021; Wang & Lu, 2019), and the mediating effect of psychological distance induced by social motivation may be small, so it is proposed that:

H5: The type of digital products moderates the impact of anthropomorphism on user experience. Compared with practical products, anthropomorphism of hedonic products can improve user experience to a greater extent.

H6: The type of digital product moderates the indirect relationship between anthropomorphism and user experience through psychological distance, and this indirect relationship is stronger for hedonic products than for practical products (Fig. 1).

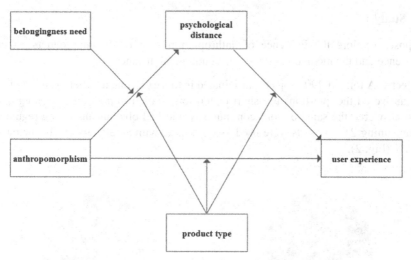

Fig. 1. Conceptual framework of the research

2 Research 1

2.1 Preliminary Study 1

Purpose. Verify material handling effectiveness.

Subjects. In this study, 54 subjects were randomly selected to participate in the experiment, 9 subjects whose response time was too short or too long were excluded, and the remaining 45 subjects were used as valid data, with an effective recovery rate of 83.33%.

Material. High and low anthropomorphic versions, the main function of this product is: language learning in the form of games. The page of Duolingo, a real product in the real market, was selected as a highly anthropomorphic version and manipulated from the aspects of image and language (Li & Sung, 2021; Gong et al., 2017; Wu, 2020; Zhao, 2021). Specific Product pages are shown in the Appendix 1.

Design and Procedure. The experiment was a single-factor (anthropomorphic: high vs. low) within-subjects design. Each participant was presented with two digital product materials and asked to evaluate the degree of anthropomorphism of the two versions of the products.

Result. Using anthropomorphism degree as the dependent variable, repeated measurement ANOVA showed that the main effect of anthropomorphism was significant. M_{high} = 5.98, SD_{high} = 1.22 vs. M_{low} = 2.29, SD_{low} = 1.49; $F(1,44)$ = 96.35, $p < 0.001$, η^2_p = 0.69, materials can be used to manipulate anthropomorphic levels.

2.2 Study 1

Purpose. Explore the influence of anthropomorphism of digital products on user experience and the mediating effect of psychological distance.

Subjects. A total of 290 subjects participated in this experiment. After excluding those who answered the questions too short or too long, failed to pass the screening questions, answered the same options continuously and had obvious answering regularity, the remaining 214 subjects were used as valid data, with an effective recovery rate of 73.79% (Fig. 2).

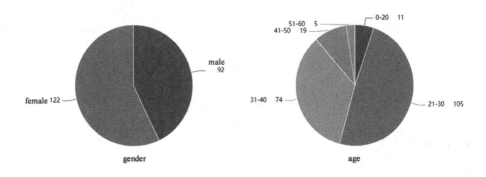

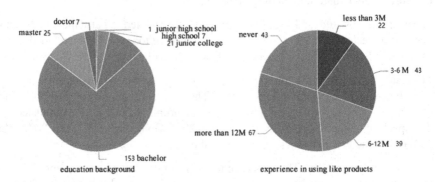

Fig. 2. Study 1 Demographic information of the subjects

Material. High/low anthropomorphic version developed in preliminary study 1.

Measurements

SUPR-Q. Used to measure users' perceptions of product usability, credibility, appearance and loyalty (Sauro, 2015), Cronbach's α coefficients of four dimensions were 0.84, 0.87, 0.87 and 0.71, respectively, in this study.

Psychological Distance Scale. According to the scale of Li and Sung (2021), Cronbach's α coefficient was 0.95 in this study.

Experimental Design and Procedure. Study 1 was a single-factor (anthropomorphic: high vs. low) between-subjects design. Each participant was presented with two digital product materials and asked to evaluate the psychological distance and four dimensions of user experiments (usability, credibility, loyalty, and appearance) of either version of the product at random.

Result
See Table 1.

Table 1. Descriptive statistical analysis in study 1

	High anthropomorphic(n = 111)		Low anthropomorphic(n = 103)	
	M	SD	M	SD
usability	6.20	0.70	5.04	1.36
credibility	5.91	0.81	5.06	1.45
loyalty	7.22	0.91	4.44	2.02
appearance	6.19	0.70	4.26	1.43
Psychological distance	6.10	0.65	3.35	1.54

The Main Effect Test of Anthropomorphism on User Experience. 0 represented the low anthropomorphic group and 1 represented the high anthropomorphic group. In the four dimensions of user experience, the high anthropomorphic group was significantly higher than the low anthropomorphic group (see Table 2), H1 was verified.

Table 2. Results of variance analysis of user experience dimensions in study 1

	M_0	SD_0	M_1	SD_1	$F(1,212)$	p	η^2_p
usability	5.04	1.36	6.20	0.70	62.91	<0.001	0.23
credibility	5.06	1.45	5.91	0.81	28.38	<0.001	0.12
loyalty	4.44	2.02	7.22	0.91	172.85	<0.001	0.45
appearance	4.26	1.43	6.19	0.70	160.76	<0.001	0.43

The Main Effect Test of Anthropomorphism on Psychological Distance. $M_{high} = 6.10$, $SD_{high} = 0.65$ vs. $M_{low} = 3.35$, $SD_{low} = 1.54$; $F(1,212) = 298.62$, $p < 0.001$, $\eta^2_p = 0.59$. The psychological distance scale was a reverse scoring scale, and H2 was verified.

An Examination of the Mediating Effect of Psychological Distance. The overall effect of anthropomorphism on usability was significant (95% confidence interval $\beta = 1.16$;

CI [0.87, 1.45]). Psychological distance mediated the influence of anthropomorphism on user experience (95% confidence interval β = 1.02; CI [0.65, 1.44]). In the four dimensions of user experience, H3 was verified as a complete mediator (Table 3).

Table 3. Psychological distance mediation analysis in study 1

	Total effect	Direct effect	Indirect effect	Mediating front	Mediating back
usability	1.16	0.14	1.02	2.75	0.37
	[0.87, 1.45]	[−0.27, 0.55]	[0.65, 1.44]	[2.44, 3.07]	[0.26, 0.48]
credibility	0.85	0.09	0.94	2.75	0.34
	[0.53, 1.16]	[−0.55, 0.37]	[0.55, 1.37]	[2.44, 3.07]	[0.21, 0.47]
loyalty	2.78	0.21	2.57	2.75	0.93
	[2.36, 3.20]	[−0.25, 0.67]	[2.12, 3.04]	[2.44, 3.07]	[0.81, 1.06]
appearance	1.93	0.10	1.84	2.75	0.67
	[1.63, 2.23]	[−0.24, 0.43]	[1.52, 2.17]	[2.44, 3.07]	[0.57, 0.76]

3 Research 2

3.1 Preliminary Study 2

Purpose. In research 2, product type was introduced to further explore the role of anthropomorphism on user experience. Preliminary study 2 was designed to manipulate testing of product type and anthropomorphism of the materials.

Subjects. A total of 47 subjects were recruited, 12 subjects whose response time was too short or too long and failed to pass the systematic screening questions were excluded, and the remaining 35 subjects were used as valid data, with an effective recovery rate of 74.47%.

Material

Practical Products. The main function of this product was to collect and manage electronic invoices. With reference to the real product "Piao Shui Bao" on the market in reality, version 1 was a high anthropomorphic version, and version 2 was a low anthropomorphic version. Specific Product pages are shown in the Appendix 2.

Hedonic Product. Same as preliminary study 1.

Experimental Design and Procedure. The experiment was a 2 (anthropomorphism: high vs. low) × 2 (product type: hedonic vs. Practical) within-subjects design. Each participant was presented with four digital product materials, namely practical products - high anthropomorphic version, practical products - low anthropomorphic version, hedonic products - high anthropomorphic version and hedonic products - low anthropomorphic version. The subjects were asked to evaluate the practical and hedonic degree of the practical product and hedonic product respectively, and evaluate the anthropomorphic degree of the two versions of the practical product and hedonic product respectively.

Result. The hedonic score of hedonic products was higher than that of practical products, $M_{practical} = 3.77$, $SD_{practical} = 1.88$ vs. $M_{hedonic} = 4.80$, $SD_{hedonic} = 1.68$; $F(1,34) = 16.79$, $p < 0.001$, $\eta^2_p = 0.33$. The practical score of practical products was higher than that of hedonic products, $M_{practical} = 6.46$, $SD_{practical} = 0.61$ vs. $M_{hedonic} = 5.94$, $SD_{hedonic} = 1.39$; $F(1,34) = 5.97$, $p = 0.02$, $\eta^2_p = 0.15$. The high anthropomorphic version of practical products scored higher than the low anthropomorphic version, $M_{high} = 6.20$, $SD_{high} = 0.93$ vs. $M_{low} = 3.03$, $SD_{low} = 1.82$; $F(1,34) = 59.56$, $p < 0.001$, $\eta^2_p = 0.64$. The high anthropomorphic version of hedonic products scored higher than the low anthropomorphic version, $M_{high} = 6.43$, $SD_{high} = 0.66$ vs. $M_{low} = 2.57$, $SD_{low} = 1.70$; $F(1,34) = 133.83$, $p < 0.001$, $\eta^2_p = 0.80$. There was no difference between the anthropomorphic degree of the two types of products, so the difference of dependent variables caused by the different manipulation of the anthropomorphic degree of the two types of products was excluded. In summary, materials can be used to manipulate product type and anthropomorphism, $M_{hedonic} = 6.43$, $SD_{hedonic} = 0.66$ vs. $M_{practical} = 6.20$, $SD_{practical} = 0.93$; $F(1,34) = 2.06$, $p = 0.16$.

3.2 Study 2

Purpose. Compared with Study 1, Study 2 added research on practical products, and discusses the more targeted impact of anthropomorphism on user experience, as well as the role of psychological distance and belonging needs.

Subjects. A total of 780 subjects participated in the experiment. After excluding those who answered the questions too short or too long, failed to pass the screening questions, answered the same options continuously and had obvious answering rules, the remaining 595 subjects were used as valid data, and the effective recovery rate was 76.28% (Fig. 3).

Material. 2 groups of pages each for practical and hedonic products, which developed in preliminary study 2.

Measurements

SUPR-Q. Used to measure users' perceptions of product usability, credibility, appearance and loyalty (Sauro, 2015), Cronbach's α coefficients of four dimensions were 0.84, 0.85, 0.84 and 0.69, respectively, in this study.

Psychological Distance Scale. The Cronbach's α coefficient of psychological distance scale was 0.93 in this study.

Belonging-Need Scale (Leary et al., 2013). The Cronbach's α coefficient was 0.86 in this study, which could be used for subsequent analysis.

Experimental Design and Procedure. The experiment was a 2 (anthropomorphism: high vs. low) × 2 (product type: hedonic vs. practical) between-subjects design. Each

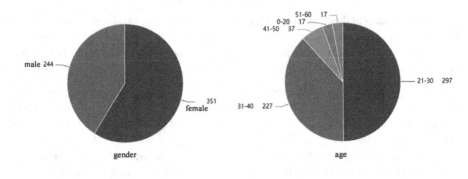

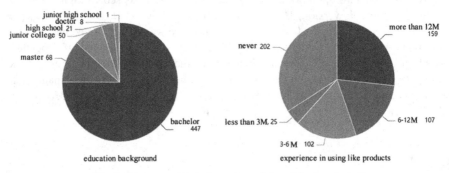

Fig. 3. Demographic information of the subject in study 2

subject was randomly assigned to one of the hedonic products or practical products. After a brief introduction of the product in text form, the subjects were presented with a high anthropomorphic version and a low anthropomorphic version of the product, and one of the versions was randomly selected by the system for the subjects to imagine and use and evaluate. After that, participants were asked to evaluate their perceived psychological distance, belonging needs, and user experience.

Results
See Table 4.

Table 4. Descriptive statistical analysis in study 2

	practical-high n = 149		practical-low n = 145		hedonic-high n = 156		hedonic-low n = 145	
	M	SD	M	SD	M	SD	M	SD
usability	5.60	1.38	5.34	1.45	5.99	0.80	5.10	1.49
credibility	5.77	1.05	5.49	1.31	5.94	0.82	5.05	1.43
loyalty	6.63	1.77	5.89	1.82	6.99	1.14	4.78	2.17

(continued)

Table 4. (*continued*)

	practical-high n = 149		practical-low n = 145		hedonic-high n = 156		hedonic-low n = 145	
	M	*SD*	*M*	*SD*	*M*	*SD*	*M*	*SD*
appearance	5.73	1.27	5.15	1.42	6.13	0.77	4.49	1.48
Psychological distance	5.77	1.13	4.43	1.59	6.02	0.82	3.97	1.74
Belongingness need	5.12	0.90	5.06	0.97	5.02	1.03	5.13	0.95

The Main Effect Test of Anthropomorphism on User Experience

Hedonic Product. The data of the subjects assigned to hedonic products were screened out, and H1a was verified in the four dimensions of user experience (see Table 5).

Table 5. Results of Variance analysis of User Experience Dimensions (Hedonic products) in study 2

	M_0	SD_0	M_1	SD_1	$F(1,299)$	p	η^2_p
usability	5.10	1.49	5.99	0.80	42.26	<0.001	0.12
credibility	5.05	1.43	5.94	0.82	44.18	<0.001	0.13
loyalty	4.78	2.17	6.99	1.14	125.09	<0.001	0.30
appearance	4.49	1.48	6.13	0.77	149.61	<0.001	0.33

Practical Product. Except for the usability dimension, H1b was partially validated in the other 3 dimensions (see Table 6).

Table 6. Results of Variance analysis of User Experience Dimensions (Practical products) in study 2

	M_0	SD_0	M_1	SD_1	$F(1,292)$	p	η^2_p
usability	5.34	1.45	5.60	1.38	2.35	0.126	0.01
credibility	5.49	1.31	5.77	1.05	4.26	0.04	0.01
loyalty	5.89	1.82	6.63	1.77	12.58	<0.001	0.04
appearance	5.15	1.42	5.73	1.27	13.87	<0.001	0.05

The Main Effect Test of Anthropomorphism on Psychological Distance

Hedonic Product. The anthropomorphism of hedonic digital products reduced the user's psychological distance from the product, $M_{high} = 6.02$, $SD_{high} = 0.82$ vs. $M_{low} = 3.97$, $SD_{low} = 1.74$; $F(1,299) = 175.43$, $p < 0.001$, $\eta^2_p = 0.37$, H2a is verified.

Practical Product. The anthropomorphism of practical digital products reduced the user's psychological distance from the product, $M_{high} = 5.77$, $SD_{high} = 1.13$ vs. $M_{low} = 4.43$, $SD_{low} = 1.59$; $F(1,292) = 69.41$, $p < 0.001$, $\eta^2_p = 0.19$, H2b is verified.

An Examination of the Mediating Effect of Psychological Distance

Hedonic Product. Psychological distance mediated the impact of anthropomorphism of hedonic digital products on user experience. The overall effect of anthropomorphism on usability was significant (95% confidence interval $\beta = 0.89$; CI [0.62, 1.16]). Psychological distance mediated the influence of anthropomorphism on user experience (95% confidence interval $\beta = 1.06$; CI [0.78, 1.36]), H3a was validated in four dimensions (see Table 7).

Table 7. Psychological distance-mediated analysis of hedonic products in study 2

	Total effect	Direct effect	Indirect effect	Mediating front	Mediating back
usability	0.89	−0.17	1.06	2.05	0.52
	[0.62, 1.16]	[−0.45, 0.10]	[0.78, 1.36]	[1.74, 2.35]	[0.44, 0.60]
credibility	0.89	−0.15	1.04	2.05	0.51
	[0.62, 1.15]	[−0.42, 0.12]	[0.77, 1.30]	[1.74, 2.35]	[0.43, 0.59]
loyalty	2.21	−0.04	2.25	2.05	1.10
	[1.82, 2.60]	[−0.29, 0.22]	[1.88, 2.63]	[1.74, 2.35]	[1.02, 1.17]
appearance	1.65	0.16	1.49	2.05	0.73
	[1.38, 1.91]	[−0.03, 0.34]	[1.23, 1.75]	[1.74, 2.35]	[0.67, 0.78]

Practical Product. Psychological distance mediated the impact of anthropomorphism of practical digital products on user experience. Psychological distance mediated the influence of anthropomorphism on user experience (95% confidence interval $\beta = 0.87$; CI [0.64, 1.12]), direct effect (95% confidence interval $\beta = −0.62$; CI [−0.90, −0.34])and indirect effect(95% confidence interval $\beta = 0.87$; CI [0.64, 1.12]) were significant, but in opposite directions. The total effect of anthropomorphism on usability was not significant due to masking effect (95% confidence interval $\beta = 0.25$; CI [−0.07, 0.58]). H3b was verified in four dimensions (see Table 8).

Testing the Moderating Effect of Belongingness Need

Hedonic Product. The interaction term did not have a significant effect on psychological distance (95% confidence interval $\beta = 0.13$, CI [−0.18, 0.44]), which was inconsistent with H4a.

Table 8. Psychological distance-mediated analysis of practical products in study 2

	Total effect	Direct effect	Indirect effect	mediating front	mediating back
usability	0.25	−0.62	0.87	1.34	0.65
	[−0.07, 0.58]	[−0.90, −0.34]	[0.64, 1.12]	[1.02, 1.66]	[0.56, 0.74]
credibility	0.29	−0.45	0.73	1.34	0.55
	[0.01, 0.56]	[−0.68, −0.21]	[0.52, 0.96]	[1.02, 1.66]	[0.47, 0.62]
loyalty	0.74	−0.63	1.37	1.34	1.02
	[0.33, 1.15]	[−0.91, −0.34]	[1.04, 1.71]	[1.02, 1.66]	[0.93, 1.11]
appearance	0.58	−0.47	1.05	1.34	0.79
	[0.28, 0.89]	[−0.67, −0.27]	[0.81, 1.31]	[1.02, 1.66]	[0.72, 0.85]

Practical Product. Belonging-need moderated the influence of anthropomorphism of practical digital products on psychological distance. Compared with users with low belonging-need, anthropomorphism reduced psychological distance to a greater extent for users with high belonging-need.The interaction term had a significant effect on psychological distance (95% confidence interval β = 0.38, CI [0.04, 0.72]), H4b was verified.

Testing the Moderating Effect of Product Type

Moderating Effect Test for Total Effect. The type of digital products moderated the impact of anthropomorphism on user experience. Compared with practical products, anthropomorphism of hedonic products improved user experience to a greater extent. Interaction items had a positive impact on usability (95% confidence interval β = 0.64, CI [0.22, 1.06]). H5 was verified in four dimensions (see Table 9).

Table 9. Test results of moderating effect of product type on total effect

	Total effect of hedonic products	Total effect of practical products	Moderating effect β & CI
usability	0.89	0.25	0.64 [0.22, 1.06]
credibility	0.89	0.29	0.60 [0.22, 0.98]
loyalty	2.21	0.74	1.47 [0.91, 2.03]
appearance	1.65	0.58	1.06 [0.66, 1.47]

Moderating Effect Test for Mediating Effect. In the dimension of user experience usability and credibility, the mediating effect of product type on psychological distance was not significant. In terms of loyalty and appearance, product type had a significant moderating effect on the mediating effect of psychological distance, and the indirect relationship between hedonic products was stronger than that between practical products. In summary, H6 was partially verified (see Table 10).

Table 10. Test results of moderating effect of product type on mediating effect

	Mediating effect of hedonic products	Mediating effect of practical products	Moderating effect β & CI
usability	1.06	0.87	0.20 [−0.19, 0.58]
credibility	1.04	0.73	0.30 [−0.04, 0.66]
loyalty	2.25	1.37	0.88 [0.37, 1.40]
appearance	1.49	1.05	0.44 [0.07, 0.80]

4 General Discussion

4.1 The Impact of Anthropomorphism on User Experience of Digital Products

For hedonic products, this paper verifies that anthropomorphism has a significant effect on improving user experience. For practical products, this study verifies that anthropomorphism can improve user experience in three dimensions of credibility, loyalty and appearance, which is consistent with most research results (Broadbent et al., 2013; Kim et al., 2019; Waytz et al., 2014; Chen & Lin, 2021).

4.2 The Mediating Effect of Psychological Distance

For hedonic products, psychological distance mediates the influence of anthropomorphism on the user experience of digital products, and is completely mediating in the four dimensions of user experience. It also plays a mediating role for practical products, but anthropomorphism will reduce the evaluation of various dimensions of user experience through other mediating paths (such as cognitive processing fluency, cognitive load, etc.), resulting in masking effect. In practice, product designers need to be more careful if they attempt to anthropomorphic design for practical products.

4.3 Moderating Effect of Belongingness Needs

For hedonic products, the effect of anthropomorphism on psychological distance is not moderated by user's belongingness needs; for practical products, the belongingness needs moderate the effect of anthropomorphism on psychological distance, which is a relatively new finding in this paper. Consumers' decision-making is often driven by two different motivations: the hedonic and practical nature of products (Choi et al., 2020). Users already expect to get emotional experience for hedonic products. Once users find the social cues stimulated by anthropomorphic characteristics, regardless of the user's belongingness needs, anthropomorphism can greatly narrow the psychological distance, so it does not reach statistical significance. As for practical products, users' attitude towards them mainly depends on practical motivation. Only users with high belongingness needs will notice the social clues brought by anthropomorphic features, thus narrowing the psychological distance.

5 Conclusion

1. Anthropomorphism improves the user experience of digital products, and product types moderate this relationship. Compared with practical products, anthropomorphism of hedonic products has a higher degree of improvement on user experience.
2. Anthropomorphism reduces users' psychological distance from digital products, and psychological distance mediates the influence of anthropomorphism on user experience. Product type moderates this mediation relationship, and the mediation relationship is stronger for hedonic products than for practical products.
3. For practical products, the user's belongingness needs moderate the influence of anthropomorphism on psychological distance positively, while hedonic products are not moderated.

Acknowledgments. This research is supported by the National Natural Science Foundation of China (32000771); the Fundamental Research Funds for the Central Universities, and the Research Funds of Renmin University of China (21XNLG13).

Disclosure of Interests. The authors have no competing interests to declare that are relevant to the content of this article.

Appendix 1

See Figs. 4, 5, 6, 7 and 8.

Fig. 4. Hedonic products page 1

Fig. 5. Hedonic products page 2

Fig. 6. Hedonic products page 3

Fig. 7. Hedonic products page 4

Fig. 8. Hedonic products page 5

Appendix 2

See Figs. 9 and 10.

Fig. 9. Practical product page 1

Fig. 10. Practical product page 2

References

Allen, K.A., Gray, D.L., Baumeister, R.F., Leary, M.R.: The need to belong: a deep dive into the origins, implications, and future of a foundational construct. Educ. Psychol. Rev. **34**(2), 1133–1156 (2022)

Baddoura, R., Venture, G.: Social vs. useful HRI: experiencing the familiar, perceiving the robot as a sociable partner and responding to its actions. Int. J. Soc. Robot. **5**, 529–547 (2013)

Bartneck, C., Bleeker, T., Bun, J., Fens, P., Riet, L.: The influence of robot anthropomorphism on the feelings of embarrassment when interacting with robots. Paladyn J. Behav. Robot. **1**(2), 109–115 (2010)

Baumeister, R.F., Leary, M.R.: The need to belong: desire for interpersonal attachments as a fundamental human motivation. Psychol. Bull. **117**(3), 497–529 (1995)

Broadbent, E., et al.: Robots with display screens: a robot with a more humanlike face display is perceived to have more mind and a better personality. PLoS ONE **8**(8), e72589 (2013)

Chen, K.J., Lin, J.S.: Revisiting the effects of anthropomorphism on brand relationship outcomes: the moderating role of psychological disposition. Eur. J. Mark. **55**(8), 2174–2200 (2021)

Chen, Z., Yang, G.: Which brand personification image is preferred: the moderating effect and boundary of belonging needs. Nankai Manage. Rev. **20**(03), 135–143 (2017). (in Chinese)

Choi, J., Madhavaram, S.R., Park, H.Y.: The role of hedonic and utilitarian motives on the effectiveness of partitioned pricing. J. Retail. **96**(2), 251–265 (2020)

Delbaere, M., McQuarrie, E.F., Phillips, B.J.: Personification in advertising. J. Advert. **40**(1), 121–130 (2011)

Dugan, R.G., Clarkson, J.J., Beck, J.T.: When cause-marketing backfires: differential effects of one-for-one promotions on hedonic and utilitarian products. J. Consum. Psychol. **31**(3), 532–550 (2021)

Du, J., Zhu, Y., Song, J.: Does anthropomorphism lead to more or less use? – Study on the interaction between anthropomorphic design and product type on post-purchase usage. Foreign Econ. Manage. **44**(12), 120–135 (2022). (in Chinese)

Epley, N., Waytz, A., Cacioppo, J.T.: On seeing human: a three-factor theory of anthropomorphism. Psychol. Rev. **114**(4), 864 (2007)

Epley, N., Waytz, A., Akalis, S., Cacioppo, J.T.: When we need a human: motivational determinants of anthropomorphism. Soc. Cogn. **26**(2), 143–155 (2008)

Fazli-Salehi, R., Torres, I.M., Madadi, R., Zúñiga, M.Á.: The impact of interpersonal traits (extraversion and agreeableness) on consumers' self-brand connection and communal-brand connection with anthropomorphized brands. J. Brand Manage. **29**(1), 13–34 (2022). https://doi.org/10.1057/s41262-021-00251-9

Gong, S., Shangguan, C., Zhai, K., Guo, Y.: The impact of emotional design on multimedia learning. Acta Psychol. Sin. **49**(06), 771–782 (2017). (in Chinese)

Ha, Q.A., Chen, J.V., Uy, H.U., Capistrano, E.P.: Exploring the privacy concerns in using Intelligent Virtual Assistants under perspectives of information sensitivity and anthropomorphism. Int. J. Hum.-Comput. Interact. **37**, 512–527 (2020)

Kidultoo: DP01- Hello, Digital Life. From the Internet, November 2020. (in Chinese). https://mp.weixin.qq.com/

Kim, A., Cho, M., Ahn, J., Sung, Y.: Effects of gender and relationship type on the response to artificial intelligence. Cyberpsychol. Behav. Soc. Netw. **22**(4), 249–253 (2019)

Leary, M.R., Kelly, K.M., Cottrell, C.A., Schreindorfer, L.S.: Construct validity of the need to belong scale: mapping the nomological network. J. Pers. Assess. **95**(6), 610–624 (2013)

Liviatan, I., Trope, Y., Liberman, N.: Interpersonal similarity as a social distance dimension: implications for perception of others' actions. J. Exp. Soc. Psychol. **44**(5), 1256–1269 (2008)

Li, X., Sung, Y.: Anthropomorphism brings us closer: the mediating role of psychological distance in User–AI assistant interactions. Comput. Hum. Behav. **118**, 106680 (2021)

Maeng, A., Aggarwal, P.: Facing dominance: anthropomorphism and the effect of product face ratio on consumer preference. J. Consum. Res. **44**(5), 1104–1122 (2018)

Meng, L.: Evaluation characteristics and eye movement mechanism of product expressions in hedonic and practical scenarios (Master's Thesis, Zhejiang Sci-Tech University) (2021). (in Chinese)

Sauro, J.: SUPR-Q: a comprehensive measure of the quality of the website user experience. J. Usability Stud. **10**(2), 68–86 (2015)

Shank, D.B., Graves, C., Gott, A., Gamez, P., Rodriguez, S.: Feeling our way to machine minds: people's emotions when perceiving mind in artificial intelligence. Comput. Hum. Behav. **98**, 256–266 (2019)

Velasco, F., Yang, Z., Janakiraman, N.: A meta-analytic investigation of consumer response to anthropomorphic appeals: the roles of product type and uncertainty avoidance. J. Bus. Res. **131**, 735–746 (2021)

Voss, K.E., Spangenberg, E.R., Grohmann, B.: Measuring the hedonic and utilitarian dimensions of consumer attitude. J. Mark. Res. **40**(3), 310–320 (2003)

Wang, Y.-Z., Lu, H.-L.: Influence of power perception on purchase intention of anthropomorphic products. Psychol. Sci. **42**(03), 660–666 (2019). (in Chinese)

Waytz, A., Epley, N.: Social connection enables dehumanization. J. Exp. Soc. Psychol. **48**(1), 70–76 (2012)

Waytz, A., Heafner, J., Epley, N.: The mind in the machine: anthropomorphism increases trust in an autonomous vehicle. J. Exp. Soc. Psychol. **52**, 113–117 (2014)

Wu, Y.: Attention processing Mechanism and Usability testing of anthropomorphic ICONS on Web pages (Master Dissertation, Zhejiang Sci-Tech University) (2020). (in Chinese)

Xie, Y., Chen, K., Guo, X.: Online anthropomorphism and consumers' privacy concern: moderating roles of need for interaction and social exclusion. J. Retail. Consum. Serv. **55**, 102119 (2020)

Xu, L., Yu, F., Zhao, L., Han, T.: Anthropomorphism in human-computer interaction. In: Chinese Psychological Society (eds.) 20th National Conference on Psychology and National Mental Health Abstracts, pp. 1135–1136 (2017). (in Chinese)

Xu, N., Wu, X., Li, S., Li, J.-W.: User diversity, emotional characteristics and adaptive innovation of digital products. Res. Sci. Sci. **41**(06), 1121–1129 (2023). (in Chinese)

Yam, K.C., et al.: Robots at work: people prefer—and forgive—service robots with perceived feelings. J. Appl. Psychol. **106**(10), 1557 (2021)

Yuan, L., Dennis, A.R.: Acting like humans? Anthropomorphism and consumer's willingness to pay in electronic commerce. J. Manag. Inf. Syst. **36**(2), 450–477 (2019)

Zhang, Y.: Research on Data-driven Internet Product R&D Management (Master thesis). Beijing Jiaotong University (2022). (in Chinese)

Zhao Y.: The impact of emotional personification on Purchase Intention (Master's Thesis, Zhejiang University) (2021). (in Chinese)

Zong, Y., Wang, G.: Anthropomorphism: psychological applications in human-computer interaction. Psychol. Tech. Appl. **4**(05), 296–305 (2016). (in Chinese)

Research on Children's Furniture Design Based on User Needs and AHP

Lin Zhang[1,2] and Danylo Kosenko[2(✉)]

[1] The College of Design and Art, Shaanxi University of Science and Technology, Xi'an 710021, Shaanxi, China
[2] Kyiv National University of Technologies and Design, Kyiv 01011, Ukraine
danylo.kosenko@gmail.com

Abstract. For a new generation of parents, children's furniture is not just a smaller version of adult furniture, but plays a crucial role in the growth of children. China's children's furniture market is huge, diverse and rich in creativity, but the design and development mainly focus on creativity and market, while the design evaluation and feedback optimization of connecting creative market are relatively ignored. Although China's research in the field of children's furniture design is fruitful, the depth is insufficient, especially in the design evaluation and optimization.

This study takes children's furniture as the research object, uses KANO model, qualitatively analyzes the needs of children's furniture users through questionnaire survey results, and preliminarily establishes the design index of children's furniture. Then the analytic hierarchy process is introduced to build a scientific and reasonable evaluation model for children's furniture design from the perspective of aesthetics and design, and quantitative analysis is carried out through the judgment matrix to calculate the weight of each level. After the consistency test, the children's furniture design evaluation system is formed. According to this system, children's furniture design products that meet the needs of users and reflect the design aesthetics can be determined, and provide reference for the design optimization of other types of products.

Keywords: kano model · AHP · Children's Furniture Design

1 Introduction

Statistics show that the number of children under the age of 16 in China exceeds 300 million, with children under the age of 6 accounting for 171 million, or a quarter of the total population. Under the "three-child" policy, the total number of children will continue to grow. Although the children's furniture market has great potential, the problem of low industry threshold and lack of uniform standards is prominent. Compared with foreign enterprises, Chinese children's furniture enterprises have a significant gap in technical content and design optimization. The recent market supervision department sampling results show that the unqualified rate of online sales of children's furniture is as high as 72%, highlighting the urgent need for the industry to improve product quality and industrial upgrading.

© The Author(s), under exclusive license to Springer Nature Switzerland AG 2024
P.-L. P. Rau (Ed.): HCII 2024, LNCS 14699, pp. 388–401, 2024.
https://doi.org/10.1007/978-3-031-60898-8_26

Although China has accumulated a lot of research results in children's furniture design, most of them focus on creativity and market. Excessive pursuit of profit leads us to blindly imitate foreign products and ignore the real needs of the domestic market. The homogenization of children's furniture design reflects the unreasonable design evaluation feedback mechanism, which makes the development of children's furniture design over-rely on the designer's personal talent, and lack of scientific and rigorous iterative process.

2 Research Methods and Research Status

KANO model, originated from professor Noriaki Kano of Tokyo Institute of Technology, aims to solve the problem of user demand classification and prioritization, and is an effective tool [1]. Based on the analysis of the effect of product functions on user satisfaction, the model constructs a nonlinear relationship between the two. Based on the two-dimensional model of satisfaction, the factors affecting satisfaction are divided into six types, and the influence relationship between each type and satisfaction is explored, thus shaping the KANO model. It should be noted that KANO model is not an accurate nonlinear relationship model and cannot directly measure user satisfaction, but can obtain and predict user satisfaction through nonlinear relationship. In the process of product design, designers need to design according to user needs, while KANO model can mine user needs and divide the attributes of user needs.

Analytical Hierarchy Process (AHP) is a multi-scheme optimization decision-making method, which was initiated by Saaty et al. [2], an American scholar and professor at the University of Pittsburgh, in the 1970s. This method is designed to assist decision makers to make decision analysis in complex environment and has high practical value.

KANO model and AHP analysis method, as common research methods in the field of modern product design, have been widely used by scholars in the study of user needs. For example, in the paper "Research Progress on Long-term Care Needs of Disabled Elderly Based on KANO Model", Kaiying Zhong and Longfeng Sun used KANO model method to explore the long-term care needs of disabled elderly people [3]. In their article "Design of Children's Interactive Toys Based on KANO Model and Synesthetic Experience", Li Xiaoying and Dong Yiyao obtain the design needs of children's interactive toys through KANO model [4].Chen Shanshan, Duan Qijun, Li Yajun et al., in Research on Design of Children's dental Service System based on SAPAD-AHP, used AHP to obtain core meaning clusters, and then conducted research and design on children's dental service system [5].

3 Research Model Analysis and Feasibility

3.1 Research Model Analysis

The ultimate goal of user demand analysis is to provide decision basis for product design. Although product attribute categories help designers to understand user needs, they should not be used as a guideline for specific decisions. When using the analytical KANO model for product design, the attribute categories of the KANO model reflect different priorities (essential attribute > desired attribute > charm attribute > Indifference attribute > reverse attribute). However, such methods cannot distinguish between functional requirements in the same category. Therefore, the applicability of KANO model to quantitative decision-making in product design function screening is limited.

Analytic hierarchy Process (AHP) is seen as a highly inclusive system that works as a subjective weighting method for making decisions based on multiple criteria. The first step in implementing this approach is to build a hierarchy of problems. The second step is to design a questionnaire and distribute it to the respondents to collect their opinions in order to realize the matching comparison. It should be noted that each decision maker makes a pairwise comparison of the mutual importance of the elements at the same level, and the final result is derived from their geometric average. The scale ranges from 1 to 9, where 1 indicates that both are equal or equally important, and the number 9 indicates that one element is of great importance relative to the other in a pairwise matrix [6].

3.2 Study the Feasibility of the Model

In the practical application scenario, the traditional KANO method does not have the function of quantitative evaluation, and its decision support ability in the field of engineering design is limited. This is because when the traditional weight calculation method is used, it mainly focuses on the user and market perspective, but fails to fully combine the limitations of the enterprise's ability to meet the user's needs (such as production cost, material technology, etc.), resulting in strong subjectivity and lack of qualitative analysis and other problems [7].

The KANO model is essentially user-centric, and its core goal is to solve the problems that users are concerned about. However, when viewed as a decision tool for engineers, the KANO model does not adequately take into account the concerns of manufacturers in meeting user needs [8]. Cost constraints are often borne by product development teams with the expertise to ensure that the product contains only the features that the manufacturer can afford. However, these cost models are relatively simple and do not fully reflect the complexity of design and manufacturing costs. From the perspective of enterprise production, product design should seek the best balance between the user's perceived value and the manufacturer's ability.

The Analytic Hierarchy Process (AHP), as a combination of qualitative and quantitative demand weight research method, has significant advantages over the traditional weight calculation method. It can start from multiple targets and make weight comparison according to different levels of targets, making data comparison more independent and scientific [9].

Therefore, in the process of children's furniture design, we use the method of combining KANO model and AHP hierarchical analysis. This method is based on the KANO model to divide the attributes of user needs, using AHP to compare the weight of user needs, and then get the ranking of user needs, so as to clarify the goal and direction of children's furniture design.

4 User Demand Analysis Based on KNAO Model

The core target group of this study is 3 to 5 years old children, through the in-depth analysis of the characteristics of children in this age group and the needs of parents, summed up 20 functional requirements of children's furniture options. These options include: Safe structure, diverse form and practical, suitable size, environmentally friendly materials and harmony, easy to operate, interesting, interactive, color coordination, with growth, high stability, easy to store, light weight, highly adjustable, intelligent, fashionable appearance, affordable price, educational significance, cartoon design, parent-child suit and game function.

4.1 Questionnaire Design

This paper analyzes the relationship between the degree of user demand and user satisfaction, and divides user demand into six types in the fuzzy KANO model: problem demand (Q), basic demand (M), opposite demand (R), excited demand (A), expectation demand (O) and irrelevant demand (I).

According to the user's answer when the requirement is implemented or not, we can find the corresponding KANO type. Table 1 lists the parameters.

Table 1. Sample KANO questionnaire

The KANO questionnaire		
Product demand 1	Positive question: What would you do if this need were met?	☐ Very much like ☐ Taken for granted ☐ It doesn't matter ☐ Reluctantly accept ☐ Very dislike
	Negative question: What happens if this need is not met?	☐ Very much like ☐ Taken for granted ☐ It doesn't matter ☐ Reluctantly accept ☐ Very dislike

4.2 Survey Implementation and Questionnaire Retrieval

The research objects of this survey are mainly distributed in four cities in Hunan province: Changsha, Zhuzhou, Xiangtan and Zhangjiajie. The survey will run from November 2023 to January 2024. The research team consisted of university students studying product design. In view of the critical period of children's growth and development, and the participants in children's furniture buying behavior are usually young parents with purchasing power, so the focus of this survey is young parents in all social classes. A total of 100 questionnaires were issued, and 97 valid questionnaires were finally recovered.

In order to fully understand users' demand tendency for products, we compiled KANO questionnaires for 20 functional requirements, conducted a survey on 100 respondents, and finally collected 97 valid survey results. Then, we sorted out the data of the KANO questionnaire according to the Kano questionnaire score Table 3 and the questionnaire item comprehensive score Table 4 (Table 2):

Table 2. Scoring table for KANO questionnaire

Options	Like very much	Take for granted	It doesn't matter	Settle for	It doesn't matter
score	1	2	3	4	5

Table 3. Comparison table of comprehensive scores of questionnaire items

Project comprehensive score comparison table

Forward score	1	1	1	1	1	2	2	2	2	2	3	3	3	3	3	4	4	4	4	4	5	5	5	5	5
Negative score	1	2	3	4	5	1	2	3	4	5	1	2	3	4	5	1	2	3	4	5	1	2	3	4	5
KANO price	Q	A	A	A	O	R	I	I	I	M	R	I	I	I	M	R	I	I	I	M	R	R	R	R	Q

Through sorting and conversion, we conclude that the user demand attributes of 20 products are shown in Table 4:

Table 4. User demand attributes of products (based on 97 respondents)

Functional options	M	O	A	I	R	Q	attributive judgment
in light weight	19	16	5	10	47	0	R
Highly adjustable	25	10	1	8	53	0	R
The size is appropriate	47	7	22	16	4	1	M
Colour collocation is reasonable	11	52	16	17	0	1	O
Material harmony and environmental protection	6	60	15	14	1	1	O
Growth	13	18	32	26	6	2	A
interesting	13	8	66	9	0	1	A
Functional forms are diverse	6	56	23	10	0	2	O

(continued)

Table 4. (*continued*)

Functional options	M	O	A	I	R	Q	attributive judgment
Puzzle	10	21	38	21	5	2	A
stability	50	4	1	38	4	0	M
Convenient storage	20	6	5	61	4	1	I
Structural safety	66	8	20	0	3	0	M
The appearance is novel and fashionable	5	62	0	18	12	0	O
cheapness	7	50	4	33	3	0	O
simplicity of operator	57	9	18	5	8	0	M
Educational sex	10	0	67	18	2	0	A
Cartoon shape design	18	2	9	63	5	0	I
interactivity	6	0	56	26	9	0	A
Parent-child suit	15	6	22	42	12	0	I
With the game function	9	10	8	24	45	1	R

4.3 Requirements Processing

We obtained the raw data through the questionnaire for statistical analysis, and initially determined the evaluation index of children's furniture design.

First, I removed the functional requirements that I identified as R (reverse attribute): light weight, adjustable height, with gaming capabilities;

Then, we refer to the following BETTER-WORSE principle of KANO model to calculate the attributes of the remaining 17 user requirements:

$$\text{BETTER} = \frac{(A+0)}{(A+O+M+I)} \quad (1)$$

$$\text{WORSE} = \frac{(-1)*(O+M)}{(A+O+M+I)} \quad (2)$$

The coefficient BETTER is positive, between 0 and 1, the larger the value, the faster the user satisfaction improvement; the coefficient WORSE is negative, between−1 and 0, the smaller, the faster the user satisfaction decreases. Through calculation, we obtained the following BETTER-WORSE control table for 17 user requirements, as shown in Table 5:

To facilitate the calculation, we took the absolute value of WORSE and summarized the BETTER-WORSE values of 12 items according to the following KANO model judgment principle.

First quadrant/no attribute: BETTER > 0.5, I WORSE I> 0.5;

Second quadrant/essential attributes: BETTER > 0.5, I WORSE I <0.5;

The third quadrant/expected attribute: BETTER < 0.5, I WORSE I <0.5;

Table 5. Shows the BETTER-WORSE comparison of 17 user requirements

Functional options	M	O	A	I	R	Q	WORSE	BETTER
The size is appropriate	47	7	22	16	4	1	−0.587	0.315
Colour collocation is reasonable	11	52	16	17	0	1	−0.656	0.708
Material harmony and environmental protection	6	60	15	14	1	1	−0.695	0.789
Growth	13	18	32	26	6	2	−0.348	0.562
interesting	13	8	66	9	0	1	−0.219	0.771
Functional forms are diverse	6	56	23	10	0	2	−0.653	0.832
Puzzle	10	21	38	21	5	2	−0.344	0.656
stability	50	4	1	38	4	0	−0.581	0.054
Convenient storage	20	6	5	61	4	1	−0.283	0.12
Structural safety	66	8	20	0	3	0	−0.787	0.298
The appearance is novel and fashionable	5	62	0	18	12	0	0.788	0.729
cheapness	7	50	4	33	3	0	−0.606	0.574
simplicity of operator	57	9	18	5	8	0	−0.742	0.303
Educational sex	10	0	67	18	2	0	−0.105	0.705
Cartoon shape design	18	2	9	63	5	0	−0.217	0.12
interactivity	6	0	56	26	9	0	−0.068	0.636
Parent-child suit	15	6	22	42	12	0	−0.247	0.329

Fourth quadrant/Charm attributes: BETTER < 0.5, |WORSE| > 0.5;

From the four-quadrant diagram:

No difference attribute I is: cartoon shape design, parent-child package, convenient storage, stability;

The necessary attribute M is: appropriate size, simple operation, structure safety and stability;

The expected attribute A is: diverse functional forms, harmonious and environmentally friendly materials, novel and fashionable appearance, reasonable color difference collocation, cheap price;

Charm attribute O is: interesting, educational, educational, interactive, growth;

Delete no difference properties, we through the KANO model preliminary identified children furniture design index 14 include: appropriate size, simple operation, structure safety, stability, functional diversity, material harmonious environmental protection, novel appearance fashion, reasonable color difference collocation, cheap, interesting, educational, educational, interactive, growth.

5   Children's Furniture Design Based on AHP Method

In this study, 20 experts in product design and industrial design, 60%, men, 12 women, 40%, 8. The average age was 37.33 years old, among which 80% were those with a graduate degree or above. There are 11 experts with associate senior title or above titles, accounting for 55%; In terms of working years, 17 experts have 6–15 years of working experience, accounting for 85%.

In the first round of screening, experts respected the design of children's furniture, removing the stability of the essential attributes of the KANO model and the affordable price of the expected attributes.

Basic attributes of children's furniture. It mainly includes children's furniture of appropriate size, safe structure and simple operation. These are the most basic demand of consumer to children's furniture.

Children's furniture willingness attributes. It mainly includes the reasonable color matching of children's furniture, harmonious environmental protection materials and diversified functional forms. With the post-90s and even post-00s becoming the main force of the children's furniture consumer market, rich color matching, novel and fashionable appearance, environmentally friendly material selection and a variety of functional choices have been used by more and more consumers as an important reference indicator for the purchase of children's furniture.

Charming attribute of children's furniture. It mainly includes growth, interest and interactivity. In today's children's furniture products, children can become more interesting and intelligent. In addition, the emphasis on children's development leads to the sustainable growth of children's furniture and the interaction between parents and children has also become a prominent selling point of products.

Based on the above evaluation indexes, the evaluation system of children's furniture design is shown in Fig. 1.

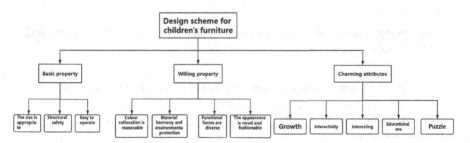

Fig. 1. Design scheme for children's furniture

Using the hierarchical analysis method, combined with the above constructed evaluation model, to evaluate different children's furniture design indicators, and the weight value of each index is finally determined and the final evaluation system of children's furniture design is obtained.

Based on the evaluation system of children's furniture design in this paper, the hierarchical analysis method is adopted to analyze the basic attributes of communication children's furniture, and the 12 factors under the willingness attributes and charm attributes are the evaluation index system of the index layer. Because it is impossible to exclude the possible investigation error caused by the subjective emotions of experts, the paper will test the consistency of the research results after quantitative analysis. The paper uses yaahp Version 10.1 software to calculate. If the consistency is less than 0.1, we can calculate the weight value of each index.

$A = (a_{ij})_{n \times n}$ A λ_{max} For the constructed judgment matrix, the corresponding maximum feature root and corresponding feature weight vector of the judgment matrix are solved. W The corresponding equation is as follows:

$$AW = \lambda_{max} W \tag{3}$$

W Among them, the desired feature weight vector is processed after normalization, which is the importance ranking of each evaluation index.

Then calculate the consistency ratio of the judgment matrix:

$$CI = \frac{\lambda_{max} - n}{n - 1} \tag{4}$$

$$CR = \frac{CI}{RI} \tag{5}$$

n CI CR Among them, it is the order of the judgment matrix, the consistency test coefficient of the judgment matrix, the consistency ratio of the judgment matrix, the RI is the average random consistency ratio, and the relevant indicators are shown in Table 6:

Table 6. Mean random agreement index table

Matrix order	1	2	3	4	5	6	7	8
RI	0	0	0.52	0.89	1.12	1.26	1.36	1.41

The ranking results of the standard layer weight of the children's furniture design evaluation body are shown in Table 7:

Table 7. The judgment matrix and weight of the criterion layer under the target layer

Children's furniture design and evaluation system	Basic property	Willing property	Charming attributes	Wi
Basic property	1	2	3	0.5396
Willing property	0.5	1	2	0.297
Charming attributes	0.3333	0.5	1	0.1634

$\lambda_{max} = 3.0092$ $CR = 0.0088 < 0.1$ Among them, the judgment matrix maximum feature root, consistency proportion, consistency test passed, do not screen out any indicators.

Table 8. Judgment matrix and weight of the index layer under the basic attributes

Basic property	The size is appropriate	Structural safety	Easy to operate	Wi
The size is appropriate	1	0.5	2	0.297
Structural safety	2	1	3	0.5396
Easy to operate	0.5	0.3333	1	0.1634

Table 8 shows the weight sorting results of indicators under basic attributes:

$\lambda_{max} = 3.0092$ $CR = 0.0088 < 0.1$ Among them, the judgment matrix maximum feature root, consistency proportion, consistency test passed, do not screen out any indicators.

The weight ranking results of each indicator under the willingness attribute are shown in Table 9:

Table 9. Judgment matrix and weight of the index layer under the willingness attribute

Willing property	Colour collocation is reasonable	Material harmony and environmental protection	Functional forms are diverse	The appearance is novel and fashionable	Wi
Colour collocation is reasonable	1	1	3	4	0.4018
Material harmony and environmental protection	1	1	2	3	0.337
Functional forms are diverse	0.3333	0.5	1	2	0.164
The appearance is novel and fashionable	0.25	0.3333	0.5	1	0.0972

$\lambda_{max} = 4.0310$ $CR = 0.0116 < 0.1$ Among them, the maximum feature root of the judgment matrix, the consistency proportion, the judgment consistency test passed, do not screen to remove any index.

The weight ranking results of the attractive indicators are shown in Table 10:

$\lambda_{max} = 5.0278$ $CR = 0.0062 < 0.1$ Among them, the judgment matrix maximum feature root, consistency proportion, consistency test passed, do not screen out any indicators.

Table 10. Judgment matrix and weight of the index layer under the attractive type attribute

Charming attributes	Growth	interactivity	interesting	Educational sex	Puzzle	Wi
Growth	1	0.5	0.3333	0.3333	2	0.108
interactivity	2	1	0.5	0.5	3	0.1818
interestingness	3	2	1	1	5	0.3293
Educational sex	3	2	1	1	4	0.3165
Puzzle	0.5	0.3333	0.2	0.25	1	0.0644

According to the single ranking results of each indicator, the relative weight of the subcriterion layer relative to the target layer is calculated by the following equation:

$$W_i^2 = \sum_{j=1}^{m} W_j^1 W_{ij} \tag{6}$$

W_i^2 i Specifically, the relative weight of the first index of the sub-criterion layer relative to the target layer, the weight of the first index of the criterion layer relative to the target layer, and the weight of the first index of the sub-criterion layer relative to the first index of the criterion layer. $W_j^1 j W_{ij} ij$ j.

Based on the results from Tables 8, 9 and 10, the total hierarchy ranking is shown in Table 11:

Table 11. Overall total ordering

Target layer	The standard layer	weight	Index layer	weight	Comprehensive weight
Design scheme for children's furniture	Basic property	0.5396	The size is appropriate	0.297	0.1602
			Structural safety	0.5396	0.2912
			Easy to operate	0.1634	0.0882
	Willing property	0.297	Colour collocation is reasonable	0.4018	0.1193
			Material harmony and environmental protection	0.337	0.1001
			Functional forms are diverse	0.164	0.0487
			The appearance is novel and fashionable	0.0972	0.0289
	Charming attributes	0.1634	Growth	0.108	0.0177
			interactivity	0.1818	0.0297
			interesting	0.3293	0.0538
			Educational sex	0.3165	0.0517
			Puzzle	0.0644	0.0105

6 Design Practice

After expert comprehensive score and weight calculation, we take children seats as children furniture design practice case, through the analysis score we from children furniture design scheme design index layer: appropriate size, structure safety, simple operation, reasonable color collocation, material harmonious environmental protection, functional diversity, growth, interest, educational and educational put forward specific design ideas, as shown in Table 12:

Table 12. Design idea

Criterion layer	Design index layer	Design ideas
essential attribute	The size is appropriate	The legs are detachable and adjustable in size as the child grows
	Structural safety	No edges and corners design, avoid bumping, remove heavy and insufficient thin board
	Easy to operate	Remove the hidden is the pull plate, the operation is more simple and convenient
essential attribute	Reasonable color matching	Add a wood tone from the original single bright yellow
	Material harmony and environmental protection	The materials are selected from ABS plastic, rubber, and frosted soft rubber
	Functional forms are diverse	A total of three functional forms, add table and chair combined furniture
Charm attributes	Growth	Adjustable size with voice stories of all ages
	interesting	After the table leg is removed, it is inserted into the holes on both sides and turned into a seesaw
	Puzzle	Drawer can store children's picture books
	Educational sex	Create possibilities for children to read

The edges and edges of the product are smooth to avoid the bumps of users in daily use. The table leg adopts a removable structure, which is combined to increase the length of the table leg with the growth of the user. When idle, it can be placed on the desktop, and cooperate with the grooves to help users to read books. At the same time, the table leg can be inserted into both sides of the hole, into a seesaw, providing fun for users in their spare time. As shown in Figs. 2, 3, 4 and 5:

Fig. 2. Design overall rendering

Fig. 3. Toy form rendering

Fig. 4. Front View of Seat

Fig. 5. Removable seat rendering

7 Conclusion

In the case study process of the design of children's multifunctional seat for children's furniture, the research method of combining KANO model with AHP hierarchical analysis provides a new solution to the importance of KANO model. Through two methods of combining research way can better solve the growth of children sit in structure, function and materials show the user demand attribute division fuzzy, user demand importance is not clear, effective reduction between children, parents and designers and the design concept, the difference between the growth of children sit design more scientific and reasonable, higher consumer acceptance of products, also for related product design research provides a new theoretical method and reference.

References

1. Kano, N., Seraku, N., Takahashi, F., et al.: Attractive quality and must-be quality. J. Jpn. Soc. Qual. **18**(2), 39–48 (1984)
2. Yin, L., He, R.K., Hao, C.J.: User demand research method based on big data user portrait and KJ-AHP method. Design **35**(1), 82–85 (2022)
3. Zhong, K.Y., Sun, L.F.: Research progress on long-term care needs of disabled elderly based on Kano model. Chin. J. Nurs. **57**(3), 368–373 (2022)
4. Li, X.Y., Dong, Y.Y.: Design of interactive children's toys based on Kano model and synesthesia experience. Design **35**(3), 60–63 (2022)
5. Chen, S.S., Duan, Q.J., Li, Y.J.: Pediatric dentistry service system design based on SAPADAHP. Packag. Eng. **42**(10), 115–123 (2021)
6. Kwong, C.K., Bai, H.: A fuzzy AHP approach to the determination of importance weights of customer requirements in quality function deployment. J. Intell. Manuf. **13**(5), 367–377 (2002)
7. Wei, F., Zhao, X.: Research on pet cat companion robot design based on Kano and AHP. Design **35**(1), 128–131 (2022)
8. Lai, X.: Optimizing product design using the Kano model and QFD. IEEE Int. Eng. Manag. Conf. **18**(21), 1085–1089 (2004)
9. Wang, H.B., Zou, J.Z., Liu, J.: Research on interactive design of cow's heat monitoring equipment based on KJ-Kano-AHP. Design **35**(3), 128–131 (2022)

Author Index

P.-L. P. Rau (Ed.): HCII 2024, LNCS 14699, pp. 403–404, 2024.
https://doi.org/10.1007/978-3-031-60898-8

Printed in the United States
by Baker & Taylor Publisher Services